MW00784473

Khrushchev Lied

The Evidence That Every "Revelation" of Stalin's (and Beria's) "Crimes" in Nikita Khrushchev's Infamous "Secret Speech" to the 20th Party Congress of the Communist Party of the Soviet Union on February 25, 1956, is Provably False*

By Grover Furr

(* All except one, which I can neither prove true nor disprove.)

Khrushchev Lied

First English Edition Published by Erythros Press and Media, LLC, February 2011; corrected edition July 2011; **second corrected edition January 2014**

Published in Russian by Algoritm Publishers, Moscow, December 2007 under the title *Antistalinskaia Podlost'*
http://www.algoritm-kniga.ru/ferr-g.-antistalinskaya-podlost.html
Republished by EKSMO Publishers, Moscow, November 2010
under the title *Teni XX S"ezda. Antistalinskaia Podlost'*
http://www.eksmo.ru/catalog/882/481650/

© Grover Furr 2007, 2010, 2011, 2014

Published and printed with permission of the author, who assumes all responsibility for the content herein.

Library of Congress Cataloguing-in-Publication Data

Furr, Grover C. (Grover Carr)
 Khrushchev Lied: The Evidence That Every "Revelation" of Stalin's (and Beria's) "Crimes" in Nikita Khrushchev's Infamous "Secret Speech" to the 20th Party Congress of the Communist Party of the Soviet Union on February 25, 1956, is Provably False / Grover C. Furr; translations by Grover C. Furr

1. Khrushchev, Nikita Sergeevich, 1894-1971. 2. Khrushchev, Nikita Sergeevich, 1894-1971. Rech' na zakrytom zasedanii dvad´t`satogo S"ezda KPSS. 3. Stalin, Joseph, 1879-1953. 4. Soviet Union--Politics and government--1917-1936. 5. Soviet Union--Politics and government--1936-1953. I. Title.

Table of Contents

Acknowledgements and Dedication

I wish to express my special gratitude to my editor, translator, and friend Vladimir L. Bobrov, of Moscow. Without his encouragement and help at every step this book would never have been written.

My special thanks to the Inter-Library Loan librarians at Harry S. Sprague Library, Montclair State University – Kevin Prendergast, Arthur Hudson, and Sergio Ferreira, for their tireless help in obtaining hard-to-find Soviet and other books and articles.

* * *

I dedicate this book to the memory of my son Joseph Furr: wonderful son and friend, skilled diesel truck mechanic, and one of "the salt of the earth."

Introduction.

The Khrushchev School of Falsification: "The 20th Century's Most Influential Speech"

The fiftieth anniversary of Nikita S. Khrushchev's "Secret Speech", delivered on February 25, 1956, elicited predictable comment. An article in the London (UK) *Telegraph* called it "the 20th century's most influential speech." In an article the same day in the *New York Times* William Taubman, whose biography of Khrushchev won the Pulitzer Prize for Biography in 2004, called it a "great deed" that "deserves to be celebrated" on its anniversary. [1]

Some time ago I reread Khrushchev's "Secret Speech" for the first time in many years. I used the HTML version of the edition of the speech published in a special issue of *The New Leader* in 1962.[2] During my reading I remarked that the noted Menshevik scholar Boris Nikolaevsky, in his annotations to Khrushchev's talk, expressed his opinion that certain of Khrushchev's statements were false. For example, early in his speech Khrushchev says the following:

> Lately, especially after the unmasking of the Beria gang, the Central Committee looked into a series of matters fabricated by this gang. This revealed a very ugly picture of brutal willfulness connected with the incorrect behavior of Stalin.

Boris Nikolaevsky's note 8 to this passage reads:

> This statement by Khrushchev is not quite true: Investigation of Stalin's terrorist acts in the last period of

---

[1] The full text of Khrushchev's speech is available online at: http://chss.montclair.edu/english/furr/research/kl/speech.html

[2] Khrushchev, Nikita S. The New Leader.The Crimes of the Stalin Era. Introduction by Anatol Shub, notes by Boris Nikolaevsky. New York: The New Leader, 1962.

his life was initiated by Beria. … Khrushchev, who now depicts himself as having well-nigh initiated the probe of Stalin's torture chambers, actually tried to block it in the first months after Stalin's death.

I remembered that Arch Getty wrote something very similar in his magisterial work *Origins of the Great Purges*

> Other inconsistencies in Khrushchev's account include an apparent confusion of Ezhov for Beria. Although Ezhov's name is mentioned occasionally, Beria is charged with as many misdeeds and repressions; however, the latter was merely a regional secretary until 1938. Further, many reports note that the police terror began to subside when Beria took over from Ezhov in 1938. Could Khrushchev have conveniently substituted Beria for Ezhov in his account? **What else might he have blurred?** At any rate, Beria's recent execution by Khrushchev and the leadership made him a convenient scapegoat. **Khrushchev's opportunistic use of Beria certainly casts suspicion on the exactitude of his other assertions.** (p. 268 n.28; emphasis added GF)

So I suspected that today, in the light of the many documents from formerly secret Soviet archives now available, serious research might discover that even more of Khrushchev's "revelations" about Stalin were false.

In fact, I made a far different discovery. **Not one specific statement of "revelation" that Khrushchev made about either Stalin or Beria turned out to be true.** Among those that can be checked for verification, every single one turns out to be false. Khrushchev, it turns out, did not just "lie" about Stalin and Beria – he did virtually nothing else except lie. The entire "Secret Speech" is made up of fabrications. This is the "great deed" Taubman praised Khrushchev for! (A separate, though much shorter, article might be written to expose the falsehoods in Taubman's own *New York Times* Op-Ed article celebrating Khrushchev's meretricious speech).[3]

---

[3] A few examples here: It was Beria, not Khrushchev, who released many prisoners, though not "millions", as Taubman claims. The "thaw" he celebrates had begun during the last Stalin years. Khrushchev **limited** it to "rightist", anti-Stalin material only. Stalin

For me, as a scholar, this was a troubling and even unwelcome discovery. If, as I had anticipated, I had found that, say, 25% or so of Khrushchev's "revelations" were falsifications, my research would surely excite some skepticism as well as surprise. But in the main I could anticipate acceptance, and praise: "Good job of research by Furr", and so on.

But I feared – and my fears have been born out by my experience with the Russian-language original of this book, published in December 2007 – that if I claimed **every one** of Khrushchev's "revelations" was false, no one would believe me. It would not make any difference how thoroughly or carefully I cited evidence in support of my arguments. To disprove the whole of Khrushchev's speech is, at the same time, to challenge the whole historical paradigm of Soviet history of the Stalin period, a paradigm to which this speech is foundational.

The most influential speech of the 20th century – if not of all time – a complete fraud? The notion was too monstrous. Who would want to come to grips with the revision of Soviet, Comintern, and even world history that the logic of such a conclusion would demand? It would be infinitely easier for everyone to believe that I had "cooked the books," shaded the truth – that **I** was falsifying things, just as I was accusing Khrushchev of doing. Then my work could be safely ignored, and the problem would "go away." Especially since I am known to have sympathy towards the worldwide communist movement of which Stalin was the recognized leader. When a researcher comes to conclusions that suspiciously appear to support his own preconceived ideas, it is only prudent to suspect him of some lack of objectivity, if not worse.

So I would have been much happier if my research had concluded that 25% of Khrushchev's "revelations" about Stalin and Beria were false. However, since virtually all of those "revelations" that can be checked are, in fact, falsehoods, the onus of evidence lies even more heavily on me as a scholar than would ordinarily be the case. Accordingly, I have organized my report on this research in a somewhat unusual way.

The entire book is divided into two separate but interrelated sections.

---

had tried to retire in October 1952, but the 19th Party Congress had refused to permit it. Taubman claims Khrushchev said he was "not involved" in the repressions, yet Khrushchev had not responded to Stalin's urgings, but had **taken the initiative**, demanding higher "quotas" for repressions than the Stalin leadership wanted. Taubman claims "Khrushchev somehow retained his humanity." It would be more accurate to say the opposite: Khrushchev appears more like a thug and murderer.

In the first sections, consisting of Chapters 1 through 9, I examine each of the statements, or assertions, that Khrushchev made in his report and that constitute the essence of his so-called "revelations." (To jump ahead a bit, I note that I have identified sixty-one such assertions).

Each of these "revelations" is preceded by a quotation from the "Secret Speech" which is then examined in the light of the documentary evidence. Most of this evidence is presented as quotations from primary sources. Only in a few cases do I quote from secondary sources. I have set myself the task of presenting the best evidence that I can find, drawn in the main from former Soviet archives in order to demonstrate the false character of Khrushchev's Speech at the 20th Party Congress. Since, if interspersed with the text, long documentary citations would make for difficult reading, I have only briefly referred to the evidence in the text and reserved the fuller quotations from the primary (and occasionally secondary) sources themselves in the sections on each chapter in the Appendix..

The second section of the book, Chapters 10 through 12, is devoted to questions of a methodological nature and to a discussion of some of the conclusions which flow from this study. I have given special attention to a typology of the falsehoods, or methods of deception that Khrushchev employed. A study of the "rehabilitation" materials of some of the Party leaders named in the Speech is included here.

I handle the references to primary sources in two ways. In addition to the traditional academic documentation through footnote and bibliography I have tried wherever possible to guide the reader to those primary documents available either in part or in full on the Internet. All of these URL references were valid at the time the English language edition of this book was completed.

In a few cases, I have placed important primary documents on the Internet myself, normally in Adobe Acrobat (pdf) format. In a few cases this has made it possible for me to refer to page numbers, something that is either clumsy or impossible if using hypertext markup language (HTML).

In conclusion I would like to thank my colleagues in the United States and in Russia who have read this work in its earlier drafts and given me the benefit of their criticism. Naturally, they bear no responsibility for any errors and shortcomings that remain in the book despite their best efforts.

My especial gratitude goes to my wonderful colleague in Moscow, Vladimir L'vovich Bobrov. Scholar, researcher, editor, and translator, master of both his native Russian and English, I would never have undertaken this work, much less completed it, without his inspiration, guidance, and assistance of all kinds.

I will be grateful for any comments and criticisms of this work by readers.

Chapter 1.

The Cult and Lenin's "Testament"

1. The Cult

Khrushchev:

> Comrades! In the report of the Central Committee of the party at the 20th Congress, in a number of speeches by delegates to the Congress, as also formerly during the plenary CC/CPSU [Central Committee of the Communist Party of the Soviet Union] sessions, quite a lot has been said about the cult of the individual and about its harmful consequences.

> After Stalin's death the Central Committee of the party began to implement a policy of explaining concisely and consistently that it is impermissible and foreign to the spirit of Marxism-Leninism to elevate one person, to transform him into a superman possessing supernatural characteristics, akin to those of a god. Such a man supposedly knows everything, sees everything, thinks for everyone, can do anything, is infallible in his behavior.

> Such a belief about a man, and specifically about Stalin, was cultivated among us for many years.

> The objective of the present report is not a thorough evaluation of Stalin's life and activity. Concerning Stalin's merits, an entirely sufficient number of books, pamphlets and studies had already been written in his lifetime. The role of Stalin in the preparation and execution of the Socialist Revolution, in the Civil War, and in the fight for the construction of socialism in our country, is universally known. Everyone knows this well.

> At present, we are concerned with a question which has immense importance for the party now and for the future – with how the cult of the person of Stalin has been gradually growing, the cult which became at a

> certain specific stage the source of a whole series of
> exceedingly serious and grave perversions of party
> principles, of party democracy, of revolutionary legality.

This Speech is often referred to as one of "revelations" by Khrushchev of crimes and misdeeds done by Stalin. The issue of the "cult of personality", or "cult of the individual", around the figure of Stalin was the main subject of the Speech. Khrushchev did not "reveal" the existence of a "cult of personality" itself. Its existence was, of course, well known. It had been discussed at Presidium meetings since immediately after Stalin's death.

Yet Khrushchev does not **specifically** state at the outset that Stalin promoted the "cult". This was clearly deliberate on Khrushchev's part. Throughout his speech Khrushchev implies – or, rather, takes it for granted – what he ought to have proven, but could not: that Stalin himself fostered this cult in order to gain dictatorial power. In fact, throughout his entire Speech, Khrushchev was unable to cite a single *truthful* example of how Stalin encouraged this "cult" – presumably, because he could not find even one such example.

Khrushchev's whole speech was built on this falsehood. All the rest of his "revelations" were fitted within the explanatory paradigm of the "cult" around himself which, according to Khrushchev, Stalin created and cultivated.

This study will show that virtually all of Khrushchev's "revelations" concerning Stalin are false. But it's worth mentioning at the outset that Khrushchev's explanatory framework itself – the notion of the "cult" constructed by Stalin and as a result of which the rest of his so-called "crimes" could be committed with impunity – this is itself a falsehood. Not only did Stalin not commit the crimes and misdeeds Khrushchev imputes to him. Stalin also did not construct the "cult" around himself. In fact, the evidence proves the opposite: that Stalin opposed the disgusting "cult" around himself.

Some have argued that Stalin's opposition to the cult around himself must have been hypocrisy. After all, Stalin was so powerful that if he had really wanted to put a stop to the cult, he could have done so. But this argument assumes what it should prove. To assume that he was that powerful is also to assume that Stalin was in fact what the "cult" absurdly made him out to be: an autocrat with supreme power over everything and everyone in the USSR.

Khrushchev mischaracterized the nature of Stalin's leadership

1. Stalin's Opposition to the Cult

Stalin protested praise and flattery directed at himself <u>over and over again</u> <u>over many years.</u> He agreed with Lenin's assessment of the "cult of the individual", and said basically the same things about it as Lenin had. <u>Khrushchev quoted Lenin, but without acknowledging that Stalin said</u> <u>the same things.</u> A long list of quotations from Stalin is given here in evidence of Stalin's opposition to the "cult" around him.[4] Many more could be added to it, for almost every memoir by persons who had personal contact with Stalin gives further anecdotes that demonstrate <u>Stalin's op-</u> <u>position to, and even disgust with, the adulation of his person.</u>

For example, the recently-published posthumous memoir *Stalin. Kak Ia Ego Znal* ("Stalin As I Knew Him", 2003) by Akakii Mgeladze, a former First Secretary of the Georgian Communist Party later punished and marginalized by Khrushchev, the author often comments on Stalin's dislike of the "cult" around him. Mgeladze, who died in 1980, recounts how Stalin wished to suppress any special celebration of his 70th birthday in 1949 and acceded to it with reluctance only because of the arguments made by other Party leaders that the event would serve to unite the communist movement by bringing together its leaders from around the <u>world.</u>

Stalin was more successful in preventing others in the Politburo from renaming Moscow "Stalinodar" (= "gift of Stalin") in 1937. But his attempt to refuse the award of <u>Hero of the Soviet Union</u> was thwarted when the award, which he never accepted, was pinned to a pillow which was placed in his coffin at his death.

2. Malenkov's Attempt to Call a CC Plenum Concerning the "Cult" April 1953

Immediately after Stalin's death, Malenkov proposed calling a Central Committee Plenum to deal with the harmful effects of the cult. Malenkov was honest enough to blame himself and his colleagues and <u>reminded</u> <u>them all that Stalin had frequently warned them against the "cult" to no</u> <u>avail. This</u> attempt failed in the Presidium; the special Plenum was never called. If it had been, Khrushchev's "Secret Speech" could not have taken place.

---

[4] See the quotations for Chapter 1 in Appendix 1 for a long list of quotations of Stalin showing his opposition to the "cult" around him.

Whether Khrushchev supported Malenkov's proposal or not – the evidence is unclear on this point – he was certainly involved in the discussion. Khrushchev knew all about Malenkov's attempt to deal with the "cult" openly and early on. But he said nothing about it, thereby effectively denying that it had occurred.

3. July 1953 Plenum – Beria Attacked for Allegedly Opposing "Cult"

At the July 1953 Plenum, called to attack an absent (and possibly already dead) Beria, a number of the figures blamed Beria for **attacking** the cult. Khrushchev's leading role at this Plenum and in the cabal of leaders against Beria shows that he was complicit in attacking Beria and so in supporting the "cult" as a weapon with which to discredit Beria.

4. Who Fostered the "Cult"?

A study of the origins of the "cult" is beyond the scope of this article. But there is good evidence that oppositionists either began the "cult" around Stalin or participated eagerly in it as a cover for their oppositional activities. In an unguarded moment during one of his *ochnye stavki* (face-to-face confrontations with accusers) Bukharin was forced to admit that he urged former Oppositionists working for *Izvestiia* to refer to Stalin with excessive praise, and used the term "cult" himself. Another Oppositionist, Karl Radek, is often said to have written the first full-blown example of the "cult", the strange futuristic *Zodchii Sotsialisticheskogo Obshchestva* ("The Architect of Socialist Society"), for the January 1, 1934 issue of *Izvestiia*, subsequently published as a separate pamphlet.

5. Khrushchev and Mikoian

Khrushchev and Mikoian, the main figures from the Stalin Politburo who instigated and avidly promoted the "de-Stalinization" movement, were among those who, in the 1930s, had fostered the "cult" most avidly.

If this were all, we might hypothetically assume that Khrushchev and Mikoian had truly respected Stalin to the point of being in awe of him. This was certainly the case with many others. Mgeladze's memoir shows one example of a leading Party official who retained his admiration for Stalin long after it was fashionable to discard it.

But Khrushchev and Mikoian had participated in the Presidium discussions of March 1953 during which Malenkov's attempt to call a Central

Committee Plenum to discuss the "cult" had been frustrated. They had been leaders in the June 1953 Plenum during which Beria had been sharply criticized for opposing the "cult" of Stalin.

These matters, together with the fact that Khrushchev's "revelations" are, in reality, fabrications means there must be something else at work here.

2. Lenin's "Testament"

Khrushchev:

> Fearing the future fate of the party and of the Soviet nation, V. I. Lenin made a completely correct characterization of Stalin, pointing out that it was necessary to consider the question of transferring Stalin from the position of the Secretary General because of the fact that Stalin is excessively rude, that he does not have a proper attitude toward his comrades, that he is capricious and abuses his power.
>
> In December 1922, in a letter to the Party Congress, Vladimir Ilyich wrote: 'After taking over the position of Secretary General, Comrade Stalin accumulated in his hands immeasurable power and I am not certain whether he will be always able to use this power with the required care.'

We must interrupt this quotation to note an important fact. Khrushchev here attributes to Lenin the accusation that Stalin "abuses his power." In reality, Lenin wrote only that he was "not certain whether he [Stalin] will be always able to use this power with the required care." There is nothing in Lenin's words about accusing Stalin of "abusing his power."

Khrushchev continues:

> This letter – a political document of tremendous importance, known in the party history as Lenin's "testament" – was distributed among the delegates to the 20th Party Congress. You have read it and will undoubtedly read it again more than once. You might reflect on Lenin's plain words, in which expression is given to Vladimir Ilyich's anxiety concerning the party, the people, the state, and the future direction of party policy.

Vladimir Ilyich said:

> Stalin is excessively rude, and this defect, which can
> be freely tolerated in our midst and in contacts
> among us Communists, becomes a defect which
> cannot be tolerated in one holding the position of
> the Secretary General. Because of this, I propose
> that the comrades consider the method by which
> Stalin would be removed from this position and by
> which another man would be selected for it, a man
> who, above all, would differ from Stalin in only one
> quality, namely, greater tolerance, greater loyalty,
> greater kindness and more considerate attitude
> toward the comrades, a less capricious temper, etc.

This document of Lenin's was made known to the
delegates at the 13th Party Congress who discussed the
question of transferring Stalin from the position of
Secretary General. The delegates declared themselves in
favor of retaining Stalin in this post, hoping that he
would heed the critical remarks of Vladimir Ilyich and
would be able to overcome the defects which caused
Lenin serious anxiety.

Comrades! The Party Congress should become
acquainted with two new documents, which confirm
Stalin's character as already outlined by Vladimir Ilyich
Lenin in his "testament." These documents are a letter
from Nadezhda Konstantinovna Krupskaia to [Lev B.]
Kamenev, who was at that time head of the Political
Bureau, and a personal letter from Vladimir Ilyich Lenin
to Stalin.

I will now read these documents:

> LEV BORISOVICH!

> Because of a short letter which I had written in
> words dictated to me by Vladimir Ilyich by
> permission of the doctors, Stalin allowed himself
> yesterday an unusually rude outburst directed at me.
> This is not my first day in the party. During all these
> 30 years I have never heard from any comrade one
> word of rudeness. The business of the party and of

Ilyich are not less dear to me than to Stalin. I need at present the maximum of self-control. What one can and what one cannot discuss with Ilyich I know better than any doctor, because I know what makes him nervous and what does not, in any case I know better than Stalin. I am turning to you and to Grigorii [E. Zinoviev] as much closer comrades of V. I. and I beg you to protect me from rude interference with my private life and from vile invectives and threats. I have no doubt as to what will be the unanimous decision of the Control Commission, with which Stalin sees fit to threaten me; however, I have neither the strength nor the time to waste on this foolish quarrel. And I am a living person and my nerves are strained to the utmost."

N. KRUPSKAIA

Nadezhda Konstantinovna wrote this letter on December 23, 1922. After two and a half months, in March 1923, Vladimir Ilyich Lenin sent Stalin the following letter:

TO COMRADE STALIN:

COPIES FOR: KAMENEV AND ZINOVIEV

Dear Comrade Stalin!

You permitted yourself a rude summons of my wife to the telephone and a rude reprimand of her. Despite the fact that she told you that she agreed to forget what was said, nevertheless Zinoviev and Kamenev heard about it from her. I have no intention to forget so easily that which is being done against me; and I need not stress here that I consider as directed against me that which is being done against my wife. I ask you, therefore, that you weigh carefully whether you are agreeable to retracting your words and apologizing or whether you prefer the severance of relations between us.

SINCERELY: LENIN

MARCH 5, 1923

(Commotion in the hall.)

Comrades! I will not comment on these documents.
They speak eloquently for themselves. Since Stalin could
behave in this manner during Lenin's life, could thus
behave toward Nadezhda Konstantinovna Krupskaia –
whom the party knows well and values highly as a loyal
friend of Lenin and as an active fighter for the cause of
the party since its creation – we can easily imagine how
Stalin treated other people. These negative characteristics
of his developed steadily and during the last years
acquired an absolutely insufferable character."

The document in question was not widely "known in the party history as
Lenin's 'Testament'". Khrushchev took this term from Trotsky, who
wrote a book with that title in 1934. It had never been known as such in
the Bolshevik Party except among oppositionists. In fact there is a history
to the very use of the term "Lenin's Testament" – one that does not reflect well on Khrushchev.

In 1925 Trotsky, in a sharp criticism of Max Eastman's book *Since Lenin
Died*, had explicitly repudiated Eastman's lie that Lenin left a "testament"
or "will." Along with the other members of the Politburo, Trotsky said
that Lenin had not done so. And that appears to be correct: there is no
evidence at all that Lenin intended these documents as a "testament" of
any kind. Then, in the 1930s, Trotsky changed his mind and began writing about "Lenin's Testament" again, this time as a part of his partisan
attack on Stalin. Therefore Khrushchev or, more likely, one of his collaborators, must have taken this usage from Trotsky – though they would
never have publicly acknowledged doing so.

Other aspects of Khrushchev's speech are similar to Trotsky's writings.
For example, Trotsky viewed the Moscow Trials as faked frame-ups –
naturally enough, because he was an absent co-defendant in them. Although the first Moscow Trial defendant, Akbal Ikramov of the March
1938 "Bukharin" Trial, was not officially "rehabilitated" until May 1957,
after the 20th Party Congress[5], Khrushchev did deplore the executions of

---

[5] Ikramov was rehabilitated on June 3, 1957. See *Reabilitatsiia. Kak Eto Bylo. Febral' 1956 –
nachalo 80-kh godov. Moskva: "Materik", 2003.* (hereafter *RKEB 2*), 851. See also
http://www.memo.ru/memory/communarka/chapter5.htm

Zinoviev, Kamenev, and Trotskyites in the Secret Speech. This constituted at least an implicit declaration of their innocence, since their punishment would not be considered too harsh for anyone really guilty of the crimes to which they confessed in 1936.

But in fact the whole tenor of Khrushchev's speech, which blamed Stalin alone for derailing socialism through immense crimes of which Khrushchev held him alone responsible, was identical to Trotsky's demonized portrait of Stalin. Trotsky's widow recognized this fact, and applied for the rehabilitation of her late husband and within a day of the "Secret Speech".[6] The fact that Natalia Sedova-Trotskaia learned of the supposedly "secret" speech immediately it happened suggests that the Trotskyites may have still had high-level informants in the CPSU.

There are good reasons to suspect that Lenin's letter to Stalin of March 5, 1923 may be a forgery. Valentin A. Sakharov has published a major scholarly book on this subject on this thesis with Moscow University Press. His general argument is outlined in several articles of his and in reviews of the book.[7]

There is no question that at the time Stalin himself, and everybody who knew about it, believed that it was genuine. But even if genuine, Lenin's letter to Stalin of March 5 1923 does not show what it has often been assumed to show – that Lenin was estranged from Stalin. For less than two weeks later his wife Nadezhda Konstantinova Krupskaia (called "c(omrade) Ul'ianova (N.K.)" in this exchange) told Stalin that Lenin had very insistently asked her to make Stalin promise to obtain cyanide capsules for him, in order to end his great suffering. Stalin agreed, but then reported to the Politburo on March 23 that he could not bring himself to do it, "no matter how humane it might be."

---

[6] Aimermakher, I., V.IU. Afiani, et al. eds. *Doklad Khrushcheva o kul'te lichnosti Stalina na XX s"ezdt KPSS. Dokumenty. Moscow: ROSSPEN, 2002.* (hereafter *Doklad Khrushcheva)* Razdel IV, Dok. No. 3, p. 610. The editors of this official volume note that the letter must be dated on or after February 25; that is, they relate it to Khrushchev's Speech, which was delivered the same day. Another possibility is that Sedova's letter was written in response to Mikoian's speech to the Congress on February 16. A facsimile of Sedova's letter to the Presidium of the 20th Party Congress is at
http://chss.montclair.edu/english/furr/research/sedovaltr022856.jpg

[7] V.A. Sakharov, *"Politicheskoe zaveshchanie"V.I. Lenina: real'nost' istorii i mify politiki.* Moscow: Izdatel'stvo MGU [Moscow State University], 2003.

These documents were quoted by Dmitrii Volkogonov in his very hostile biography of Lenin.[8] Copies of them remain in the Volkogonov Papers in the Library of Congress. There is no doubt about their authenticity. Lidia Fotieva, one of Lenin's secretaries, had made a note in 1922 that Lenin had told her he would request cyanide capsules if his illness progressed beyond a certain point.[9]

Therefore, even if Lenin's letter of March 5, 1923 be genuine — and Sakharov's study calls this into serious question — Lenin still trusted and relied upon Stalin. There was no estrangement between them.

According to Volkogonov (and others),

> In the morning of December 24 Stalin, Kamenev and
> Bukharin discussed the situation. They did not have the
> right to force their leader [Lenin] to be silent. But care,
> foresight, the greatest possible quite, were essential. A
> decision was taken:
>
> 1. Vladimir Ilich is given the right to dictate daily for 5-
> 10 minutes, but this must not be in the form of
> correspondence, and Vladimir Ilich must not expect
> answers to these notes. No meetings are allowed.
>
> 2. Neither friends nor family are permitted to
> communicate anything of political life to Vladimir Ilich,
> so as not to thereby present materials for consideration
> and excitement.[10]

According to Robert Service (*Lenin*), Lenin suffered serious "events" (probably strokes) on the following dates:

- May 25, 1922 – a "massive stroke" (p. 443);
- December 22-23, 1922 – Lenin "lost the use of his whole right side" (p.461);

---

[8] A facsimile of Stalin's letter to the Politburo of March 23, 1923 is published in D.A. Volkogonov, *Lenin. Politicheskii portret. V 2-kh knigakh. Kn. II*. Moscow: Novosti, 1994, pp. 384-385. Stalin's letter to the Politburo of March 23, 1923 is reproduced, with commentary, at http://www.hrono.ru/libris/stalin/16-67.html and in Appendix 1 of the present book.

[9] This note was published in 1991 and can be consulted at http://www.hrono.ru/libris/stalin/16-9.html

[10] Volkogonov, Dmitri. *Stalin*. Vol. I. M., 1992, Ch. 2, par. 156; cited at http://militera.lib.ru/bio/volkogonov_dv/02.html

- The night of March 6-7, 1923 – Lenin "lost the use of the extremities of the right side of his body." (pp. 473-4).

On December 18 the Politburo put Stalin in charge of Lenin's health and forbade anyone to discuss politics with him. Krupskaia violated this rule and was reprimanded for it by Stalin, on December 22. That very night Lenin suffered a serious stroke.

On March 5, 1923 Krupskaia told Lenin that Stalin had spoken rudely to her back in December. Incensed, Lenin wrote Stalin the famous note. According to Krupskaia's secretary V. Dridzo, whose version of this event was published in in 1989, it happened this way:

> Now, when Nadezhda Konstantinovna's name and Stalin's relationship with her is more frequently mentioned in some publications, I wish to tell about those matters I know for certain.

> Why was it only two months after Stalin's rude conversation with Nadezhda Konstantinovna that V.I Lenin wrote him the letter in which he demanded that Stalin excuse himself to her? It is possible that I am the only one who really knows how it happened, since Nadezhda Konstantinova often told me about it.

> It happened at the very beginning of March 1923. Nadezhda Konstantinovna and Vladimir Ilich were talking about something. The phone rang. Nadezhda Konstantinovna went to the phone (in Lenin's apartment the phone always stood in the corridor). When she returned Vladimir Ilich asked her: 'Who called?' – 'It was Stalin, he and I have reconciled.' – 'What do you mean?'

> And Nadezhda Konstantinovna had to tell everything that had happened when Stalin called her, talked with her very rudely, and threatened to bring her before the Control commission. Nadezhda Konstantinovna asked Vladimir Ilich to pay it no mind since everything had been settled and she had forgotten about it.

> But Vladimir Ilich was adamant. He was deeply offended by I.V. Stalin's disrespectful behavior towards Nadezhda Konstantinovna and on March 5 1923 dictated the latter to Stalin with a copy to Zinoviev and Kamenev in which

he insisted that Stalin excuse himself. Stalin had to
excuse himself, but he never forgot it and did not forgive
Nadezhda Konstantinovna, and this had an effect on his
relationship with her."[11]

The next day Lenin had a further serious stroke.

In each case Lenin had a stroke shortly after Krupskaia discussed political
matter with him – something that, as a Party member, she was not supposed to do. This cannot have been a coincidence, for Lenin's doctors
had specifically warned against getting Lenin upset about anything. So it
seems more than possible that, in fact, it was Krupskaia's actions that
precipitated Lenin's last two serious strokes.

As one of Lenin's long-time secretaries Lidia Fotieva said,

Nadezhda Konstantinovna did not always conduct
herself as she should have done. She might have said too
much to Vladimir Ilich. She was used to sharing
everything with him, even in situations when she should
not have done that at all…For example, why did she tell
Vladimir Ilich that Stalin had been rude to her on the
telephone?…[12]

Incidentally, when Stalin's wife committed suicide in 1932, Krupskaia
wrote the following letter of consolation to Stalin, which was published
in *Pravda* on November 16, 1932:

Dear Iosif Vissarionych:

These days everything somehow makes me think about
you, makes me want to hold your hand. It is hard to lose
a person who is close to you. I keep remembering those
talks with you in Ilich's office during his illness. They
gave me courage at that time.

\I press your hand yet again. N. Krupskaia.[13]

---

[11] V.S. Dridzo, "Vospominania." *Kommunist* 5 (1989).

[12] L. Fotieva. Cited in A. Bek, "K istorii poslednikh leninskikh dokumentov. Iz arkhiva
pisatelia, besedovavshego v 1967 s lichnymi sekretariami Lenina." *Moskovskie Novosti* No.
17, April 23, 1989, pp. 8-9.

[13] Cited in E.N. Gusliarov, *Stalin v zhizni. Sistematizirovannyi svod vospominanii sovremennikov,
dokumentov zpokhi, versii istorikov.* Moscow: OLMA-Press, p. 237. Online at
http://www.stalin.su/book.php?action=page&fr_page=6&fr_book_id=1 Also cited in
Novoe Vremia No. 46, Nov. 14, 2004.

This letter shows once again that Stalin was not estranged from Lenin's wife after the December 1922 dispute.

Stalin was held in very high esteem by all those in Lenin's household. The writer Aleksandr Bek wrote down the reminiscences of Lidia Fotieva, in which she said:

> You do not understand those times. You don't understand what great significance Stalin had. Stalin was great... Maria Il'inichna [Ul'ianova, Lenin's sister] during Vladimir Ilich's lifetime told me: 'After Lenin, Stalin is the most intelligent person in the party... Stalin was an authority for us. We loved Stalin. He was a great man. Yet he often said: 'I am only a pupil of Lenin's.' (In Bek, *op.cit.*)

Khrushchev was simply trying to make Stalin "look bad," rather than transmit any understanding of what went on.

It is obvious that Khrushchev took Lenin's letter to Stalin out of context, and in so doing he seriously distorted the situation. He omitted the fact that the Central Committee had instructed Stalin to make sure Lenin was isolated from political issues for the sake of his health. This prohibition explicitly mentioned "friends" and "domestic persons." Since Lenin's secretaries were not likely to violate a Central Committee directive, probably the term "domestic persons" was specifically intended to include Lenin's sister and Krupskaia, his wife. Stalin had criticized Krupskaia for violating this isolation.

Nor did Khrushchev mention Stalin's reply of March 7, 1923 to Lenin's note, or Lenin's later request to Stalin for poison. By omitting these facts, Khrushchev seriously distorted the context in which Lenin's note to Stalin of March 5 1923 occurred, and deliberately distorted Lenin's relationship with Stalin.

Khrushchev omitted the accounts of Lenin's sister Maria Il'inichna. Lenin's secretaries Volodicheva and Fotieva, and Krupskaia's secretary Dridzo, were still alive, but their testimony was not sought. He omitted the evidence that Krupskaia's actions in violating the CC's prohibition about getting Lenin upset may well have been the cause of two Lenin's strokes. He omitted the fact that, far from making any break with Stalin, two weeks **later** Lenin trusted only Stalin with the secret request to be given poison if he asked for it. Finally, he omitted Krupskaia's reconciliation with Stalin.

Khrushchev strove to depict Stalin in a bad light in this affair at all costs. He showed no interest in what had really happened or an understanding of the events in their context.

Chapter 2.

Collegiality "Trampled"

3. "Collegiality" In Work

At several points in his speech, Khrushchev complains about Stalin's lack of collegiality and violation of collective leadership. Here is a typical passage:

> We have to consider seriously and analyze correctly this matter in order that we may preclude any possibility of a repetition in any form whatever of what took place during the life of Stalin, who absolutely did not tolerate collegiality in leadership and in work, and who practiced brutal violence, not only toward everything which opposed him, but also toward that which seemed, to his capricious and despotic character, contrary to his concepts.

This very general accusation can be easily refuted, but only in similarly general terms, by citing the testimony of many others who worked with Stalin, some more closely than Khrushchev ever had. Marshal Georgii Zhukov had worked with him closely during the war, and testifies to Stalin's method of work. In the first quotation he obviously has the "Secret Speech" in mind and calls Khrushchev a liar. General Shtemenko says much the same thing.[14]

According to Ivan A. Benediktov, long-time Minister for Agriculture, decisions were always taken collegially. Dmitrii T. Shepilov, by far Stalin's junior, did not work as closely with Stalin, but his anecdote is revealing. Even Khrushchev himself, in his memoirs, contradicted himself and called Stalin's ability to change his own mind when faced with someone who disagreed with him and defended his viewpoint well, "characteristic."

---

[14] These and other quotations are given in Appendix 1.

Anastas Mikoian supported Khrushchev wholeheartedly and was very antagonistic to Stalin. Yet Mikoian complained that democracy and collective leadership were never achieved at any time under Khrushchev or Brezhnev.

It was Khrushchev himself who refused to lead collectively, and was removed in large part for that in 1964. It appears that Mikhail A. Suslov, who gave the main speech against Khrushchev, echoed in his wording **both** Lenin's "characteristics" letter about Stalin of 1922 **and** Khrushchev's "Secret Speech" attacks on the "cult" around Stalin. The irony could not have been lost on Khrushchev or his audience.

4. Stalin "Morally and Physically Annihilated" Leaders Who Opposed Him

> Stalin acted not through persuasion, explanation and patient cooperation with people, but by imposing his concepts and demanding absolute submission to his opinion. Whoever opposed this concept or tried to prove his viewpoint and the correctness of his position was doomed to removal from the leading collective and to subsequent moral and physical annihilation.

There is not one single example, during Stalin's whole life, of his "removing" someone "from the collective leadership" because that person disagreed with Stalin. It is significant that Khrushchev himself does not even allege a specific instance.

Stalin was the General Secretary of the Party's Central Committee. He could be removed by the Central Committee at any time. His was only one vote in the Politburo and in the Central Committee. Stalin tried to resign from his post as General Secretary four times. Each time his attempt was rejected. The last such attempt was at the 19th Party Congress, in October 1952. It too was rejected.

Khrushchev and the rest not only could have opposed Stalin, but did in fact oppose him. Some examples are given below – for example, that of the taxes on the peasantry, which apparently came up in February 1953.[15] None of those who opposed the tax increase were "removed from the

---

[15] This claim of Khrushchev's is discussed in Chapter 9.

leading collective," "morally annihilated" – whatever that means – or "physically annihilated."

Although Stalin never removed anyone from the leadership for opposing him, Khrushchev did. Khrushchev and the others had Lavrentii Beria arrested suddenly on June 26, 1953, on false charges and without any evidence. Subsequently they had Beria killed, together with six others – Merkulov, Dekanozov, Kobulov, Goglidze, Meshik, and Vlodzimirskii – who had been close associates of his.

Nor was Beria the only person in the leadership of the Party whom Khrushchev had removed for disagreeing with him. In July 1957 Khrushchev called a CC Plenum to have Malenkov, Molotov, Kaganovich, and Shepilov removed from the leadership simply because they disagreed with his policies and had tried to get Khrushchev voted out of the Party leadership. Khrushchev's high-handedness was a main reason for his removal by the Central Committee in 1964.

Khrushchev and those who supported him needed to have some kind of explanation or excuse for failing to oppose Stalin in all his alleged "crimes" during all the years they shared the Party leadership with him. It seems that this – the threat of "annihilation" – became their alibi. Khrushchev evidently said many times that, if "they" had tried to "restore Leninist norms to the Party," or to ask him to retire, "not even a wet spot would have remained of us."[16]

Others in the communist movement saw through this thin excuse:

> When the Soviet leader Anastas Mikoian led the CPSU delegation to China to attend the CCP's 8th Congress in 1956, P'eng [Te-huai] asked him face to face why it was only now that the Soviet party was criticizing Stalin. Mikoian apparently replied: 'We did not dare advance our opinion at that time. To have done so would have meant death.' To which P'eng retorted: 'What kind of a communist is it who fears death?'[17]

But of course the accusation itself was false.

---

[16] E.g. by IUrii Shapoval, "Proshchanie s vlast'iu", *Zerkalo Nedeli* Oct. 23-29, 2004. At http://www.zerkalo-nedeli.com/nn/print/48113/

[17] Roderick Macfarquhar, *The Origins of the Cultural Revolution. Vol. 2* (New York: Columbia University Press, 1983), p. 194.

5. Mass Repressions Generally

Khrushchev:

> Worth noting is the fact that, even during the progress of
> the furious ideological fight against the Trotskyites, the
> Zinovievites, the Bukharinites and others, extreme
> repressive measures were not used against them. The
> fight was on ideological grounds. But some years later,
> when socialism in our country was fundamentally
> constructed, when the exploiting classes were generally
> liquidated, when the Soviet social structure had radically
> changed, when the social basis for political movements
> and groups hostile to the party had violently contracted,
> when the ideological opponents of the party were long
> since defeated politically – then the repression directed
> against them began. It was precisely during this period
> (1935-1937-1938) that the practice of mass repression
> through the Government apparatus was born, first
> against the enemies of Leninism – Trotskyites,
> Zinovievites, Bukharinites, long since politically defeated
> by the party – and subsequently also against many honest
> Communists, against those party cadres who had borne
> the heavy load of the Civil War and the first and most
> difficult years of industrialization and collectivization,
> who actively fought against the Trotskyites and the
> rightists for the Leninist party line.

Nothing in Khrushchev's speech was more shocking than his accusation
that Stalin had instigated massive and unjustified repression against high-
ranking Bolsheviks. We will examine his specific allegations below, and
preface those remarks here by stressing a few basic points.

Khrushchev himself was responsible for massive repressions, possibly
more than any other single individual aside from Nikolai Ezhov, head of
the NKVD from 1936 to late 1938, who was certainly bloodier than anyone else.[18] Unlike Stalin and the central Party leadership to whom he reported, but like Ezhov and many others, Khrushchev either had to know

---

[18] IUrii Zhukov adds Robert I. Eikhe to this group of bloodiest repressors. See
"Podlinnaia istoriia Iosifa Stalina?" *Literaturnaia Gazeta* No. 8 , February 28, 2007. We will
return to this question below.

that many, probably the vast majority of those he repressed were innocent or, at the very least, that their fates were decided without detailed investigation.

Khrushchev was defending both Ezhov and Genrikh Iagoda (Ezhov's predecessor as head of the NKVD) as late as February 1 1956, twenty-four days before the "Secret Speech". He reiterated this defense, though in somewhat more moderate terms, in the "rough draft" of his speech dated February 18, 1956. This is hard to explain unless Khrushchev were already trying to deny that **any** conspiracies had actually taken place, and therefore that all those who had been repressed were innocent. Khrushchev did in fact take that position, though not till well after the 20th Party Congress. In his Speech Khrushchev claimed Stalin must have been responsible for all of Ezhov's repressions. He had to know this was false, since he had far more evidence at his disposal than we do today. It is clear from what relatively little we now have that Ezhov was guilty of huge illegal repressions.

Khrushchev was either candidate or full Politburo member during the investigations that established Ezhov's guilt. However, so were others, such as Mikoian, Molotov, Kaganovich, and Voroshilov. Mikoian was a close accomplice of Khrushchev's. But the acquiescence to Khrushchev's speech by Molotov, Kaganovich, and Voroshilov, though only temporary, can't be explained in the same way.[19]

Khrushchev declared many executed Party leaders "rehabilitated", innocent, in defiance of the evidence we have today, after the release of a small fraction of the documents relating to them. Sometimes he declared them to have been innocent victims of unfounded repression *a priori*, even before the formality of a study of the evidence, Prosecutor's protest, and Supreme Court decision had been completed or even begun. The Pospelov Report[20] was drawn up to provide evidence for Khrushchev that the Party leaders had been unjustly executed, and came to foregone

---

[19] We return to this question in the final chapter.

[20] The "Pospelov Commission Report" or simply "Pospelov Report" is dated February 9, 1956. Its official title is "The Report of the Commission of the CC CPSU to the Presidium of the CC CPSU to Establish the Causes of the Mass Repressions Against Members and Candidate Members of the CC CPSU Elected at the 17th Party Congress." The Report was signed by A.B. Aristov, N.M. Shvernik, and P.T. Komarov in addition to Pospelov. For the Russian text see *Doklad Khrushcheva* 185-230; *RKEB 1* 317-348 does not contain the appendices, including Eikhe's letter.

conclusions. It failed to consider a great deal of the evidence we know exists. Even as it stands it does not prove the innocence of the persons whose repression it studies.

All the evidence we presently have points to the existence of a wide-spread Rightist-Trotskyist series of anti-government conspiracies involving many leading Party leaders, both NKVD chiefs Iagoda and Ezhov, high-ranking military leaders, and many others.[21] Broadly speaking, this is more or less the picture drawn by the Stalin government at the time, except that some vital details, such as Ezhov's involvement in the leadership of the Rightist conspiracy, were never publicly revealed. *why not?*

There is a lot of circumstantial evidence to suggest that Khrushchev himself may well have been a participant in this Right-Trotskyite conspiracy.[22] Such an hypothesis makes sense of much of the evidence we have, but it is suggestive rather than conclusive. However, such a hypothesis would go far towards explaining Khrushchev's attack on Stalin, and even the subsequent history of the CPSU.

Included in the Appendix section below and online in Russia and English are:

- evidence of Khrushchev's massive repressions;
- excerpts from confessions by Iagoda, Ezhov, and Frinovskii (Ezhov's second-in-command) concerning their participation in the Rightist-Trotskyist conspiracy, in the separate section on Ezhov.

6. "Enemy of the People"

Khrushchev:

> Stalin originated the concept "enemy of the people."
> This term automatically rendered it unnecessary that the ideological errors of a man or men engaged in a controversy be proven; this term made possible the usage of the most cruel repression, violating all norms of revolutionary legality, against anyone who in any way disagreed with Stalin, against those who were only suspected of hostile intent, against those who had bad

---

[21] See Chapter 4.

[22] For some of this see the Appendix on the present chapter.

reputations. This concept "enemy of the people" actually
eliminated the possibility of any kind of ideological fight
or the making of one's views known on this or that issue,
even those of a practical character. In the main, and in
actuality, the only proof of guilt used, against all norms
of current legal science, was the "confession" of the
accused himself; and, as subsequent probing proved,
"confessions" were acquired through physical pressures
against the accused. This led to glaring violations of
revolutionary legality and to the fact that many entirely
innocent persons, who in the past had defended the
party line, became victims.

We must assert that, in regard to those persons who in
their time had opposed the party line, there were often
no sufficiently serious reasons for their physical
annihilation. The formula "enemy of the people" was
specifically introduced for the purpose of physically
annihilating such individuals.

Stalin certainly did not "originate the concept." The phrase *l'ennemi du*
peuple was widely used during the great French Revolution. It was used by
the writer Jean-Paul Marat in the very first issue of his revolutionary
newsletter *L'Ami du Peuple* in 1793.[23] Subsequent use of the term derives
from the French Revolution. It is famously the name of a play by Ibsen.
Maxim Gorky used the term in his sketch "The Tauride Chersonese"
("Khersones Tavricheskii") in the "Oath of the Chersonesers," a sketch
published in 1897.

Because all the revolutionaries of 1917 tended to view the revolution in
Russia through the lenses of the revolution of 1789, the term was used
widely from the very beginning. Lenin used the term before the revolution. The Constitutional Democratic Party, called the "Cadets", which
was the party of the rich bourgeoisie, was banned by the Council of People's Commissars on November 28 1917 as an "enemy of the people." It
was signed by Lenin.

A *locus classicus* for the use of the term "enemy of the people" during the
1930s is the Decree of the Central Executive Committee and the Soviet
of People's Commissars of August 7, 1932, also known as "the law of the

---

[23] See http://membres.lycos.fr/jpmarat/jpmif.html

three ears." Here the term "enemy of the people" does not refer at all to oppositionists in the Party, but rather to the pursuit, within the bounds of legality, of thieves, robbers, and swindlers of various kinds. The law was signed by Kalinin, Chairman of the Central Executive Committee (the Legislative Branch), Molotov, Chairman of the Council of People's Commissars (the Executive Branch), and Enukidze, Secretary of the CEC. Since he was not a leading member of either the Legislative or the Executive branches of the Soviet government Stalin did not sign it.

The phrase "enemy of the people" – in Russian, *vrag naroda* – occurs about a dozen times in Stalin's works after the beginning of 1917. Khrushchev himself also used it frequently.[24]

7. Zinoviev and Kamenev

Khrushchev:

> In his "testament" Lenin warned that "Zinoviev's and Kamenev's October episode was of course not an accident." But Lenin did not pose the question of their arrest and certainly not their shooting.

By implication Khrushchev here accused Stalin of having Zinoviev and Kamenev shot without justification. He sidesteps the whole question of their confessions to serious crimes at their 1936 trial. This, of course, is the main issue.

Lenin was furious with Zinoviev and Kamenev for their "strikebreaking" activity near the time of the Bolshevik Revolution. But of course their arrest and execution were not contemplated – they were not charged with involvement in assassinations at that time.

No evidence has ever emerged to suggest that Zinoviev's or Kamenev's confessions were other than genuine. Evidence has emerged since 1991 that corroborates their confessions of guilt. The Russian government has so far refused to release the investigative materials of their case. We now have additional evidence of their guilt, however.

One such piece of evidence – at least, evidence that Stalin himself was convinced they were guilty, and just as convinced that their conspiracy

---

[24] The last time Khrushchev used this term before the "Secret Speech" was just 11 days before in his regular report to the 20th Party Congress. See IU. V. Emel'ianov, *Khrushchev. Smut'ian v Kremle.* Moscow: Veche, p. 32.

really existed – is a private letter from Stalin to Kaganovich, first published in 2001. It's clear from this letter that Stalin is reading the confessions of the defendants at trial and trying to learn and draw conclusions from them.

The section of Dmitriev's confession first published in 2004 is part of an investigative report sent to Stalin by Beria on October 23, 1938. Beria was in the process of rooting out NKVD men who had conspired to frame innocent people, mislead investigations, and aid the Rightists Bukharin, Rykov and others to overthrow the government. The accused.here, D.M. Dmitriev, had been head of the NKVD in Sverdlovsk *oblast'*. He refers directly to the interrogation of Kamenev's wife to which Stalin had referred, and so provides striking verification of the genuine nature of Stalin's letter to Kaganovich of August 23, 1936 printed among the documents in the Appendix. It is completely consistent with a Rightist plot.

We now have a few of Zinoviev's, Kamenev's, and Bukharin's pre-trial interrogations from the Volkogonov Papers, in which all mutually accuse one another – that is, all their confessions are mutually reinforcing, and consistent with their testimony at trial.

We also possess their appeals for clemency to the Supreme Court, which they wrote after their sentencing. In them they again reaffirm their guilt. Even the Rehabilitation report on them published in 1989, though heavily edited, contains suggestions of their guilt, for in it Zinoviev twice states that he is "no longer" an "enemy."

Sentencing Zinoviev and Kamenev, among others, to be shot for treason was not arbitrary if they were guilty, as all the evidence at our disposal at present suggests. We may assume Khrushchev had no evidence of their innocence, or he surely would have had it released. Therefore, we have every reason to conclude that Khrushchev lied hypocritically when he deplored Zinoviev's and Kamenev's fates.

8. Trotskyites

Khrushchev:

> Or, let us take the example of the Trotskyites. At
> present, after a sufficiently long historical period, we can
> speak about the fight with the Trotskyites with complete
> calm and can analyze this matter with sufficient
> objectivity. After all, around Trotsky were people whose

origin cannot by any means be traced to bourgeois
society. Part of them belonged to the party intelligentsia
and a certain part were recruited from among the
workers. We can name many individuals who, in their
time, joined the Trotskyites; however, these same
individuals took an active part in the workers' movement
before the Revolution, during the Socialist October
Revolution itself, and also in the consolidation of the
victory of this greatest of revolutions. Many of them
broke with Trotskyism and returned to Leninist
positions. Was it necessary to annihilate such people?

In a speech to the February-March 1937 Plenum on March 3, Stalin did
refer to Trotskyites in very hostile terms. But he did not advocate perse-
cuting former Trotskyites. While stressing the need for renewed vigilance
Stalin also proposed the establishment of special ideological courses for
all leading party workers. That is, Stalin saw the problem of Trotskyism
as a result of a low level of political understanding among Bolsheviks.

Meanwhile at the same Plenum, in his concluding speech on March 5,
Stalin argued strongly **against** punishing everyone who had ever been a
Trotskyist, and called for "an individual, differentiated approach." This is
precisely what Khrushchev, in the "Secret Speech," claimed that Stalin
did **not** do. So Khrushchev advocated exactly what Stalin advocated at
the Feb.-March 1937 Plenum,[25] while denying that Stalin did this. The
parallel between Khrushchev's and Stalin's speeches are so close that
Khrushchev may in fact have copied this passage out of Stalin's very
speech!

There's a great deal of documentary evidence that Trotsky and his sup-
porters were involved in anti-Soviet conspiracies, including with the
Nazis. Full documentation must await a separate study,[26] but General
Pavel A. Sudoplatov's claim, together with some Nazi documentation

---

[25] There is now considerable evidence to support Soviet allegations of the 1930s that
Trotsky was involved with other Oppositionists within the USSR in a conspiracy to
overthrow the Stalin government, and even that he was in touch with the German and
Japanese military. There is also evidence that clandestine Trotskyist groups, both outside
and inside the Party, were involved in sabotage and espionage within the USSR, and in
spreading false accusations of treason against others.

[26] See Grover Furr, "Evidence of Leon Trotsky's Collaboration with Germany and
Japan." *Cultural Logic* (2009), at http://clogic.eserver.org/2009/Furr.pdf

showing that Sudoplatov was telling the truth, is cited in Appendix 1 at this point.

9. Stalin neglected Party

Whereas, during the first few years after Lenin's death, party congresses and Central Committee plenums took place more or less regularly, later, when Stalin began increasingly to abuse his power, these principles were brutally violated. This was especially evident during the last 15 years of his life. Was it a normal situation when over 13 years elapsed between the 18th and 19th Party Congresses, years during which our party and our country had experienced so many important events?

Khrushchev implies that Stalin failed to call any such Congress. The little evidence that has been published so far from the former Soviet archives suggests that the Stalin leadership wished to call a Congress in 1947 or 1948, but that this suggestion was rejected by the Politburo for some reason that has not been disclosed. The proposal was made by Andrei Zhdanov, who was very close to Stalin. It is highly unlikely that Zhdanov would have made this proposal without Stalin's agreement.

Furthermore, as a member of the Politburo Khrushchev would have been there to hear it! This makes the fact that Khrushchev does not actually **state**, in so many words, that Stalin "refused" or "failed" to call a Congress, significant: many in his audience may have been aware of the plan for an earlier conference. Nor did Khrushchev mention the war of 1941-45 or the Russo-Finnish War of 1939-40. If peacetime years only are counted, then a Congress in 1947 or 1948 would have been timely – three **peacetime** years (1940-1, 1946, 1947) since the Eighteenth Party Congress in 1939.[27]

So once again Khrushchev was not being honest: a Congress **was** planned for 1947 or 1948, but was never held. Khrushchev must have known the details of this very interesting discussion, including the reasons for not calling the Congress. But he never alluded to the fact at all. Nor did he or any of his successors ever release the transcript of this and succeeding CC Plenums. It has not been released to date.

[27] See Ustav Vsesoiuznoi Kommunisticheskoi Partii (bol'shevikov) ... Moscow, 1945, p. 13.

Khrushchev also made the following similar and equally false accusation:

> It should be sufficient to mention that during all the
> years of the Patriotic War not a single Central
> Committee plenum took place. It is true that there was
> an attempt to call a Central Committee plenum in
> October 1941, when Central Committee members from
> the whole country were called to Moscow. They waited
> two days for the opening of the plenum, but in vain.
> Stalin did not even want to meet and talk to the Central
> Committee members. This fact shows how demoralized
> Stalin was in the first months of the war and how
> haughtily and disdainfully he treated the Central
> Committee members.

Even Boris Nikolaevsky's note to the original *New Leader* edition of this speech recognized that this is a lie, though in his final sentence Nikolaevsky shows that he prefers to believe Khrushchev rather than Stalin-era Soviet sources.

> If one were to trust official Soviet sources, this statement
> by Khrushchev would not be true: According to the
> collection, The Communist Party of the Soviet Union in
> the Resolutions and Decisions of Congresses,
> Conferences and Central Committee Plenums (published
> by the Marx-Engels-Lenin-Stalin Institute of the Party
> Central Committee in 1954), one Central Committee
> plenum was held during the war (January 27, 1944),
> when it was decided to give the various Union Republics
> the right to have their own foreign ministries and it was
> also decided to replace the Internationale by the new
> Soviet national anthem. But it is likely that Khrushchev
> is correct, that there was no Central Committee plenum
> in 1944 and a fraud was perpetrated: The plenum was
> announced as having occurred although it never had.

Wishful thinking on Nikolaevsky's part! For if Khrushchev lied here, where else might he have lied? The 1989 Russian edition of Khrushchev's Speech acknowledges that these two Plena were scheduled,[28] and that

---

[28] Doklad Khrushcheva 152 n. 23.

one of them took place, though without pointing up the obvious conclusion – that Khrushchev had lied.

In October 1941 leading party members were at the front and at this, the most crucial time of the war. With the Nazi armies near Moscow, they could not be recalled for a CC meeting. And not only was there, in fact, a CC Plenum on January 27, 1944 – it was the Plenum at which the Soviet National Anthem was changed. Virtually everyone in Khrushchev's 1956 audience had to know this! Yet Khrushchev still said it![29] Perhaps this is best explained as one of Khrushchev's blunders. It was certainly one of many falsehoods in his speech that must have been obvious even at the time.

---

[29] Further decisions of the January 1944 Plenum of the CC are described in a 1985 Soviet textbook *Velikaia Otechestvennaia Voina. Voprosy i Otvety*. Eds. P.N. Bobylev et al. Moscow: Politizdat, 1985. At

http://www.biografia.ru/cgi-bin/quotes.pl?oaction=show&name=voyna083

Chapter 3.

Stalin's "Arbitrariness" Towards the Party

10. Reference to "a party commission under the control of the Central Committee Presidium"; fabrication of materials during repressions

Khrushchev:

> The commission has become acquainted with a large quantity of materials in the NKVD archives and with other documents and has established many facts pertaining to the fabrication of cases against Communists, to false accusations, to glaring abuses of socialist legality, which resulted in the death of innocent people. It became apparent that many party, Soviet and economic activists, who were branded in 1937-1938 as "enemies," were actually never enemies, spies, wreckers, etc., but were always honest Communists; they were only so stigmatized and, often, no longer able to bear barbaric tortures, they charged themselves (at the order of the investigative judges -falsifiers) with all kinds of grave and unlikely crimes.

> [...]

> It was determined that of the 139 members and candidates of the party's Central Committee who were elected at the 17th Congress, 98 persons, i.e., 70 per cent, were arrested and shot (mostly in 1937-1938).
> (Indignation in the hall.) ... The same fate met not only the Central Committee members but also the majority of the delegates to the 17th Party Congress. Of 1,966

> delegates with either voting or advisory rights, 1,108
> persons were arrested on charges of anti-revolutionary
> crimes, i.e., decidedly more than a majority.

This statement is one of my three "Special Cases"[30] for the following reason: Khrushchev implies that Stalin was responsible for something, but does not say precisely what. Nor does he make an explicit accusation. Therefore, strictly speaking, there is no "revelation," and nothing to expose.

However, Khrushchev's statement was certainly meant to imply that Stalin simply had all these Party members murdered. That implication is completely false, and it will be refuted in the present section of this essay. However, even though this implication was clearly intentional and is, as we shall see, false, Stalin is not **explicitly** accused of anything.

We now have the report of this commission, known as the Pospelov Commission,"[31] after Petr N. Pospelov, director of the Institute of Marx-Engels-Lenin and secretary of the Central Committee. An historian, Pospelov directed this commission and later wrote the first draft of Khrushchev's "Secret Speech." During Stalin's lifetime Pospelov's works were among the most flagrant examples of the "cult." He became a close ally of Khrushchev's. Pospelov is considered to have been a very politically-biased historian. Given his position, it would be surprising if he had not been. Even if we knew nothing about him, however, the report that bears his name would suggest that this was the case.

The Pospelov Commission report does indeed conclude that many executed Party figures were innocent. **But the evidence cited in the report does not demonstrate their innocence.** The Commission simply **declared** them innocent. The whole structure of the report makes it clear that its purpose was to find Stalin guilty of massive repressions and to hush up any evidence that contradicted this foregone conclusion.

We also have the summary reports prepared for the "rehabilitations" of those leading Party figures repressed during the 1930s. Some of these

---

[30] See Chapter 10, "A Typology of Khrushchev's Prevarications," for discussion of this and other categories of Khrushchev's prevarications.

[31] Cr. *Reabilitatsiia. Kak Eto Bylo. Dokumenty Prezidiuma TsK KPSS i drugie materialy. V 3-kh tomakh. Tom I. Mart 1953 – Fevral' 1956.* Moscow: Mezhdunarodnyi Fond Demokratiia, 2000, pp. 317-348. Also at http://www.alexanderyakovlev.org/almanah/inside/almanah-doc/55752

reports were prepared before the Pospelov Report, and most of them were prepared afterwards. Edited and published by Alexandr N. Iakovlev's "Memorial" fund, they include the Pospelov Report within them, but much other material too. "Memorial" is a very anti-communist organization extremely hostile to Stalin. It can be assumed that they would have included any and all evidence that tended to make Stalin look guilty of repressing innocent people.[32]

In this section we cover the following matters:

- There is a great deal of evidence suggesting that a significant number of the high-ranking Party members whose repression is cited by Khrushchev appear to have been guilty after all! At the very least, there is sufficient evidence of their guilt that the short summaries of their cases given in the Pospelov Report are utterly insufficient to establish their innocence.

- Ezhov was responsible for fabricating cases against many Soviet citizens. It is possible that this includes a few of the Party members cited by Khrushchev. Ezhov confessed to doing this and was tried and executed for it (See the separate section 17 on Ezhov, below).

- Many, if not most, of the investigations that established the fact of fabrications of confessions and torture against those arrested, were done during Beria's tenure as head of the NKVD, after he replaced Ezhov in late 1938.

- Khrushchev initiated a coverup of the specific reasons for arrests, investigative and trial information, and executions of Central Committee members.

Khrushchev referred to the large per centage of the Central Committee elected at, and Delegates to, the 17th Party Congress in 1934 who were subsequently the victims of repression. As with the more detailed "ac-

---

[32] *Op. cit.* We have also studied the two further volumes of "rehabilitation" materials, but as they publish materials later than the 20th Party Congress, they have no direct bearing on Khrushchev's "Secret Speech."

counting" of the CC delegates later published[33] Khrushchev gives no details about when and why different delegates were arrested, tried, and many of them executed. His account gives the impression that his was done in an undifferentiated way by "Stalin."

But Khrushchev knew better. We can be sure of that, because we have the "rehabilitation" reports, including the Pospelov Commission report. Their contents make clear that there were several different reasons for these arrests and executions.

According to the Commission,

- "Most" were innocent. That implies that some were not, although the Commission did not specify which were guilty, except for Ezhov.

- Some were falsely implicated by others. Both Eikhe and E.G. Evdokimov speak of falsely accusing others, including CC members, when they were beaten or otherwise tortured.

- Some were tortured into signing false confessions and accusations against others.

In addition the Commission emphasizes that Stalin was sent confessions and interrogations of many of those accused, which he then sent on to others on the Politburo. We know this is true, since a few of these have now been published.

Both Khrushchev and the Pospelov Commission try to blame Beria for repression as well as Ezhov. But their own facts – many gathered during Beria's investigation of NKVD crimes and excesses during Ezhov's tenure – and their own statistics, give the lie to this theory. The reality is that Beria **put an end to** the "Ezhovshchina".

The Pospelov Commission report lifts the curtain a tiny bit on what was really going on, while Khrushchev's "Secret Speech" keeps it all resolutely hidden. But neither during the existence of the USSR nor since 1991 have the relevant materials been made available to researchers. So the truth of what went on continues to be covered up. It is reasonable to surmise that this is so because such a study would tend to exculpate both Stalin and Beria, whom Khrushchev and Co. went to great lengths to blame for everything.

---

[33] In *Izvestiia TsK KPSS* No. 12, 1989, pp. 82-113.

In fact Khrushchev himself was one of those most guilty of mass repression. We discussed this briefly in the previous chapter and cite documents as evidence in the Appendix.

In this chapter and the following one, we will examine the case of each of the repressed Party figures named by Khrushchev. In none of these cases did the "rehabilitation" materials, including the Pospelov Commission report, cite sufficient evidence to establish their innocence. In fact, in a number of cases the report itself admits the existence of contradictory evidence.

Since the end of the USSR and the very partial opening of former Soviet archives to a few researchers some evidence relating to the charges against the high Party officials mentioned by Khrushchev and discussed in the Pospelov Commission's report has come to light. The Russian government has refused to make public the full investigative materials about any of these figures. Therefore, we cannot be certain that these men were guilty. But the evidence available to us today demonstrates the utter inadequacy of the Pospelov Commission's conclusions that these men were innocent. The vast preponderance of evidence available to us today points towards their guilt.

11. December 1, 1934 "directive" signed by Enukidze

Khrushchev:

> On the evening of December 1, 1934 on Stalin's
> initiative (without the approval of the Political Bureau –
> which was passed two days later, casually)…

This is a false statement. Khrushchev was complaining to the Party leadership that this law had been signed by the Governmental body – the Presidium of the TsIK – but **not** by the Politburo of the Party.

But the Soviet Constitution said nothing about the Politburo of the Party, and there was thus no reason for the Politburo to pass on this decision. It was signed by Kalinin and Enukidze, Chairman and Secretary of the Central Executive Committee respectively. Khrushchev gives no evidence that it was passed "on Stalin's initiative." Stalin wrote a note on the draft that he was "for publication." This means it had been submitted to him to ask him if he agreed with publishing it. Since it had been submitted to him, this draft at least cannot have come from him in the first place.[34]

The question of this decree is distorted in the 1989 official Russian edition of Khrushchev's Speech, which states that it was not submitted for confirmation by a session of the Central Executive Committee of the USSR. No evidence is given in support of this statement. But even if this is so – what does it have to do with Stalin? He was not Chairman of the CEC. And it is irrelevant to our purpose anyway, as Khrushchev was not referring to ratification by the CEC at all. He was complaining that the Politburo – a Party organ – had not passed on it beforehand. But there was no need for it to do so.

The fact that Khrushchev complained Stalin had not sought approval by the Politburo for this decree supports the theory put forward by some researchers that one of Khrushchev's motives in attacking Stalin was Stalin's attempt to move the Party out of governing society and running the economy. This theory has been supported in various ways by researchers such as Iurii Zhukov, Arch Getty, and Iurii Mukhin, as well as the author of this present work.[35]

12. Khrushchev Implies Stalin's involvement in Kirov's murder.

Khrushchev:

> It must be asserted that to this day the circumstances surrounding Kirov's murder hide many things which are inexplicable and mysterious and demand a most careful examination. There are reasons for the suspicion that the killer of Kirov, Nikolaev, was assisted by someone from among the people whose duty it was to protect the person of Kirov. A month and a half before the killing, Nikolayev was arrested on the grounds of suspicious

---

[34] Volkogonov's photocopy shows that Stalin and Molotov agreed to the publication of the decision, then passed it back to Enukidze, whose signature appears a second time, dated December 2, 1934, to note it had been sent to the newspapers. See http://chss.montclair.edu/english/furr/research/12_01_34_law.pdf

[35] For all these references see Grover Furr, "Stalin and the Struggle for Democratic Reform" (two parts) in *Cultural Logic* (2005). At http://clogic.eserver.org/2005/furr.html and http://clogic.eserver.org/2005/furr2.html

behavior but he was released and not even searched. It is
/ an unusually suspicious circumstance that when the
Chekist assigned to protect Kirov was being brought for
an interrogation, on December 2, 1934, he was killed in a
car "accident" in which no other occupants of the car
\were harmed. After the murder of Kirov, top
functionaries of the Leningrad NKVD were given very
light sentences, but in 1937 they were shot. We can
assume that they were shot in order to cover the traces
of the organizers of Kirov's killing.

In this passage Khrushchev implied, though without stating it overtly, that Stalin was involved in Kirov's murder. As Arch Getty has pointed out, several Soviet and post-Soviet commissions tried to find evidence that Stalin was involve in Kirov's assassination, and all failed. In a longer discussion in *The Road To Terror* (141-7) Getty concludes that there is no evidence at present that Stalin had anything to do with Kirov's assassination. Sudoplatov too concluded there was no reason to suspect Stalin in this assassination.

Getty, along with most Russian researchers, believes that Stalin "framed" – fabricated a false case against – the Oppositionists who were tried, convicted, and executed for involvement in Kirov's assassination. But there is good evidence that they were not framed at all. For example, though only a tiny amount of the investigative material from the Kirov assassination is even open to researchers, and much less than that has been published, we have a partial transcript of an interrogation of Nikolaev, the assassin, in which he incriminates an underground Zinovievist group that included Kotolynov, and a partial interrogation of Kotolynov of the day **before** in which he accepts "political and moral responsibility" for the assassination of Kirov by Nikolaev.[36]

13. Stalin's and Zhdanov's telegram to the Politburo of September 25 1936.

Khrushchev:

---

[36] *Lubianka. Stalin I VChK-GPU-OGPU-NIKVD. IAnvar' 1922 – dekabr' 1936.* Moscow: IDF, 2003, Nos. 481 and 482, pp. 575-577. Vladimir Bobrov and I are preparing a detailed study of the Kirov Assassination.

Mass repressions grew tremendously from the end of 1936 after a telegram from Stalin and [Andrei] Zhdanov, dated from Sochi on September 25, 1936, was addressed to Kaganovich, Molotov and other members of the Political Bureau. The content of the telegram was as follows:

> 'We deem it absolutely necessary and urgent that Comrade Ezhov be nominated to the post of People's Commissar for Internal Affairs. Yagoda has definitely proved himself to be incapable of unmasking the Trotskyite-Zinovievite bloc. The OGPU is four years behind in this matter. This is noted by all party workers and by the majority of the representatives of the NKVD.'

This Stalinist formulation that the "NKVD is four years behind" in applying mass repression and that there is a necessity for "catching up" with the neglected work directly pushed the NKVD workers on the path of mass arrests and executions.

Stalin's phrase did not refer to repression, much less mass repression, at all but to dissatisfaction with the investigation of the recently-discovered Trotskyite-Zinovievite bloc. Getty[37] shows that the phrase "four years behind" must mean four years, not from the Riutin Platform but from the discovery of the bloc of Rights and Trotskyites formed in 1932. That is, it showed suspicion of Iagoda. Thurston and Jansen and Petrov agree.[38]

In fact, Khrushchev knew this too, but hid the fact in the "Secret Speech." The Pospelov-Aristov draft of Khrushchev's speech stated directly that the "four years" was since the formation of the bloc in 1932. (*Doklad Khrushcheva*, 125). Pospelov and Aristov introduced the words *naverstat' upushchennoe* ("catch up what has been neglected"). But this was an invention of theirs. Stalin had not used these words.

---

[37] Getty, *Origins*, Chapter 5; Getty, "The Great Purges Reconsidered". Unpub. PhD diss. Boston College, 1979, p. 326.

[38] Robert Thurston. *Life and Terror in Stalin's Russia, 1934–1941*. (Yale University Press; 1998), p.35; Marc Jansen, Nikita Petrov. *Stalin's Loyal Executioner: People's Commissar Nikolai Ezhov, 1895–1940*. (Hoover Institution Press, 2002), p.54.

Khrushchev picked up this expression, but omitted the fact that the "four years" was since the formation of the bloc. The Pospelov Report also omitted reference to the "bloc," interpreting the "four years" to mean the need for repression (*Doklad Khrushcheva*, 220). An important part of Khrushchev's and Pospelov's basic premise is that no bloc existed.

It's clear that the "neglected work" Stalin and Zhdanov meant in their telegram was the investigation of the Right-Trotskyite bloc and its involvement with representatives of foreign governments in planning a "palace coup" and with "terror" (*terror* = assassination, murder). Both Getty and prominent Trotskyist scholar Pierre Broué affirm that such a bloc really existed. Their studies in Trotsky's own archives at Harvard University, opened in 1980, prove this beyond doubt.[39]

14. Stalin's report at the February-March 1937 CC Plenum

Khrushchev:

> Stalin's report at the February-March Central Committee plenum in 1937, 'Deficiencies of party work and methods for the liquidation of the Trotskyites and of other two-facers', contained an attempt at theoretical justification of the mass terror policy under the pretext that as we march forward toward socialism class war must allegedly sharpen. Stalin asserted that both history and Lenin taught him this.

Stalin's report at this Plenum did not contain any such theoretical justification. Khrushchev seriously distorted Stalin's words. Stalin never said that "as we march forward towards socialism class war must sharpen." What he said was:

> ... the further forward we advance, the greater the successes we achieve, the greater will be the fury of the remnants of the broken exploiting classes, the sooner will they resort to sharper forms of struggle, the more

---

[39] J. Arch Getty, "Trotsky in Exile: The Founding of the Fourth International." *Soviet Studies* 38 No. 1 (January 1986), 28 and n. 19 p. 34; Pierre Broué, "Trotsky et le bloc des oppositions de 1932." *Cahiers Leon Trotsky* 5 (1980) 5-37.

> will they seek to harm the Soviet state and the more will
> they clutch at the most desperate means of struggle, as
> the last resort of doomed people. It should be borne in
> mind that the remnants of the broken classes in the
> U.S.S.R. are not alone. They have the direct support of
> our enemies beyond the bounds of the U.S.S.R.[40]

Stalin went on to call for an individual approach and for political education, not for anything like repressions or "terror." But about the "direct
support of enemies beyond the bounds of the USSR" Stalin was correct.
A great deal of evidence that foreign agents were recruiting Soviet citizens into sabotage and espionage had already been gathered, and a lot
more would be uncovered in the months after the Plenum.

And, in fact, Lenin **had** said something very similar to this in a passage
Stalin had quoted in a speech of April 1929. Even in this speech the solutions Stalin called for were vigilance, along with political education
courses to be organized for all Party leaders above a certain rank. This
call for political education, not mass repression, marks the culminating
point of his speech.

On March 5 1937 Stalin also made another, concluding report at the February-March CC Plenum. This closing speech of the Plenum could never
be termed a "theoretical justification of the mass terror policy". Stalin
explicitly argued that "there must be an individual, differentiated approach. Further on in the report Stalin made the same point again, explicitly arguing **against** a mass approach. Stalin argues that there are, at
most, only a few thousand Party members who could be said to have
sympathized with the Trotskyites, or "about 12,000 Party members who
sympathized with Trotskyism to some extent or other. Here you see the
total forces of the Trotskyite gentlemen."[41]

Rather than calling for a "mass terror policy," Stalin made a strong argument **against** it. Iurii Zhukov (*Inoi Stalin*, 360 ff.) agrees that Stalin's
speech was very mild. A resolution was prepared on his report. It was
passed unanimously, but has never been published. Zhukov quotes it
from an archival copy (362-3).

---

[40] J.V. Stalin, *Mastering Bolshevism* (New York: Workers Library, 1937), p. 30. At
http://www.marx2mao.com/Stalin/MB37.html

[41] *Ibid.,* 60.

Far from calling for "mass repression", as Khrushchev falsely claimed, Stalin called for more inner-Party political education, especially for Party leaders such as those at the Central Committee Plenum. He called for each such Party leader to pick two replacements for him so he could go to Party courses that would last four months, while more local Party leaders would go to courses lasting six months.

Many or most of the Delegates to the Plenum were First Secretaries and local Party secretaries. They could have interpreted this plan as a threat. In effect, they were to choose their own potential replacements. A kind of "competition" for these high Party posts seemed to be in the offing. If the Party Secretaries went off to these courses, who could say that they would return?

In reality, it was the Party First Secretaries and others around the country – including, as we have seen, Khrushchev himself – who turned to "mass repression." These courses were never set up. At the next Plenum in June 1937, the Secretaries instead turned to Stalin with frightening stories of threats by reactionaries and returning *kulaks*. They demanded extraordinary powers to shoot and imprison tens of thousands of these people. This will be discussed in more detail below.

Earlier in the Plenum also, on February 27, Stalin gave the report of the commission on the investigation of Bukharin and Rykov. This marked a total of three reports by Stalin – the most he ever made at any Plenum. In this report he recommended a very mild resolution. Getty and Naumov (411-416) study the voting of the commission and point out that Stalin's recommendations were mildest of all – internal exile. Ezhov, the original reporter, along with Budienniy, Manuil'skii, Shvernik, Kosarev and Iakir all voted to "turn [them] over to trial with a recommendation to shoot them."

See the detailed discussion by Vladimir Bobrov and Igor' Pykhalov[42] in an article that examines a rumor, spread by Bukharin's widow Larina in her memoirs, that **Stalin** had been for execution and and **Iakir** had opposed it – exactly the opposite of what really occurred, but a bit of anti-Stalin "folklore" that became elevated to the status of historical "fact" until the documents were published in post-Soviet times.

---

[42] "Iakir I Bukharin: Spletni I Dokumenty." http://delostalina.ru/?p=333 and elsewhere. It is reprinted in Igor' Pykhalov, *Velikii Obolgannyi Vozhd'* (Moscow: Yauza, 2010), Chapter 6, 355-366.

Stalin had outlined a view that the class struggle had to sharpen as the Soviet Union developed towards socialism. But this was not in 1937, but at the April 1928 Joint Plenum of the Central Committee and the Central Control Commission:

> What is the issue here? It's not at all the issue that the further ahead we drive, the stronger the task of socialist construction becomes developed, then the stronger will grow the opposition of the capitalists. **That isn't the issue**. The issue is why does the opposition of the capitalists grow stronger? (Emphasis added, GF)[43]

According to Bordiugov and Kozlov this thesis had been further developed by Valerian Kuibyshev at the September 1928 Plenum. They add that Bukharin had opposed it at the April 1929 Plenum, but in an equivocal way: Bukharin had agreed that class struggle sharpened at certain times – and agreed that 1929 was one of those times – but said that it was not a general principle.

15. "Many Members questioned mass repression", especially Pavel Postyshev

Khrushchev:

> At the February-March Central Committee plenum in 1937 many members actually questioned the rightness of the established course regarding mass repressions under the pretext of combating "two-facedness.
>
> Comrade Postyshev most ably expressed these doubts. He said:
>
>> I have philosophized that the severe years of fighting have passed. Party members who have lost their backbones have broken down or have joined the camp of the enemy; healthy elements have fought for the party. These were the years of industrialization and collectivization. I never thought it possible that after this severe era had passed

---

[43] Uncorrected transcript of Stalin's speech at the Joint Plenum of the CC and the CCC of the AUCP(b) April 22, 1929, in *Kak lomali NEP. Stenogrammy Plenumov TsK VKP(b) 1928-1929 gg. V 5 tomakh. Tom 4.* (Moscow: MDF, 2000), p.655.

Karpov and people like him would find themselves
in the camp of the enemy. (Karpov was a worker in
the Ukrainian Central Committee whom Postyshev
knew well.) And now, according to the testimony, it
appears that Karpov was recruited in 1934 by the
Trotskyites. I personally do not believe that in 1934
an honest party member who had trod the long road
of unrelenting fight against enemies for the party
and for socialism would now be in the camp of the
enemies. I do not believe it… I cannot imagine how
it would be possible to travel with the party during
the difficult years and then, in 1934, join the
Trotskyites. It is an odd thing… [44]

In the mid-1990s the transcript of this February- March 1937 Central
Committee Plenum was finally published. We can now see that, while this
quotation of Postyshev is genuine, Khrushchev's commentary is deliberately false.

Khrushchev obviously knew he was lying about it. Khrushchev said
"many members…questioned the rightness…" In fact, **not a single
member** did so. Even Postyshev did not do so! After the section quoted
by Khrushchev, Postyshev went on to condemn Karpov, and anyone else
who had joined forces with the enemy.

Postyshev was actually harshest of all at expelling large numbers of people, and was removed as candidate member of Politburo for this at the
January 1938 CC Plenum. Getty demonstrates at length how Postyshev
was raked over the coals at this Plenum for excessive repression, speaking of "the overvigilant Postyshev as being sacrificed for the sake of ending mass expulsions in the party…"[45] (Getty & Naumov 517; cf 533ff.)

---

[44] See *Lubianka. Stalin i Glavnoe upravlenie gosbezopasnosti NKVD 1937-1938*. Moscow: MDF,
2004 (hereafter Lubianka 2) No. 17, pp. 69 ff., a report made to Stalin by Ezhov on
February 2, 1937 of an interrogation of Asranf'ian about a "Right-Leftist" organization in
the Ukraine that was collaborating with the Trotskyist and Ukrainian Nationalist
undergrounds. In the transcript of Asranf'ian's confession of January 14, 1937 Stalin
circled Karpov's name and wrote "Who is this?" in the margin – p. 71-2.

[45] Getty, J. Arch and Oleg V. Naumov, *The Road to Terror. Stalin and the Self-Destruction of the
Bolsheviks, 1932-1939*. New Haven: Yale University Press, 1999 (hereafter Getty &
Naumov)., 517; cf. 533 ff. The document confirming Postyshev's expulsion and arrest is
reproduced on pp. 514-516.

Iuri Zhukov's analysis agrees that at the January 1938 Plenum the Stalin leadership again tried to put brakes on the First Secretaries' illegal repressions. The document confirming Postyshev's expulsion and arrest for repressing innocent people in a mass way is quoted at length, in translation, by Getty and Naumov.

Khrushchev was present at the January 1938 CC Plenum, and certainly knew all about Postyshev's fate and why he was sacked. As a Plenum participant Khrushchev also had to know that "many members" did **not** "question the rightness" of the repressions. Khrushchev himself made a harsh, repressive speech at the February-March 1937 CC Plenum in which he supported the repression wholeheartedly.

Furthermore, it was Khrushchev who replaced Postyshev as candidate member of Politburo.[46] According to Getty and Naumov Khrushchev himself was one of those who were "speaking up forcefully against Postyshev."[47]

Therefore, Khrushchev was lying. Far from "questioning" the mass repressions, Postyshev was one of those who most flagrantly engaged in them himself, to the point where he was the first to be removed from candidate membership in the Politburo, and soon after that expelled from the Party and arrested. The partial transcript of this Plenum now available confirms this. Postyshev's lawless and arbitrary repressions are documented in a letter from Andreev to Stalin of January 31, 1938.

Postyshev was soon arrested, and later confessed to involvement in some kind of conspiracy to participating in a Rightist conspiracy, naming a number of others, including other First Secretaries and CC members. According to Vladimir Karpov, Postyshev confirmed his confession to Molotov.

Given the documentation cited above – a small fraction of all that is available but not yet released – there is every reason to believe that Postyshev's arrest, trial and execution were justified. His execution came more than a year after his arrest. We know there is a lengthy investigative file on him, and a trial transcript, but virtually none of this has been released by the Russian government.

---

[46] Stalinskoe Politbiuro v 30-e gody. Sbornik dokumentov (Moscow: AIRO-XX, 1995), p.167.

[47] Getty & Naumov, 512.

Chapter 4.

The "Cases" Against Party Members and Related Questions

16. Eikhe

Khrushchev:

> The Central Committee considers it absolutely necessary
> to inform the Congress of many such fabricated "cases"
> against the members of the party's Central Committee
> elected at the 17th Party Congress. An example of vile
> provocation, of odious falsification and of criminal
> violation of revolutionary legality is the case of the
> former candidate for the Central Committee Political
> Bureau, one of the most eminent workers of the party
> and of the Soviet Government, Comrade Eikhe, who
> was a party member since 1905.

Khrushchev goes on to quote from several documents pertaining to
Eikhe's case, including part of the text of Eikhe's letter to Stalin of October 27, 1939. This letter – really a declaration of a complaint of mistreatment – exists. There's no reason to doubt Eikhe's claim in it, that he was
beaten by the interrogators into confessing things he never did. However,
there is no reason to believe that Eikhe was telling the truth, or the whole
truth, either.[48]

The Pospelov Report quotes somewhat more from the text of Eikhe's
letter, but does not contain any evidence concerning Eikhe's guilt or innocence. It concludes with the single sentence: "At the present time it
has been unquestionably established that Eikhe's case was falsified." [49]

---

[48] The letter is published in *Doklad Khrushcheva,* pp. 225-229, without archival identifiers.
The original letter, as well as perhaps much else from Eikhe's investigation file, is still
kept top secret by Russian authorities today. Even the editors of this official publication
were not permitted to cite its exact location in the archives. We have translated and annotated it in Chapter 11 below.

[49] *RKEB* 1, p. 328.

Concerning "Torture"

We should keep in mind some things that are, or should be, obvious. The fact that somebody has been beaten or tortured does not mean that that person was "innocent." The fact that a person may have given false confessions under torture does not mean that person was not guilty of yet other offenses. The fact that a person claims that he was beaten, tortured, intimidated, etc., into giving a false confession does not mean that he is telling the truth – that he was, in fact, tortured or that the confessions he gave were false. Of course, it doesn't mean that he is lying, either.

In short, there is no substitute for evidence. Eikhe's letter is not sufficient evidence to establish anything, including whether he was tortured or not.

In one of the few quotations we have from his own trial in 1940, Ezhov claims to have been beaten into false confessions as well. Yet there can be no doubt that Ezhov was guilty of falsifying confessions, beatings and torture, fabricating cases against many innocent people and executing them.

However, this is only part of the Eikhe story. We do not know all of it, because neither Khrushchev, nor any of his successors as heads of the CPSU, nor Gorbachev, Yeltsin, or Putin, have ever seen fit to publish the documents in Eikhe's case, or even to make Eikhe's case available to researchers.

There is good evidence suggesting that it was precisely Eikhe who led the way for the First Secretaries in demanding extraordinary powers to shoot thousands of people and send thousands more to what became the GU-LAG – that it was, in fact, Eikhe who began the mass repression that Khrushchev is claiming to denounce.[50] Iuri Zhukov outlines the details we know. (*KP* Nov. 16, 2002). He believes that Ezhov was working with the First Secretaries on this, and would have arrested and executed Stalin if Stalin had refused them (Nov. 16 2002; Nov. 20, 2002).

In early 2006 a volume was published with transcripts of a single, long interrogation each from Ezhov and Frinovskii, Ezhov's second-in-

---

[50] See S.N. Mironov's note to Nikolai Ezhov of June 17, 1937, printed in Ezhov's "special communication" to Stalin of June 22, 1937, in Vladimir Khaustov and Lennart Samuel'son, *Stalin, NKVD i repressii 1936-1938 gg.* (Moscow: ROSSPEN, 2009) 332-333. Mironov explicitly names Eikhe in this note.

command in the NKVD.[51] Both confess to being a part of the conspiracy
of the Rights that included Bukharin, Rykov, and Ezhov's predecessor as
head of the NKVD Iagoda. Frinovskii names Evdokimov and Ezhov, as
well as Iagoda, as leading Rightist conspirators. He specifically mentions
Eikhe, once as a visitor of Evdokimov's, a second time together with
both Ezhov and Evdokimov.[52] Evdokimov was very close to Ezhov, and
was tried, convicted, and executed together with Ezhov in February 1940.
It is clear that Frinovskii suspected Eikhe was involved in the same
Rightist conspiratorial group that he, Ezhov, Evdokimov and others
were, or he would not have mentioned him in this connection. But he
does not give specifics concerning Eikhe.

Zhukov's hypothesis best explained the known facts even before the
publication of Frinovskii's statement of April 11, 1939. In it Frinovskii
confirms the existence of a very broad Rightist conspiracy all over the
Soviet Union. Evdokimov, who outlined this conspiracy to Frinovskii in
1934, told him that already by 1934 the Rights had recruited a large number of leading Soviet officials around the USSR.[53] It was precisely the
trials and executions of such people that Khrushchev claimed Stalin had
fabricated. Frinovskii's statement makes it clear this was no fabrication.

Evdokimov emphasized that it was now necessary to recruit among the
lower levels of Party, state, and peasant – i.e., kolkhoz – members, in order to take charge of the wave of uprisings which were already under
way, and which the Rights hoped to organize into a movement for a
coup.[54]

According to documents available to Jansen and Petrov, many of which
have been re-classified by the Russian government, Eikhe interfered in
NKVD matters, insisting on the arrest of persons against whom there
was no evidence.[55] Ezhov told his subordinates not to oppose Eikhe but
to cooperate with him. This is consistent with Frinovskii's statement

---

[51] *Lubianka. Stalin i NKVD-NKGB-GUKR "Smersh". 1939 – mart 1946.* Moscow: MDF,
2006, Doc. No. 37, pp. 52-72, and Doc. No. 33, pp. 33-50. This volume will be cited
hereafter as Lubianka 3.

[52] Eikhe confirms one such visit to Ezhov's together with Evdokimov in the letter to
Stalin. Cf. *Doklad* p. 228.

[53] Lubianka 3, p. 38.

[54] Ibid.

[55] M.Jansen, N.Petrov. *Stalin's Loyal Executioner: People's Commissar Nikolai Ezhov. 1895–
1940* (Hoover Inst4itution Press, 2002), p.91.

about the way Ezhov, and he himself, operated – beating and framing innocent persons in order to appear to be fighting a conspiracy while hiding their own conspiracy.

Zhukov believes that the goal of Eikhe, together with other First Secretaries, was to avoid at all costs the contested elections scheduled for December 1937, by claiming that the oppositional conspiracies were too dangerous.[56] Whether they really believed this or not, at the October 1937 CC Plenum they were successful in persuading Stalin and Molotov to cancel the contested elections.

Stalin was under other pressures, too. One of his closest collaborators on the Constitution and election issues, Ia. A. Iakovlev, was suddenly arrested on October 12, 1937. In a confession-interrogation that was first published only in 2004 Iakovlev said he had been working for the Trotskyist underground since the time of Lenin's death, and was cooperating with Trotsky through a German spy.[57] Given this avalanche of evidence that **real** and extremely dangerous conspiracies involving highly-placed persons in the Soviet government, Party and military, Stalin and the Politburo were in no position to ignore firm demands from a number of First Secretaries for an all-out war against the danger.

It is interesting that Eikhe appears to have been tried and executed at the same time as Ezhov and Ezhov's associates. Can it be that the *real* charges against Eikhe at trial were not those of espionage, but that he conspired with Ezhov to accuse, perhaps to torture, and to execute without evidence? A.S. Iakovlev, the famous aircraft designer, wrote in his memoirs that Stalin had told him Ezhov had been executed because he had "killed many innocent people."[58] It appears that Ezhov was executed

---

[56] Stalin wanted elections to the Supreme Soviet of the USSR to take place with 2-3 candidates for a given position. Candidates would be proposed not just by the Communist Party (ACP(b)) but also by union-wide social organizations. As evidence Zhukov published a sample ballot for the December 1937 elections on which is written: "Leave on this ballot the last name of ONE candidate for whom you wish to vote. Cross out the rest." It is the sixth illustration after p. 256 in Zhukov, IU. *Inoi Stalin*. Moscow: Vagrius, 2003. I have put it online at
http://chss.montclair.edu/english/furr/research/sample_ballot_1937.html

[57] Lubianka 2 Doc. No. 26, pp. 387-395.

[58] A.S. Iakovlev, *Tsel' Zhizni*. Moscow: Politizdat, 1973, p. 264. This book is also available online at http://militera.lib.ru/memo/russian/yakovlev-as/20.html

for that, and for his own participation in the Rightist conspiracy. Perhaps that was so with Eikhe.

The whole text Eikhe's letter to Stalin of October 27, 1939 was appended to the Pospelov Commission's report. In it, Eikhe makes clear that he was charged with either conspiring, or working closely with, Ezhov. (p. 229) The evidence we cite here, which was available to Petrov, strongly suggest that Eikhe was deeply involved in Ezhov's mass repression.

Eikhe's claims in his letter to Stalin that he was beaten and tortured into making false confessions is very credible, since he names Ushakov and Nikolaev [-Zhurid] as his torturers. We know independently that these two specific NKVD officers tortured many others, and in fact were tried and executed for precisely this under Beria.

Nikolaev-Zhurid was finally arrested in October 1939 under Beria. This is the same month that Eikhe wrote his letter to Stalin. Nikolaev-Zhurid was also executed, and therefore probably tried, at the same time as were Ezhov and Eikhe, in early February 1940. So was Ushakov.

This suggests that Ezhov and his men may have been trying to put the blame on each other in order to disguise their own responsibility. This is consistent with the way Frinovskii described Ezhov. Frinovskii explicitly describes Ezhov as demanding that Zakovskii be shot so that Beria would not be able to question him and, possibly, learn about Ezhov's role in massive illegal repressions and in the Rightist conspiracy.[59]

Eikhe was arrested on April 29, 1938, long before Beria joined the NKVD, and therefore long before Ezhov had to fear Beria's interrogating Eikhe. Given what we know from Jansen and Petrov's summary of the documents they got to see, it seems clear that Ezhov and Eikhe had some kind of falling out. We know from Frinovskii's statements and from other sources that Ezhov and his men routinely tortured those they arrested, whether guilty or not, to force them to make confessions incriminating themselves.

What we do not have is the rest of Eikhe's case file, including the trial documents – the actual accusations made against him at his trial in February 1940, evidence, testimony, the prosecution's charge (*obvinitel'noe zakliuchenie*) and sentence. We know that the "archival-investigatory file"

---

[59] Lubianka 3, 45.

on Eikhe exists – or did in Khrushchev's day, because it was cited as the place where Eikhe's letter was taken from (p.229).

But the only thing released from the Eikhe case file was the letter to Stalin. The rest of the contents of that file have not been released. And not all of Eikhe's letter to Stalin was in either Khrushchev's Speech or in the Pospelov Report. Specifically, Eikhe wrote that he was not willing to

> …undergo beatings again for Ezhov, who had been
> arrested and exposed as a counter-revolutionary, and
> who was the undoing of me [or, "who has destroyed
> me"] was beyond my strength.[60]

The underlined section was carefully excised from the Pospelov Report, as were the following words:

> My confessions about counter-revolutionary ties with
> Ezhov are the blackest spot on my conscience.

Eikhe evidently believed that Ezhov was a counter-revolutionary; had confessed to counter-revolutionary ties with Ezhov which he here denies; and blamed Ezhov, rather than Beria, for his downfall.

Khrushchev wanted to blame Beria rather than Ezhov. Eikhe blamed Ezhov, so it's easy to see why Khrushchev omitted these passages. Eikhe's claim that Ezhov was in reality a counter-revolutionary would have raised questions in the minds of the Central Committee – questions inconvenient for Khrushchev. The recently-published interrogations of Ezhov and statement by Frinovskii flesh out Ezhov's conspiratorial activity and his frame-ups of innocent people. Khrushchev and Pospelov covered them up too, for the sake of casting all the blame on Stalin and Beria.

Though we'd like to know a lot more, the interrogation /confessions of Frinovskii and Ezhov are fully consistent with the facts outlined above.

17. Ezhov

Although it breaks the order of the original somewhat, it is convenient to examine what Khrushchev says about Ezhov here, since it is closely linked to Eikhe.

Khrushchev:

---

[60] Doklad Khrushcheva, p. 229.

We are justly accusing Ezhov for the degenerate
practices of 1937. But we have to answer these
questions: Could Ezhov have arrested Kossior, for
instance, without the knowledge of Stalin? Was there an
exchange of opinions or a Political Bureau decision
concerning this? No, there was not, as there was none
regarding other cases of this type. Could Ezhov have
decided such important matters as the fate of such
eminent party figures? No, it would be a display of
naiveté to consider this the work of Ezhov alone. It is
clear that these matters were decided by Stalin, and that
without his orders and his sanction Ezhov could not
have done this.

The interrogations of both Ezhov and Frinovskii published in early 2006
fully confirm Ezhov's deliberate torturing and killing of a great many innocent people. He organized these massive atrocities to cover up his own
involvement in the Rightist conspiracy and with German military espionage, as well as in a conspiracy to assassinate Stalin or another Politburo
member, and to seize power by *coup d'état.*

These confessions are the most dramatic new documents to appear in
years that bear upon our subject. They completely contradict Khrushchev's allegations on every point: his contention that Ezhov was just doing Stalin's bidding; that the Military leaders were "framed"; and that the
Moscow Trials were faked (as Khrushchev suggests). We now (2010)
have a great many more interrogations of Ezhov's, all of which confirm
the existence of his very serious conspiracy and give much detail about
it.[61]

Khrushchev, his supporters, and those who did the "research" for the
Pospelov Report and the "rehabilitation" reports, had all this information
at their disposal. So why did they not deal with it in those reports? The
most obvious reason is that they covered it up in order to reach conclusions exactly the opposite from the truth.

---

[61] English translations of the texts of all of Ezhov's interrogations published as of 2010
are in Grover Furr, "Interrogations of Nikolai Ezhov, former People's Commissar for
Internal Affairs," at
http://chss.montclair.edu/english/furr/research/ezhovinterrogs.html

The question naturally arises: Why did Ezhov do all this? Zhukov thinks he may have been in league with a number of the First Secretaries in some kind of conspiracy. Ezhov's men functioned together with the First Secretaries in the provinces. In documents available to Jansen and Petrov in the early '90s and extensively quoted by them in their book, S.N. Mironov, head of the NKVD of the Western Siberian region, tells of being instructed by Ezhov not to interfere with Eikhe even though the latter was insisting on the arrest of persons without evidence and was personally interfering in the investigations.[62] The trial transcripts for those tried at the same time as Ezhov have not been released. But it seems very likely that a number of these men, of whom Eikhe was one, were tried and convicted of working with Ezhov to kill innocent people.

The recently published confessions of Frinovskii and Ezhov now confirm that Ezhov himself headed an important Rightist conspiracy, in collusion with the German military, and that he conspired to seize power in the USSR himself.

All this information, and much more, was of course available to Khrushchev and his investigators. Yet as late as February 1, 1956, Khrushchev took the position that Ezhov was completely innocent, and Stalin was to blame![63] He modified this view of Ezhov only slightly in the "Secret Speech" as he tried to shift all the responsibility for Ezhov's actions onto Stalin.

Stalin, however, blamed Ezhov, and his testimony is entirely consistent with the evidence presented by Jansen and Petrov. In Russia, at least, the passage from aircraft designer A. Iakovlev's memoirs, in which Stalin explained to him how Ezhov had innocent men framed, is very well known. Molotov and Kaganovich said similar things in their interviews with Felix Chuev.

Ezhov was removed from office, evidently with difficulty. In April 1939 Ezhov was arrested for, and immediately confessed to, gross abuses in investigations: beatings, falsified confessions, torture, and illegal executions. Jansen and Petrov, relying in part on documents no longer available to researchers and in part on some documents only released in 2006, show the tremendous extent of these abuses and describe the criminal methods of Ezhov and his men. There is **zero** evidence – none at all --

---

[62] See the Appendix to this chapter for quotations.

[63] See *RKEB 1*, pp. 308-9 and Appendix to this chapter.

that Stalin or the central leadership wanted him in any way to act like this, and plenty of evidence that they thought this criminal.

18. Rudzutak

Khrushchev:

> Comrade Rudzutak, candidate-member of the Political Bureau, member of the party since 1905, who spent 10 years in a Tsarist hard-labor camp, completely retracted in court the confession which was forced from him. ... After careful examination of the case in 1955, it was established that the accusation against Rudzutak was false and that it was based on slanderous materials. Rudzutak has been rehabilitated posthumously.

According to the rehabilitation materials Rudzutak did, in fact, confess.[64] Evidently this was a very detailed confession in which he named "more than sixty people" with whom he was involved in the conspiracy – including Eikhe, who is named twice in the two pages of his rehabilitation report. Then he retracted this confession at trial, stating that he was "forced" to confess by "an abcess [*gnoynik*] not yet uprooted from the NKVD." It is interesting that he evidently did not claim he had been tortured, or the Rudenko's report would have so stated. Molotov later told Chuev Rudzutak had been tortured and did not confess.[65]

There is a great deal of testimony against him. The Rehabilitation Materials by Rudenko of December 24, 1955 do **not** establish Rudzutak's innocence. Furthermore, they acknowledge that Rudzutak was inculpated by a great many other defendants.

Obviously it is problematic to convict someone of a serious crime based only upon his own confession. By the same token, a person cannot be declared innocent solely because he denies consistently denies his guilt. But multiple, independent accusations by different defendants, interrogated by different investigators, is strong evidence in any judicial system. For example, in the United States today, defendants are routinely convicted of conspiracy solely on the testimony of alleged confederates. And

---

[64] *RKEB 1* pp. 294-5.
[65] F.I Chuev. *Molotov: Poluderzhavnyi Vlastelin.* Moscow: OLMA-PRESS, 1999, p. 484.

co-conspirators are guilty of crimes committed by other members of the conspiracy.

There is no evidence in that "rehabilitation" that Rudzutak was innocent, as Khrushchev claimed. The only "evidence" the rehabilitation report can come up with is that the testimonies against him are "contradictory." This is not evidence that they are false. Just the opposite: if a substantial number of confessions or testimonies were identical that would be *prima facie* evidence that they had been "orchestrated" in some way.

Rudzutak evidently retracted his confession at trial. But we can't be sure he retracted **all** of it. The Rudenko Rehabilitation Materials of 1955 give much more extensive information on the accusations against Rudzutak. The Pospelov Report mentions only the accusation that he was in a "Latvian nationalist organization, engaged in sabotage, and was a spy for foreign intelligence."[66]. Khrushchev falsified even this:

> They did not even call him to the Politburo, Stalin did
> not want to speak with him. ... Through an exhaustive
> verification carried out in 1955 it was established that the
> case against Rudzutak was falsified. And he was
> condemned on the basis of slanderous evidence.

There's nothing in either the Rudenko materials or the Pospelov Report about these things. Perhaps Khrushchev just made them up.

And a great deal is omitted. For instance, the Rehabilitation materials on Rudzutak do not even mention Tukhachevsky, though Rudzutak was closely associated with him in expulsions, etc.[67]

This is how we know Khrushchev lied – if the "rehabilitation" report on Rudzutak does not clear him, then Khrushchev did not know, in reality, whether Rudzutak was guilty or not. Khrushchev spoke "in flagrant disregard for the truth" – he may not have known what it was, but he claimed to know. And of course Khrushchev and Pospelov had access to all of Rudzutak's file and to all of the investigative materials linked with it. If exculpatory evidence existed, why did they not cite it?

Still, we do know now that Ezhov and, at his instruction, his men, were fabricating confessions against many thousands of people. It's quite possible that there was some falsification in Rudzutak's case. Ezhov and his

---

[66] *RKEB 1,* p.328.

[67] *RKEB 1* ,pp. 294-5.

interrogators could have falsified some information against Rudzutak even though Rudzutak had admitted his guilt on some matters, and had been implicated by a great many others.

It is all the more important, then to be able to carefully scrutinize all the evidence available to Soviet investigators and courts at the time. But this is exactly what we cannot do. Neither in Khrushchev's day, in Gorbachev's time when "glastnost'", or "openness", was supposed to lead to the archives being "opened", nor to this day, have any but a tiny proportion of the investigative materials against even the major defendants at the three famous Moscow Trials of 1936, 1937, and 1938 been released.

No materials from Rudzutak's case have ever been published, either during the USSR or since. This in itself is suspicious, as Rudzutak was arrested in close association with Tukhachevsky.

Rudzutak was one of the people accused by Stalin of involvement in the Military Conspiracy on June 2, 1937 at the expanded extraordinary expanded session of the Military Soviet.[68] Yet he was not executed until July 28, 1938, over a year after the Tukhachevsky group. This suggests that a long, serious investigation occurred. But we do not have access to any of it.

Rudzutak was convicted through the testimony of others, despite the lack of any confession of his own. He is named in several NKVD documents published in Lubianka 2, such as

- No. 290, M.L. Rukhimovich's very detailed confession. Rudzutak is named on p. 484.
- No. 323, pp. 527-37; Rudzutak is named on p. 530.

Of course these do not prove his guilt, all the more so since they are "Ezhov" documents, confessions made during Ezhov's tenure as head of the NKVD – and we have seen above the kind of stuff that went on under Ezhov. But they are incompatible with any claim Rudzutak was innocent – that is, with his "rehabilitation." A defendant's confession of guilt may not be truthful, for one reason or another. But it can never be evidence of innocence.

Stalin's private annotations on these[69] as well as other documents are consistent with someone trying to learn from the police reports being

---

[68] Lubianka 2, No. 92 pp. 202 ff. On Rudzutak particularly see 204-5.
[69] *Ibid.* p. 537.

submitted to him, but not at all with someone "fabricating" anything. It is hard to imagine anyone making such annotations, intended only for the eyes of his closest supporters, if he did not in fact accept them as true.

Rudzutak is named many times in the 1938 Moscow Trial by defendants Grin'ko, Rozengol'ts and Krestinsky, who testify about him at length and in great detail. In another interrogation – confession just published in early 2006 Rozengol'ts is named by Tamarin as the person who recruited him into the Right-Trotskyite conspiracy.[70]

According to Krestinsky, Rudzutak was central to the whole conspiracy. Molotov agrees Rudzutak told him he had been beaten and tortured, but still refused to confess. However, there was much testimony against him.[71]

19. Rozenblium

Khrushchev:

> The way in which the former NKVD workers manufactured various fictitious "anti-Soviet centers" and "blocs" with the help of provocatory methods is seen from the confession of Comrade Rozenblum, party member since 1906, who was arrested in 1937 by the Leningrad NKVD.
>
> During the examination in 1955 of the Komarov case Rozenblum revealed the following fact: When Rozenblum was arrested in 1937, he was subjected to terrible torture during which he was ordered to confess false information concerning himself and other persons. He was then brought to the office of Zakovskii, who offered him freedom on condition that he make before the court a false confession fabricated in 1937 by the NKVD concerning "sabotage, espionage and diversion in a terroristic center in Leningrad." (Movement in the hall.) With unbelievable cynicism, Zakovskii told about the vile "mechanism" for the crafty creation of fabricated "anti- Soviet plots."

---

[70] Lubianka 3, 84-90, 92-93.

[71] Chuev, *Molotov*, 483-5.

"In order to illustrate it to me," stated Rozenblum, "Zakovskii gave me several possible variants of the organization of this center and of its branches. After he detailed the organization to me, Zakovskii told me that the NKVD would prepare the case of this center, remarking that the trial would be public. Before the court were to be brought 4 or 5 members of this center: Chudov, Ugarov, Smorodin, Pozern, Shaposhnikova (Chudov's wife) and others together with 2 or 3 members from the branches of this center...

"... The case of the Leningrad center has to be built solidly, and for this reason witnesses are needed. Social origin (of course, in the past) and the party standing of the witness will play more than a small role.

"'You, yourself,' said Zakovskii, 'will not need to invent anything. The NKVD will prepare for you a ready outline for every branch of the center; you will have to study it carefully and to remember well all questions and answers which the Court might ask. This case will be ready in four-five months, or perhaps a half year. During all this time you will be preparing yourself so that you will not compromise the investigation and yourself. Your future will depend on how the trial goes and on its results. If you begin to lie and to testify falsely, blame yourself. If you manage to endure it, you will save your head and we will feed and clothe you at the Government's cost until your death.'"

This is the kind of vile things which were then practiced. (Movement in the hall.)

Khrushchev never explicitly states, but strongly implies, that Stalin was involved in this. In reality, the evidence we have today – and that Khrushchev had then – shows that Zakovskii was Ezhov's man.

Rozenblium testified about Zakovskii's fabrication of cases. Zakovskii was "one of Ezhov's closest coworkers."[72] Zakovskii was arrested on April 30, 1938, and sentenced to death on August 29, 1938. Beria was named as Ezhov's second-in-command in August 1938.

If Rozenblium[73] was telling the truth here, then two conclusions emerge. First, Zakovskii would not have done all this without Ezhov's leadership. Therefore it's clear that Ezhov was involved in some kind of major conspiracy to build himself up by fabricating large-scale conspiracies. This is consistent with the details available to, and reported by, Jansen and Petrov concerning Ezhov's conspiracy, which we have examined briefly above.

Second, Beria – which means Stalin and those around him in the Politburo – was involved in investigating, and ultimately uncovering and eliminating, this conspiracy. Stalin and Beria were involved in smashing Ezhov's conspiracy, not in fomenting it. This is consistent with Zhukov's deductions.

Jansen and Petrov (151) quote Ezhov as having Zakovskii shot in August 1938 to get him out of the way, so he could not testify against him (Ezhov). Frinovskii affirms this in his recently-published (February 2006) confession statement of April 11, 1939. According to Frinovskii and the other evidence we have, Zakovskii was part of Ezhov's conspiracy. Frinovskii quotes Ezhov as telling him in October 1937 that Zakovskii "is completely 'ours'". Then on August 27-28 1938 Evdokimov, Ezhov's right-hand man, told Frinovskii to make sure Zakovskii and "all of Iagoda's men" had been shot, because Beria might reopen their cases and "these cases could turn against us."[74]

Zakovskii was explicitly blamed for torturing people "as a rule" in Stalin's telegram of Jan. 10, 1939 (which may in fact have been sent, or resent, in July – for this telegram, see below). Even without the recent statements

---

[72] Ezhov is called "one of the closest coworkers of N.I. Ezhov" in the Zakovskii biography from Zalesky, *Imperiia Stalina*, at http://www.hrono.ru/biograf/zakovski.html

[73] A.M. Rozenblium, according to the Pospelov Report of Feb. 9, 1956 – see *Doklad Khrushcheva*, p. 193, 865; *RKEB* 1, 323. When arrested in 1937 he was the chief of the Political department of the October railroad. In his speech Khrushchev did not refer to Rosenblium's criminal case file but to his statements to the Commission of the CC CPSU in 1955.

[74] Jansen & Petrov, 151. Lubianka 3, p. 45. Cf text at http://chss.montclair.edu/english/furr/research/frinovskyeng.html

and confessions by Ezhov, Frinovskii and others, this would be strong evidence that Stalin was opposed to this kind of behavior.

But Khrushchev omitted this part of the Stalin telegram in the "Secret Speech" – undoubtedly because it would conflict with the impression he was attempting to produce here. Therefore Khrushchev is blaming Stalin for Ezhov's conspiracy, while in fact Stalin had Ezhov arrested, tried, and executed for precisely this conspiracy.

20. I.D. Kabakov

Khrushchev:

> Even more widely was the falsification of cases practiced in the provinces. The NKVD headquarters of the Sverdlov Oblast "discovered" the so-called "Ural uprising staff" – an organ of the bloc of rightists, Trotskyites, Socialist Revolutionaries, church leaders – whose chief supposedly was the Secretary of the Sverdlov Oblast Party Committee and member of the Central Committee, All-Union Communist Party (Bolsheviks), Kabakov, who had been a party member since 1914. The investigative materials of that time show that in almost all krais, oblasts [provinces] and republics there supposedly existed "rightist Trotskyite, espionage-terror and diversionary-sabotage organizations and centers" and that the heads of such organizations as a rule – for no known reason – were first secretaries of oblast or republic Communist party committees or central committees.

Despite the Russian government's refusal to release investigative materials of this period, there is quite a lot of evidence against Kabakov.

The American mining engineer John D. Littlepage was hired during the Depression to work in the USSR developing the mining industry, and wrote a memoir of his years there upon his return to the USA (he was from Alaska). In *In Search of Soviet Gold* NY: Harcourt, Brace and Co., 1938 (1937) Littlepage discusses sabotage in Urals. He specifically suspects Kabakov; claims that Kabakov had never competently seen to the fruitful exploitation of the rich mineral area under his stewardship; claims he suspected some kind of conspiracy in all this; and expressed no surprise when Kabakov was arrested shortly after the Piatakov trial, since the two had long been closely associated. More recently, James Harris has seen and quoted evidence against Kabakov from Kabakov's criminal case without suggesting any fakery in it.[75]

Kabakov was dismissed from both the CC and the Party itself by a resolution circulated to the CC on May 17-19, 1937 and confirmed at the June 1937 on June 29th. This may suggest some kind of relationship either with the Tukhachevsky – military conspiracy, which was being unraveled at that time, or with the Rightist conspiracy generally, as Iagoda was being intensively questioned about this time.

Kabakov was named by L.I. Mirzoian, former First Secretary of the Central Committee of the Communist Party of Kazakhstan, as a leader of the Right-Trotskyite underground.[76] He figured in Ezhov's report to the June 1937 CC Plenum on the widespread nature of the conspiracy.[77]

Kabakov was named by P.T. Zubarev, one of the defendants in the March 1938 "Bukharin" Moscow Trial, as known by him to be a member of the Rightist conspiracy in the Urals as early as 1929. Zubarev claimed to have worked closely with Kabakov in this conspiracy since that time. Rykov, one of the main defendants along with Bukharin, also named Kabakov as an important member of the Rightist conspiracy. There is no evidence that Rykov or, indeed, any of the defendants in this Trial were subjected to torture.

Kabakov was named as head of a counterrevolutionary organization in Urals in a note to the Politburo signed by Kabakov's successor, First Secretary of the Sverdlovsk Obkom A. Ia. Stoliar. NKVD man D.M. Dmitriev of Sverdlovsk later confessed to being involved in a conspiracy himself, and fingered Stoliar as a conspirator too. But he also speaks of the "liquidation of the *kabakovshchina*" in the Urals in 1937 – that is, Kabakov was the first to go but other conspirators, including him and Stoliar, remained. Stalin's annotation on Stoliar's note suggests he is not organizing this news, but learning of it.[78]

In declaring Kabakov "rehabilitated", therefore, Khrushchev was casting the strongest doubt on the 1938 Moscow Trial, as he had already done

---

[75] James R. Harris. *The Great Urals: regionalism and the evolution of the Soviet system* (Ithaca NY: Cornell University Press, 1999) 163 at notes 78 and 81.

[76] *RKEB 1*, Doc. No. 52, p. 280; cf Pospelov report, *ibid.*, p. 323.

[77] Jansen & Petrov, p. 75.

[78] Lubianka 2, Doc. No. 276, p. 463.

on the 1936 Trial in declaring that Zinoviev and Kamenev had been treated too harshly. For present purposes, though, it's clear that Khrushchev did not speak the truth about Kabakov in his "Secret Speech."

21-24. S.V. Kossior; V. Ia. Chubar'; P.P. Postyshev; A.V. Kosarev

Khrushchev:

> Many thousands of honest and innocent Communists have died as a result of this monstrous falsification of such "cases," as a result of the fact that all kinds of slanderous "confessions" were accepted, and as a result of the practice of forcing accusations against oneself and others. In the same manner were fabricated the "cases" against eminent party and state workers -- Kossior, Chubar, Postyshev, Kosarev and others.

(For Postyshev, see Chapters 3 and 9.)

Kosior, Chubar', Postyshev, and Kosarev are listed in that precise order in a letter of March 16, 1939, to Stalin from V. V. Ul'rikh, Chairman of the Military College of the Supreme Court of the USSR, which is reproduced in facsimile at:

http://www.memo.ru/history/vkvs/images/ulrih-39.jpg

The relevant section reads as follows:

> Military Collegium
>
> Of the Supreme Court
>
> Of the Union of SSR
>
> - - - - -
>
> March 15, 1939
>
> No. 001119...
>
> Re: No. I-68/112
>
> TOP SECRET
>
> Copy No. 1
>
> TO THE CENTRAL COMMITTEE OF THE ACP(b)
>
> To Comrade J.V. STALIN

> Between February 21 and March 14 1939 the Military
> Collegium of the Supreme Court of the USSR in closed
> court sessions in Moscow heard the cases of 436
> persons.
>
> 413 were sentenced to be shot. The sentences have been
> carried out on the basis of the law of December 1, 1934.
>
> At court sessions of the Military Collegium the following
> persons fully confessed their guilt: KOSIOR S.V.,
> CHUBAR', V. IA., POSTYSHEV P.I., KOSAREV
> A.V,...

According to the rest of Ulrikh's note others among the accused renounced their confessions but "were exposed by other evidence in the
case." That is, Kosior, Chubar', Kosarev, and Postyshev did **not** re-
nounce their confessions, as others did, but reaffirmed them at trial.

Kosior and Chubar'

In his confession-interrogation of April 26 1939 Ezhov names Chubar'
and Kosior as two of a number of high-ranking Soviet officials who were
passing information to German intelligence – in plain language, German
spies. Ezhov says that the German agent Norden was in touch with "a
great many" others. [79]

According to the Rehabilitation materials of Postyshev prepared for
Khrushchev, Kosior implicated Postyshev, then withdrew his confessions, but then reiterated them again.[80] In his own confessions Postyshev
implicated Kosior, as well as Iakir, Chubar', and others. (*ibid.*, 218) Chubar' was implicated in the Right-Trotskyite conspiracy by Antipov,
Kosior, Pramnek, Sukhomlin, Postyshev, Boldyrev, and others.[81]

Interviewed by Felix Chuev the aged Lazar' M. Kaganovich said that he
had defended Kosior and Chubar', but had given up when he was shown
a lengthy handwritten confession of Chubar's.[82] Molotov told Chuev that
he himself was present when Antipov, Chubar's friend, accused Chubar'.

---

[79] Lubianka 3, p. 57.

[80] *RKEB 1*, p. 219.

[81] *Ibid.*, p. 251.

[82] F.I. Chuev. *Kaganovich. Shepilov.* Moscow: OLMA-PRESS, 2001, p. 117

Chubar' denied it heatedly and got very angry at Antipov. Molotov knew both of them very well.[83]

According to the Pospelov Report prepared for Khrushchev, Kosior was arrested on May 3, 1938 – that is, under Ezhov – and both tortured (no details are given) and subjected to prolonged interrogations of up to 14 hours at a stretch. Of 54 interrogations of Kosior only 4 were preserved.[84] So far this has all the earmarks of a Ezhov frameup.

However, Kosior was sentenced on February 26, 1939, three months after Ezhov's ouster. By this time cases were being reviewed, and it had long been recognized that Ezhov and his men had tortured innocent men.

We know, from the Ul'rikh letter cited above, that Kosior and Chubar' acknowledged their guilt at trial, though others did not. But no details of this trial have been released, either in the Pospelov Report or in the Rehabilitation Materials. Once again, it appears that the Khrushchev-era materials were not an objective study of the investigative materials, but rather a falsified attempt to make all those convicted **appear** to have been "innocent."

In the long transcript of the October 1938 confession - interrogation of Dmitriev, former head of the NKVD in Sverdlovsk. Dmitriev speaks of the "counterrevolutionary underground headed by Kosior, who was one of the most clandestine of the Rights in the Ukraine."[85]

Ezhov's confession makes it clearer than ever that Chubar' and Kosior were guilty of being involved in the underground organization of Rights without more information. Even without it, it's obvious that there was a great deal of evidence against him. Khrushchev failed to release it, and it has never been released since.

Kosarev

It is not true that, as Khrushchev stated, the Rehabilitation Materials established that the case against Kosarev had been fabricated.

There is very little information about Kosarev in the published Rehabilitation materials. (*Reabilitatsiia Kak Eto Bylo* 1, 79-80; 166-8; 219; in future

---

[83] Chuev, *Molotov*, pp. 486-7.

[84] *RKEB 1*, p. 326.

[85] Lubianka 3, p. 590.

RKEB 1) He did confess, and short parts are published – though the re-habilitation report of 1954 claims Kosarev was tortured into making the confession by Beria (167). His own dossier – interrogations, trial, etc. – has never been made available to researchers.

Kosarev is named in the Ul'rikh letter of March 16, 1939, as one of the accused who confirmed his admission of guilt at trial (see above). We also know that Postyshev accused Kosarev.

According to the rehabilitation report Kosarev had been hostile towards Beria when Beria was First Secretary of the Georgian party. They continue that Kosarev was tortured into confessing, and also perhaps framed. Kosarev did confess at trial. According to the rehabilitation report he was duped into thinking this would save him. We do know of examples in which defendants claimed they were beaten into confessing during interrogations but renounced those confessions at trial. But it is hard to imagine why anyone would confess to a capital crime at trial in order to save himself!

The Rehabilitation Materials on Kosarev are very concerned to blame Beria for everything, as is a letter written by Kosarev's widow in December 1953, at the time Beria and others were supposedly on trial. (*RKEB 1*, 79-80) And Khrushchev was quick to claim that virtually anyone arrested and convicted during Beria's tenure as head of the NKVD was "framed."

Kosarev was arrested on November 29, 1937 after Ezhov was effectively ousted. He had had some contact with Ezhov, having been editor of the Komsomol newspaper that Ezhov's wife worked on. Jansen and Petrov speculate that he may have been involved with Ezhov in some way, though they caution that this was unlikely. (185)

But in a recently-published interrogation (February 2006) A.N. Babulin, Ezhov's live-in nephew, fellow conspirator, and witness to Ezhov's and Ezhov's wife Evgeniia's "moral degeneration," names Kosarev as one of the "most frequent guests in the Ezhov home," along with Piatakov, Uritsky, Mikhail Kol'tsov, Glikina, Iagoda, Frinovskii, Mironov, Agranov, and other NKVD men later tried and executed along with Ezhov. It was strange company for an "innocent" leader of the Komsomol to be keeping! In his own recently-published interrogation Ezhov himself names Kol'tsov and Glikina – both on Babulin's list of "most frequent guests" – as English spies, along with his late wife Evgeniia.

Vadim Rogovin wrote that Kosarev was dismissed from his post as head of the Komsomol and arrested for unjustified repression of Komsomol workers. A number of articles have appeared in the popular press, some by Kosarev's family, setting forth the view that he was unjustly accused and that Ol'ga P. Mishakova, the Komsomol worker Kosarev had purportedly maltreated, had wrongly denounced him.[86]

Whoever was at fault, this does seem to be the reason for Kosarev's arrest, since it is referred to by Mgeladze in his memoirs. The rehabilitation report of 1954 does not mention it at all. Rather, it sets Kosarev's arrest down to a personal hatred of him by Beria, for some negative things Kosarev had reputedly said about Beria.

After Beria's arrest in June 1953 Khrushchev, abetted by the rest of the CPSU leadership, went about demonizing Beria in every possible way. This failure to even mention the real reason for Kosarev's arrest is further evidence that the rehabilitation reports were fabricated for political purposes, not serious studies of the evidence against those repressed.

We don't have enough information about Kosarev that is reliable – that is, not based upon anecdote or rumor – to say more than that he had a very suspicious relationship with Ezhov and his wife, and many other associates of the Ezhovs, all of whom seem to have been involved in Ezhov's NKVD-centered Rightist conspiracy.

The Rehabilitation reports on Kosarev allege that he was tortured. (*RKEB* 1, 79-80; 166-8 ; 219). Since Frinovskii says that, in order to deflect the investigation away from his own conspiracy, Ezhov had the guilty as well as the innocent tortured, including some friends of his, it may well be that he had Kosarev tortured too. (See under 16. Ezhov, above).

We certainly do not have any evidence at all that either Stalin or Beria "framed" Kosarev. Even the anecdotal information merely accuses Stalin of being too credulous. What we do know is that Khrushchev and the "rehabilitation commission" hid a great deal of information about Kosarev, as about many others.

In the case of Kosarev, they hid his connections to Ezhov, which seem to have been his undoing. These are not even mentioned in the Khrush-

---

[86] Some of these articles insist that Kosarev never confessed, despite the fact that the Khrushchev-era rehabilitation materials affirm that he was "tricked" into a confession while the Ulrikh letter states definitely that he confessed. Therefore, it's unlikely that these articles are reliable in the least. Without more evidence from interrogation and trial materials, we just can't tell.

chev-era rehabilitation materials. The most cautious conclusion we can reach is that Khrushchev declared Kosarev innocent "in flagrant disregard for the truth," without any serious study of his guilt or innocent.

Akakii Mgeladze, later First Secretary of the Georgian Party but in the 1930s a leading Komsomol figure, had liked and respected Kosarev when the latter was the head of the Komsomol. According to his recently-published memoirs written in the 1960s Mgeladze discussed Kosarev with Stalin in 1947 (p. 165). Stalin listened and then patiently explained that Kosarev's guilt had been carefully verified by Zhdanov and Andreev.[87]

This is consistent with what we know from other sources – that these Politburo members, as well as others, had been assigned to check up on NKVD arrests and accusations against leading Party members.[88] Mgeladze, who clearly wished to believe that Kosarev was either entirely innocent and had been framed by Beria for personal reasons, or had simply made some mistake or other, then told Stalin he himself had read these reports, as well as one by Shkiriatov, and found it impossible to doubt what they said.

If Mgeladze's account is significant at all, it is because Mgeladze had great difficulty believing Kosarev was guilty – to the point where he confronted Stalin, however politely, on this question – and Stalin calmly repeated his belief, based on investigation, that Kosarev had been guilty. According to Mgeladze, Stalin went on to explain that everybody made mistakes, and that many mistakes were made in 1937. But Stalin did not apply this to Kosarev's case.

To this day all of the documentary materials relating to Kosarev's dismissal, arrest, investigation, and trial are kept secret by the Russian government. Kosarev was criticized and removed from leadership of the Komsomol at the 7th Plenum of the Central Committee of the Komsomol, held in Moscow on November 19-22 1938. The transcript of this Plenum exists; it is quoted in a recent biography of Georgii M. Popov,

---

[87] A.I. Mgeladze. Stalin. Kakim ia ego znal. Stranitsy nedavnogo proshlogo. N.pl., 2001, pp. 165; 172.

[88] *Sovetskoe Rukovodstvo. Perepiska 1928-1941.* Moscow: Rosspen, 1999, reprints a number of these letters by both Andreev and Zhdanov.

who spoke at this Plenum. Therefore it existed in Khrushchev's day. But Khrushchev never mentioned it.[89]

25. The Lists

Khrushchev:

> The vicious practice was condoned of having the NKVD prepare lists of persons whose cases were under the jurisdiction of the Military Collegium and whose sentences were prepared in advance. Yezhov would send these lists to Stalin personally for his approval of the proposed punishment. In 1937-1938, 383 such lists containing the names of many thousands of party, Soviet, Komsomol, Army and economic workers were sent to Stalin. He approved these lists.

These lists exist, and have been edited and published, first on CD[90] and now on the Internet, as the "Stalinist 'Shooting' Lists". But this is a tendentious, inaccurate name, for these were not lists of persons "to be shot" at all.

As Khrushchev did, the very anti-Stalin editors of these lists do in fact call the lists "sentences" prepared in advance. But their own research disproves this claim. The lists give the sentences that the prosecution would seek if the individual was convicted – that is, the sentence the Prosecution would ask the court to apply. In reality these were lists sent to Stalin (and other Politburo or Secretariat members) for "review" – *rassmotrenie* – a word that is used many times in the introduction to the lists. (http://www.memo.ru/history/vkvs/images/intro1.htm)

Many examples are given of people who were **not** convicted, or who were convicted of lesser offenses, and so not shot. A.V. Snegov, whom Khrushchev mentions by name later in this speech, is on the lists at least twice.

- At http://stalin.memo.ru/spiski/pg13026.htm No. 383;

---

[89] E.V. Taranov, *"Partiinii gubernator Moskvy Georgii Popov* (Moscow: Izd-vo Glavarkhiva Moskvy, 2004), 12-14 and note 17 p. 104.

[90] Zhertvy politicheskogo terrora v SSSR. Na 2-kh diskakh. Disk 2. Stalinskie rasstrel'nye spiski. Moscow: Zven'ia, 2004. At http://www.memo.ru/history/vkvs/

- At http://stalin.memo.ru/spiski/pg05245.htm
  No. 133.

In this last reference Snegov is specifically put into "1st Category", meaning: **maximum** sentence of death in the event of conviction. A brief summary of the Prosecutor's evidence against him is provided, and there seems to have been a lot of it. Nevertheless Snegov was not sentenced to death but instead to a long term in a labor camp.

According to the editors of these lists "many" people whose names are on them were not in fact executed, and some were freed.

> For example, a selective study of the list for the Kuibyshev oblast' signed on September 29, 1938 has shows that not a single person on this list was convicted by the VK VS (the Military Collegium of the Supreme Court), and a significant number of the cases were dismissed altogether.

- -
  http://www.memo.ru/history/vkvs/images/intro.ht
  m

So Khrushchev knew that Stalin was not "sentencing" anybody but rather reviewing the lists in case he had any objections. We can be certain that Khrushchev knew this because the note from S. N. Kruglov, Minister of Internal Affairs (MVD) to Khrushchev of February 3, 1954 has survived. It says nothing about "sentences prepared in advance," but gives the truth:

> These lists were compiled in 1937 and 1938 by the NKVD of the USSR and presented to the the CC of the ACP(b) **for review** right away. [emphasis added, GF][91]

The Prosecutor went to trial not only with evidence, but with a sentence to recommend to the judges in case of conviction.

It appears that the names of **Party** members, but not of non-Party members, were sent on for review. The disingenuous Introduction notes that those signing the lists comprised "not all the Politburo members but only

---

[91] At http://www.memo.ru/history/vkvs/images/intro1.htm

those of its members who were closest to Stalin" [92] But the evidence suggests that it was the members of the Party Secretariat rather than the Politburo to whom the lists were submitted. Even the editors note that Ezhov – a member of the Secretariat but not of the Politburo – signed "as a secretary of the Central Committee."[93]

Khrushchev concealed the fact that not Stalin, but he himself, was deeply involved in selecting the persons for inclusion on these lists, and for choosing the category of punishment proposed for them. Khrushchev mentions that the NKVD prepared the lists. But he does not mention the fact that the NKVD acted together with the Party leadership, and that a great many of the names on these lists – perhaps more than from any other region of the USSR – originated in the areas under Khrushchev's own power.

Until January 1938 Khrushchev was First Secretary of the Party in Moscow and Moscow *oblast'* (province). After that he was First Secretary in the Ukraine. The letter to Stalin (see section 4) asking for permission to shoot 8500 people is dated July 10, 1937, the same date as the first of the "shooting lists" from Moscow.[94]

In the same letter Khrushchev also confirms his own participation in the *troika* responsible for selecting these names, along with the head of the directorate of the NKVD for Moscow, S.F. Redens, and the assistant prosecutor K.I. Maslov (Khrushchev does admit that "when necessary" he was replaced by the second secretary A.A. Volkov).

Volkov served as second secretary of the Moscow Region of the AUCP(b) only till the beginning of August 1937, when he left to serve as First Secretary of the Belorussian party. After that he was no longer Khrushchev's subordinate, which may have saved his life.[95] Maslov re-

---

[92] "Not all the members of the Politburo, but only the members who were closest to Stalin, took part in the review (in reality, the cosigning) of the lists." At http://www.memo.ru/history/vkvs/images/intro.htm

[93] "On 8 lists we find the signature of Ezhov (evidently here he was acting not as the People's Commissar for Internal Affairs, but as a secretary of the CC)", *ibid.*

[94] Cf. http://www.memo.ru/history/vkvs/spiski/pg02049.htm

[95] On August 11 1937 Volkov was chosen First Secretary of the CC of the Communist Party (b) of Belorussia, and from October 1938 to February 1940 occupied the post of First Secretary of the Chuvash Obkom of the ACP(b). As far as we can tell he died in 1941 or 1942. A more detailed account of Volkov was published in the newspaper *Sovetskaia Belorussia* of April 21, 2001. Cf http://sb.by/article.php?articleID=4039

mained the Procuror (prosecutor) of the Moscow *oblast'* (province) until November 1937. In 1938 he was arrested and executed in March 1939, after having been found guilty of subversive counterrevolutionary activity. [96] The same fate befell K.I. Mamonov who at first occupied Maslov's position and was later shot the same day as Maslov.[97] Nor did Redens escape punishment. He was arrested in November 1938 as a member of a "Polish diversionist-espionage group", tried and sentenced, and shot on January 21, 1940. Jansen and Petrov describe Redens as one of "Ezhov's men."[98] During the years of the "thaw" Redens was rehabilitated at Khrushchev's insistence but by such crude violations of legal procedures that in 1988 Redens' rehabilitation was reversed — at a time when a huge wave of rehabilitations was under way![99]

In other words, with the exception of Volkov all of Khrushchev's closest co-workers who took part in repressions in Moscow and Moscow *oblast'* were severely punished. How did Khrushchev manage to escape the same punishment? The answer to this puzzle remains to be uncovered. In the final chapter we will examine some interesting facts concerning Khrushchev's successor as Moscow Party leader, A.S. Shcherbakov, that may bear on this question.

26. Resolutions of the January 1938 CC Plenum

Khrushchev:

> Resolutions of the January plenum of the Central
> Committee, All-Union Communist Party (Bolsheviks), in
> 1938 had brought some measure of improvement to the
> party organizations. However, widespread repression
> also existed in 1938.

Khrushchev implies — and states a little further on — that the repression was driven by Stalin. As we have already seen, though, the evidence

---

[96] Cf. http://www.mosoblproc.ru/history/prokurors/7/ and http://www.memo.ru/memory/donskoe/d39.htm

[97] Cf. http://www.mosoblproc.ru/history/prokurors/8/ and http://mos.memo.ru/shot-63.htm

[98] Jansen & Petrov, pp. 84; 148.

[99] *RKEB 3*, p. 660.

strongly suggests that it was driven by Ezhov and a number of First Secretaries, including Khrushchev himself as one of the leading "repressers." Stalin and the central party leadership who were **not** involved in the Rightist conspiracy wanted the repression limited. Eventually they severely punished those who were proven to have fabricated cases and killed or punished innocent people.

Getty and Naumov have made the longest study so far of this January 1938 Plenum.[100] Their account makes it clear that the Stalin central Party leadership was very concerned about irresponsible repressions. It was at this Plenum that Postyshev was removed on just such grounds. Thurston's discussion confirms the fact that Stalin was trying to rein in the First Secretaries, the NKVD and repression generally.[101]

At the January 1938 CC Plenum, Malenkov gave the report, obviously echoing Stalin, that far too many and capricious expulsions had taken place. For our present purposes it is most significant that Postyshev was the person singled out as most guilty. The Resolution of January 9, 1938 specifically blamed Postyshev for this, reprimanded him, and removed him from his post as first secretary of the Kuybyshev *obkom* (city committee).

According to I.A. Benediktov, who was a high official in agriculture (either People's Commissar or First Deputy Minister of Agriculture) from 1938 to 1953, on the CC and a frequent participant in Politburo meetings, Stalin began to correct the illegalities of the repressions at this Plenum. Lev Balaian, whose study of Khrushchev's falsifications, while incomplete, is very useful, gives additional details.

Khrushchev's head of NKVD in Ukraine from January 1938 was A.I. Uspensky. Having been warned by Ezhov, Uspensky fled arrest on November 14, 1938 and feigned suicide by leaving a note that he would jump into the Dnepr river. Uspensky was at length located and arrested on April 14, 1939. Stalin believed Ezhov had warned Uspensky by eavesdropping on his telephone call to Khrushchev.

---

[100] Getty & Naumov 498–512.

[101] Robert Thurston. *Life and Terror in Stalin's Russia, 1934–1941.* (Yale University Press; 1998), p.109, 112; also see Part 4 of his book.

Whatever Uspensky was guilty of, Khrushchev must have been guilty of framing innocent people as well – they were both in the same *troika*.[102] In interrogations no longer available to researchers today Uspensky revealed Ezhov's directions to falsify cases massively.[103] (Jansen and Petrov 84; 148).

27. "Beria's gang"

Khrushchev:

> Meanwhile, Beria's gang, which ran the organs of state security, outdid itself in proving the guilt of the arrested and the truth of materials which it falsified.

This is false. Thurston discusses Khrushchev's distortion of what really happened once Beria took over the NKVD, and the "astonishing liberalism" that was instituted immediately under Beria. Torture ended, and inmates received privileges again. Ezhov's men were removed from office, many of them tried and convicted of repressions.[104]

According to the Pospelov report, arrests dropped hugely, by over 90%, in 1939 and 1940 in comparison to 1937 and 1938. **Executions in 1939 and 1940 dropped to far less than 1% of the levels of mass executions in 1937 and 1938.**[105] Beria took over as head of the NKVD in December, 1938, so this corresponds precisely with Beria's period in command. Khrushchev, therefore, knew of this, but omitted it from the "Secret Speech" and so concealed it from his audience.

It was during the Beria years that trials and executions of men convicted of illegal repressions, mass killings, torture, and falsifications took place. Many – certainly more than 100,000 – persons wrongly repressed were released from GULAG camps and prisons.[106] Khrushchev knew, and concealed, this too.

---

[102] Khrushchev, *Vremia, Liudi, Vlast'. Kn. I, chast'1* (Moscow: Moskovskie Novosti, 1999), pp. 172-3

[103] Jansen & Petrov p. 84; p. 148.

[104] Thurston, pp. 118-119.

[105] *RKEB* 1, p. 317. Cf. http://www.alexanderyakovlev.org/almanah/inside/almanah-doc/55752

[106] See the note by Okhotin and Roginskii in Danilov,V., et al., ed., *Tragediia Sovetskoi Derevni* vol. 5 No. 2 (Moscow: ROSSPEN 2006) 517. Also Mark IUnge, Gennadii

28. "Torture telegram"

Khrushchev:

> When the wave of mass arrests began to recede in 1939, and the leaders of territorial party organizations began to accuse the NKVD workers of using methods of physical pressure on the arrested, Stalin dispatched a coded telegram on January 10, 1939 to the committee secretaries of oblasts and krais, to the central committees of republic Communist parties, to the People's Commissars of Internal Affairs and to the heads of NKVD organizations. This telegram stated:
>
>> "The Central Committee of the All-Union Communist Party (Bolsheviks) explains that the application of methods of physical pressure in NKVD practice is permissible from 1937 on in accordance with permission of the Central Committee of the All-Union Communist Party (Bolsheviks)... It is known that all bourgeois intelligence services use methods of physical influence against the representatives of the socialist proletariat and that they use them in their most scandalous forms.
>>
>> "The question arises as to why the socialist intelligence service should be more humanitarian against the mad agents of the bourgeoisie, against the deadly enemies of the working class and of the kolkhoz workers. The Central Committee of the All-Union Communist Party (Bolsheviks) considers that physical pressure should still be used obligatorily, as an exception applicable to known and obstinate enemies of the people, as a method both justifiable and appropriate."
>
> Thus, Stalin had sanctioned in the name of the Central Committee of the All-Union Communist Party

Bordiugov, Rol'f Binner, *Vertikal' Bol'shogo Terrora* (Moscow: Novyi Khronograf, 2008), 490, n. 55.

(Bolsheviks) the most brutal violation of socialist legality, torture and oppression, which led as we have seen to the slandering and self-accusation of innocent people.

Khrushchev deliberately deceived his audience in at least three, and possibly four ways.

- He omitted important parts of the text of the telegram that undermined his assertions.

- He did not tell his audience that the text of the "telegram" he had was certainly never sent. In fact, the text we have looks like a copy made in 1956.

- Khrushchev did not divulge the doubtful nature of the text of this supposed telegram. We know of it because it was discussed in the later June 1957 Central Committee Plenum called to punish Malenkov, Molotov, and Kaganovich.

- Khrushchev may, in fact, have had this "telegram" forged.

- There are many problems with the text of the "original" of this telegram, which was published during the 1990s. It would take a full article-length study to disentangle all the problems with it. Some of them will become clear in the discussion below.

This entire "telegram"part of the speech is highly suspicious, beginning with the first sentence, which makes the Party Secretaries look like angels. And Khrushchev makes exactly this point in his speech – the "leaders of the local party organizations" were complaining about torture, and it was all Stalin's and Beria's fault! Stalin, with his henchman Beria, were the "bad guys" – the Party First Secretaries were trying to resist them!

Thanks to Zhukov's primary document research published in *Inoy Stalin,* we know that it was, in fact, these same Party First Secretaries that insisted on the mass executions to begin with. Stalin and that the central party leadership of the Politburo (the "narrow leadership", as Zhukov puts it) strongly resisted it. Zhukov claims he has seen the document in which Khrushchev asks for permission to raise "Category one" to 20,000

– a number, with no names. Getty cites Khrushchev's request for 41,000 people in both categories.[107]

It appears, therefore, that a main purpose of the "Secret Speech" was to cover up the bloodthirstiness of the First Secretaries such as himself. Khrushchev does blame Ezhov somewhat – he mentions him a few times. But Khrushchev mainly blames Beria, whom he really hates, but who actually **stopped** the Ezhovshchina and corrected its abuses by reviewing sentences. And, of course, Khrushchev lays the main blame on Stalin, who was more responsible than anyone else for **stopping** the repression.

The first thing we should note, for our purposes, is what Khrushchev omitted – the entire passage in boldface (see Quotations). This passage does several things:

- It qualifies, limits, and restricts the conditions under which "means of physical pressure" are to be used.
- It names well-known, high-ranking NKVD men, close associates of Ezhov's, by name, and stresses that they have been punished.

This includes Zakovskii, whom Khrushchev, through Rozenblium, cited as a chief fabricator of false charges (see section 18. above). Had Khrushchev quoted this part of the telegram's text it would have undermined Khrushchev's main contention throughout the "Speech" that Stalin had been promoting the massive repressions rather than trying to rein them in. In the recently released confession-interrogation Ezhov names Zakovskii as one of his most devoted men, and confirms that he ordered Zakovskii killed so that he would not tell Beria about the falsifications and murders Ezhov and his men were engaged in.

The "Torture Telegram" is a complicated example of Khrushchev's prevaricating, and deserving of a lengthy analytical study. The main points for our purposes are these:

1. The document we have – the "January 10, 1939" document – is, at best, a draft copy. It is not on official stationery. It contains no signature, not Stalin's or anyone else's. The most recent, semi-official edition, no longer claims it was "signed" by Stalin, but contains the claim that hand-

---

[107] *Komsomolskaia Pravda* December 3 2002; J. Arch Getty. "Excesses are not permitted.: Mass Terror and Stalinist Governance in the Late 1930s". *The Russian Review*. Vol.61 (January 2002), p.127.

written emendations are in Stalin's handwriting.[108] This is pure bluff; the editors cite no evidence this is the case. What is clear is that the editors wish to convince readers that this is a genuine document from 1939.

2. If it is not a forgery it may or may not be an unsent "draft." It **looks** like a copy typed up in 1956, as this is stated directly on it. Furthermore, the typeface of the 1956 addition and that of the rest of the telegram looks identical.

All this would have to be scientifically and objectively verified. But the Russian government is not about to carry out this kind of study either with this document or with any of the many other documents of questionable veracity supposedly discovered since the end of the USSR. But if it is a copy, as seems likely, where is the original document of which it is a copy?

3. At the July 1957 Central Committee Plenum, at which the "anti-Party group" of Molotov, Malenkov, Kaganovich, and Shepilov was arraigned for trying to have Khrushchev ousted the year before, Molotov states that a decision to use "physical pressure" against certain arrestees did exist, but that all Politburo members signed it. Khrushchev then insists that there were **two** such documents, and that he is talking about the **second** one. He never returns to the subject of the first one. What was this first document? We never learn.

As for the supposed second document, according to another CC member in this discussion the original has been destroyed, but one copy remained in the Dagestan *obkom* (regional committee). However, **that** copy is certainly not the copy we have, because the text we have is not on any stationery and is, at best, a draft, perhaps a later (1956) typed copy of a draft, and possibly even a forgery altogether. No other such copy has turned up, and the "Dagestan *obkom*" document has never turned up either.

Surely Khrushchev would never have destroyed such valuable evidence against Stalin – unless it incriminated himself, in some way. Or, unless it never existed in the first place! In this case A.B. Aristov's (one of Khrushchev's main supporters in the Central Committee) mention of the

---

[108] *Lubianka 3,* No. 8, pp. 14-15 and n. p. 15.

"copy from the Dagestan *obkom*" was a bluff to intimidate the "anti-Party group" in front of the rest of the C.C.[109]

Getty has stated that he has found the text of a similar telegram dated July 27, 1939.[110] If it is genuine (it has not been published), and if Molotov was correct in July 1957 that all Politburo members had signed such a telegram, then **Khrushchev would have signed it too**, as Khrushchev was made a Politburo member on March 22, 1939, and was a candidate member (taking the disgraced Postyshev's place) after the January 1938 CC meeting). This would have made Khrushchev just as responsible as Molotov, Malenkov, and Kaganovich.

If the telegram had really been sent on January 10, 1939, as stated by Khrushchev in the "Secret Speech", he would not have signed it. However, he would certainly have (a) seen it, and (b) been responsible for carrying it out, i.e. applying "physical pressure" to prisoners, since he was First Secretary of the Ukraine, where he was repressing thousands of people.

Therefore it's possible that Khrushchev searched for genuine copies of the July 27, 1939 telegram, and had all those he could find destroyed. Before doing that, he had a copy made with the same text (omitting Ezhov's name, which is in the later version), but predated to a period before he had joined the Politburo. We can't be sure.

Many scholars and others have assured us that Khrushchev had a great number of documents destroyed. Iuri Zhukov, Nikita Petrov, and Mark Junge and Rolf Binner all attest to the fact that it appears that Khrushchev destroyed more documents than anyone else.[111] Benediktov, former agriculture minister, said the same thing in an article published in 1989. In this scenario, the document Getty has found is a copy that Khrushchev failed to find and destroy. We don't really know.

What we do know is that, at the **very least**, Khrushchev quoted selectively from this document with the intent to deceive his audience.

---

[109] *Molotov, Malenkov, Kaganovich, 1957. Stenogramma iiun'skogo plenuma TsK KPSS I drugie dokumenty.* Ed. A.N. Iakovlev, N. Kovaleva, A. Korotkov, et al. Moscow: MDF, 1998, pp. 121-2.

[110] Getty, "Excesses" p. 114, n.4.

[111] IU. Zhukov, "Zhupel Stalina", Part 3. *Komsomol'skaia Pravda*, Nov. 12, 2002), Nikita Petrov, *Ivan Serov*, Moscow 2005, pp. 157-162; Mark Junge and Rolf Binner, *Kak Terror Stal Bol'shim*. Moscow, 2003, p. 16, n. 14.

29. Rodos tortured Chubar' and Kosior on Beria's orders

Khrushchev:

> Not long ago – only several days before the present
> Congress – we called to the Central Committee
> Presidium session and interrogated the investigative
> judge Rodos, who in his time investigated and
> interrogated Kossior, Chubar and Kosarev. He is a vile
> person, with the brain of a bird, and morally completely
> degenerate. And it was this man who was deciding the
> fate of prominent party workers; he was making
> judgments also concerning the politics in these matters,
> because, having established their "crime," he provided
> therewith materials from which important political
> implications could be drawn.

> The question arises whether a man with such an intellect
> could alone make the investigation in a manner to prove
> the guilt of people such as Kossior and others. No, he
> could not have done it without proper directives. At the
> Central Committee Presidium session he told us: "I was
> told that Kossior and Chubar were people's enemies and
> for this reason I, as an investigative judge, had to make
> them confess that they are enemies."

> (Indignation in the hall.)

> He would do this only through long tortures, which he
> did, receiving detailed instructions from Beria. We must
> say that at the Central Committee Presidium session he
> cynically declared: "I thought that I was executing the
> orders of the party." In this manner, Stalin's orders
> concerning the use of methods of physical pressure
> against the arrested were in practice executed.

> These and many other facts show that all norms of
> correct party solution of problems were invalidated and
> everything was dependent upon the willfulness of one
> man.

Khrushchev's deception here is in his implication that confessions, obtained by Rodos' beatings, were the only grounds on which Chubar' and

Kosior were convicted and executed. As we have already seen, there is plenty of evidence against both Chubar' and Kosior that has nothing to do with "means of physical pressure." For example, they were both named by Ezhov in his confession-interrogation of April 26, 1939 as members of the Rightist conspiracy and German spies.

Khrushchev implies that Rodos was Beria's man.[112] But rehabilitation materials state that he was involved in the investigation of suspects during Ezhov's tenure too (*RKEB 1*, 176).

It is possible that Rodos had simply "followed orders", as he claimed he had done. If, as alleged by Khrushchev and the "torture telegram," torture had been authorized by the Central Committee, and if Rodos had been told to torture some defendants, as he seems to have admitted, then he had merely been following orders. It so, he had committed no crime. Perhaps his real crime was to have been an investigator under Beria as well as under Ezhov. Khrushchev did his best to blame everything on Beria.

Rodos was tried and sentenced during the period February 21-26, 1956 – **during** the 20th Party Congress itself![113] (*RKEB 1* 411, n. 13). Why? This suggests that Rodos may have been "tried" and executed to shut him up. As the chief of the Investigative Section of the NKVD Rodos would have taken an active part in the investigations of Ezhov's activities and would have been in charge of the cases of those who were in the close circle around Ezhov's wife, including Isaac Babel, Vsevolod Meierkhol'd, and others.

Another possibility is that his fate was intended to warn others to get them to cooperate with Khrushchev's "rehabilitations", say what he wanted them to say. Pavel' Sudoplatov, one of Beria's subordinates, was evidently imprisoned for fifteen years because he refused to falsify charg-

---

[112] Nikita Petrov states that Rodos was arrested on October 5 1953, during the same period that others in "Beria's gang" were under arrest and being interrogated. N. Petrov, *Pervyi predsedatel' KGB Ivan Serov.* Moscow, 2006, p. 393.

[113] *RKEB 1*, p. 411, note 13. Rodos's investigative file has not yet been declassified. In the exhibition "1953 god. Mezhu proshlym i budushchim" (2004) in the Exhibition Hall of the Federal Archives in Moscow there were on exhibit two documents concerning Rodos. See the catalog of the exhibition at http://www.rusarchives.ru/evants/exhibitions/stalin_sp.shtml , Nos 269 and 270. It seems likely that Rodos' investigative file still exists.

charges against Beria, only escaping execution by the difficult strategem of feigning insanity for a few years.

Rodos' trial materials have never been released. He had obviously not been prosecuted after Ezhov's dismissal, as had so many other NKVDers who had tortured defendants and fabricated cases. It was surely convenient for Khrushchev to have Rodos and Beria on whom to blame repressions. This rush to get rid of Rodos suggests that there may have been some kind of connection between Khrushchev and Ezhov that remains unknown to us today and whose origins go back to the years in which Khrushchev was one of the First Secretaries.

General Pavel Sudoplatov was asked by Roman Rudenko, head Soviet Prosecutor and a creature of Khrushchev's, to write false testimony against Beria after the latter's death. When Sudoplatov refused he was arrested and accused of being a participant in an imaginary "conspiracy" of Beria's. According to Sudoplatov's account General Ivan I. Maslennikov, a Hero of the Soviet Union, committed suicide rather than do the same thing. Sudoplatov evaded execution only by successfully feigning insanity but remained in prison for 15 years.[114] It's possible that something similar happened to Rodos.

---

[114] Pavel Sudoplatov, *Spetsoperatsii. Lubianka i Kreml' 1930-1950 gody.* Moscow: Sovremennik, 1997. The chapter in question is online at http://www.hrono.ru/libris/lib_s/beria1.php

Chapter 5.

Stalin and the War

30. Stalin didn't heed warnings about war

Khrushchev:

> The power accumulated in the hands of one person,
> Stalin, led to serious consequences during the Great
> Patriotic War...During the war and after the war, Stalin
> put forward the thesis that the tragedy which our nation
> experienced in the first part of the war was the result of
> the "unexpected" attack of the Germans against the
> Soviet Union. ...Stalin took no heed of these warnings.
> What is more, Stalin ordered that no credence be given
> to information of this sort, in order not to provoke the
> initiation of military operations...everything was ignored:
> warnings of certain Army commanders, declarations of
> deserters from the enemy army, and even the open
> hostility of the enemy. ...Is this an example of the
> alertness of the chief of the party and of the state at this
> particularly significant historical moment?

Germany did indeed commit aggression against the Soviet Union, and so this is one assertion of Khrushchev's that is unquestionably correct. There is a huge amount of evidence to refute the rest of what he says.

Still, the attack did occur. Marshal A. E. Golovanov believed that any responsibility should be shared by all the top military commanders, as was the glory of victory.

Documents published since the end of the USSR have shown that Stalin and the Soviet leadership were expecting a German attack, but that the warnings from intelligence and other sources were contradictory and uncertain. V.V. Kozhinov points out the problems of distinguishing deliberate disinformation and just plain error from accurate information in the evaluation of intelligence, and how contradictory the intelligence available to Soviet leaders was.

The German Army had a disinformation plan to spread false rumors to
the Soviet leadership. A detailed order to this effect by Field Marshal
Wilhelm Keitel, dated February 15, 1941, has been published.[115]

As Kozhinov points out, Khrushchev's accusations here can be turned
around on his own thesis. Historians do not blame President Roosevelt
for failing to foresee the attack on Pearl Harbor. Therefore to blame
Stalin for not foreseeing the precise time and place of the Nazi attack is
to fall prey to the "cult of personality", to believe Stalin was supposed to
have superhuman abilities and inexplicably failed to use them.[116]

The Soviets could not declare a mobilization because that was universally
understood as a declaration of war. It was precisely such a mobilization
that had set off the First World War. It would have given Hitler the opportunity to declare war, leaving the USSR vulnerable to a separate deal
between Hitler and the Allies. And in a plan for "Operation 'Ost'" drawn
up in 1940 German General-Major Marks make the regretful remark that
"The Russians will not do us the favor of attacking us [first]."[117]

The Soviets could not rely upon British warnings, for the British clearly
wanted to set Hitler against the Soviet Union and weaken both, if not use
the opportunity to make peace with Hitler against the Soviets, as many in
the British establishment wanted.

Marshal K.A. Meretskov, no admirer of Stalin, believed the situation immediately preceding the war was very complex, impossible to predict. His
memoirs were published after Khrushchev's ouster, in 1968. Zhukov,
who had been demoted in disgrace after the war by Stalin and had helped
Khrushchev attack Stalin in 1957, thought the Soviet Union under Stalin
had done everything it could to prepare for the war.

---

[115] *1941 god. Dokumenty. V. 2-kh kn. Kn.1* . Moscow, 1998, pp. 661-664. The document is
"Ukazanie Shtaba Operativnogo Rukovodstva O Meropriiatiiakh Dezinformatsii." I have
put it on line at http://chss.montclair.edu/english/furr/research/germandisinfo.html

[116] Although Khrushchev does not directly address the question here, we wish to mention
that good evidence has now been published that General Dmitry Pavlov, commander of
the Western front, where the Red Army was taken completely unprepared, where the
greatest losses were suffered, and where the Germans effected their greatest penetration
into the USSR after June 22, was in fact guilty of plotting defeat to benefit the Germans.
Some quotations and bibliography on this question are included in the Russian language
section at this point.

[117] 1941 god v 2-kh knigakh. Kniga pervaia (Moscow: MFD, 1998) p. 154.

Marshals Vasilevskii and Zhukov disagreed about whether Stalin should
have ordered all the troops to take positions along the border. Comment-
ing on Vasilevskii's article in 1965, after Khrushchev's ouster, Zhukov
wrote said he believed this would have been a serious error.

Although Khrushchev does not refer to it here, it's worth mentioning the
most famous "warning" of an impending German attack, that from the
famous Soviet spy Richard Sorge who was in the German embassy in
Japan, has recently been denounced as a fake created during the years of
Khrushchev's "Thaw."[118]

31. Vorontsov's Letter

Khrushchev:

> We must assert that information of this sort concerning
> the threat of German armed invasion of Soviet territory
> was coming in also from our own military and
> diplomatic sources; however, because the leadership was
> conditioned against such information, such data was
> dispatched with fear and assessed with reservation.
>
> Thus, for instance, information sent from Berlin on May
> 6, 1941 by the Soviet military attaché, Captain
> Vorontsov, stated: "Soviet citizen
> Bozer…communicated to the deputy naval attaché that,
> according to a statement of a certain German officer
> from Hitler's headquarters, Germany is preparing to
> invade the USSR on May 14 through Finland, the Baltic
> countries and Latvia. At the same time Moscow and
> Leningrad will be heavily raided and paratroopers landed
> in border cities…"

In this case we know that Khrushchev deliberately lied, because we now
have the full text of the Vorontsov letter. Khrushchev omitted Admiral
Kuznetsov's evaluation of it, which changes the whole meaning of the
letter. Khrushchev deliberately concealed from his audience the fact that
the Navy had decided this was disinformation intended to mislead the
Soviet leadership! (See Appendix)

---

[118] "22 iiunia 1941 goda. Moglo li vse byt' po-inomu?" ("June 22, 1941: Could it have all
been otherwise?"), *Krasnaia Zvezda* June 16 2001. Online at
http://www.redstar.ru/2001/06/16_06/4_01.html

Khrushchev's dishonest reference to the Vorontsov letter was evidently his own idea. It is not mentioned in the Pospelov Report; in the Pospelov-Aristov draft of Khrushchev's Speech of February 18, 1956, or in Khrushchev's additions to that draft of February 19, 1956. We do not know how or from whom Khrushchev obtained the letter.

The editors of *Doklad Khrushcheva* do not reprint it, or identify where the original was published, or discuss it in any way. They could not possibly have been ignorant of the original of the letter, for it was published in the major military journal *Voenno-Istoricheskii Zhurnal* (No. 2, 1992, 39-40). They erroneously identify "Bozer" with the Soviet spy within the German SS Schulze-Boysen, even though Bozer is clearly identified as a "Soviet citizen."

It appears as though they wished to conceal Khrushchev's lie by not identifying it. All this points to a deliberate coverup by the editors of this supposedly authoritative book.

Examples such as Vorontsov's letter demand that we examine Khrushchev's possible motives for lying in the Secret Speech.

32. German soldier

A little later in the "Secret Speech" Khrushchev returned to this theme of "warnings":

> The following fact is also known: On the eve of the invasion of the territory of the Soviet Union by the Hitlerite army, a certain German citizen crossed our border and stated that the German armies had received orders to start the offensive against the Soviet Union on the night of June 22 at 3 o'clock. Stalin was informed about this immediately, but even this warning was ignored.

This statement of Khrushchev's is also false. Unlike the Vorontsov letter, which was secret until recently, the story of the German soldier must have been remembered by many people in Khrushchev's audience.

The soldier in question was Alfred Liskow. His warning was not ignored at all. His desertion, at 9 p.m. on June 21, was reported at 3:10 a.m. on June 22 by telephone, 40 minutes before the Nazi invasion. Therefore Stalin was **not** "informed immediately", nor is there any evidence that he "ignored" it, as Khrushchev said. Liskow's platoon commander, a Lieut.

Schulz, had told his men "towards evening" (*pod vecherom*) of the impending invasion.

Liskow was sent to Moscow. On June 27 1941 his story was printed in *Pravda*[119]. A leaflet with his story, picture, and a call for German soldiers to desert to the Soviet side, was produced. According to one account, one unit immediately blew a bridge and went to defensive positions, where they were wiped out to a man with the German attack a few hours later

In his memoirs, written in the 1960s, Khrushchev himself does not repeat the claim that the German soldier's warning was ignored.

33. Commanders Killed

Khrushchev:

> Very grievous consequences, especially in reference to
> the beginning of the war, followed Stalin's annihilation
> of many military commanders and political workers
> during 1937-1941 because of his suspiciousness and
> through slanderous accusations. During these years
> repressions were instituted against certain parts of
> military cadres beginning literally at the company and
> battalion commander level and extending to the higher
> military centers; during this time the cadre of leaders
> who had gained military experience in Spain and in the
> Far East was almost completely liquidated.

Khrushchev does not directly state, but instead alludes to, the following claims which he and others made subsequently:

- Marshal Tukhachevsky and the seven other commanders condemned and executed with him on June 11, 1937, were innocent of what they were charged with – conspiring to overthrow the government and with espionage contacts with Germany and Japan.

- So many military commanders were executed or dismissed that Soviet military preparedness was

---

[119] I have put this article online at
http://chss.montclair.edu/english/furr/research/liskowpravda062741.pdf

greatly harmed. The military commanders executed
or dismissed were better commanders – more
educated, with more military experience – than those
who replaced them.

Research has disproven these statements. The facts are otherwise.)

1. Since the end of the USSR a large mass of evidence has been published)
that confirms that Tukhachevsky and these other commanders were
guilty as charged. Since Khrushchev's time these same commanders have
been considered heroes in the USSR and, now, in post-Soviet Russia. The
government, which controls the Presidential archive where the materials
for this and the 1936-1938 trials and investigations are kept today, has
only released small bits of this documentation, and official historians still
deny that the commanders were guilty.

But even that documentation demonstrates their guilt beyond any reasonable doubt. For example, in his recently-published (February 2006)
confession-interrogation of April 26 1939 Ezhov fully confirms the exist-)
ence of **three** separate, competing military conspiracies: one consisting of
"major military leaders" headed by Marshal A.I. Egorov; a Trotskyist
group led by Gamarnik, Iakir and Uborevich; and a "Bonapartist group
of officers" led by Tukhachevsky.[120]

To compound his dishonesty, Khrushchev had Tukhachevsky and most
of the others "rehabilitated" in 1957. But Khrushchev did not set up a
commission to study the question of their guilt until 1962. Its report, with
additional evidence of their guilt, was kept secret until 1994.[121]

2. Khrushchev and the anti-communist historians who have come after
him have greatly exaggerated the number and per centage of military
commanders executed and dismissed during 1937-38. Good studies of
this subject existed in Khrushchev's time, and have been done today.
Likewise, the level of military training, and even of battlefield experience
– at least, experience in the First World War – increased as a result of the

---

[120] I have put this confession-interrogation of Ezhov's online at
http://chss.montclair.edu/english/furr/research/ezhov042639eng.html (Russian text:
../ezhovru.html).The full bibliographical reference to it is at the top of the article there.

[121] There is an enormous amount of evidence that Tukhachevsky and the other
commanders tried and executed with him were guilty as charged. The author and)
Moscow historian Vladimir L. Bobrov are preparing a lengthy study on the whole
"Tukhachevsky Affair" question.

replacement of executed, arrested, and dismissed officers with those promoted to replace them.

The best summaries of recent Russian publications on these subjects are:

- Gerasimov, G.I. "Destvitel'noe vliyanie repressiy 1937-1938 gg. Na ofitserskiy korpus RKKA. *Rossiiskiy Istoricheskiy Zhurnal* No. 1, 1999. Also at http://www.hrono.ru/statii/2001/rkka_repr.html

- Pykhalov, Igor'. *Velikaya Obolgannaya Voyna.* Moscow: "Yauza", "Eksmo", 2005, Ch. 2: "Byla li 'Obezglavlena' Krasnaya Armiya?" Also at http://militera.lib.ru/research/pyhalov_i/02.html

Marshal Konev, speaking in 1965 with writer Konstantin Simonov, disagreed sharply with Khrushchev.

What's more, Khrushchev himself was directly responsible for "annihilating" most of the commanders in the Kiev (Ukraine) Military District. Volkogonov quotes a directive from Khrushchev, dated March 1938. The longer version, from the Russian edition, is translated here (see Appendix); a much shorter version is given in the English edition, Dmitrii A. Volkogonov, *Stalin: Triumph and Tragedy.* (NY: Grove Weidenfeld, 1991), p. 329.

34. Stalin's "Demoralization" after the beginning of the war

Khrushchev:

> It would be incorrect to forget that, after the first severe disaster and defeat at the front, Stalin thought that this was the end. In one of his speeches in those days he said:
>
> > "All that which Lenin created we have lost forever."
>
> After this Stalin for a long time actually did not direct the military operations and ceased to do anything whatever.

This is completely false, and Khrushchev had to know that it was. Most of those who worked closely with Stalin during the first weeks of the war (and afterwards) were still alive and in high positions. Yet they never reported anything like this. Khrushchev himself was in the Ukraine during this whole period, and could have had no first-hand knowledge of anything Stalin said or did.

The logbooks of those who came to Stalin's office to work with him have been published now. They demonstrate that Stalin was extremely active from the very first day of the war. Of course, they were available to Khrushchev as well. The logbooks for June 21-28 1941 were published in *Istoricheskii Arkhiv* No. 2, 1996, pp. 51-54, and document Stalin's continuous activity. We have also put facsimile copies of the original handwritten pages online.[122]

Marshal Zhukov had no particular love for Stalin. Stalin had demoted him after the war when Zhukov had been caught stealing German war booty for himself. Zhukov had also supported Khrushchev in his 1957 ouster of the "Stalinists" Malenkov, Molotov and Kaganovich. Nevertheless Zhukov appears to have retained a good deal of respect for Stalin, and he refuted Khrushchev's claim in his memoirs.

Georgi Dimitrov, the Bulgarian head of the Comintern, wrote in his diary that he was summoned to the Kremlin at 7 a.m. on June 22 1941, where he found Poskrebyshev (Stalin's secretary), Marshal Timoshenko, Admiral Kuznetsov, Lev Mekhlis, editor of *Pravda* and head of the Political Directorate of the Army, and Beria, head of the NKVD. He remarked: "Striking calmness, resoluteness, confidence of Stalin and all the others."[123]

Attempting to rescue Khrushchev's falsehood about Stalin's alleged inactivity Cold-War biographers of Stalin have seized on the fact that there are no entries in the logbook of visitors to Stalin's office for June 29 and 30. Therefore, they conclude, his supposed breakdown must have occurred then.

Even Soviet dissident historian and ferocious anti-Stalinist Roi Medvedev has given the lie to this version of events. Khrushchev's version, says

---

[122] They have been reproduced at http://www.hrono.ru/libris/stalin/16-13.html. One convenient source for this information is in Igor' Pykhalov's article "Did Stalin Collapse into Inactivity?" ("Did Stalin Fall into Prostration?"), Chapter 10 of his book *Velikaya Obolgannaya Voina* (The Great Calumniated War), also online at

http://militera.lib.ru/research/pyhalov_i/10.html

Facsimiles of the original archival copies are at
http://chss.montclair.edu/english/furr/research/stalinvisitors41.pdf

The pages from *Istoricheskii Arkhiv* No. 2, 1996, are reproduced at
http://chss.montclair.edu/english/furr/research/stalinvisitors41_istarkh96.pdf

[123] *The Diary of Georgi Dimitrov*, ed. Ivo Banac (Yale U.P., 2003), p. 166

Medvedev, is "a complete fabrication,"[124] but has appeared in biographies of Stalin by Jonathan Lewis and Phillip Whitehead (1990), Alan Bullock (1991), and the *Oxford Encyclopaedia of the Second World War* (1995). Medvedev goes on to cite the evidence.

Stalin was continuously very active from June 22 onward, including June 29 and 30. On June 29 occurred a famous argument with his commanders, including Timoshenko and Zhukov. Mikoian described it to G.A. Kumanev (*Riadom so Stalinym*, pp. 28-9). Also on June 29 Stalin formulated and signed the important directive concerning partisan warfare. On June 30 the Decree of the Supreme Soviet, the Council of People's Commissars, and the Central Committee of the Party, forming the State Defense Committee, was issued.

General Dmitri Volkogonov and Pavel' Sudoplatov agree that Khrushchev was lying. Both were hostile towards Stalin, Volkogonov extremely so, in the '90s, when they wrote their books.

35. Stalin A Bad Commander

Khrushchev:

> Stalin was very far from an understanding of the real situation which was developing at the front. This was natural because, during the whole Patriotic War, he never visited any section of the front or any liberated city except for one short ride on the Mozhaisk highway during a stabilized situation at the front. To this incident were dedicated many literary works full of fantasies of all sorts and so many paintings. Simultaneously, Stalin was interfering with operations and issuing orders which did not take into consideration the real situation at a given section of the front and which could not help but result in huge personnel losses.

Aside from Khrushchev, nobody says this! By contrast, writing after Khrushchev's fall Marshal Zhukov thought Stalin an extremely competent military leader. In his memoirs Marshal Vasilevsky specifically mentioned Khrushchev's statement here and strongly disagreed with it. Mar-

---

[124] R.Medvedev, Z.Medvedev. *The Unknown Stalin* (Woodstock, NY: The Overlook Press, 2003), p. 242.

shal Golovanov spoke of Stalin and his abilities as a commander in the highest terms.

36. Khar'kov 1942

Khrushchev:

> I will allow myself in this connection to bring out one characteristic fact which illustrates how Stalin directed operations at the fronts. There is present at this Congress Marshal Bagramian, who was once the chief of operations in the headquarters of the southwestern front and who can corroborate what I will tell you. When there developed an exceptionally serious situation for our Army in 1942 in the Kharkov region…And what was the result of this? The worst that we had expected. The Germans surrounded our Army concentrations and consequently we lost hundreds of thousands of our soldiers. This is Stalin's military "genius"; this is what it cost us.

Not only is this wrong – most generals do not blame Stalin – but some) say Khrushchev himself is to blame!

In an anniversary article on the subject of Khrushchev's "Secret Speech" writer Sergei Konstantinov summed up the reactions of many military leaders at Khrushchev's remarks about Stalin. (See Appendix) According to Academician A.M. Samsonov Zhukov disagreed with Khrushchev's account. In his memoirs Zhukov does blame Stalin, but only in part.[125]

As we have seen (see section 35, Appendix) Marshal Vasilevskii directly called Khrushchev's version of the Khar'kov defense a lie. He says that Khrushchev and General Kirponos were in fact given plans and sample rocket-launchers, as well as advice on how to build their own weapons. In effect, Vasilevskii says, the fault was Khrushchev's, not Stalin's. Historian Vadim Kozhinov points out that Khrushchev used this story to

+ or booty

---

[125] However, Zhukov was very angry at Stalin – Stalin demoted him for stealing German) trophies. This is fully documented in *Voennie Arkhivy Rossii*, 1993, pp. 175 ff.; for Zhukov's confession see pp. 241-44. Khrushchev knew this, and had it all quashed, undoubtedly to get Zhukov on his side.

discredit Malenkov[126], and completely avoided the obvious point that, as First Secretary of the Ukraine for over three years already, Khrushchev could have seen to the preparation of rifles long beforehand.

The *Short History of the Great Patriotic War* (1970 edition, pp. 164-5) published after Khrushchev's ouster carries this version, which blames the front command rather than Stalin and the GKO. This is consistent with Stalin's letter of June 26 1942 quoted by many sources, including Portugal'skii et al.'s biography of Timoshenko, and which blamed not only Bagramian, but also Timoshenko and Khrushchev himself.

Earlier in the "Secret Speech" Khrushchev claimed that "Whoever opposed this concept or tried to prove his viewpoint and the correctness of his position was doomed to removal from the leading collective and to subsequent moral and physical annihilation." This is not true, and Khrushchev did not even give a single example of it. Marshal Timoshenko outlived Stalin by 17 years, Khrushchev, by 18, Marshal Bagramian by 29 years. They all had insisted on their "viewpoint", and yet none was punished, much less "annihilated."

Dmitry Volkogonov, who was intensely hostile to Stalin, suggests that Khrushchev had either misremembered after so many years, or was simply lying on this point in his "Secret Speech."

37. Stalin Planned Military Operations on a Globe

Khrushchev:

> I telephoned to Vasilevsky and begged him: "Alexander Mikhailovich, take a map" – Vasilevsky is present here – "and show Comrade Stalin the situation which has developed." We should note that Stalin planned operations on a globe. (Animation in the hall.) Yes, comrades, he used to take the globe and trace the front line on it. I said to Comrade Vasilevsky: "Show him the situation on a map…

---

[126] Vadim Kozhinov, *Rossiia. Vek XX (1939-1964)*. Moscow: Algoritm, 1999, p. 75. IUrii Emel'ianov says much the same thing in "Mif XX S'ezda". *Slovo* No. 3, 2000. Cf. http://stalinism.newmail.ru/emelian2.htm.

This is perhaps the most obvious lie in Khrushchev's entire speech. No
one has ever defended this statement. Many authorities refute it, some
indignantly. I refer to the reader to the quotations from military leaders as
well as from Molotov.

38. Stalin Downgraded Zhukov

Khrushchev:

> Stalin was very much interested in the assessment of
> Comrade Zhukov as a military leader. He asked me often
> for my opinion of Zhukov. I told him then, "I have
> known Zhukov for a long time; he is a good general and
> a good military leader."
>
> After the war Stalin began to tell all kinds of nonsense
> about Zhukov, among others the following, "You
> praised Zhukov, but he does not deserve it. It is said that
> before each operation at the front Zhukov used to
> behave as follows: He used to take a handful of earth,
> smell it and say, 'We can begin the attack,' or the
> opposite, 'The planned operation cannot be carried
> out.'" I stated at that time, "Comrade Stalin, I do not
> know who invented this, but it is not true."
>
> It is possible that Stalin himself invented these things for
> the purpose of minimizing the role and military talents of
> Marshal Zhukov.

No one else ever heard Stalin say this. According to a remark by Zhukov
himself that is quoted by several writers, Stalin demoted him but never
insulted him. This remark of Zhukov's was probably a direct rebuke to
Khrushchev here, since it's hard to imagine any other reason he might
have made it.

Stalin did have Zhukov demoted after the war when it was discovered
that the Marshal had been stealing German war booty on a grand scale,
instead of contributing it to the State to be used in rebuilding the immense destruction wrought by the Germans during the war.[127] Since

---

[127] The details were published in an obscure but evidently official journal *Voenniye Arkhivy
Rossii* 1, 1993, pp. 175-245. There was never another issue of this mysterious journal. A
facsimile of these specific pages may be downloaded from
http://chss.montclair.edu/english/furr/research/zhukovtheft4648_var93.pdf

everybody knew of Zhukov's demotion after the war, but few knew the details of why it had occurred, Khrushchev was probably just currying favor with Zhukov here. He needed Zhukov the following year, to help him defeat the "Stalinists" Malenkov, Molotov, Kaganovich, and Shepilov, who tried to get him voted out of office.

Chapter 6.

Of Plots and Affairs

39. Deportations of nationalities

Khrushchev:

> Comrades, let us reach for some other facts. The Soviet
> Union is justly considered as a model of a multinational
> state because we have in practice assured the equality and
> friendship of all nations which live in our great
> Fatherland.
>
> All the more monstrous are the acts whose initiator was
> Stalin and which are rude violations of the basic Leninist
> principles of the nationality policy of the Soviet state. We
> refer to the mass deportations from their native places of
> whole nations, together with all Communists and
> Komsomols without any exception; this deportation
> action was not dictated by any military considerations....
>
> Not only a Marxist-Leninist but also no man of common
> sense can grasp how it is possible to make whole nations
> responsible for inimical activity, including women,
> children, old people, Communists and Komsomols, to
> use mass repression against them, and to expose them to
> misery and suffering for the hostile acts of individual
> persons or groups of persons.

Khrushchev is not "revealing" these deportations; they were well known
at the time they happened. What was "new" was his three accusations
against Stalin here: (1) the deportations were made "without any exception"; (2) the deportations were "not dictated by any military consideration;" (3) "whole nations" were punished "for the hostile acts of individual persons or groups of persons." These are the "revelations" we will
deal with.

Khrushchev mentions Karachai, Kalmyks, Chechen-Ingush, Balkars. For
some reason he does not mention Crimean Tatars or Volga Germans.

The events leading up to these deportations, the deportations themselves, and the aftermath, are extremely well documented in Soviet archives. Though none of this archival information was published until after the end of the USSR, Khrushchev undoubtedly had access to it. He, or his aides, had to know that each of the criticisms Khrushchev made was false.

1. Examples of exceptions to the deportations are cited by Pykhalov, from Soviet documents published by N.F. Bugai, the main Russian expert on this question and an extremely anti-Stalin researcher.

2. The military necessity for the deportations was to secure the Red Army's rear. In each of the cases of the deported nationalities, very large parts of the population were either actively or passively aiding the Germans in rebelling against the Soviet government, and constituted a serious danger to Soviet forces. In addition, the Soviets could not be sure that the German armies would not push eastward again in 1944, as they had done in each of the three previous years.

According to Bugai and A.M. Gomov, who are hostile to Stalin and do not approve of the deportations at all,

> ...the Soviet government had by and large allocated its priorities correctly, basing those priorities on its right to maintain order behind the front lines, and in the North Caucasus in particular. [128]

In the "Secret Speech" Khrushchev noted with an attempt at humor:

> The Ukrainians avoided meeting this fate only because there were too many of them and there was no place to which to deport them. Otherwise, he would have deported them also. (*Laughter and animation in the hall.*)

This was supposed to be a joke, since Khrushchev did not seriously claim Stalin had wanted to deport the Ukrainians. But perhaps Khrushchev mentioned the Ukrainians for a reason, because, as he well knew, a tiny number of Ukrainians, most of whom had entered the Soviet Union along with the Nazis and who had abetted the Nazis' crimes, was in revolt, on the Nazis' side and against the Soviet Union. This caused huge problems in the rear of the Red Army as it advanced westward towards

---

[128] N.F. Bugai and A.M. Gonov. "The Forced Evacuation of the Chechens and the Ingush." *Russian Studies in History.* vol. 41, no. 2, Fall 2002, pp. 43–61, at p. 59.

Poland and Germany in 1944-45.[129] In the light of the massive nature of the anti-Soviet rebellions going on in Chechen-Ingushia and among the Crimean Tatars, the Soviets had every reason to fear that the same thing would have occurred there.

3. The question of whether whole nationalities should have been deported or not resolves down to two points. First, how massive were the rebellions among these ethnic groups? Were they so massive that they involved a majority of the population? We'll cite evidence below that, in the case of two of these nationalities that we pick for examples here, the rebellions were massive, involving much more than half the population.

Second, there is also the question of genocide. To split up a small national group that is tightly knit by a unique language, history, and culture, is in fact to destroy it.

In the case of the Chechen-Ingush and the Crimean Tatars, collaboration with the Nazis was massive, involving most of the population. To try to isolate and punish "only the guilty" would have been to split the nation up, and would likely have indeed destroyed the nationality. Instead, the national group was kept together, and their population grew.

I assume that my readers, like I myself, support punishing individuals for the crimes of individuals. However, the Nazi collaboration of these groups was so massive that to punish the individuals involved would have endangered the survival of these ethnic groups as groups. It would have meant depleting these groups of young men, through imprisonment and execution, leaving very few young men for the young women to marry.

Deportation kept these groups intact. The deportations themselves were almost completely free of casualties. This enabled the populations of these groups to increase in future years, right up to the present. So their cultures and languages, and in fact their existence as peoples, did in fact remain alive. Furthermore, they became so well established in the places of their deportation that many of them never returned to their aboriginal areas when they were permitted to do so.

Here is the conundrum: to punish only the individuals guilty of desertion or Nazi collaboration would have been consistent with Enlightenment views of individual, not collective, punishment -- views that I myself

---

[129] Zhukov, IU. *Stalin: Tainy Vlasti*. Moscow: Vagrius, 2005, pp. 432-3.

share. But it would also have led to a greater evil: the destruction of these ethnic groups as "peoples" – in short, to genocide!

Crimean Tartars

The Crimean Tartars were deported en masse. Many documents concerning their deportation have been published in Russia, from formerly classified Soviet archives. Naturally, they have been published by anti-communist researchers, whose commentaries are very tendentious. But the documents themselves are very interesting!

In 1939 there were 218,000 Crimean Tartars. That should mean about 22,000 men of military age – about 10% of the population. In 1941, according to contemporary Soviet figures, 20,000 Crimean Tartar soldiers deserted the Red Army. By 1944 20,000 Crimean Tartar soldiers had joined the Nazi forces and were fighting against the Red Army.

So the charge of **massive** collaboration sticks.[130] The question is: What should the Soviets have done about this?

They could have done nothing – let them all go unpunished. Well, they weren't going to do that!

They could have shot the 20,000 deserters. Or, they could have imprisoned – deported –just them, the young men of military age. Either would have meant virtually the end of the Crimean Tartar nation, for there would have been no husbands for the next generation of young Tartar women.

Instead, the Soviet government decided to deport the whole nationality to Central Asia, which they did in 1944. They were given land, and some years of relief from all taxation. The Tartar nation remained intact, and had grown in size by the late 1950s.

The Chechens and Ingush

In 1943 there were about 450,000 Chechens and Ingush in the Chechen-Ingush Autonomous Soviet Socialist Republic (CHASSR). This should

---

[130] Researcher J. Otto Pohl, an extremely anticommunist author, has argued from German sources that not all these men joined Nazi forces. See "The False Charges of Treason against the Crimean Tatars." (International Committee for Crimea, Washington, DC, 18 May 2010). But even if true this makes no difference. The Soviets could not have known this; desertion was still a serious offense; and most men would have joined anti-Soviet partisan or bandit groups.

have meant about 40,000-50,000 men of age for military service. In 1942, at the height of the Nazis' military successes, 14576 men were called to military service, of whom 13560, or 93%, deserted and either hid or joined rebel or bandit groups in the mountains.

There was massive collaboration with German forces on the part of the Chechen and Ingush population. On February 23 2000 Radio Svoboda interviewed Chechen nationalists who boasted proudly of a pro-German anti-Soviet armed rebellion in February 1943, when the German penetration towards the Caucasus was at its greatest.

The problem with this account is that it lies by omission. The revolt in question took place, but it was under a Nazi flag, and with the goal of a Nazi alliance.

Casualties among the deportees during the deportation were low – 0.25% of those deported, according to Bugai and Gomov.

> NKVD records attest to 180 convoy trains carrying 493,269 Chechen and Ingush nationals and members of other nationalities seized at the same time. Fifty people were killed in the course of the operation, and 1,272 died on the journey. (p. 56)

Since it happened in the winter, and during the fiercest war in European, perhaps world, history, that figure does not seem very high.

But that is not our concern here, which is simply to verify or disprove Khrushchev's accusations. Khrushchev claimed: (1) that the national groups were deported "without any exception;" (2) there was no military reason for the deportations; (3) that the collaboration and treason were the "acts of individual persons or groups of persons." All three of these assertions of Khrushchev's are false: (1) exceptions existed; (2) as did military reason; and (3) there was massive, not merely individual, betrayal. Khrushchev's assertions were not truthful. The question of exceptions is covered by the quotations in the Appendix.

40. The Leningrad Affair

Khrushchev:

> After the conclusion of the Patriotic War, the Soviet nation stressed with pride the magnificent victories gained through great sacrifices and tremendous efforts.

> The country experienced a period of political
> enthusiasm. …
>
> And it was precisely at this time that the so-called
> "Leningrad affair" was born. As we have now proven,
> this case was fabricated. Those who innocently lost their
> lives included Comrades Voznesensky, Kuznetsov,
> Rodionov, Popkov, and others….
>
> How did it happen that these persons were branded as
> enemies of the people and liquidated?
>
> Facts prove that the "Leningrad affair" is also the result
> of willfulness which Stalin exercised against party cadres.

The Leningrad Affair is mysterious, important, and fascinating. There is plenty of reason to think that it was **not** simply a question of falsification, but that serious crimes were involved.

Fortunately for us, we do not have to try to unravel it here. We simply have to prove that Khrushchev was lying when he claimed the case was a result of "Stalin's willfulness."[131] This is a case of Khrushchev's "flagrant disregard for the truth."

Khrushchev changed his story about who was responsible for the "Leningrad Affair" several times, evidently to suit his needs of the moment. On June 25, 1953, the day before his arrest (and, possibly, his murder) at Khrushchev's hand, Beria wrote to the Presidiium concerning the investigation of former NKVD man M.D. Riumin. In this document Beria accuses Riumin of falsifying the Leningrad Affair. The problem for Khrushchev seems to have been that this directly implicated Ignat'ev, the former head of the MVD and a man dismissed by Stalin.

A year later, on May 3 1954, the Presidium headed by Khrushchev issued a "Resolution [*postanovlenie*] of the Presidium of the CC CPSU on the 'Leningrad Affair.' " This document blames Abakumov and – Beria! But Beria had nothing to do with the MGB or MVD at the time of the "Leningrad Affair" or anything close to it.

Two years later in the "Secret Speech" Khrushchev laid all the blame on Stalin. Than again, little more than a year after the "Secret Speech", in June 1957 Khrushchev said that Stalin had been **against** the arrests of

---

[131] In fact there is good evidence that no fabrication was involved in the "Leningrad Affair" either, but we will not undertake a study of this complicated matter here.

Voznesenskii and the others, and that Beria and Malenkov had instigated it!

Whatever Malenkov's role may have been, Beria was certainly not involved in it, since he was not in the MVD at the time. But there is no more reason to think Khrushchev was telling the truth in 1957 than there is to believe him at any other time.

41. The Mingrelian Affair

Khrushchev:

> Instructive in the same way is the case of the Mingrelian nationalist organization which supposedly existed in Georgia. As is known, resolutions by the Central Committee, Communist Party of the Soviet Union, were made concerning this case in November 1951 and in March 1952. These resolutions were made without prior discussion with the Political Bureau. Stalin had personally dictated them. They made serious accusations against many loyal Communists. On the basis of falsified documents, it was proven that there existed in Georgia a supposedly nationalistic organization whose objective was the liquidation of the Soviet power in that republic with the help of imperialist powers.

> In this connection, a number of responsible party and Soviet workers were arrested in Georgia. As was later proven, this was a slander directed against the Georgian party organization.

The only specific accusation Khrushchev makes here is that Stalin personally dictated the CC decisions of November 1951 and March 1952, and without prior discussion of them at the Politburo. We know this is not true.

A critical edition of the Politburo resolution of November 9, 1951 has been published. The editors note Stalin's corrections to the original text: in some cases to make it more precise, but in other places to soften harsher accusations of nationalism.[132] However, it and the March 27 1952

---

[132] Politbiuro TsK VKP(b) i Sovet Ministrov SSSR. 1945-1953 gg. Moscow, 2002, p. 350-352.

Politburo resolution (*ibid.*, 352-4) were both taken at Politburo sessions (*ibid.*, p. 351 n. 1; p. 354 no.1). In the latter case Stalin wrote in the title, but the resolution was on the agenda of the Politburo.[133]

But Khrushchev's main claim is that Stalin was responsible for fabricating this case – that "All of this happened under the 'genial' leadership of Stalin, 'the great son of the Georgian nation,' as Georgians like to refer to Stalin." This is untrue. Documents cited by Nikita Petrov, an extremely anti-Stalin researcher with the extremely anticommunist "Memorial" organization, suggest that the real matter was "the struggle against 'clannishness' in the Georgian leadership."[134]

On April 10 1953, a month after Stalin's death, the Presidium of the CC of the CPSU adopted a decision blaming, above all others, S. D. Ignat'ev, the head of the MGB, for fabricating the entire affair and for subjecting a number of those arrested to prolonged torture, imprisonment, and maltreatment. Khrushchev himself was a member of the Presidium!

Ignat'ev was explicitly named as responsible at the least for not controlling his subordinates M.D. Riumin, Tsepkov, and others. On April 1 1953 Ignat'ev was also blamed by the Presidium in the frameup of the "Doctors' Plot" and on April 3 dismissed from his position as secretary of the CC for his negligence (p. 24). A report made by Beria on June 25, 1953 to the Presidium blames Ignat'ev for permitting Riumin and other subordinates to use torture against, among others, the "Leningrad Affair" defendants (p.66).[135]

Yet it was Khrushchev himself who restored Ignat'ev to responsible posts once Beria had been arrested or killed! Ignat'ev was present at the 20th Congress, and Khrushchev referred specifically to him with regard to the "Doctors' Plot" – for his role in which the Presidium had already sharply criticized and demoted him!

Boris Nikolaevsky's note to the *New Leader* edition also points to Ignat'ev's responsibility in the "Mingrelian conspiracy."

> Khrushchev's statement on the "Mingrelian conspiracy" does explain the purges in Georgia in 1952. Though he

---

[133] For the texts see Appendix and facsimiles of the pages from *ibid.*, 349-354, at http://chss.montclair.edu/english/furr/research/mingrelianres.pdf

[134] Petrov, Nikita. *Pervyi predsedatel' KGB. Ivan Serov.* Moscow: Materik, 2005, p. 114.

[135] See facsimiles of Beria's reports from *RKEB* 1at http://chss.montclair.edu/english/furr/research/mingrelianaff.pdf

implies that the "Mingrelian case," like the "Leningrad case," was also staged by Beria and Abakumov, this is a deliberate distortion. It was precisely in November 1951 that S. D. Ignatiev, one of Beria's bitterest enemies, was appointed Minister of State Security; the "Mingrelian case" was, therefore, trumped up as a blow at Beria.

42. Yugoslavia

Khrushchev:

> The willfulness of Stalin showed itself not only in decisions concerning the internal life of the country but also in the international relations of the Soviet Union.
>
> The July plenum of the Central Committee studied in detail the reasons for the development of conflict with Yugoslavia. It was a shameful role which Stalin played here. The "Yugoslav affair" contained no problems which could not have been solved through party discussions among comrades. There was no significant basis for the development of this "affair"; it was completely possible to have prevented the rupture of relations with that country. This does not mean, however, that the Yugoslav leaders did not make mistakes or did not have shortcomings. But these mistakes and shortcomings were magnified in a monstrous manner by Stalin, which resulted in a break of relations with a friendly country.

This is another lie. In July 1953 Khrushchev, Molotov, and Malenkov attacked Beria for planning to improve relations with Yugoslavia. Meanwhile, they themselves called Tito and Rankovich "agents of the capitalists" who "behave like enemies of the Soviet Union."

But here Khrushchev refers to them as "comrades!" In other words, Khrushchev et al. attacked Beria for beginning a rapprochement with the Yugoslavs, and calling them "comrades," which is precisely what Khrushchev is doing here, and what he attacked Stalin for **not** doing!

43. The Doctors' Plot

Khrushchev:

Let us also recall the "affair of the doctor-plotters."
(Animation in the hall.) Actually there was no "affair"
outside of the declaration of the woman doctor
Timashuk, who was probably influenced or ordered by
someone (after all, she was an unofficial collaborator of
the organs of state security) to write Stalin a letter in
which she declared that doctors were applying
supposedly improper methods of medical treatment.

Such a letter was sufficient for Stalin to reach an
immediate conclusion that there are doctor-plotters in
the Soviet Union. He issued orders to arrest a group of
eminent Soviet medical specialists. He personally issued
advice on the conduct of the investigation and the
method of interrogation of the arrested persons. He said
that the academician Vinogradov should be put in
chains, another one should be beaten. Present at this
Congress as a delegate is the former Minister of State
Security, Comrade Ignatiev. Stalin told him curtly, "If
you do not obtain confessions from the doctors we will
shorten you by a head."

Stalin personally called the investigative judge, gave him
instructions, advised him on which investigative methods
should be used; these methods were simple – beat, beat
and, once again, beat.

Shortly after the doctors were arrested, we members of
the Political Bureau received protocols with the doctors'
confessions of guilt. After distributing these protocols,
Stalin told us, "You are blind like young kittens; what
will happen without me? The country will perish because
you do not know how to recognize enemies."

The case was so presented that no one could verify the
facts on which the investigation was based. There was no
possibility of trying to verify facts by contacting those
who had made the confessions of guilt.

We felt, however, that the case of the arrested doctors
was questionable. We knew some of these people
personally because they had once treated us. When we

examined this "case" after Stalin's death, we found it to be fabricated from beginning to end.

This ignominious "case" was set up by Stalin; he did not, however, have the time in which to bring it to an end (as he conceived that end), and for this reason the doctors are still alive. Now all have been rehabilitated; they are working in the same places they were working before; they treat top individuals, not excluding members of the Government; they have our full confidence; and they execute their duties honestly, as they did before.

In organizing the various dirty and shameful cases, a very base role was played by the rabid enemy of our party, an agent of a foreign intelligence service – Beria, who had stolen into Stalin's confidence.

This is a completely false account of the "Doctors' Plot."[136]

- The "Doctors' Plot" was taken up by the MGB in 1952. Timashuk's letters were written in 1948. They concerned Zhdanov's treatment in his final illness. They mentioned no Jewish doctors at all. At no time did Dr. Timashuk have any connection with the "Doctors' Plot" whatsoever, which did not even arise until three to four years later. Khrushchev simply slanders her here.

- Ignat'ev was head of the KGB at this time, not Beria. On April 1 1953, less than a month after Stalin's death the Presidium – of which Khrushchev was a member – had criticized Ignat'ev for his responsibility in the "Doctors' Plot" frameups (Beria p. 22). It did not occur to them to blame Stalin.

- It was Beria who stopped the Doctors' Plot frame-ups, who freed the doctors, and arrested those responsible, including Ignat'ev, who was released shortly after Beria was done away with (arrested or killed) in late June 1953.

---

[136] All sources are quoted and identified in the Appendix to this chapter.

- According to his daughter Svetlana Stalin did not
  believe the Jewish doctors were guilty.

Stalin was in semi-retirement, and was not kept current with developments. Stalin had thought that the MGB had serious problems (Maly-
shev, about the Dec.1, 1952 Presidium meeting, in *Vestnik* 5 (1997), p.
141). It's possible that Stalin planned to put Beria in charge to clean up
these problems, especially the phony "Doctors' Plot", though he may
have had the "Mingrelian Affair" on his mind as well.

It is hard to imagine how Beria could have been chosen to head both the
MVD and the MGB at the same time, at the emergency Presidium meeting at the dying Stalin's bedside – a great concentration of power in the
hands of a single man -- unless there had been a previous agreement. It's
unlikely such an agreement would have been made during the preceding
days while Stalin was ill, because no one could be sure that Stalin would
die. Therefore, it seems most likely that Beria's joint appointment to
these two ministries was decided with Stalin's agreement and perhaps,
even probably, even at his suggestion.

The "Doctors' Plot" articles stopped appearing in the newspapers before
Stalin died. Anti-Stalinist and former Soviet dissident Zhores Medvedev
argues that this, together with other facts, shows it was Stalin himself
who ended the "Doctors' Plot" attacks in the press. Medevedev points
out that Stalin opposed the anti-semitism that had been a part of the
campaign from the outset. (Zhores Medvedev, *Stalin i Evreiskaia Problema.*(Moscow, 2003), 208ff; 216 f.) Stalin himself was famously opposed
to anti-semitism, as Medvedev admits.[137]

---

[137] In *The Unknown Stalin*, a collection of essays written at various times, Roi and Zhores
Medvedev both accuse Stalin of inciting anti-Semitism and then of decisively ending the
press campaign about, and preparations for a trial in, the "Doctors' Plot" . That is, these
two anti-Stalin authors decide that it was Stalin who put an end to the "Doctors' Plot"
campaign. *The Unknown Stalin* (Woodstock and New York: Overlook Press, 2004), 32.

Chapter 7.

Beria, His "Machinations" and "Crimes"

44. Beria

Khrushchev:

> In organizing the various dirty and shameful cases, a very base role was played by the rabid enemy of our party, an agent of a foreign intelligence service – Beria, who had stolen into Stalin's confidence.

Nobody today supports Khrushchev's tale of Beria's being a "foreign agent." It has been completely exploded by the evidence. Furthermore, neither Molotov nor Kaganovich believed it even at that time, though they did not say so in 1953.

No one mentioned such a charge during the vicious attacks upon him at the July 1953 Central Committee Plenum, as Mikoian admitted. [138] Khrushchev said that Beria's proposal for a united, neutralist Germany was "yielding to the West." But Stalin had suggested a neutral united Germany to the Allies in March 1952. *Pravda* repeated variations of this offer in April and May 1953, after Stalin's death. Beria could never have gotten this into the Party's newspaper by himself.

And in fact Khrushchev's claim that this was "yielding to the West" was not true – the Allies were very much opposed to this, and turned down any consideration of a unified Germany. Had the Soviet Union chosen to stick with this offer, it would have been very embarrassing to the West, since it would have been extremely tempting to almost all Germans. If the West had continued to oppose it, it would have been they, not the USSR, who would have appeared unfriendly to Germany after the war.

---

[138] Lavrentii Beriia. 1953. Stenogramma iul'skogo Plenuma TsK KPSS i drugie dokumenty. Moscow: MDF, 1999, p. 315.

In conversations with Felix Chuev the aged Molotov went on to explain (409-10) that he considers Beria's acts as an "agent of imperialism" to be that of proposing a neutral Germany.[139] This was the same charge raised, at the July 1953 Plenum. But Beria was only one member of the Presidium, and it was only a proposal. There was nothing at all wrong with his raising the question; it could not have been put into practice without the Presidium's approval. To Chuev's direct question whether Beria really was an agent of foreign intelligence and whether that had been confirmed by evidence, Molotov answered in the negative.

45. Kaminsky accuses Beria of working with the Mussavat

Khrushchev:

> Were there any signs that Beria was an enemy of the party? Yes, there were. Already in 1937, at a Central Committee plenum, former People's Commissar of Health Kaminsky said that Beria worked for the Mussavat intelligence service. But the Central Committee plenum had barely concluded when Kaminsky was arrested and then shot. Had Stalin examined Kaminsky's statement? No, because Stalin believed in Beria, and that was enough for him.

Much material to refute this fabrication of Khrushchev's has been published since the end of the Soviet Union. For example, Pavlunovsky's letter of June 1937, testifying that Beria had indeed done Party underground work among nationalists, has only recently been published.

Beria's own Party autobiography cites his underground work among nationalists, something he would never have done if he had thought it would not distinguish his Party service.[140]

Zalessky's biographical encyclopedia, *Imperiia Stalina*, is extremely anti-Stalin, but agrees with Beria's contention that he did underground work. Indeed, it's impossible to imagine Sergei Kirov's intercession on Beria's behalf, or the Beria family's closeness to the Ordzhonikidze family as

---

[139] See also Feliks Chuev, *Kaganovich. Ispoved' stalinskogo apostola.* Moscow, 1992, p. 66.

[140] *Beriia: Konets kar'ery.* Ed. V.F. Nekrasov. Moscow: Politizdat, 1991, pp. 320-325; 323. This tendentious and poorly-document volume nonetheless contains interesting materials.

attested in Sergo Beria's memoirs, unless Beria's loyalty to the Party had been crystal clear.

It seems clear that Khrushchev simply revived an old rumor about Beria dating from his days in the nationalist underground. Undercover work is very dangerous, and Beria's "cover" had to be good enough to fool the Mussavat Party itself into believing Beria was working for them. It's not surprising that it would also fool rank-and-file Bolsheviks. Beria's own letter of 1933 to Ordzhonikidze shows that he was still trying to quash this vicious rumor. He would hardly have written a leading Politburo member about this unless he wanted to put it "on record."

Khrushchev had access to all the information we now have, and more. He had to know that this was a lie. It was another tool with which to smear Beria.

46. Kartvelishvili

Khrushchev:

> The long, unfriendly relations between Kartvelishvili and Beria were widely known; they date back to the time when Comrade Sergo [Ordzhonikidze] was active in the Transcaucasus; Kartvelishvili was the closest assistant of Sergo. The unfriendly relationship impelled Beria to fabricate a "case" against Kartvelishvili. It is a characteristic thing that in this "case" Kartvelishvili was charged with a terroristic act against Beria.

Kartvelishvili (who was also known by his Russianized name Lavrent'ev) was expelled from the Party and arrested on June 22, 1937, at the June 1937 CC Plenum, and executed on August 22, 1938, under Ezhov, not Beria.

There exists a note from Beria to Stalin about Beria's alleged uncovering of an underground Rightist group in Georgia that included Kartvelishvili. However,

- The note is from July 20 1937, a month after Kartvelishvili's arrest. (Lubianka 2, No. 142 p. 252)

- Kartvelishvili is mentioned in other documents by Liushkov, one of Ezhov's, not Beria's, men (No. 196 of Sept. 11, 1937, pp. 347 ff; No. 207 of September 19, 1937, pp. 368 ff.; No. 309 of March 29, 1938)

Liushkov was involved in Ezhov's conspiracy, and had many innocent men tortured and killed. But Ezhov was 100% against Beria. There was no way that Liushkov was abetting Beria in naming Kartvelishvili.

- According to Postyshev's rehabilitation documents Kartvelishvili was identified as a conspirator by Postyshev too (*RKEB 1*, 219).

- Kartvelishvili was named by Ia. A Iakovlev, a close associate of Stalin's in the drafting of the 1936 Constitution, vice-Chairman of the Party Control Commission, and member of the CC. Iakovlev was arrested suddenly on October 12, 1937, and in his extensive confession of October 15-18 1937 he names Kartvelishvili, among many others. It is clear from the annotations and followup note by Stalin that Stalin was taken by surprise by Iakovlev's confession.

The Rehabilitation file on Kartvelishvili (*RKEB* 1, 331-2) blames Beria for everything. Even if Kartvelishvili was framed, though, this cannot be true. Most of the documents against him are by Liushkov or, in the case of Iakovlev's confession, have nothing to do with Beria at all.

Kartvelishvili was arrested in June 1937, long before Beria had anything to do with the Soviet NKVD. It's hard to find a firm date for his execution. One "Memorial" webpage gives it as August 1938.[141] If that is accurate, then Beria could not have been involved in his interrogation and, if any, torture, because Beria had just become Ezhov's second-in-command in the NKVD on August 21 or 22, 1938. Beria seems to have remained in his post as First Secretary of the Central Committee of the Georgian Communist Party until August 31 1938, and evidently did not arrive in Moscow to take his position until around the first of September.[142]

According to the Pospelov Report (*RKEB* 1, 332), Lavrent'ev-Kartvelishvili was tortured into confessing and naming others. This is

---

[141] See http://www.memo.ru/memory/communarka/Chapt10.htm#_KMi_2450.

[142] *Lubianka 2*, No. 334, p. 545; N.V. Petrov, K.V. Skorkin. *Kto rukovodil NKVD. 1934-1941. Spravochnik*. Moscow: Zven'ia, 1999, 107. Cf.
http://www.memo.ru/history/NKVD/kto/biogr/gb42.htm

plausible, since we have Frinovskii's statement that Ezhov and his subordinates, including Frinovskii himself, regularly did this.

Given the dates, though, Beria could not have been responsible for Lavrent'ev-Kartvelishvili's fate. Khrushchev had to know this. This is probably the reason that the date of Lavrent'ev-Kartvelishvili's execution is not given in the Pospelov Report, which was drawn up to help Khrushchev blame Beria. Citing a date for the execution before Beria had even arrived at the NKVD would have contradicted the whole purpose of the Pospelov Report, which was certainly not to arrive at the truth!

47. Kedrov

Khrushchev:

> Here is what the old Communist, Comrade Kedrov, wrote to the Central Committee through Comrade Andreyev (Comrade Andreyev was then a Central Committee secretary): "I am calling to you for help from a gloomy cell of the Lefortovsky prison. Let my cry of horror reach your ears; do not remain deaf, take me under your protection; please, help remove the nightmare of interrogations and show that this is all a mistake.
>
> "I suffer innocently…"
>
> The old Bolshevik, Comrade Kedrov, was found innocent by the Military Collegium. But, despite this, he was shot at Beria's order.

We don't know the details of Kedrov's case because the materials have not been made available to researchers. But for our purposes, we do not need to do so. A Russian government agency has now published a collection of documents from which we can tell with certainty that the order for Kedrov's execution was signed by the State Prosecutor, Bochkov.[143] Beria was merely carrying it out. It was not "his order."

---

[143] Organy gosudarstvennoi bezopasnosti SSSR v Velikoi Otechestvennoi voine. T.2 Nachalo. Kn. 2 1 sentiabria – 31 dekabria 1941 goda. Moscow: Rus', 2000, p. 215-6 and note on p. 215. The facts laid out in these documents were confirmed by Vlodzimirskii and Kobulov during the investigation on the "Beria Affair"; see A.V. Sukhomlinov, Kto vy, Lavrentii Beriia? Moscow: Detektiv-Press, 1993, p. 153 and 219-220. There is more information available about Kedrov. It is almost certain that he did, in fact, get sentenced

In fact we now know more about Kedrov's case. For example, there seems to be no doubt that his death sentence was handed down by a court. We don't have the space to explore all the aspects of the Kedrov matter here. But all of it was available to Khrushchev, who was once again lying when he made his statements about Beria and Kedrov.

48. Ordzhonikidze's brother

Khrushchev:

> Beria also handled cruelly the family of Comrade Ordzhonikidze. Why? Because Ordzhonikidze had tried to prevent Beria from realizing his shameful plans. Beria had cleared from his way all persons who could possibly interfere with him. Ordzhonikidze was always an opponent of Beria, which he told to Stalin. Instead of examining this affair and taking appropriate steps, Stalin allowed the liquidation of Ordzhonikidze's brother and brought Ordzhonikidze himself to such a state that he was forced to shoot himself.

According to Oleg Khlevniuk's research (*In Stalin's Shadow: the career of 'Sergo' Ordzhonikidze.* NY: Sharpe, 1995), Sergo committed suicide, most likely from bad health. He had been very sick a long time and, in fact, had had a normal work routine his last day of life.[144]

His death had nothing whatsoever to do with Stalin, his brother, or Beria. On the contrary: "Judging from well-known facts, Ordzhonikidze actively protected Beria and maintained good relations with him right up to the middle of the 1930s." (106)

Research by Vladimir L. Bobrov has recently (October 2008) proven that even the story that Ordzhonikidze committed suicide is without foundation, yet another Khrushchev-era fabrication. Ordzhonikidze undoubtedly died of natural causes – of heart failure – as was reported at the

---

to death at a trial. See texts in the Appendix for this section. Suffice it to say that Khrushchev had all this information at his disposal, and lied about Beria's part in this.

[144] Khevniuk, Chapters 12-13; cf. O.V. Khevniuk, *Stalin i Ordzhonikidze. Konflikty v Politbiuro v 1930-e gody.* Moscow: Rossiia molodaia, 1993, p. 115. The English language version of Khlevniuk's book is somewhat different from the Russian original.

time.[145] Khlevniuk simply continues to repeat as fact the lies in an unattributed introduction to a Khrushchev-era biography of Ordzhonikidze. This introduction was omitted when the book was republished four years later, after Khrushchev's ouster.[146]

On or about Oct. 24, 1936, his 50th birthday, Sergo heard his brother Papulia had been arrested in Georgia (p. 105)[147]. Sergo's brother Valiko defended Papulia at the Georgian Central Committee, and was fired as a result. Beria was head of Georgian party, so Sergo phoned Beria in mid-December to ask for help. According to Khevniuk "Beria showed remarkable concern…," looked into it, got Valiko reinstated, and sent a polite note to Sergo (p. 108)[148]

Sergo died of heart failure during the night of February 17-18, 1937 (147)[149]. He had had a completely normal workday that day. But he had long suffered from ill health, and it was getting worse. Khlevniuk, who has great hatred for Stalin, tries hard to come up with evidence that Stalin had something to do with Sergo's death, and attempts to "reconstruct" an argument over the telephone between the two men, but is finally unable to do so. Khlevniuk could not prove that such a phone call ever took place, much less what was said in it!

Papulia was shot in November, 1937 (173). Khlevniuk gives no further information on this, since evidently he did not have any. It's obvious that Sergo's death could not have been related to Papulia's execution.

According to Sergo Beria, Sergo's relations with his brother Papulia were poor. Papulia himself was hostile to the Soviet Union; and Sergo always stayed with the Berias rather than with his own brother when he came to Tbilisi.

---

[145] Vladimir L. Bobrov, "Taina smerti Ordzhonikidze", at
http://vif2ne.ru/nvz/forum/archive/238/238967.htm ; fully footnoted Russian version at http://chss.montclair.edu/english/furr/research/bobrov-ordzhon08.html ; English translation at http://chss.montclair.edu/english/furr/research/bobrov-ordzhon08eng.html

[146] Compare the opening section of the 1963 version of I. Dubinskii-Mukhadze, *Ordzhonikidze* with that of the "second, corrected edition" of 1967 (both editions Moscow: Molodaia Gvardiia).

[147] Cf. Russian version, p. 77.

[148] Cf. Russian version, p. 80.

[149] Cf. Russian version, pp. 116-129.

In Khrushchev's, and again in Gorbachev's day stories circulated as "fact" that Ordzhonikidze was a "liberal", opposed to the Moscow Trials, and so on. There is no evidence for this. According to Arch Getty:

> ...Ordzhonikidze does not seem to have objected to terror in general, including that directed against Zinoviev, Kamenev, and Bukharin, and was in fact asked by Stalin to give the main speech on wrecking in industry to the February 1937 Plenum of the Central Committee. [n. 64] The draft of the speech Ordzhonikidze was preparing to give to the February 1937 Plenum, as chief reporter on wrecking in industry, was approved by Stalin and was in character with the hard line of the times: RTsKhIDNI (TsPA), f.558, op.1 d. 3350, ll. 1-16. [150]

To sum up: every statement Khrushchev made about Beria and the Ordzhonikidzes is a lie.

- Ordzhonikidze was not Beria's opponent. Rather he stayed with the Beria family when he went to Tbilisi, instead of staying with his older brother Papulia.

- According to Khevniuk, Papulia was executed in November 1937, long after Sergo's death (February 17-18 1937), which therefore could not possibly have been motivated by Papulia's "liquidation."

- Ordzhonikidze's death had nothing to do with Beria. The very anti-Stalin Oleg Khlevniuk concludes that Ordzhonikidze killed himself because of his own poor health. But all the evidence suggests that the "suicide" story is a Khrushchev-era falsification.

---

[150] J. Arch Getty, "The Politics of Repression Revisited," p. 131 and n. 64, p. 140. In Ward, Chris, ed. *The Stalinist Dictatorship*. London, New York: Arnold, 1998.

Chapter 8.

Ideology and Culture

49. Stalin, Short Biography

Khrushchev:

Comrades: The cult of the individual acquired such monstrous size chiefly because Stalin himself, using all conceivable methods, supported the glorification of his own person. This is supported by numerous facts. One of the most characteristic examples of Stalin's self-glorification and of his lack of even elementary modesty is the edition of his Short Biography, which was published in 1948.

This book is an expression of the most dissolute flattery, an example of making a man into a godhead, of transforming him into an infallible sage, "the greatest leader, sublime strategist of all times and nations." Finally, no other words could be found with which to lift Stalin up to the heavens.

We need not give here examples of the loathesome adulation filling this book. All we need to add is that they all were approved and edited by Stalin personally and some of them were added in his own handwriting to the draft text of the book.

What did Stalin consider essential to write into this book? Did he want to cool the ardor of his flatterers who were composing his Short Biography? No! He marked the very places where he thought that the praise of his services was insufficient. Here are some examples characterizing Stalin's activity, added in Stalin's own hand:

In this fight against the skeptics and capitulators, the Trotskyites, Zinovievites, Bukharinites and Kamenevites, there was definitely welded together,

> after Lenin's death, that leading core of the party...
> that upheld the great banner of Lenin, rallied the
> party behind Lenin's behests, and brought the Soviet
> people into the broad road of industrializing the
> country and collectivizing the rural economy. The
> leader of this core and the guiding force of the party
> and the state was Comrade Stalin. [(1) – see below
> for discussion, GF]

Thus writes Stalin himself! Then he adds:

> Although he performed his task as leader of the
> party and the people with consummate skill and
> enjoyed the unreserved support of the entire Soviet
> people, Stalin never allowed his work to be marred
> by the slightest hint of vanity, conceit or self-
> adulation. [(2) – see below for discussion, GF]

Where and when could a leader so praise himself? Is this
worthy of a leader of the Marxist- Leninist type? No.
Precisely against this did Marx and Engels take such a
strong position. This also was always sharply condemned
by Vladimir Ilyich Lenin.

In the draft text of his book appeared the following
sentence: "Stalin is the Lenin of today."

This sentence appeared to Stalin to be too weak, so, in
his own handwriting, he changed it to read: "Stalin is the
worthy continuer of Lenin's work, or, as it is said in our
party, Stalin is the Lenin of today." [(3) – see below for
discussion, GF]

You see how well it is said, not by the nation but by
Stalin himself.

It is possible to give many such self-praising appraisals
written into the draft text of that book in Stalin's hand.
Especially generously does he endow himself with
praises pertaining to his military genius, to his talent for
strategy.

I will cite one more insertion made by Stalin concerning
the theme of the Stalinist military genius. "The advanced
Soviet science of war received further development," he

writes, "at Comrade Stalin's hands. Comrade Stalin
elaborated the theory of the permanently operating
factors that decide the issue of wars, of active defense
and the laws of counteroffensive and offensive, of the
cooperation of all services and arms in modern warfare,
of the role of big tank masses and air forces in modern
war, and of the artillery as the most formidable of the
armed services. At the various stages of the war Stalin's
genius found the correct solutions that took account of
all the circumstances of the situation." [(4) – see below
for discussion, GF]

And, further, writes Stalin:

> Stalin's military mastership was displayed both in
> defense and offense. Comrade Stalin's genius
> enabled him to divine the enemy's plans and defeat
> them. The battles in which Comrade Stalin directed
> the Soviet armies are brilliant examples of
> operational military skill. [(5) – see below for
> discussion, GF]

In this manner was Stalin praised as a strategist. Who did
this? Stalin himself, not in his role as a strategist but in
the role of an author-editor, one of the main creators of
his self-adulatory biography. Such, comrades, are the
facts. We should rather say shameful facts.

The changes made by Stalin in this biography have now been published,
first in *Izvestiia TsK KPSS* No. 9, 1990, and then reprinted widely. This
allows us to see how Khrushchev lied about Stalin's changes to this biography. Even the anti-Stalin editor of these selections for the journal,
V.A. Belianov, admitted that many of Stalin's corrections were in the direction of removing fulsome praise given him by the authors and make
Stalin appear modest.

Khrushchev deliberately distorted the character of some of the quotations he himself cites. For example, Khrushchev cited only the first part
of the following phrase, marked (2) in the passage above. In this way
Khrushchev deliberately changed the meaning of the whole. Here is the
part omitted by Khrushchev:

> In his interview with the German writer Ludwig, where
> he remarks on the great role of the genius Lenin in the

> matter of transforming our country, Stalin said simply
> about himself: "As concerns myself, I am only a pupil of
> Lenin's, and my goal is to be worthy of him.

In the passage above marked (1), at the point of the ellipsis (three dots), Khrushchev omitted the names, inserted by Stalin, of many other Party leaders. Here is the full passage; the words omitted by Khrushchev are underlined.

> In this fight against the skeptics and capitulators, the
> Trotskyites, Zinovievites, Bukharinites and Kamenevites,
> there was definitely welded together, after Lenin's death,
> that leading core of the party…that upheld the great
> banner of Lenin, rallied the party behind Lenin's behests,
> and brought the Soviet people into the broad road of
> industrializing the country and collectivizing the rural
> economy. The leading core was composed of Stalin,
> Molotov, Kalinin, Voroshilov, Kuibyshev, Frunze,
> Dzerzhinskii, Kaganovich, Ordzhonikidze, Kirov,
> Iaroslavskii, Mikoian, Andreev, Shvernik, Zhdanov,
> Shkiriatov, and others…

In the passage marked (3) above, it is obvious even without the original that Stalin transformed a passage which equated him with Lenin, into a passage which makes it clear that he is only a continuer of Lenin's work.

Khrushchev attributed selections (4) and (5) above to Stalin. This is an error. In fact, they were written by General-Major M.R. Galaktionov, who wrote this section of the biography. L. V. Maksimenkov, who points this out, continues:

> What's more, in contradiction to Khrushchev's
> accusation Stalin, in editing this text, systematically
> lowered its triumphant character. For example, the
> bureaucratic-pseudodemocratic title "comrade Stalin"
> replaced the original "Generalissimo Stalin", "teaching"
> ["of the permanently operating factors"] was replaced by
> Stalin with "position," and "immortal forms of the
> military-operational art" became "significant."[151]

---

[151] L.V. Maksimenkov. "Kul't. Zametki o slovakh-simvolakh v sovetskoi politichestoi kul'ture." *Svobodnaia mysl'*. No. 10, 1993. At :
http://www.situation.ru/app/j_artp_677.htm

Maksimenkov discusses at length Stalin's very critical remarks, now available, about the draft of the second, postwar edition of his biography. The original document shows that Stalin's first directive was to write a new biography of Lenin – a fact not mentioned during the Khrushchev era or even later during Gorbachev's "perestroika."

Stalin strongly criticized the "Socialist-Revolutionary character" of the praise given to him by the authors of the "Short Biography", reproaching it as "the education of idol-worshippers." Stalin rejected any credit for any of the teachings attributed in the draft to him, giving credit to Lenin instead.

Maksimenkov concludes that Khrushchev completely distorted the nature of Stalin's changes to this biography, and points out that other writers of the Khrushchev and post-Khrushchev Soviet period did not correct them either. Other passages omitted by the original authors and inserted by Stalin include a long passage about the importance of women in the revolution and Soviet society.

In 1998, while going through the personal papers of V.D. Mochalov, one of the members of the biographical team, Richard Kosolapov found his handwritten notes of two meetings with Stalin concerning the biography. He published them on pp. 451-476 of his book *Slovo Tovarishchu Stalinu*.

Kosolapov is an admirer of Stalin and leads one of the neo-communist parties in Russia. But this specific work of his is cited several times in the footnotes to Robert Service's recent biography of Stalin, a work very hostile towards Stalin.[152] So we may consider it appropriate to cite it here as well. An excerpt showing how Stalin condemned the adulation of himself in the first draft of the biography may be consulted in the Appendix.

50. The 'Short Course'

Khrushchev:

> As is known, The Short Course of the History of the All-Union Communist Party (Bolsheviks) was written by a commission of the party Central Committee. ... This fact was reflected in the following formulation on the proof copy of the Short Biography of Stalin: "A

---

[152] E.g. Robert Service. *Stalin. A Biography* (Harvard University Press, 2005) p. 654, note 1 to Chapter 50.

commission of the Central Committee, All-Union Communist Party (Bolsheviks), under the direction of Comrade Stalin and with his most active personal participation, has prepared a Short Course of the History of the All-Union Communist Party (Bolsheviks)."

But even this phrase did not satisfy Stalin: The following sentence replaced it in the final version of the Short Biography: "In 1938 appeared the book, History of the All-Union Communist Party (Bolsheviks), Short Course, written by Comrade Stalin and approved by a commission of the Central Committee, All-Union Communist Party (Bolsheviks)." Can one add anything more?

As you see, a surprising metamorphosis changed the work created by a group into a book written by Stalin. It is not necessary to state how and why this metamorphosis took place....

And when Stalin himself asserts that he himself wrote *The Short Course of the History of the All-Union Communist Party (Bolsheviks),* this calls at least for amazement. Can a Marxist- Leninist thus write about himself, praising his own person to the heavens?

It appears that no one but Khrushchev ever asserted that Stalin claimed authorship of the *Short Course.* Neither Khrushchev nor anyone else has ever adduced any evidence that Stalin claimed to have written it. Molotov flatly stated that Stalin never claimed to have written it.

Be that as it may, in reality the first indication of the authorship of the "Short Course" first appeared in the first edition of the "Short Biography" of Stalin (1940) — a book to which, according to Maksimenkov (cited above) Stalin had no relationship as either author or editor. Maksimenkov explains:

Occupied with directing the Soviet-Finnish "Winter" war he [Stalin] distanced himself from the editing of the book ... On December 14, 1939, a week before Stalin's sixtieth birthday, the first draft of the biography in his name was sent with an accompanying letter signed by Mitin and Pospelov: "Dear Comrade Stalin. We are sending you this draft of your "Short biography",

prepared by the Marx-Engels-Lenin Institute, along with
the directions for propaganda and agitation. We request
that you look through this work and give us your
directions concerning the possibility of its publication."
Stalin underlined the whole text of the accompanying
letter and wrote with a green-pencil across the page: "No
time to 'look through' it. Return it to the MELI [Marx-
Engels-Lenin Institute]. J. Stalin"[153]

The sentence about Stalin's role in the making of the "Short Course" was
not inserted by Stalin himself about himself, but belongs to the pen of
one of the many authors and editors who worked on the book. And here
Khrushchev lied again.

There remains only to clarify the question: What was Stalin's actual role
in the writing of the "Short Course"?

In one of his sketches Roi Medvedev, scarcely a sympathizer of Stalin's,
writes of him as "the principal author of the 'Short Course'." The historians notes that Khrushchev's virtual arraignment of Stalin for plagiarism
is utterly without foundation. In evidence of his position he refers to the
publication in *Voprosy Istorii* of the typewritten texts with Stalin's corrections and a number of other materials.[154]

Regardless of the obvious lacunae and incomplete nature of the primary
documents in Medvedev's opinion there is no doubt that work on the
"Short Course" was conducted under the direction and with the active
participation of Stalin as one of the principal authors of the textbook.

Khrushchev had asserted that Stalin had had no right to write that he was
the author of the "Short Course" because, he said, he had not written it.
As it turns out, in reality Stalin had every basis to claim that he had been
one of the principal authors, but never made this claim to anyone or
anywhere. Even Molotov, who had been one of Stalin's closest collaborators, did not know precisely how much Stalin had written and believed
that he had only written the section on dialectics, since they had discussed this at some point.

---

[153] Maksimenkov, "Kul't".

[154] "I.V. Stalin v rabote nad 'Kratkim kursom istorii VKP(b)'. Publikatsiia, kommentarii i vstupitel'naia stat'ia M.V. Zelenova." *Voprosy Istorii* Nos 11-12 (2002), Nos. 3-4 (2003).

In this instance Khrushchev outsmarted himself. He said Stalin claimed an authorship he did not deserve. In reality, Stalin was indeed the principal author, but never claimed to be such.

51. Stalin Signed Order for Monument to Himself on July 2, 1951

Khrushchev:

> It is a fact that Stalin himself had signed on July 2, 1951 a resolution of the USSR Council of Ministers concerning the erection on the Volga-Don Canal of an impressive monument to Stalin; on September 4 of the same year he issued an order making 33 tons of copper available for the construction of this impressive monument.

This is no "fact", but a bare assertion. We have only Khrushchev's word for this. The relevant documents have never been reproduced, and no one else has claimed to have seen them. Khrushchev never claims that Stalin **introduced** or **suggested** this monument, so we can assume he did not.

According to the "Journal of visitors to Stalin's Kremlin office," on July 2 1951 Stalin did work for 1 hour and 45 minutes. The Presidium had met on June 26 and its "Bureau", consisting of Beria, Bulganin, Kaganovich, Mikoian, Molotov, and Khrushchev himself, met with him on July 2 from 9:30 to 11:15 p.m.[155] So he **could** have signed such a resolution of the Council of Ministers, if it were presented on that date. We do not know whether it was or not.

But it is important to note here that the mere fact of "Stalin's signature" in and of itself means nothing at this period. On February 16, 1951 the Politburo adopted a decision that the Presidium would be chaired by others, and that a rubber stamp would be used for Stalin's signature when it was necessary as the Head of State (Chairman of Council of Ministers). This document, and the rubber stamps, have been exhibited in Moscow[156] (see the Appendix for the URLs for these exhibits).

---

[155] *Istoricheskii Arkhiv* No. 1, 1997, p. 24.

[156] A photograph of these stamps may be viewed at http://chss.montclair.edu/english/furr/research/stalinsigstamps51.jpg

That is, Stalin no longer signed "decisions and instructions of the Council of Ministers of the USSR", but they were still issued under his signature, in his absence. Since that was the case since February 1951, it is logical to assume it was still the case in July of that same year. But we cannot tell one way or the other for certain whether Stalin personally signed these documents without seeing the originals, and perhaps not even then.

As for the September 4, 1951 "order" it is unlikely that Stalin could have issued it. He was on leave, or "vacation", probably for ill health, between August 10, 1951 and February 11, 1952, when he returned to his office.[157]

The main point is this – and Khrushchev knew it – Stalin was politically active only sporadically by this time. Politburo members, including Khrushchev himself, declared in 1953 that Stalin had not been politically active. Stalin said as much at the 19th Party Congress in October 1952: "I no longer read papers."[158]

According to the "Journal of visitors to Stalin's Kremlin office" Stalin's workload began to decrease in February 1950. Judging from this source, Stalin worked 73 days in 1950, but only 48 days in 1951, and 45 days in 1952.[159]

Therefore, it is very doubtful that Stalin personally signed the September 4, 1951 order. As for that of July 2, 1951, we simply do not know.

But even if Stalin did in fact personally sign this document – that is, even if this was not a case of the Politburo's voting to affixing his signature with the stamp – it has little significance. Even Khrushchev does not claim Stalin initiated the order for the monument.

---

[157] These pages from "Visitors to Stalin's Kremlin Office" may be consulted at http://chss.montclair.edu/english/furr/research/istarkh197.pdf

[158] "'V ch'i ruki vruchim estafetu nashego velikogo dela?' Neopublikovannaia rech' I.V. Stalina na Plenume Tsentral'nogo Komiteta KPSS 16 oktiabria 1952 goda (po zapisi L.N. Efremova)." *Sovetskaka Rossiia* January 13, 2000. At http://chss.montclair.edu/english/furr/research/stalinoct1652.pdf , and also at http://grachev62.narod.ru/stalin/t18/t18_262.htm

[159] IU.N.Zhukov, *Tainy Kremlia. Stalin, Molotov, Beriia, Malenkov.* Moscow: TERRA, 2000, p. 549. Cf. also sources at note 7 above. The monument to Stalin was built but taken down during Khrushchev's time and later replaced by a monument to Lenin. Monument to Stalin: http://elefantmuller.users.photofile.ru/photo/elefantmuller/2911172/xlarge/115411211.jpg; to Lenin: http://foto-fleet.users.photofile.ru/photo/foto-fleet/95172224/xlarge/115411831.jpg

52. The Palace of Soviets

Khrushchev:

> At the same time Stalin gave proofs of his lack of respect
> for Lenin's memory. It is not a coincidence that, despite
> the decision taken over 30 years ago to build a Palace of
> Soviets as a monument to Vladimir Ilyich, this palace
> was not built, its construction was always postponed and
> the project allowed to lapse.

In his recent article on the history of the plans, architectural contests, and
ultimate abandonment of the project to build the Palace of Soviets, Maksim Volchenkov directly references Khrushchev's Speech, showing that
the latter's statement here is simply not true. Nor did Khrushchev erect
this building either. The committee in charge of it gradually changed its
focus to other buildings. The plan to build a Palace of Soviets was aban-
doned – not by Stalin, but by his successors.

53. The Lenin Prize

Khrushchev:

> We cannot forget to recall the Soviet Government
> resolution of August 14, 1925 concerning "the founding
> of Lenin prizes for educational work." This resolution
> was published in the press, but until this day there are no
> Lenin prizes. This, too, should be corrected.

This is not true, and most of the audience at the 20th Party Congress
must have known it. In fact, there had been Lenin prizes, from 1925 to
1934, in the fields of science, technology, literature, art, and architecture.
It's not clear why they were ended, but nobody seems to have blamed
Stalin for it.[160]

---

[160] It is likely that the pause, and then cessation in the award of the Lenin prizes was
related to the closing of the Communist Academy, to which the commission on the Lenin
prizes was attached. The question of closing the Communist Academy "in view of the
inexpediency of two parallel Academies, the Academy of Sciences and the Communist
Academy," a matter under discussion after the beginning of 1935. The Lenin prize awards
ceased at this same time. See the Decree "Concerning the Liquidation of the Communist
Academy", by the C.C. and the Council of People's Commissars dated February 7, 1936,
reproduced at http://www.ihst.ru/projects/sohist/document/an/181.htm

However, the Order of Lenin (*Orden Lenina*) was the highest decoration given by the USSR. It was continuously awarded for outstanding achievements in many fields from 1930 until the end of the Soviet Union.

Stalin also **rejected** the proposal that an "Order of Stalin" be created in his honor. Information about that is given in the Appendix. Khrushchev would have known about this, of course.

At the time of preparing for the celebration of Stalin's sixtieth birthday in December 1939 the question of instituting prizes in Stalin's name arose again.[161] We have no indication that Stalin had anything to do with this initiative. But one thing is well known: the Stalin prizes were **not** initiated instead of or in replacement of the Lenin prizes. They were instituted at a time when there were **no** annual prizes in sciences and arts in the USSR. Consequently Khrushchev's counterposition of the Lenin and Stalin prizes is incorrect and dishonest.

---

[161] The Decree of the Sovnarkom of the USSR of December 20, 1939 on the establishment of prizes and awards in honor of Stalin was signed by the Chairman of the SNK V.M. Molotov and its chief of staff M.D. Khlomov (*Pravda* December 21, 1939). At first these awards did not include the fields of artistic creation and criticism. At the beginning of 1940 a similar decree was passed titled "Concerning the establishment of Stalin prizes in literature". It was also signed by Molotov and Khlomov (*Pravda* February 2, 1940). See http://feb-web.ru/feb/sholokh/critics/nos/nos-486-.htm.

Chapter 9.

Stalin's Last Years in Power

54. Stalin Suggested Huge Tax Increase on Kolkhozes

Khrushchev:

> What is more, while reviewing this project ["to raise the prices of such products in order to create material incentives for the kolkhoz, MTS [machine-tractor station] and sovkhoz workers in the development of cattle breeding"] Stalin proposed that the taxes paid by the kolkhozes and by the kolkhoz workers should be raised by 40 billion rubles; according to him the peasants are well off and the kolkhoz worker would need to sell only one more chicken to pay his tax in full.
>
> Imagine what this meant. Certainly, 40 billion rubles is a sum which the kolkhoz workers did not realize for all the products which they sold to the Government. In 1952, for instance, the kolkhozes and the kolkhoz workers received 26,280 million rubles for all their products delivered and sold to the Government.
>
> Did Stalin's position, then, rest on data of any sort whatever? Of course not. In such cases facts and figures did not interest him.

According to Khrushchev, Stalin said this in February, 1953, just before his death. No one else records this. We have only Khrushchev's word for this.

Khrushchev first mentioned this alleged tax increase during the July 1953 CC Plenum devoted exclusively to the condemnation of Beria. Mikoian and Malenkov both referred to the "40 billion ruble" figure after Khrushchev mentions it. But both do so in a way that makes it clear they had not heard of it prior to Khrushchev's mentioning it.

Mikoian, who spoke up against additional taxes on the peasantry at the October 1952 C.C. Plenum, affirms that Stalin suggested "only one more chicken" in taxes from the peasants. But Mikoian admits he did not hear this personally, since he was not present. Mikoian does not mention the "40 billion rubles" in his discussion of this incident in his memoirs.[162]

55. Stalin Insulted Postyshev

Khrushchev:

> In one of his speeches Stalin expressed his dissatisfaction with Postyshev and asked him, "What are you actually?"
>
> Postyshev answered clearly, "I am a Bolshevik, Comrade Stalin, a Bolshevik."
>
> This assertion was at first considered to show a lack of respect for Stalin; later it was considered a harmful act and consequently resulted in Postyshev's annihilation and branding without any reason as a 'people's enemy.'

We have already seen that Postyshev was dismissed, then arrested, and finally tried and executed, for repressing a huge number of Party members without any evidence. Khrushchev was present at this Plenum (January 1938), and knew this. Therefore Khrushchev lied when he said Postyshev was repressed "without any reason."

It's most likely that Khrushchev is lying about the exchange above too. Only Khrushchev records this purported exchange between Postyshev and Stalin, and only in his Secret Speech. No one else, apparently, ever claimed to have heard Stalin say it. It is not in Khrushchev's memoirs either.

According to Getty and Naumov there is no evidence of any particular friction between Stalin and Postyshev until the January 1938 Plenum. As we have seen, Postyshev was dismissed from candidate membership in the Politburo at that Plenum, and arrested not long afterwards. Therefore this "speech" of Stalin's – if it ever took place at all – must have happened at this January 1938 Plenum.

Commentators like Boris Nikolaevsky thought it was made at the February-March 1937 CC Plenum. That is because they believed Khrushchev's earlier assertion in this "Secret Speech" that Postyshev had opposed Stalin at this Plenum. But the voluminous transcript of that long

---

[162] A.I. Mikoian, *Tak Bylo*. Moscow: Vagrius, 1999, Ch. 46, pp. 559-568.

Plenum was published in 1992-5. Again, as we have already seen, that transcript proves Khrushchev lied: Postyshev did not oppose Stalin at all at that Plenum. Nor did this purported exchange between Stalin and Postyshev take place there.

The transcripts of the January 1938 Plenum have not been published in full. But they have been published in excerpt, and some researchers have read the whole transcripts in the archives. None of them have mentioned finding this exchange. So it is most probable that Khrushchev is lying again. But we can't be absolutely certain.

Even if, some day, evidence comes to light that Stalin did say it, it was certainly not the reason for Postyshev's arrest, trial, conviction and execution. They were the punishment for Postyshev's guilt in repressing large numbers of Party members. Whether Stalin said these words or not therefore – and, to repeat, there is no evidence that he did, aside from Khrushchev's assertion here – Khrushchev lied in saying this was the reason for Postyshev's fate.

So why did Khrushchev make the latter claim? Probably in order to provide an "alibi" for Politburo members who had worked closely with Stalin for many years.

Many communists and Soviet citizens would likely wonder: Why did Stalin's closest associates never call him on any of the "crimes" Khrushchev was accusing him of? Why did they not take steps to stop Stalin, since they knew of these things? Lame as it is, the only answer Khrushchev and the rest could give was this: "We'd be killed if we protested. Look what happened to Postyshev, just for saying 'I am a Bolshevik'!"

56. "Disorganization" of Politburo Work

Khrushchev:

> The importance of the Central Committee's Political
> Bureau was reduced and its work was disorganized by
> the creation within the Political Bureau of various
> commissions – the so-called "quintets," "sextets,"
> "septets" and "novenaries." Here is, for instance, a
> resolution of the Political Bureau of October 3, 1946:
>
> Stalin's Proposal:
>
>> 1. The Political Bureau Commission for Foreign
>> Affairs ('Sextet') is to concern itself in the future, in

> addition to foreign affairs, also with matters of
> internal construction and domestic policy.
>
> 2. The Sextet is to add to its roster the Chairman of
> the State Commission of Economic Planning of the
> USSR, Comrade Voznesensky, and is to be known
> as a Septet.
>
> Signed: Secretary of the Central Committee, J. Stalin.
>
> What a terminology of a card player! (Laughter in the
> hall.) It is clear that the creation within the Political
> Bureau of this type of commissions – "quintets,"
> "sextets," "septets" and "novenaries" – was against the
> principle of collective leadership. The result of this was
> that some members of the Political Bureau were in this
> way kept away from participation in reaching the most
> important state matters.

As Edvard Radzinsky, a ferociously hostile biographer of Stalin, admits, Khrushchev was lying. Subcommittees within the Politburo were simply a way of dividing up the work to be done. This was nothing new, and not Stalin's innovation.

57. Stalin Suspected Voroshilov an "English Agent"

Khrushchev:

> Because of his extreme suspicion, Stalin toyed also with
> the absurd and ridiculous suspicion that Voroshilov was
> an English agent. (Laughter in the hall.) It's true – an
> English agent.

In his memoirs Khrushchev relates many rumors that he said were known only to "a few of us". In this case there is no other documentation of it.

For example, it is not in Mikoian's memoirs, which have a lot of false "memories", like Stalin's telling him Benes had assured him about Tukhachevsky' guilt – an event which never occurred.[163] So even if Mikoian

---

163 *Ibid.*, p.553.

had "remembered" this, one might legitimately question it. In fact, he did not.

58. Andreev; 59. Molotov; 60. Mikoian

These all have to do with the CC Plenum of October 16, 1952 that took place immediately after the 19th Party Congress.

Andreev

Khrushchev:

> By unilateral decision, Stalin had also separated one other man from the work of the Political Bureau – Andrei Andreyevich Andreyev. This was one of the most unbridled acts of willfulness.

Strictly speaking, we don't know precisely what Stalin said, because no official transcript has ever been published (according to Mikoian, none was made). Neither has the transcript of the 19th Party Congress ever been published.[164] Immediately after Stalin's death the Party leadership did their best to change the major decisions taken at both these sessions and to obliterate any memory of them.

Therefore we do not have any **official** reason why Andreev was not retained in the newly renamed Presidium (formerly the Politburo). But we have enough information from other sources to see that Khrushchev is not telling the truth.

Andreev lost his position in the Council of Ministers on March 15, 1953, ten days after Stalin's death.[165] If it had been an "unbridled act of willfulness" not to reappoint Andreev to the Presidium of the CC of the CPSU, why did Khrushchev, Malenkov and Beria remove him also from the Soviet of Ministers? (He was appointed to the Presidium of the Supreme Soviet, a far less demanding position)

According to the only part of Stalin's Speech at the CC Plenum of October 16 1952 that we have, he actually did not nominate Andreev to the

---

[164] At least, not as a separate publication. Formal speeches were all published in *Pravda* in October 1952, at the time of the Congress. Perhaps this is all there was.

[165] Cf. the biographical entry on Andreev at Hrono.ru / hrono.info - http://www.hrono.ru/biograf/andreev_aa.html

new Presidium because Andreev was deaf.[166] Konstantin Simonov says something similar.[167] These are the only accounts of the Plenum that mention Andreev at all. Both of them affirm that Stalin explicitly excluded Andreev because of his health.

Despite the lack of any official transcript, therefore, this is good evidence that Khrushchev lied. Andreev was not excluded out of any "willfulness" on Stalin's part.

Molotov and Mikoian

Khrushchev:

> Let us consider the first Central Committee plenum after the 19th Party Congress when Stalin, in his talk at the plenum, characterized Vyacheslav Mikhailovich Molotov and Anastas Ivanovich Mikoian and suggested that these old workers of our party were guilty of some baseless charges. It is not excluded that had Stalin remained at the helm for another several months, Comrades Molotov and Mikoian would probably have not delivered any speeches at this Congress.

From what we know about this Plenum from a few who were present and wrote down their notes on it, it is clear that Stalin did criticize Molotov and Mikoian.

To determine whether Khrushchev is telling the truth here, we need to examine

- Whether the "charges" Stalin leveled at Molotov and Mikoian were "baseless" or not; and

- Whether it's true that they would not have spoken at the 20th Party Congress if Stalin had lived.

- There are four accounts of Stalin's talk at this Plenum from people who were in attendance. They are: that of Mikoian himself (*Tak Bylo*, Ch. 46); that of the

---

[166] According to L.N. Efremov's notes on the Plenum published in *Sovetskaia Rossia* January13, 2000. At http://chss.montclair.edu/english/furr/research/stalinoct1652.pdf and also at http://grachev62.narod.ru/stalin/t18/t18_262.htm

[167] Konstantin M. Simonov, *Glazami cheloveka moego pokoleniia*. Moscow: Novosti, 1988, p. 246.

writer Konstantin Simonov (*Glazami cheloveka moego
pokolenia*), that of Dmitrii Shepilov (*Neprimknuvshii*,
pp. 225-8.), and that of Leonid Nikolaevich Efremov
(*Sovetskaia Rossiia*, January 13, 2000, p. 6). Mikoian
was, of course, a long-time CC and Politburo
member; the other three were brand-new members of
the CC. Except for a short note by Simonov which
he wrote in March 1953, the rest were written down
years after the event.

Shepilov relates Stalin's criticisms of Molotov in a few paragraphs. He is
far briefer about Stalin's remarks about Mikoian. Shepilov claims that
Mikoian defended himself and attacked Molotov for being close to the
executed Voznesenskii, whom he called "a great criminal." Shepilov did
not consider the charges "baseless", or see any kind of threat in them,
but only Stalin's reasons for not including them in the new Bureau of the
Presidium.

In his first short note on the Plenum made in March 1953 Simonov did
not remark at all on Stalin's criticism of Molotov and Mikoian, but only
noted Stalin's insistence that they be as fearless as Lenin was. In 1979
what Simonov remembered was the vehemence of Stalin's criticism of
Molotov, and a vague feeling that he and Mikoian were for "capitulationism". Simonov agrees that Stalin then criticized Mikoian, but could not
recall why. He says that both men replied to Stalin's criticisms – something that in and of itself refutes Khrushchev's claim that Stalin demanded "absolute submission". Simonov believed that these criticisms,
whatever their cause, served to justify Molotov's and Mikoian's exclusion
from the new Bureau of the Presidium.

Mikoian's account, also written years later, agrees that Stalin criticized
Molotov for his weakness in foreign policy and both Molotov and himself, Mikoian, in domestic policy. But in Mikoian's account Stalin was
critical yet respectful of them. Mikoian does not mention anything about
feeling threatened. Efremov's account outlines Stalin's criticisms of the
two men but it too does not make these criticisms sound threatening at
all.

In his whole voluminous memoirs Khrushchev has only a few sentences
to say about the October 1952 Plenum, and says nothing about any
"danger" to Mikoian or Molotov.

Mikoian, Molotov, and Voroshilov too, were all named to the Presidium, and Voroshilov – but not Mikoian or Molotov – to the "Bureau of the Presidium."

But what about the truthfulness of Khrushchev's allegation? The charges – a better word would be "criticisms" – do not appear to have been "baseless". They may or may not have been correct. In essence, they reflected political differences between Stalin and these two Politburo members.

Strictly speaking Khrushchev's statement – that it is "possible" Molotov and Mikoian would not have addressed the 20th Party Congress if Stalin had lived – cannot be either proven or disproven. But it is inconsistent with Stalin's actions at the 19th Party Congress. Mikoian and Molotov, though not in the very highest body (the Bureau of the Presidium), were still in the Presidium of 25 members and, as such, would certainly have been in a position to address the next Congress.

In his own memoirs Khrushchev does not repeat the story that Molotov and Mikoian were under any kind of threat.

61. Expansion of the Presidium

Khrushchev:

> Stalin evidently had plans to finish off the old members of the Political Bureau. He often stated that Political Bureau members should be replaced by new ones.
>
> His proposal, after the 19th Congress, concerning the election of 25 persons to the Central Committee Presidium, was aimed at the removal of the old Political Bureau members and the bringing in of less experienced persons so that these would extol him in all sorts of ways.
>
> We can assume that this was also a design for the future annihilation of the old Political Bureau members and, in this way, a cover for all shameful acts of Stalin, acts which we are now considering.

Khrushchev lied here, for there is no evidence that his accusation had the slightest basis in fact. It is not supported at all by the accounts of the Plenum that survive. According to Efremov's notes on the October 1952 Central Committee Plenum Stalin was extremely clear in explaining his proposal to expand the Presidium beyond the limits of the old Politburo. Efremov, a young man at his first Plenum, may have been especially struck by Stalin's emphasis on the need for new blood in the Party leadership, for Stalin's explanation takes up a substantial place in his notes.

Chapter 10.

A Typology of Prevarication

A Typology of Khrushchev's Prevarication

Before proceeding to discuss Khrushchev's **specific** methods of distortion, we should understand that the published version before us is itself falsified.

> Published earlier in *Izvestiia TsK KPSS*, the text of Khrushchev's report is based upon the text presented by Khrushchev to the Presidium of the CC CPSU on March 1 [1956], edited and accepted for dissemination to local party organizations by a decision of the Presidium of the C.C. of March 7, 1956. **This text is not identical to that which Khrushchev read from the podium of the Congress.** For example, according to the way all the participants in the Congress remembered it, total silence reigned in the hall as the report was read. But audience reactions were inserted into the text published in *Izvestiia TsK KPSS*: "Commotion in the hall", "Indignation in the hall", "Applause", etc. which, of course, completely failed to reflect the real atmosphere of the closed session.
>
> - V.IU. Afiani, Z.K. Vodop'ianova, "Arkheograficheskoe predislovie" ['Archeographical preface'], in Aimermakher, K, et al., *Doklad N.S. Khrushcheva o Kul'te Lichnosti Stalina na XX S"ezde KPSS. Dokumenty.* Moscow: ROSSPEN, 2002, p. 44. (Emphasis added, GF.)

These same "audience reactions" were inserted into the English translation. Therefore we are examining a text that has been falsified not only in its content but in its presentation as well. We have left most of the "audience reactions" in the quotations from Khrushchev's speech cited in previous chapters as a continual reminder of the deliberate distortions introduced into this text.[168]

I have determined that in the so-called "Secret Speech" Khrushchev made **sixty-one** "revelations", or hitherto unknown and derogatory accusations, against Stalin or Beria. These statements constitute the substance of the Speech. It was these assertions that shocked the world when it was made public.

It would, of course, be absurd to say that every one of Khrushchev's statements is false. A dramatic example of a "revelation" Khrushchev made that is true is the following:

> It was determined that of the 139 members and candidates of the party's Central Committee who were elected at the 17th Congress, 98[169] persons, i.e., 70 per cent, were arrested and shot (mostly in 1937-1938). (Indignation in the hall.) What was the composition of the delegates to the 17th Congress? It is known that 80 per cent of the voting participants of the 17th Congress joined the party during the years of conspiracy before the Revolution and during the civil war; this means before 1921. By social origin the basic mass of the delegates to the Congress were workers (60 per cent of the voting members).

When I claim that every supposed "revelation" or accusation in Khrushchev's speech against Stalin and Beria[170] is false, I do not include the statement above, because Khrushchev is careful **not** to claim here that Stalin had them all killed. Had he made this claim explicitly, this statement would be demonstrably false, to be added to the list of other false accusations in the Speech.[171]

---

[168] In his memoirs, published first in *Life* magazine and then in book form, Khrushchev admitted these "audience reactions" were a lie. "The delegates listened in absolute silence. It was so quiet in the huge hall you could hear a fly buzzing." *Life*, December 11, 1970,.p. 63; Strobe Talbot (trans. & ed.), *Khrushchev Remembers: The Last Testament*. (Boston: Little, Brown, 1974), 494.

[169] In the report published by the official journal *Izvestiia TsK KPSS* No. 12 (1989), p. 86 the number of delegatesis given as 97 (44 + 53), not 98. Of course this does not change the essence of the matter.

[170] Except for the one I have marked as "Don't Know."

[171] The statement just quoted is one of my three "S", or "special cases."

Khrushchev does mention a number of the more prominent of the Central Committee members executed during the late 1930s. In the case of one very prominent full member of the 1934 Central Committee – Nikolai Ezhov – Khrushchev fails to mention the fact that he too was executed! We will examine the evidence on all the C.C. members Khrushchev explicitly names in the Speech.

The Problem of Introducing a New Paradigm

The usual problem a researcher confronts is that of assembling the evidence needed to prove his thesis, and arranging it logically so that his thesis is proven. But in writing the present essay I soon realized that another problem, much larger and more intractable, confronted me.

Khrushchev's "Secret Speech" is not just a series of assertions that can, in principle, be proven either valid or invalid. It soon became the foundational document for a whole new paradigm of Soviet history. This paradigm was not entirely new. It confirmed in part, and itself drew upon, earlier Trotskyist, Menshevik, and Soviet émigré interpretations of Soviet reality.

But because it was rapidly accepted by the worldwide communist movement itself, and was soon followed by a huge wave of "rehabilitations" of those convicted of treasonable activity during the Stalin years, the "Khrushchev" paradigm attained a degree of widespread acceptance that the earlier versions never had. It became the dominant paradigm.

As a result, to attack the veracity of Khrushchev's speech is to attack the foundation of what I will call the "anti-Stalin" paradigm. Here are a couple of illustrations of what I mean.

- I gave a talk summarizing a few of the results of my research on Khrushchev's speech at an annual conference of a Marxist academic group. During the Q&A period one long-time Marxist said to me in an accusatory tone: "You are rehabilitating Stalin!"

- Another question was: "What about Trotsky?" Khrushchev does not mention Trotsky in the speech.

- When a colleague mentioned my research project on Khrushchev's speech to an editor of a prominent Marxist journal, his derisive response was: "Does he

claim there was no GULAG?" (Khrushchev never)
mentions the GULAG in his speech).

- A sympathetic and helpful reader of an earlier draft
  suggested that I should write a history of the
  repressions of the 1930s instead.

- At first I could not understand remarks like this. But
  I came to realize that these responses were not
  directed towards my talk. Instead, they were
  responding to what they felt my talk implied. They
  reflected the fact that Khrushchev's speech is not
  only the foundational document of the "anti-Stalin
  paradigm" of Soviet history. It is also a synecdoche
  for that paradigm: it represents that paradigm as the
  part represents the whole. To prove, as I attempt to
  do, that the statements made in Khrushchev's speech
  are false is taken to be a claim that all the other
  components of this paradigm, most of which
  Khrushchev never mentions, are also false.

It's reasonable to expect a paper or book to prove what it sets out to
prove. It's not reasonable to expect a paper or book on a single topic to
refute a whole historical paradigm, disproving in the process an unde-
fined – in fact, an infinite – number of fact claims that are not part of the
paper.

The present book, therefore, confronts a strange rhetorical situation. It
evokes, if not a "totalitarian", at least a "totalizing" response. Khrushchev's "secret speech" represents the "anti-Stalin paradigm" to such an
extent that any reference to it conjures up the entire paradigm. Sometimes the response that results is one of indignation: How can I presume
to smuggle in a refutation of the whole "anti-Stalin" paradigm when I am
actually disproving only a part of it? But to others the paper is simply a
disappointment. It fails to deal with the GULAG, or Trotsky, or Bukharin, or the Katyn massacre, or something else that does not feature at
all in Khrushchev's speech, and so the paper is a failure and a disappointment, no matter how thoroughly it manages to prove the falsity of
what Khrushchev **did** say.

I agree that Khrushchev's speech is the foundational document of the
"anti-Stalin" paradigm. Moreover, the fact that Khrushchev's speech is a
tissue of fabrications virtually from beginning to end also has implica-

tions for further research. Given this degree of falsehood at the very beginning of what purported to be an exposure of "Stalin's crimes", it's unlikely that the story ends here. One is justified in suspecting that at least some of the other "revelations" over which Khrushchev presided may prove to be false as well.

And then the "anti-Stalin" paradigm is well and truly in play. For Roi Medvedev's *Let History Judge* (1971) and Robert Conquest's *The Great Terror. Stalin's Purge of the Thirties* (1968), the two major syntheses of Khrushchev-era "revelations," are precisely the formative popularizations of the "anti-Stalin" paradigm. They summarize what their authors gleaned from the Soviet press, "rehabilitation" announcements, and public and private memoirs. (For the account of Aleksandr Solzhenitsyn see the note.)[172] Both Medvedev and Conquest took these "revelations" – including Khrushchev's Secret Speech, but going far beyond it – at face value, as "true." If Khrushchev's speech were proven false, what about these other materials?

My attempt to test the accuracy of the accusations made by Khrushchev in his speech, and my resulting conclusions that virtually all of them are false, does not comprise a direct attempt on my part to destroy the "anti-Stalin" paradigm. However, it does at least remove one of the main supporting pillars on which the whole edifice of this paradigm stands. Once convinced that Khrushchev's speech is little more than a long, carefully-planned and elaborate lie, no student can ever view Soviet history of the Stalin period in the same way again.

Statements of fact can only be evaluated on the level of their factuality – whether, given the evidence we have, such statements are the most accurate conclusions that can be drawn. No paradigm can be "disproven" by the disproving of one, or any particular number, of assertions of fact.

---

[172] Solzhenitsyn's various accounts, most famously in *The GULAG Archipelago* in its various editions, are not, strictly speaking, historical works. Solzhenitsyn relied on rumor and unpublished memoirs almost exclusively. Critical interrogation of sources is virtually unknown to him. Solzhenitsyn also made a great many deliberately false statements, including many about his own life. Furthermore, it is clear that he did not compose all of *The GULAG Archipelago*. The extent to which Solzhenitsyn's life has itself been "constructed" and falsified has to be studied to be believed. For a very detailed and highly documented account of all the problems with Solzhenitsyn and his work see Aleksandr V. Ostrovskii, *Solzhenitsyn: proshchanie s mifom* ("Solzhenitsyn: Farewell to the myth") Moscow: IAuza, 2004.

Those colleagues and critics whom I've mentioned, and no doubt innumerable others, are – as another colleague put it – "reasonable people in the grip of an unreasonable narrative." That unreasonable narrative is the "cult of personality" around Stalin in its Khrushchevian disguise.

Although he claimed to be critiquing and exorcizing what is better translated as the "cult of the great man" (*kul't lichnosti*), what Khrushchev really did was to reinforce it in an inverted form. He tried to replace the "all-knowing, all-good" Stalin of the "cult" with another Stalin who was equally all-powerful but malevolent. In this Khrushchev resembled Trotsky, who also focused on what he claimed were the personal failings of his arch rival and explained Stalin's rise to leadership, policies, oppositions, and repressions, by attributing them to Stalin's combination of cunning, ruthlessness, and moral defects.

In an outline of Noam Chomsky's criticism of the mass media Mark Grimsley has written:

> A statement that fits an accepted world view requires
> little explanation and can therefore be outlined in a few
> words. In order to have any chance of being persuasive,
> a statement that challenges an accepted world view needs
> more than a sound bite."[173]

This also applies to scholarship that challenges a "received", widely accepted, historical paradigm.

Under such conditions, "equality is inequality." It is not only that it takes far greater time, effort, and space on the page to refute a falsehood than it does to state it. It is that the scholar whose work challenges the existing paradigm has **two** tasks, while the scholar whose research fits neatly into the prevailing paradigm has only one. The latter need only make sure his research follows the accepted canons of method, and his work will be greeted with approbation. In a certain sense, he is telling his readers what they already know to be true. He is "filling in a blank" in the greater model of an accepted, because acceptable, history.

But the scholar who challenges the prevailing paradigm has a far more demanding job. His research must not only meet the demands of method – use of evidence, logic, and so on – incumbent on all scholars. He must also persuade his readers to question the overall pattern of historical cau-

---

[173] Mark Grimsley, "Noam Chomsky (1928 -)". At http://people.cohums.ohio-state.edu/grimsley1/h582/2001/Chomsky.htm

sation which has heretofore given shape to their vision of the past itself. He challenges them to take seriously the possibility that their whole model of history may be wrong – a challenge that many will simply dismiss, and some will denounce as outrageous.

So I have to reiterate what should be obvious but, obviously, is not. The subject of this paper is Khrushchev's "Secret Speech" of February 25, 1956 in its published form. The surprising – to my mind at least, astounding – result of my research is this: that speech is comprised, virtually in its entirety, of falsifications. My aim in the present book is to demonstrate that result with the best evidence that exists, much of it from former Soviet archives.

I entered this project knowing that a few, at least, of Khrushchev's statements were untrue, and suspecting that some assiduous research would find that at least a few more of those statements were also untrue. I was very surprised – "shocked" is not too strong a word – to find that virtually every one of Khrushchev's "revelations" is, in fact, false.

I realize that the whole is more than the sum of its parts – that my conclusion that **all** of Khrushchev's "revelations" were false will be greeted with far more skepticism than would a more modest result that, say, half, or two-thirds, of his "revelations" were false. And I think this is so because a Khrushchev that lied about everything does not "fit" into the prevailing "anti-Stalin" paradigm, in which the Khrushchev who, in Taubman's words, "somehow retained his humanity," whose speech constitutes a "great deed," is an essential part of that paradigm.

Exposing a Lie is Not the Same as Establishing the Truth

Analysis of Khrushchev's prevarications suggests two related but distinct tasks. By far the easier and shorter job is to show that Khrushchev was not telling the truth. This is the subject of the present book.

The interested student will naturally want to know more than the mere fact that Khrushchev lied. Once convinced that Khrushchev's version of reality is false, she or he will want to know the truth – *what really happened.*

But the present study cannot satisfy that curiosity. A separate investigation would be necessary in each case – virtually, sixty-one studies for as many falsehoods. Some would be short, in the main because we do not have enough evidence to settle the matter.

Others of these studies would have to be very lengthy, as there is a great deal of information, often contradictory, to be gathered and examined. Some, perhaps many, would be inconclusive, since not enough evidence has been made available to permit us to arrive at a definite solution. In any case, to study in depth each of the false assertions made by Khrushchev with an eye to discovering – as nearly as possible, given the present state of the evidence – what really happened, is necessarily beyond the scope of this essay.

The image of Stalin as "mass murderer" originated, for all practical purposes, during Khrushchev's time.[174] The very first such accusations, those that laid the foundation for the myth – and it is precisely a myth with which we are concerned here – are in the "Secret Speech." And of all Khrushchev's "revelations" those that made by far the greatest impression remain the accusations that Stalin initiated or approved the deliberate annihilation of many prominent Bolsheviks.

After the "Secret Speech" the quantity of "crimes" attributed to Stalin continued to grow. For example, not long afterwards Stalin began to be blamed for the executions on false charges of prominent Soviet military leaders. While Khrushchev remained in power a pleiade of semi-official writers continued to work indefatigably on adding to the list of victims of supposedly unjust sentences, and many of those persons were "rehabilitated" – declared to have been guilty of nothing.

In October 1964 Khrushchev was forced into retirement. By that time the image of Stalin as a mass murderer of innocent victims was already firmly established. In the late '60s and early '70s the weighty volumes of Soviet dissident Roi Medvedev and British Sovietologist Robert Conquest with their detailed descriptions of Stalin's so-called "crimes" were published in the West. They relied very heavily upon works published under Khrushchev. The years of Gorbachev and Eltsin saw the publication of even more such tendentious, blood-curdling "histories".

For this reason careful research on just what Khrushchev said about massive repressions in his "Secret Speech" may turn out to be even more useful than simply identifying more and more examples of Khrushchev's

---

[174] In fact there is good reason to believe that Khrushchev took this view, along with others, from Trotsky. He certainly took other anti-Stalin stories from Trotsky, such as the notion that Stalin may have been involved in the murder of Sergei Kirov on December 1, 1934.

lies. Such research makes it possible to identify the sources of the myth of Stalin as "mass murderer", and begin to disclose some of the reasons this myth was created in the first place.

Historical vs. Judicial Evidence

There's a qualitative difference between history and the legal process — what counts as evidence in a trial, and what counts as evidence in history.

The "rehabilitation" reports normally relied on determining that some legal procedure or other was not observed in the (late) defendant's investigation or trial. They asserted these violations of procedure; determined that therefore the late defendant should not have been convicted; and set aside the conviction. Sometimes they provided evidence that procedures had been violated, sometimes they merely claimed this was so.

Since a defendant whose conviction has been set aside, and who has not been retried, must be considered "innocent", the late defendant is, therefore, "innocent." Rehabilitated! For an historian this is all wrong.

A court has to be concerned with a prisoner's rights, some of which concern the legal process. For example, a defendant's confession to a crime, absent any other evidence, or absent any other evidence that a crime has been committed, is normally not enough for conviction. The burden of proof on the prosecution — the defendant is not required to prove his innocence, though if he is able to do so, he may.

Evidence obtained through torture is invalid. One reason is to protect the defendant's rights. Also, if the police were allowed to abuse prisoners in order to get confessions, they might never do any actual investigation, and so never solve any cases, though they would no doubt get lots of convictions!

But history is not a "trial", where the defendant has various rights. Dead people have no rights that need to be preserved. Likewise, we are not interested in whether the defendants got a "fair trial" (however that is defined). We are interested in whether they were guilty or not.

Whether or not they got a "fair trial" may be a separate issue to look into. But it is not the same thing as guilt or innocence. For example, the question of the guilt or innocence of at least one of the "Haymarket martyrs" legally lynched by the State of Illinois in 1886-7 has recently been raised again in some academic articles. But nobody has questioned whether or

not they got a "fair trial" – they did not, and were posthumously par-
doned a few years later by the succeeding governor of Illinois.

In the Sacco-Vanzetti case there is now some evidence that Sacco, at
least, may have been guilty. But it is clear that the two men did not have a
"fair trial" by the standards of the day. There has been a lively discussion
about whether or not Julius Rosenberg did pass atomic secrets or plan to
do so if he could. But there can be no doubt that he and his wife Ethel
did not receive a fair trial.

Nor do historians need to be concerned with legal procedure. Whether
you think a defendant has received a "fair trial" or not depends on whatever the legal procedures of the day and time were, as opposed to what
procedures were actually observed, all compared with what you yourself
actually think is "fair."

Historians are concerned with gathering and assessing all the evidence we
have, and reaching a conclusion on that basis. This is not the same thing
as determining whether a given person received a "fair trial" or not. A
defendant may be guilty and still not receive a fair trial. An historian is
interested in the "guilty or innocent" part. It is possible that no black
person ever received a "fair trial" in the American South until the 1960s.
But that does not mean that every black defendant was innocent.

This paper is not concerned with whether the defendants received a "fair
trial" according to the standards of the Soviet judicial system of the
1930s. Neither is it concerned with the legal basis of the trials – whether
accelerated trials, under emergency conditions, are "legal" or not. We are
concerned with evidence that goes to the guilt or innocence of the defendant.

In all the cases of defendants mentioned in Khrushchev's speech we have
ample evidence pointing towards their guilt. But our real point is the following. In all these cases, we know what Khrushchev and his advisers
knew, because we have their reports. None of those reports demonstrates
the innocence of those accused, as Khrushchev alleged.

In not one single case do I rely on the self-incrimination of anybody as
the sole evidence. Though, frankly, if that were all the evidence we had,
then we'd have to rely on it – there'd be nothing else. Likewise, if "here-
say" evidence were the **only** evidence we had, then we'd have to rely on
it, with appropriate scepticism and caveats.

Torture and the Historical Problems Related To It

From Stalin's day on no one has denied that many prisoners arrested on political charges during the 1930s in the USSR were tortured. "Rehabilitation" courts in Khrushchev and post-Khrushchev times have often "rehabilitated" defendants on the basis that they were tortured. Normally this took the form of declaring their convictions invalid. In a judicial procedure, even in the USSR during Stalin's time, evidence obtained from a defendant by torture was invalid and could not be validly used.

The fact that a defendant was tortured does not mean that defendant was innocent. It is not **evidence** that the defendant was innocent. But it is often erroneously assumed to be.

In reality, there are many different possibilities:

- A person may be guilty, be tortured, and confess;
- A person may be guilty, be tortured, and not confess;
- A person may be innocent, be tortured, and confess (to stop the torture);
- A person may be innocent, be tortured, and still not confess.
- A person may be innocent, not be tortured, and still confess to guilt to another crime. (Examples of this occur in the Rehabilitation documents).
- A person may have been tortured, but be found guilty by other evidence, such as testimony of other defendants or physical evidence. Other testimony, from other individuals, and other evidence, usually come into play.

Establishing the fact that someone really has been tortured is not always easy. The mere fact that someone claims he confessed because he was tortured is hardly foolproof. There are many reasons why people sometimes want to retract a confession of guilt. Claiming one was tortured is a way of doing this while preserving some dignity. So to be certain a person was tortured there has to be further evidence of the fact, such as a statement or confession by a person who actually did the torturing, or a first-hand witness.

When there is no evidence at all that a defendant was tortured objective scholars have no business concluding that he was tortured. This obvious point is often overlooked, probably because a "paradigm" that everybody was tortured, and everybody was innocent, acts powerfully on the minds of both researchers and readers.

Investigators can have different reasons for torturing a suspect. Convinced that a person is a dangerous criminal or spy, they may use torture to force him to yield information that may save lives or property, inculpate his confederates, or lead to the solution of previous crimes.

Or, investigators can torture suspects in order to get them to confess to crimes they never committed – perhaps in order to enhance the reputation of the investigators themselves. They can use torture to force the detainee to inculpate other persons, who can then be tortured for the same purpose. In that way a story about a huge conspiracy can be fabricated out of nothing.

Mikhail Frinovskii, deputy to Nikolai Ezhov, head of the NKVD (Commissar of Internal Affairs), in a confessional statement that has been quoted many times but was only published in its entirety in February 2006, stated that Ezhov and he had instructed some of their subordinates to do exactly that.[175]

But Frinovskii said that this was not always the case. Not all his subordinates confessed to doing that. Also, many defendants were not arrested during Ezhov's tenure. Also, we know that Stalin, and high-level commissions sent to investigate allegations of massive abuses like this, took strong, immediate efforts to stop them and arrest those responsible. Formerly secret internal documents make that clear.

In the interrogations I have cited above Ezhov also confessed to torturing and framing innocent persons on an enormous scale in order to sow discontent with the Soviet system and thus facilitate the overthrow of the Soviet government and Party leadership in the event of invasion by Japan and/or Germany.

For our purposes all this should just serve to remind us of the need for evidence.

---

[175] See Frinovskii's statement published in *Lubianka* 3 No. 33 pp. 33-50; my translation at http://chss.montclair.edu/english/furr/research/frinovskyeng.html. See also the transcript of N.I. Ezhov's confession, ibid. No. 37 pp. 52-72; my translation at http://chss.montclair.edu/english/furr/research/ezhov042639eng.html

- We can't assume a person was tortured without evidence that he was.

- We can't assume a person was guilty or innocent just because he was tortured, much less on the basis of a mere allegation that he was tortured.

- Each case has to be decided by itself, according to the evidence we have.

In most cases we simply do not have all the evidence that the Soviet investigators had. Neither the post-Stalin Soviet regimes nor the post-Soviet Russian regime has ever released it. What has been released has been selected according to some criteria. We are almost never told what those criteria are. But often it seems that the information was selected to make it appear as though the subject had been "framed" by the Stalin government.

Fortunately information often comes from different sources, at different times, and those who released it appear to have acted according to differing motives. The contradictions among the various bits of evidence are often very enlightening.

Still, we virtually never have the "whole story", all the evidence the prosecutors had. But the anti-Stalin bias of the Khrushchev, Gorbachev, Eltsin, and subsequent Russian governments can help us evaluate the evidence they do release: we may be reasonably certain that they would have released any evidence inculpating Stalin or his close associates, if it existed.

During Khrushchev's time (1956-64) and since Gorbachev's time, roughly 1987 to the present, the Soviet, and then later the Russian state, have put a lot of resources into an effort to criminalize Stalin. The Rehabilitation documents that have been published make this clear. It is hard to imagine that any evidence tending to show Stalin guilty of framing innocent persons would have been ignored.

By the same token, we may expect that a good deal of the material that has **not** been released tends to cast doubt on the "official" anti-Stalin version. And in fact documents have been released here and there that tend to exculpate Stalin. Sometimes it appears that this has been done because of bureaucratic infighting. Usually we simply do not know why it has been done. Sometimes, too, documents are released several times, the later versions contradicting the earlier versions in such a way that it is clear that "primary" documents are being fabricated until a final forged version is declared "official" by its being inserted into an archive.

As always in the writing of history our conclusions must be provisional. There is no "certainty." Historians are seldom, if ever, in the comfortable position of dealing with "certainties." As more evidence comes to light in future, we have to be prepared to adjust or even discard our earlier conclusions, if necessary.

We have to be prepared to question our own preconceived ideas and historical paradigms. It's not easy to do this. But if we don't keep the need to do it in the forefront of our consciousness, we risk looking with favor on evidence that tends to support our own preconceived ideas, while looking critically only at evidence that tends to disprove those same preconceived ideas.

A typology of Khrushchevian prevarication

The typology of "revelations" by Khrushchev, and the evidence in each case, represents my attempt to parse the different kinds of falsification, to distinguish the different ways Khrushchev misled his audience.

The American Heritage Dictionary of the English Language defines "lie" as:

1. A false statement deliberately presented as being true; a falsehood.

2. Something meant to deceive or give a wrong impression.

As here, definitions of "lie" normally require that the liar know in advance that the statement s/he is making is false. This is often, though not by any means always, hard to demonstrate in historical research. Therefore I have used a broader definition in this article. When I call a statement by Khrushchev a "lie" I mean **either** one of two things:

1. Khrushchev must have known the statement in question was false when he made it.

2. Khrushchev made the statement "in flagrant disregard for the truth." In this latter case we cannot be certain that Khrushchev knew for certain his statement was false. Rather, he represented the statement as true without any good grounds for doing so.

In every case, however, Khrushchev and his researchers had access to all the evidence now available to us, and to a huge amount more – in practice, to all of the documentation. Therefore it is more than probable that Khrushchev did know these statements were false.

The normal practice among scholars is to consider the word "lie" a harsh term that ought to be used sparingly in serious research. I will do my best to avoid it.

More important than issues of propriety are those of analysis. There are different kinds of falsifications, and to apply any single term to them all, whether "lie" or another word, fails to bring out the subtleties of the means of rhetorical misdirection Khrushchev applied.

A typology is an attempt to lump together otherwise different things because of something they have in common. In this case all the false "revelations" by Khrushchev have in common an intention to deceive, but try to effect deception in somewhat different ways.

The "Revelations"

No.	Khrushchev's "Revelation"	Typological Description
1.	"Cult of Personality"	L
2.	Lenin's "Testament"	L
3.	Lack of collegiality	L
4.	Stalin "morally and physically annihilated" those who disagreed with him	L
5.	The practice of mass repressions as a whole	S
6.	The term "enemy of the people"	L
7.	Zinoviev and Kamenev	S
8.	Trotskyites	L
9.	Stalin's "neglect" of the norms of Party life	L
10.	Politburo Commission	S
11.	Directive of December 1, 1934 signed by Enukidze	L
12.	Khrushchev hints that Stalin was responsible for Kirov's assassination	L
13.	Telegram from Stalin and Zhdanov to Politburo of September 25, 1936	L
14.	Stalin's Speech to the February-March 1937 Central Committee Plenum	L
15.	"A number of Central Committee members doubted the correctness of the policy of mass repression." Especially Postyshev	L
16.	The case of R.I. Eikhe	LW
17.	N.I. Ezhov	LW
18.	The case of Ia. E. Rudzutak	LW
19.	Confessions of A.M. Rozenblium	LW
20.	The case of I.D. Kabakov	LW
21–24.	S.V. Kosior, V.Ia. Chubar', P.P. Postyshev, A.V. Kosarev	LW
25.	The "Stalin shooting lists"	L
26.	The decision of the January 1938 Central Committee Plenum	L
27.	"Beria's gang"	L
28.	The "torture telegram"	L
29.	On Beria's order Rodos tortured Kosior and Chubar'	LW
30.	Stalin "disregarded" warnings about the outbreak of the war	L

31. Vorontsov's Letter	L
32. The German deserter	L
33. The executed military commanders	LW
34. Stalin's "depression and passivity" at the outbreak of the war	L
35. Stalin a "poor military commander"	L
36. Khar'kov campaign of 1942	L
37. Stalin "planned military operations on a globe"	L
38. Stalin "belittled" Marshal Zhukov's services	KW
39. Mass deportations of peoples	L
40. "The Leningrad Affair"	L
41. "The Mingrelian Affair"	L
42. Relations with Yugoslavia	KW
43. "The Doctors' Plot"	L
44. Beria an "agent of foreign intelligence"	L
45. Kaminsky about Beria's work for the Mussavetists	L
46. The "Kartvelishvili – Lavrent'ev case"	L
47. Vengeance on M.S. Kedrov	LW
48. Papulia, Sergo Ordzhonikidze's brother	L
49. "J.V. Stalin. A Short Biography"	L
50. "History of the AUCB(b): A Short Course"	L
51. Stalin signed a decree of June 2, 1951 to erect a statue in his own honor	DK
52. The Palace of Soviets	L
53. The Lenin and Stalin prizes	L
54. Stalin's proposal to raise taxes on the kolkhozes	KW
55. Stalin's insult to Postyshev	KW
56. "Disorganization" of the work of the Politburo	L
57. Stalin suspected Voroshilov was an "English spy"	L
58. "Unbridled arbitrariness" with regard to Andreev	L
59.– "Unfounded" accusations against Molotov and Mikoian	Lx2
60.	
61. Increasing the membership of the Presidium of the C.C.	L

The typology

DK - "Don't Know" – 1 statement (#51). Without studying the original of the relevant document, we cannot determine whether Khrushchev was telling the truth when he claimed Stalin personally signed the order for a monument to himself on July 2 1951. Khrushchev certainly distorted the **context** by omission.

What would constitute proof of this statement one way or the other is not certain. For example, a photocopy alone would not be sufficient, as will be explained when we consider this claim of Khrushchev's.

KW – "Khrushchev's Word (only)" – 4 statements. Khrushchev claims Stalin said something, but no one else has confirmed it. Even if others have denied it, it still can't be definitively established as false.

However, these statements probably **are** lies, since in only one case does Khrushchev say he was the sole person to hear these remarks of Stalin's. If the rest of these statements had been made in the presence of others, surely somebody would have confirmed them, since they all became well known after the Secret Speech. We can't be certain of this, however, hence the special "KW" classification.

LW – "Lie, information Withheld" – 12 statements. These are statements which give a false impression because essential context – other information – is omitted. Khrushchev himself may, or may not, have known this context, but those who did the research and reported to him certainly knew it, on the principle that what we know today, and much more, was certainly knowable then. It's more than unlikely his researchers would have dared to withhold this information from Khrushchev.

S – "Special case" – 3 instances. These are very broad statements that, when examined carefully, do not really make any specific accusation against Stalin, but rather imply an accusation, and so create a false impression without actually making a specific claim.

L – "Lie" – 41 statements, by far the largest category. These statements are either demonstrably false, or made in flagrant disregard of the facts. In this latter case we can show that Khrushchev did not know whether they were true or not.

An example or two from each category (except, of course, the first, which has already been cited) should give an idea of the kind of classification and deception that is involved in each.

KW – Khrushchev's Word

According to Khrushchev Stalin said, in Khrushchev's presence, "I will shake my little finger – and there will be no more Tito. He will fall." (p. 35) Khrushchev implies, though he does not explicitly state, that he was the only witness to these words of Stalin's. If so, there is no way to verify this incident. No one has confirmed this.

A second example is the question of Stalin's proposing to raise taxes on the peasantry by 40 billion rubles. Khrushchev claimed that in late 1952 or early 1953 Stalin suggested a 40 billion ruble tax increase on the peasantry. We show that either Stalin said this to Khrushchev alone, or Khrushchev made it up.

The other two examples are Stalin's alleged insult against Marshal Zhukov and Khrushchev's allegation that Stalin insulted Pavel Postyshev.

If Khrushchev had been an honest man, one whose statements on all other occasions had proven to be worthy of believe, then here we might rely on an unblemished reputation for veracity and presume these statements true. But Khrushchev was only rarely truthful. Therefore it's most likely that what he said on his own witness alone is false. But we cannot be completely certain; hence this classification.

LW – Lie, Information Withheld

Khrushchev said "In the same manner were fabricated the "cases" against eminent party and state workers -- Kossior, Chubar, Postyshev, Kosarev and others." (Nos 21-24)

The situation is not nearly as clear as Khrushchev claims it was. Some very incriminating information is now available to us concerning Kosarev, and much more is available about Kossior, Chubar', and Postyshev. For example, Postyshev was rebuked, removed, and finally arrested and convicted of massive, unfounded repressions against Party members in his area. Khrushchev was at the January 1938 C. C. Plenum at which Postyshev reported and was severely criticized.

Khrushchev had to know that Molotov had visited Postyshev in prison, where Postyshev had confessed his guilt to Molotov. Likewise Khrushchev had to know that Postyshev, and many others, had inculpated Kossior and Chubar', and that Kaganovich said he had seen a whole notebook of Chubar's confessions. A recently published document has shown that all four of these men confessed at trial, although other defendants retracted their confessions at trial. Khrushchev had to know this too.

A fifth example is Rozenblium's story about how Zakovskii fabricated confessions. Khrushchev implies, though without affirming it in so many words, that Stalin was behind this. In fact we have good evidence that

Zakovskii was acting under Ezhov's orders as part of a conspiracy. We have documentary proof that Stalin strongly condemned Zakovskii for torturing suspects.

It should be noted that some cases of "lie, information withheld" (LW) shade over into the category of "lie" (L). Examples of this are Nos 33 and 47. In the case of the "executed military commanders" (No. 33) Khrushchev expressed himself so vaguely that it's impossible to know exactly what, if anything, he was asserting; for the same reason it is impossible to say for sure that he was lying. There is ample published evidence that Marshal Tukhachevsky and the commanders condemned together with him in June 1937 were really guilty of the charges against them. So it is hard to classify this statement of Khrushchev's, but we have put it into the category of "lie, information withheld."

"The cruel vengeance on M.S. Kedrov" (No. 47) is another such example. It is easy to see that Kedrov was not shot "on Beria's order", meaning "at his instigation." The initiating document did not originate with Beria. After confirmation with Bochkov, Prosecutor of the USSR Beria, as Commissar of Internal Affairs, received the decision to shoot Kedrov. So that it would also be incorrect to say that Beria had nothing to do with Kedrov's execution, and he certainly must have issued an "order."

In both cases we have to make do with crumbs of declassified evidence, on the basis of which it is quite impossible to gain a full understanding of those events. Still, the information we do have is sufficient to establish the fact that Khrushchev lied at least in some aspects of these cases (and possibly a great deal more). So both cases are both "lies" (L) and also "lies, information withheld" (LW), or a combination of the two.

S – Special Case

Khrushchev discusses mass repressions generally (No. 5) before getting into specifics. He neglects to mention that he himself was heavily involved in mass repressions, as Party First Secretary of Moscow *oblast'* (province) and city committees during 1935-38 and then, after January 1938, of the Ukraine (1938-49).

The studies that are available to us today suggest that Khrushchev may well have repressed more people than any other single Party leader. Certainly he was among the leaders in repression. This context is entirely missing from the Secret Speech. I classify this here as S, "special case" rather than as LW, "lie, information withheld," because Khrushchev does not **explicitly** blame Stalin or Beria for all this repression, though that is the impression he no doubt intended to leave his audience with.

Another example of this category is Khrushchev's statement about Zinoviev and Kamenev:

> In his "testament" Lenin warned that "Zinoviev's and
> Kamenev's October episode was of course not an
> accident." But Lenin did not pose the question of their
> arrest and certainly not their shooting. (p. 9)

This statement sidesteps the whole question of Zinoviev's and Kamenev's innocence or guilt in plotting to overthrow the Soviet government and indirect involvement in Kirov's assassination. These were the charges brought against them in the first public "show trial" in Moscow in August 1936, and to which they confessed. These confessions together with all the rest of the investigation material were available to Khrushchev.

The very small portion of this information available to us today suggests that Zinoviev and Kamenev were guilty of what they confessed to. Even Khrushchev did not declare them innocent, as he did a number of other high-ranking Party leaders of whose guilt we have a good deal of evidence today. Instead Khrushchev just sets down their shooting to Stalin's "arbitrariness." But if indeed they were guilty, as the evidence suggests, then their executions were anything but "arbitrary."

The final example of category "S" is Khrushchev's reference to No. 10:

> a party commission under the control of the Central
> Committee Presidium… charged with investigating what
> made possible the mass repressions against the majority
> of the Central Committee members and candidates
> elected at the 17th Congress …"

Khrushchev claimed that this commission "established many facts pertaining to the fabrication of cases against Communists, to false accusations, to glaring abuses of socialist legality, which resulted in the death of innocent people."

In reality, this "Pospelov Commission," whose text has been published,[176] did **not** "establish" these facts. This tendentious study followed a predetermined agenda to reach conclusions convenient to Khrushchev, but in most cases unsupported by any evidence. Furthermore the Com-

---

[176] For example in *Doklad Khrushcheva* (cited above), pp. 185-230.

mission never established that Stalin was guilty of these abuses. Nor, of course, is this statement really a revelation at all, since it was widely acknowledged, even at the time (1939 and thereafter) that many persons had been executed wrongly.

L - Lie

By far the largest category is "L" – the outright lies. All lies rely on context – something with reference to which they can be recognized as contrary to fact. So depending upon the specific context some of them shade off into the "LW, or "Lie, information Withheld," category.

But some are just blatant falsehoods. Examples of these include "Vorontsov's letter" (No. 31). Here Khrushchev omits the last paragraph, which reverses the meaning of the whole letter and in fact **disproves** his point.

Another is the "Torture Telegram" (No. 28), where again Khrushchev omitted crucial parts of the document. In it Stalin,[177] while reaffirming the use of "physical pressure" on "hardened" criminals, forcefully rejects this save as an "exception" while revealing that certain well-known NKVDists have been punished for making it a "rule." Khrushchev's quotation removes Stalin's order that torture only be used "in exceptional circumstances."

A third example is Stalin's purported "demoralization" at the war's outset (No. 34). This is refuted by virtually all the people who were present and working with Stalin at the time. And Khrushchev was not with Stalin or even in Moscow at all but in Kiev!

---

[177] Or "Stalin" – the document itself is of questionable authenticity, as I explain separately in Chapter 4.

Chapter 11.

The Results of Khrushchev's "Revelations";

Falsified Rehabilitations

Falsified Rehabilitations

Tivel - Postyshev - Kosarev - Rudzutak - Kabakov - Eikhe

In his Speech Khrushchev announced that "a party commission under the control of the Central Committee Presidium" had determined that

> ...many party, Soviet and economic activists, who were branded in 1937-1938 as 'enemies', were actually never enemies, spies, wreckers, etc., but were always honest Communists.

He then went on to discuss a number of specific cases whose innocence, he said, had been established.

After the collapse of the USSR the documents of this commission headed by Petr Pospelov were published. So were the rehabilitation reports signed by Chief Prosecutor of the USSR Rudenko on which Pospelov relied.[178] Verbatim quotations and other similarities show that the rehabilitation reports were the factual basis for the Pospelov Report, which draws directly from them.

The Pospelov Report has been discussed a few times in a very credulous vein that has failed to expose the falsifications it contains. Some of these are very obvious ones. For example, one section of the report concludes that all the so-called "blocs" and "centers" of oppositional activity were

---

[178] *Reabilitatsia. Kak Eto Bylo. Dokumenty Prezidiuma Ts KPSS I Drugie Materialy. V 3-x tomakh. T. 1. Mart 1953 – Fevral' 1956 gg.* (rehabilitation. How It Happened. Documents of the Presidium of the CC CPSU and Other Materials. In 3 volumes. Volume 1. March 1953-February 1956.") Moscow: MDF, 2000. Hereafter *RKEB* 1. The Pospelov Report is on pp. 317-348; online at http://www.alexanderyakovlev.org/almanah/inside/almanah-doc/55752

fabricated by NKVD investigators. We know this is not so, since Trotsky's own papers mention a "bloc" of his supporters with the Rights.[179]

But the rehabilitation reports have never been subject to any scrutiny. Previous studies of the rehabilitations referred to in Khrushchev's Speech, such as those by Rogovin and Naumov, have been little more than summaries of Khrushchev's own memoirs and have credulously accepted Khrushchev's own self-aggrandizing accounts.[180]

In the pages that follow we discuss rehabilitation reports on a few of the Party figures who feature in Khrushchev's Speech and compare their contents with what we know from other sources published since the end of the USSR. We conclude that the rehabilitation reports in question were not compiled to discover the truth about the guilt or innocence of the defendants. They could not have been, because they did not review even all the materials we now have about these individuals. Who knows what else is in their investigative and judicial files that we do not know about?

So why were the rehabilitation reports prepared? As concerns the persons who figure in Khrushchev's Speech, all Central Committee members, the only logical explanation is that their purpose was to provide Khrushchev with plausible documentation for his claims that they were all innocent.

This can't have been the reason for the thousands of rehabilitation reports on lesser officials, Party members of lesser rank, and of private individuals. Most, if not all, of these were prepared as a result of petitions by the relatives of the defendants, and few of these have been published.

---

[179] *RKEB* 1, 322-3. See J. Arch Getty, "Trotsky in Exile: The Founding of the Fourth International," *Soviet Studies* 38, No. 1 (January 1986), p. 28 & notes 18-21, p. 34; Pierre Broué, "Trotsky et le bloc des oppositions de 1932," *Cahiers Léon Trotsky* 5 (January-March 1980), pp. 5-37.

[180] Naumov, V.V. "K istorii sekretnogo doklada N.S. Khrushcheva na XX s"ezd KPSS," *Novaia i Noveishaia Istoriia* No. 4 (1996); also at http://vivovoco.rsl.ru/VV/PAPERS/HISTORY/ANTIST.HTM; Rogovin, Vadim. "Prilozhenie I: Iz istorii razoblacheniia stalinskikh prestupleniy." *Partiia rasstreliannykh*. Also at http://web.mit.edu/people/fjk/Rogovin/volume5/pi.html Rogovin naively repeats Khrushchev's self-serving version of events. Naumov is a bit more critical of Khrushchev's and Mikoian's memoir accounts, but never questions the validity of the process itself, starting with the rehabilitation reports.

But even in these cases we cannot be confident that proper investigations to determine guilt or innocence were in fact carried out. One example is that of Alexandr Iul'evich Tivel'-Levit.

Tivel'

Getty got to see Tivel''s unpublished party file and briefly summarized Tivel''s case as it is reflected in that file. In May 1957 the Supreme Court of the USSR overturned Tivel''s 1937 conviction and expulsion from the Party. But there is no evidence that any serious study of Tivel''s case was ever carried out, the Supreme Court merely stating that his conviction "had been based on contradictory and dubious materials."[181]

In fact we now have a good deal of information about Tivel'. That is because, as it turns out, he was hardly a "Soviet Everyman," as Getty termed him.[182] Tivel' had coauthored an official history of the first ten years of the Comintern. Tivel' was referred to by name as the interpreter in the transcript of the 17th Party Congress when, on February 2, 1934, Okano, a representative of the Japanese Communist Party, spoke.

Alexander Barmine, a Soviet official who fled to the West, wrote that Tivel' had been Zinoviev's secretary. Radek called him "my collaborator" and testified that Tivel' was connected with a Zinovievist group. He was named as a conspirator by both Iuri Piatakov and Grigorii Sokol'nikov, two of the major defendants in the 1937 Trial. Sokol'nikov said Tivel' had approached **him**, Sokol'nikov, as a member of a Trotskyist group that was planning to assassinate Stalin.

> Sokolnikov: In 1935 Tivel came to me and informed me that he was connected with the Zaks-Gladnyev terrorist group. Tivel asked for instructions about the further activities of this group....
>
> The President: On whose life was this group preparing to make an attempt?
>
> Sokolnikov: Tivel told me then that they had instructions to prepare for a terrorist act against Stalin... I was personally connected with Tivel, Tivel was personally connected with the Zaks-

---

[181] Getty, J. Arch and Oleg V. Naumov, *The Road to Terror. Stalin and the Self-Destruction of the Bolsheviks, 1932-1939*. New Haven: Yale University Press, 1999, p. 5; Tivel' is discussed on pp. 1-5.

[182] Getty & Naumov, p.1.

Gladnyev group. Whether Tivel himself was a member of this group, I do not know[183]

There is quite a bit more. Zaks-Gladnev, who had been editor of *Leningradskaia Pravda* while Zinoviev headed the Leningrad Party, was Zinoviev's brother-in-law. Victor Serge wrote about meeting with Zinoviev in 1927 at Zaks' apartment after the unsuccessful Trotskyist demonstration against the Party leadership – Bukharin and Stalin at that time – and Adolf Yoffe's suicide protest (Yoffe was a devoted Trotskyite), where they planned an underground opposition.

Since Sokolnikov and Piatakov discussed Tivel' in their trial testimony they no doubt also mentioned him, and possibly at greater length, in pre-trial investigative interrogations.[184] When they named him at trial Tivel' was not only still alive at the time – he had not yet been arrested, although he had evidently been expelled from the Party in August 1936. Perhaps his name came up in connection with the Zinoviev-Kamenev Trial of that same month. Tivel''s name was mentioned by Ezhov in the face-to-face confrontation between Bukharin and Kulikov, one of Bukharin's accusers, in December 1936.[185]

According to Getty, Tivel''s rehabilitation was the result of appeals from his widow, who wanted the blot of "child of an enemy of the people" removed from her son. From the little documentation that has been made available so far it is clear that despite his rehabilitation there was a good deal of evidence implicating Tivel' in the network of conspiracies alleged during the late 1930s. This is even more obviously true in the case of the far more prominent Bolsheviks whose examples are cited by Khrushchev in his Speech.

Postyshev

Khrushchev claimed in his Speech that at the February-March 1937 Plenum "many members" of the Central Committee "questioned the right-

---

[183] Report of Court Proceedings in the Case of the Anti-Soviet Trotskyite Centre. … Verbatim Report. Moscow: People's Commissariat of Justice of the U.S.S.R., 1937, pp. 162-3,165.

[184] We know these pre-trial interrogations exist because a very short section of an interrogation of Sokol'nikov was published in 1991 in *Reabilitatsia: Politicheskie Protsessy 30-x - 50-x gg.* ((Moscow, 1991), pp. 228-9.

[185] "Stenogramma ochnykh stavok v TsK VKP(b). Dekabr' 1936 goda." *Voprosy Istorii* No. 3, 2002, pp. 3-31, at p. 6.

ness" of "mass repressions," and that "Postyshev most ably expressed these doubts." This assertion could not be checked until the corresponding section of the transcript of that Plenum was published in mid-1995.[186]

The statement turns out to be a deliberate lie. In reality neither Pavel Postyshev nor a single other member questioned the repressions.

But Khrushchev's deception is far greater than this. Postyshev himself was guilty of massive repressions. Stalin called Postyshev's actions "a massacre ... shooting" of innocent Party members in his area. This was the reason that Postyshev himself was removed from his Party post, removed as candidate member of the Politburo, expelled from the Central Committee, then from the Party, arrested, tried, and executed (See our more detailed analysis of what Khrushchev said about Postyshev, and the evidence we have amassed, in Chapter Three).

To this day the Russian government continues to forbid the publication of, or even access to, Postyshev's case file.[187] Without access to such investigative materials as the statements and confessions made by Postyshev himself, by those who accused him and those whom he accused, and the transcript of his trial, we cannot possibly have a full account of what really happened. This is the case with all the figures who Khrushchev claimed were executed though innocent.

Therefore, we can't know the whole story either in the case of Postyshev or that of any of the others. What we can do is to compare the rehabilitation reports which have now been published, with what we know about Postyshev from other sources that have become public.

The Pospelov Report section on Postyshev's rehabilitation is far shorter even than the brief rehabilitation report, and is taken wholly from it, with

---

[186] In *Voprosy Istorii*, 5/6, 1995. The Postyshev quotation Khrushchev cited dishonestly is on p. 4.

[187] One reason given for this is the passage of a strange law according to which the next of kin of those tried and executed must give their permission before such materials can be made public. Postyshev's son Leonid, a noted economist, has given some interviews in which he warmly recalls his father and takes for granted that he was innocent. Rehabilitation was advantageous for the family of those "rehabilitated", since there were various formal and informal ways in which family members of those executed for treason suffered discrimination. It seems that in most cases it was family members who petitioned for the rehabilitation of their executed relatives, though in Postyshev's case Khrushchev may have initiated it himself.

a personal attack on Stalin added.[188] Khrushchev certainly saw these reports, as they were all sent to the Presidium members. A few are signed by them, and a few more are even addressed personally to Khrushchev.[189] We'll concentrate on the more detailed rehabilitation report here.

One thing immediately becomes apparent: Postyshev's rehabilitation report[190] says nothing at all about his involvement in massive extra-legal executions of Party members, concerning which we do have a great deal of documentation. Raising this issue would not have induced sympathy towards Postyshev and hostility towards Stalin.

It is significant that nothing about this occurs in the report, since to really exculpate Postyshev it would have to be included. Any bona fide review of Postyshev's case would naturally have to re-examine the issue of mass murder! Had it been included, Khrushchev could have simply disregarded this information. But this would have left a paper trail. One of Khrushchev's political opponents like Molotov or Kaganovich might have wanted to read the rehabilitation report and seen through the fakery.

Khrushchev himself was present at the January 1938 Central Committee Plenum at which Postyshev was criticized, and expelled from the C.C., for this repression. Khrushchev certainly knew all about what Postyshev had done and the reasons for his expulsion from the C.C. No doubt he voted for it himself.

From the evidence it is clear that both the Pospelov Report and the rehabilitation report itself are faked. They were a put-up job to provide an excuse for declaring Postyshev innocent, rather than any genuine attempt to review his case. Khrushchev certainly knew this. No one would have dared to do this without Khrushchev's order.

It is remarkable that in the case of Postyshev's rehabilitation as well as in most, or all, of the others, those members of the Presidium who had

---

[188] *RKEB* 1, 325.

[189] Signed by Presidium members: pp. 203, 207, 217, 220, 227, 229, 231, 233, 236, 237, 251, 260, 261, 263. Addressed to Khrushchev: p. 192, In some cases the reports were not specifically addressed to Khrushchev but notes on them make it clear that they went directly to him. See p. 188, 191, 208, 233, 236, 237, 251, 264. A few were either sent first to Malenkov or Bulganin, or theirs are the copies that were found in the archives and printed.

[190] *RKEB* 1,218-220. Dated May 19, 1955.

been on the Politburo in 1938 – Molotov, Kaganovich, Mikoian, and Voroshilov – must have known this just as Khrushchev did.[191]

It is quite possible that Postyshev was only tried on one, or a limited number, of capital offenses – for example, for being involved in a Right-Trotskyite conspiracy. It is common in the USA as well for a defendant not to be tried consecutively for every capital offense. It is likely that Postyshev never stood trial on other capital offenses – after all, a person can only be executed once.

But in that case, in order to "completely rehabilitate" him, all that would be necessary would be to have his conviction **on the offense of which he was convicted** set aside. If **that** conviction could be set aside, he would then be "innocent", meaning: his only conviction had quashed. It looks as though this is what happened. It is probably the case of many, if not all, of those "rehabilitated" in the reports used by the Pospelov Report.

The report confirms that Postyshev confessed both to participation in a Right-Trotskyite conspiracy and to espionage for Poland, but that some of those those whom Postyshev named as his accomplices either failed to name him in their own confessions or named Postyshev as one of the targets of their own conspiracies.[192]

Some of the material in this report reads very strangely.

- Popov confessed that he, Balitskii and Iakir "attempted to use Postshev in their anti-Soviet plans but were not successful." This is interesting! If Postyshev were "innocent", he would have reported such attempts to recruit him to a conspiracy. If he had done so, this fact would surely have been noted

---

[191] Aside from the Presidium members already mentioned (Khrushchev, Bulganin, Molotov, Kaganovich, Mikoian) the only other person who was a C.C. member before 1939 and also in 1956 was Shvernik, a close ally of Khrushchev's. Marshal Semion Budionniy was a candidate member in 1934, 1939 and 1956; and A.P. Zaveniagin was a candidate member in 1934, evidently in 1939 as well, and 1956. Bulganin was a candidate member in 1934.

[192] We know from a letter of Judge Ul'rikh to Stalin on March 16 1939 that Postyshev was among those who confessed at trial. Ul'rikh is quoted at http://stalin.memo.ru/images/intro1.htm . See the facsimile of the actual letter is at http://stalin.memo.ru/images/ulrih-39.jpg or, a more readable copy, http://chss.montclair.edu/english/furr/research/ulrih-39.jpg

in his favor. But if there's no evidence he did so, how can he be "innocent"?

- Iona Iakir, one of the military commanders tried and executed in the Tukhachevskii case, was named by Postyshev as one of his co-conspirators but "did not name Postyshev in any of his confessions." Was Iakir specifically asked about Postyshev? If not, the fact he did not mention Postyshev may not be important at all. Why is this detail not included?

- "Kosior S.V. at the beginning of the investigation named Postyshev as one of the participants of the military conspiracy in the Ukraine, then recanted this confession, then afterwards reaffirmed it." This hardly exculpates Postyshev. A confession does not prove guilt, any more than a recantation disproves it.

- "In Kosior's case file there is a statement by N.K. Antipov in which he affirms that there were very abnormal personal relations between Kosior and Postyshev and that Postyshev was not a member of the general center of counterrevolutionary organizations in the Ukraine."

- After March 1937 Postyshev was transferred from the Ukraine to the post of Oblast' (province) secretary in Kuibyshev. The fact that he was not in the leadership of the Ukrainian conspiracies does not prove him "innocent" of anything.

- "At the preliminary investigation Postyshev confessed that he carried out his espionage contacts with Japanese intelligence through B.N. Mel'nikov and B.I. Kozlovskii, members of the eastern division of the People's Commissariat of Foreign Affairs of the USSR. As a verification has established, although B.N. Mel'nikov admitted guilt in contact with Japanese intelligence, he gave no confession about Postyshev, and B.I. Kozlovskii was not even arrested. In this way Postyshev's 'confessions' about his counterrevolutionary activities in the Ukraine and connections to Japanese intelligence were not

confirmed, and as has been established at the present
time they were falsified by the organs of the NKVD."

On the contrary: If Postyshev confessed to being a Japanese agent,
named Mel'nikov, and Mel'nikov himself confessed to being a Japanese
agent, this tends to confirm rather than to rebut Postyshev's guilt regardless of whether Mel'nikov mentioned him or not!

We are informed that investigator P.I Tserpento confessed to the NKVD
that one specific interrogation transcript was written by himself and another interrogator, Vizel', on the instructions of G.N. Lulov – presumably their superior – and that Lulov had, evidently, warned Postyshev to
confirm its contents. We are told that Tserpento himself was involved in
falsifying cases, and confessed to collaborating in falsifying a single interrogation of Postyshev. However, there's no indication of the contents of
this specific interrogation, and we are specifically informed that there is
only a single interrogation in question here.

The final statement of the Postyshev rehabilitation report says merely:

> The Prosecutor's office considers it possible to institute
> a protest against the sentence passed against Postyshev
> by the Military Collegium of the Supreme Court of the
> USSR with the object of closing his case and a
> posthumous rehabilitation. We request your agreement.

This rehabilitation note (**zapiska**) is dated May 19, 1955. Two months
later, on July 18 1955 in the rehabilitation report of Ukhanov we are told:

> It has been established by a process of verification that
> the investigation on the case of Ukhanov was carried out
> by the former associates of the NKVD of the USSR,
> Lulov and Tserpento, who were later exposed as
> criminals who had wormed their way into working for
> the organs of State Security and who were sentenced to
> be shot for a series of crimes, including that of falsifying
> investigations.

> From Lulov's criminal case file it is clear that he
> stemmed from a socially foreign milieu: Lulov's brother
> Mendel' was a big capitalist who lived in Palestine. In
> Lulov's case file is his note to Zinoviev in which Lulov
> expresses his approval of one of Zinoviev's speeches.
> From Tserpento's case file it is clear that in 1934 he was
> a participant in a counter-revolutionary Trotskyite group

at Saratov University. At that time Tserpento was recruited as a non-public agent-observer by the organs of the NKVD. In 1937 Tserpento was transferred to a government position in the central apparatus of the NKVD of the USSR.

In the confessions of Tserpento and Lulov are contained many facts that testify to the fact that, in interrogating arrested persons, they forced them to name innocent persons and in particular forced from them false accusations against leading Party and Soviet workers. In falsifying criminal cases Tserpento and Lulov did not stop at compelling false testimony in relations to certain leaders of the government and Party. In this way Tserpento and Lulov falsified many investigative cases, including the case against Postyshev, now posthumously completely rehabilitated, and other persons.[193]

Lulov and Tserpento, in short, are accused of having been supporters of the Rights (Lulov – Zinoviev) and of Trotsky (Tserpento) respectively. What this means about Postyshev we will see below. But it also confirms the existence of Trotskyite conspiracies, something that the Pospelov Report denied outright fewer than nine months later.

The Ukhanov report goes on to quote verbatim from an interrogation-statement by Ezhov's right-hand man in the NKVD Mikhail Frinovskii. In it Frinovskii details how Ezhov directed massive fabrications of confessions with the help of torture in order to cover up his own leadership in an anti-government Right-Trotskyite conspiracy of his own. Often selectively quoted, this document has only recently been published in Russia for the first time (February 2006).[194]

All of this tells us some important things.

- One interrogation of Postyshev's was composed by the interrogators before Postyshev was tried and executed.

---

[193] *RKEB 1* 233-4). The entire Postyshev rehabilitation report is at
http://chss.montclair.edu/english/furr/research/postyshevrehab.html

[194] *RKEB* 1, 234. The Russian text of the Frinovskii statement is at
http://chss.montclair.edu/english/furr/research/frinovskyru.html ; the English at
http://chss.montclair.edu/english/furr/research/frinovskyeng.html

- Frinovskii, Ezhov's right-hand man, is quoted as describing a method of falsifying confessions and framing people very similar to that allegedly used by Lulov and Tserpento against Postyshev.

- This means Postyshev's case was reviewed under Beria, after he replaced Ezhov in late November 1938, but evidently before Postyshev was tried and executed on February 26, 1939.[195] His interrogator Tserpento and his commander Lulov were tried and executed for falsifying cases, so this was under Beria too.

- The issue of massive repression of Party leaders did not even arise in Postyshev's rehabilitation report. Yet Postyshev was "completely rehabilitated" two months after the original rehabilitation report.

- A number of those implicated by Postyshev in his own confessions either implicated him in turn (Kosior) or failed to name him but did not necessarily clear him either (Iakir, Antipov, Mel'nikov).

- Some of those who confessed to plotting against Postyshev did, by the same token, confirm the existence of conspiracies.

- If Postyshev really had been in a conspiracy this would not have been known beyond a very restricted number of people. So the fact that other conspirators confessed to plotting against Postyshev does not exculpate him in the least.

Conclusion

There's only one theory that can account for all these issues: the rehabilitation report on Postyshev is a fraud. None of the important charges against Postyshev were really investigated, and so he was not really cleared of any of them. The purpose of the report was not to verify

---

[195] Tserpento is quoted as saying that his statements could easily be verified by calling Postyshev and Bubnov – another arrestee – and talking with them (*RKEB 1* 219). It's possible too that Postyshev had already been executed and Tserpento just did not know that.

whether Postyshev was really guilty or not. It was to provide Khrushchev's phony research with a fig-leaf to justify his blaming Stalin for Postyshev's execution.

The Pospelov Report, which bases itself on these rehabilitation reports, is
a fraud too. Its passage on Postyshev is much less detailed, blames Stalin
more directly, and was clearly drafted for polemic rather than analytical
purposes.

Kosarev

We have a rehabilitation report on Alexandr Kosarev.[196] But there is no
section devoted to him in the Pospelov Report; in the draft of the Speech
by Pospelov and Aristov;[197] or in the draft of Khrushchev's additions.[198]
Therefore it was added by Khrushchev himself, and constitutes the best
evidence possible that Khrushchev worked not only from the Pospelov
Report and the Pospelov-Aristov draft, but from the rehabilitation reports themselves.

We know much less about Kosarev's fate than about Postyshev's, but
only because the Russian authorities have not released anything. The rehabilitation report on him, dated August 4, 1954, sets down Beria's arrest
of Kosarev, dated November 28 1938, to a personal grudge. At first
Kosarev refused to confess to any treasonable activities, but was beaten
until he signed a false confession on December 5 in which he admitted to
being a part of the Right-Trotskyite conspiracy to overthrow the Soviet
government.

Everything is blamed on Beria, who is said to have hated Kosarev because Kosarev despised Beria for distorting the history of the Bolshevik
Party in Georgia and for oppressing old Georgian Bolsheviks. Beria took
his first opportunity as head of the NKVD to arrest Kosarev and his
wife. When Kosarev refused to "confess", Beria had him beaten into a
false confession.

---

[196] *RKEB* 1, 166-168

[197] "Proekt doklada 'O kul'te lichnosti I ego postledstviiakh', predstavlenniy P.N.
Pospelovym I A.B. Aristovym. 18 fevralia 1956 g." *Doklad N.S. Khrushcheva O Kul'te
Lichnosti Stalina na XX S"ezde KPSS. Dokumenty.* Ed K. Aimermakher et al. Moscow:
ROSSPEN, 2002, pp. 120-133; also in *RKEB* 1, 353-364.

[198] "Dopolneniia N.S. Khrushcheva k proektu doklada 'O kul'te lichnosti i ego
posledstviiakh'". *Doklad Khrushcheva,* pp. 134-150; also in *RKEB* 1, 365-379.

Beria allegedly had Bogdan Kobulov, one of his right-hand men, and the main investigator Lev Shvartsman beat Valentina Pikina, a former co-worker of Kosarev's in the Komsomol, though Pikina still refused to falsely accuse Kosarev. We are told that Kosarev confessed at his trial only because Beria and Kobulov assured him that by so doing his life would be spared. Beria then refused to pass on Kosarev's appeal to the court, and Kosarev was shot.

Khrushchev had already had Beria and seven of his closest associates, including Kobulov, shot in 1953. Investigator Shvartsman, who along with Kosarev's widow provided virtually all the information in the reha-bilitation report, was to be executed under Khrushchev in 1955. So the report tells a Beria "horror story" similar to many others Khrushchev was spreading. Beria is said to have done all this just out of revenge, without any political motive at all.

This itself is suspicious, since we know from other documents that there were political charges against Kosarev. We review them briefly below (#24), and in somewhat more detail in the body of this study. The reha-bilitation report does not even mention them, much less refute them.

Rogovin cites an account in which in March 1938 Kosarev met with a former Leningrad Komsomol leader named Sergei Utkin, who had com-plained that the NKVD had forced him to make false accusations. Kosarev then denounced Utkin to Ezhov and Utkin was sent to a camp for 16 years. A close relationship between Kosarev and Ezhov is also attested by Anatoly Babulin, a nephew of Ezhov's whose statement was recently published.

According to Rogovin, who based his summary on Gorbachev-era publi-cations, Kosarev was really arrested right after a plenum of the Komso-mol Central Committee which met November 19-22 1938 and at which most of the Politburo of the Party appeared and spoke: Stalin, Molotov, Kaganovich, Andreev, Zhdanov, Malenkov and Shkiriatov. Kosarev and others had dismissed and persecuted a certain Mishakova, an instructor of the Central Committee of the Komsomol, who had denounced a number of Komsomol figures in Chuvashiia.

The memoirs of Akakii Mgeladze, a former Komsomol and, later, Geor-gian Party leader were published in 2001.They were written in the 1960s and concern his meetings with Stalin. Mgeladze recalled that sometime around 1950 he had asked Stalin about Kosarev, whom he had greatly admired. Mgeladze told Stalin that he could not believe the charges against Kosarev, and wondered if a mistake had been made.

Stalin listened quietly, and replied to Mgeladze that everybody made mistakes, including himself (Stalin). But, Stalin continued, the Politburo had discussed the Kosarev case twice, and had assigned Andreev and Zhdanov to verify the charges against him and to check the NKVD reports. Mgeladze then states that he himself had read the transcript of the Komsomol Plenum, including Andreev's and Zhdanov's speeches and Shkiriatov's report, and had found them entirely convincing in their evidence against Kosarev.

Obviously there were serious political charges made against Kosarev. They probably included involvement with Ezhov, who also confessed to being the head of a Right-Trotskyite conspiracy himself. The transcript of the Komsomol Plenum, NKVD investigation reports, and probably much other evidence too, existed in Khrushchev's day, and probably still does. It has never been open to researchers.

In his memoirs, published after he was deposed in 1964, Khrushchev mentions Kosarev, Mishakova and the charges against Kosarev. He says nothing there about any "revenge" by Beria at all.[199] Yet Rudenko's report of August 1954 makes no mention of any of these matters, and everything is blamed on Beria's desire for revenge!

Whatever the truth may be, we can be sure that this isn't it. And this is the rehabilitation report Khrushchev based his speech on.

Rudzutak

IAn Rudzutak was arrested in May 1937, at the same time as Tukhachevsky and the other military leaders, and was accused of being involved with their conspiracy.[200] When Stalin spoke to the Expanded Session of the Military Soviet about the Right-Trotskyite-Tukhachevsky con-

---

[199] Khrushchev, N.S. *Vremia, Liudy, Vlast'* (Time, People, Power). Moscow: 'Moskovskie Novosti', 1999. I, Ch. 11, p. 119. Available at
http://kursk1943.mil.ru/kursk/arch/books/memo/hruschev_ns/11.html

[200] Rudzutak and Tukhachevsky were named in the same Politburo resolution accusing them of participation in an anti-Soviet Right-Trotskyite conspiracy and espionage for Germany, on May 24 1937, and expelled by the Central Committee Plenum on May 25-26 1937 (Lubianka 2, Nos. 86 & 87, p.190).

spiracy, he named Rudzutak as one of the thirteen persons identified to that date.[201]

The rehabilitation report, dated December 24, 1955, says nothing at all about this.[202] We are told that Rudzutak confirmed "anti-Soviet activity" in his preliminary confession but that these confession statements are "contradictory, not concrete (i.e. specific), and unconvincing", and that at trial Rudzutak recanted them, saying that they were "imagined." Nothing at all is said about the involvement with the military conspiracy.

The corresponding short section on Rudzutak in the Pospelov Report[203] is based entirely on this rehabilitation report, adding that "a meticulous verification carried out in 1955 determined that the case against Rudzutak was falsified and he was condemned on the basis of slanderous materials." As we show below, this is false. The rehabilitation report on Rudzutak is a whitewash.

A large number of defendants inculpated Rudzutak. The Rehabilitation report dispenses with these in various ways:

• Some (Magalif, Eikhe, and others) named Rudzutak in their confessions but later recanted their confessions.

The fact that a confession is recanted does not make that recantation more "true" than the original confession.

- Some (Alksnis, German, "and other Soviet and Party workers of Latvian nationality") named Rudzutak, but their investigation had been carried out "with the most serious violations of legality" and so were discounted.

- The rehabilitation report on Iakov Alksnis[204] was not prepared until three weeks later. It says that Alksnis confessed and confirmed his confession at his trial, but says that he did so because he had been tortured, though no details, such as names of investigator – torturers, etc., are given in support of this statement.

---

[201] Stalin's speech is in *Istochnik* No.3, 1994; Lubianka 2, No. 92, pp. 202-209 and is reprinted widely, e.g. http://grachev62.narod.ru/stalin/t14/t14_48.htm

[202] *RKEB* 1, 294-5.

[203] *RKEB* 1, 328-329.

[204] *RKEB* 1, 300-1, January 14 1956.

- Some (Chubar', Knorin, Gamarnik and Bauman) had already been declared innocent, "consequently they could not have had anti-Soviet ties with Rudzutak."

- According to the rehabilitation report on Chubar' himself (251-2) Chubar' had confessed to participating in a Right-Trotskyite conspiracy, and was named by a number of others such as Antipov, who himself was named by Rykov. Chubar also confessed to espionage for Germany. Chubar' also confessed fully at trial, a point we have documented in the body of this book.

- The confessions of Bukharin and Rykov stated only that Rudzutak was a "Rightist" and sympathized with them but was afraid to say so openly.

- The confessions of Krestinsky, Rozengol'ts, Grin'ko, Postnikov, Antipov, Zhukov and others are "extremely contradictory and lacking in concreteness", and "therefore cannot be accepted as evidence of Rudzutak's guilt."

There are a few rhetorical techniques used here that we should note.

- The fact that a confession is recanted does not mean the recantation is "true" and the confession "false." In this case we simply do not know which, if either, statement is true.

- Nor do we know whether Rudzutak recanted all of his confessions, or only a part of them. We actually know that in other cases, like that of Airforce General-Lieutenant Rychagov and former NKVD chief Iagoda, defendants admitted to conspiracy to overthrow the government and to sabotage, but vigorously denied claims that they had spied for Germany.[205] Bukharin too confessed to certain specific serious crimes but firmly denied others.

---

[205] For Rychagov see *RKEB* 1, 165. For Iagoda, see his final statement at the March 1938 "Bukharin" Moscow Trial; English text at *The great purge trial*. Edited, and with notes, by Robert C. Tucker and Stephen F. Cohen. With an introd. by Robert C. Tucker. New

- Chubar' and the other three men had been "rehabilitated", which usually means that their convictions had been set aside for procedural reasons. It is not the same thing as a finding of "innocence", though it was in fact accepted as such.

- There is no basis for dismissing such confessions on the basis of "contradictions." It is to be expected that confessions from many different defendants will have "contradictions" among them. This is far from meaning that they are worthless as evidence. On the contrary: identical confessions from different persons would be highly suspicious.

Rudzutak is named by Grin'ko and Rozengol'ts, and many times by Krestinskii, in the transcript of the March 1938 "Bukharin" trial. The rehabilitation report simply ignores this testimony.

In recently published confessions Rozengol'ts is named both by Ezhov himself and by his associate and relative A.M. Tamarin as having been involved with Ezhov himself in his own Rightist conspiracy. This fact tends to add credence to Rozengol'ts' incrimination of Rudzutak and of others too.

Rudzutak is also named in Rukhimovich's confession of February 8, 1938 (Lubianka 2, No. 290). There's no question that Ezhov and his men were fabricating confessions and forcing defendants to sign them by torturing them, as Frinovskii's recently-published statement confirms. There is eye-witness testimony that Rukhimovich was beaten (Lubianka 2, 656-7), though not by one of Ezhov's men, many of whom were later punished for fabricating confessions.[206] However, the fact that someone was

---

York: Grosset & Dunlap, 1965, p. 675. Russian text at
http://magister.msk.ru/library/trotsky/trotlsud.htm

[206] The eye-witness account says Rukhimovich was beaten by Meshik, later an associate of Beria's and executed with others in December 1953. The rehabilitation report on Rudzutak names Iartsev as a fabricator of one of Rudzutak's confessions, and notes that Iartsev was later executed for such falsifications (p. 295). Iartsev was arrested in June 1939 and executed along with Ezhov and many of Ezhov's NKVD men – under Beria. This would mean the accusation against Meshik, and therefore against Beria, is false. See Nikita Petrov and K.V. Skorkin, *Kto rukovodil NKVD 1934-1941. Spravochnik* (Moscow, 1999). At http://www.memo.ru/history/nkvd/kto/biogr/gb572.htm

beaten does not mean their statements, or confessions, were either true or false.

Kabakov

There is no rehabilitation report on Ivan Kabakov, who was simply included in the list of 36 along with Eikhe and Evdokimov, and no attempt to confront the charges against him. From the materials now available to us today (No. 19), and of course available, along with much more, to Khrushchev in 1956, there is a lot of testimony against Kabakov.

Rykov and Zubarev, both defendants in the March 1938 "Bukharin" Trial, named Kabakov as a conspirator. No one claims these defendants were subject to torture or threats of any kind. This well-known testimony is simply ignored by the Pospelov Report and Khrushchev. The American mining engineer John Littlepage expressed his conviction that Kabakov must have been involved in some kind of sabotage. American scholar John Harris has seen, and quotes from, Kabakov's *delo*, or investigative file. Harris cites no indication that Kabakov's confessions were other than genuine.

Eikhe

Robert I. Eikhe was the first person Khrushchev named as unjustly repressed by Stalin. We have saved Eikhe's case for last because it reveals more than the other cases.

Our section on him (No. 16) details what we know about Eikhe's arrest and trial. As with other defendants neither the Soviet nor Russian authorities have released the investigative file and trial information to researchers. But it is clear that Eikhe himself was involved in large-scale repressions of innocent people, in concert with the NKVD. He was most likely punished for this, among other offenses. The fact that he worked so closely with Ezhov in these repressions would lead any investigator to wonder whether the two were conspiratorially linked – though we cannot be certain without more evidence.

At the end of the section of his speech on Eikhe, Khrushchev says:

> It has been definitely established now that Eikhe's case
> was fabricated; he has been posthumously rehabilitated.

This statement is false. Khrushchev delivered his Speech on February 25, 1956. According to the rehabilitation materials Eikhe was not rehabilitated until March 6. Although Khrushchev devotes more space to Eikhe than to any other repressed Party official there was no rehabilitation report about Eikhe. He was one of 36 repressed Party officials all recommended for rehabilitation **en masse** on March 2 1956.[207] This document is merely a list; there are no details about any specific individual.

The main part, and the only substantive section, of Khrushchev's Speech devoted to Eikhe consists of a long quotation from his letter to Stalin dated October 27, 1939. Without question, this is one of the most emotionally charged sections of the Speech. Eikhe vehemently protests his innocence, recounts how he has been tortured into signing confessions of crimes he never committed, and repeatedly affirms his loyalty to the Party and to Stalin personally.

The impression given is one of a wholly devoted communist going to his death on trumped-up charges. It is damning testimony. Since the full text was finally published in 2002, we can also tell this: as read by Khrushchev the letter was heavily falsified by significant omission.

The parts of Eikhe's "letter to Stalin" of October 27 1939 published in the Pospelov Report are not always the same parts Khrushchev cited in his Speech. Both documents contain significant ellipses from the full text of what is apparently the original letter. I say "apparently", because the published text is acknowledged by its editors to be a copy.

There are no archival identifiers at the end of the document, just the note that the original is in the "Eikhe's archival investigative file." That has no archival identifiers either. That means that the Russian government does not want researchers to know where the Eikhe investigative materials are – if, indeed, they still exist.

Even the compilers and editors of this official volume were not permitted to see the original, or Eikhe's original file![208] We don't know why, but a study of the sections of Eikhe's letter that are not included in either the Pospelov Report or Khrushchev's Speech suggests some possible answers.[209]

---

[207] *Reabilitatsia. Kak Eto Bylo. Fevral' 1956 – Nachalo 80-kh godov.* Ed. Artisov et al. Moscow Materik, 2003, pp. 16-18. Hereafter *RKEB 2.* See pp. 18-19 for the Presidium resolution rehabilitating them.

[208] "Pis'mo R.I. Eikhe I.V. Stalinu" [Letter of R.I. Eikhe to J.V. Stalin], *Doklad Khrushcheva* 225-229.

[209] The following remarks do not pretend to be a comprehensive study of this very important document.

A translation of the full text of Eikhe's letter is appended to this chapter. It is annotated to make it clear which sections are quoted in Khrushchev's Speech, which parts are in the Pospelov Report, and which parts are quoted in both of them. Most important for our purposes, the sections omitted from both the Speech and the Pospelov Report are highlighted.

It is immediately clear that it would not have been useful for Khrushchev's purposes to make the full text of this letter public.

- Eikhe refers to a letter he wrote to "Commissar L.P. Beria" – meaning he wrote it long after his arrest, which took place on April 29, 1938. Beria did not become Commissar until late November 1938, replacing Ezhov.

- Eikhe says that "Commissar Kobulov" had agreed with Eikhe that he could not have invented all the stories of treasonable activity he had confessed to. Kobulov was one of the seven KGB men who were judicially murdered in December 1953 for having been close to Beria. This passage would tend to make Kobulov, and hence Beria, look like responsible men, and so Khrushchev could not permit it to become public.

- Eikhe's letter reveals that he had been accused of conspiracy by a great many other Party officials. He calls all these accusations "provocations" and gives various explanations for them. This naturally suggests that his arrest was warranted. A person named as a co-conspirator by many other conspirators may, in fact, be guilty. Anyone would conclude that the whole investigative file must be examined to determine whether Eikhe was telling the truth or not. Such an examination would have shown that it was Khrushchev who was not telling the truth.

- Eikhe blames two NKVD investigators for torturing (beating) him: Ushakov and Nikolaev-Zhurid. We know something about the activities of these two men. They acted under Ezhov's orders and were arrested, tried and executed for fabricating confessions and torturing arrestees. Both Ushakov and Nikolaev [-Zhurid] wer so closely associated with Ezhov that they were tried and executed at virtually the same time.[210]

- The arrests and investigations of NKVD men who tortured prisoners and fabricated confessions was carried out by Beria. Khrushchev had been the leading figure in the judicial murder of Beria in 1953, and never missed a chance to blame Beria for anything he could. Since in his Speech Khrushchev tries to blame Beria for Eikhe's plight – and for much else Beria did not do – it would not have been in Khrushchev's interest to release the text of Eikhe's letter.

- Likewise, Eikhe's letter makes it clear that some kind of proper investigatorial, i.e. judicial, procedure was now in place. He had been allowed to write to Beria, who was now the head of the NKVD (People's Commissar for Internal Affairs). NKVD investigator Kobulov, one of Beria's men, had expressed some degree of agreement with his, Eikhe's, professions of innocence or, at least, was trying to figure out what was true and what was not. And of course Eikhe had been permitted to write this letter to Stalin, which Khrushchev implies was delivered to its recipient.

- All this implies that Beria, and Stalin as well, were trying to carry out a serious investigation, sort out the rights and wrongs. This is what Khrushchev's audience would have expected of Stalin, at least. But it goes directly contrary to the whole purpose of Khrushchev's Speech, which was to claim that Stalin and Beria did **not** act responsibly.

---

[210] Petrov and Skorkin, op.cit, http://www.memo.ru/history/nkvd/kto/biogr/gb355.htm. Both Nikolaev and Ushakov are on the same "list" of January 16, 1940 as Ezhov; see "Stalinskie rasstrel'nye spiski" [= "Stalin Shooting Lists"] http://stalin.memo.ru/spiski/pg12117.htm and ff.

- Eikhe makes it clear that conspiracies did exist, and names a number of prominent CC members as having been implicated in them or in false accusations against himself. The whole thrust of Khrushchev's Speech is to cast doubt on all conspiracies.

- * Eikhe states that both Evdokimov and Frinovskii implicated him as involved with Ezhov in conspiratorial activities. Eikhe blames Ezhov and Ushakov for having him beaten into false confessions. Eikhe claimed he had no conspiratorial ties with Ezhov, though Frinovskii had said he did.

- Eikhe calls Ezhov an "arrested and exposed counter-revolutionary", raising the issue of Ezhov's own conspiracy. This is a fact only revealed very recently when a single confession statement each by both Ezhov and Frinovskii have been published (February 2006).

There's no reason to doubt that Eikhe was beaten into false confessions by Ezhov's men, for Frinovskii and Ezhov admit to doing just that to many people. But in this case that fact does not necessarily suggest innocence on the part of Eikhe. Frinovskii admits that he and Ezhov fabricated cases against their own men, and had them shot as well, in order to avert any chance that they would "turn" on them when questioned by Beria.

Reproducing Eikhe's whole letter – to say nothing of the whole Eikhe investigation file – would have "muddied the waters" considerably. It would have raised the issue of Ezhov's conspiracy, a story which would have interfered with Khrushchev's goal of blaming everything on Stalin. It would have introduced the names of many other high-raking Party members, revealing that all these cases had to be looked into before the genuine confessions could be separated from the false ones.

- It would have introduced Evdokimov, named by both Frinovskii and Ezhov as a close co-conspirator of theirs. But Evdokimov's name is on the same "rehabilitation" of March 2, 1956 list as Eikhe's!

- Eikhe also names CC members Pramnek, Pakhomov,
  Mezhlauk, and Kosior. He says that Pramnek and
  Pakhomov have falsely implicated him.

A denial of guilt such as Eikhe's letter to Stalin is no more credible in itself than an admission of guilt. Yet the only exculpatory information cited by either Khrushchev or the Pospelov Report were the carefully selected excerpts from Eikhe's letter.

When the full text of this letter is put side by side with the other information about Eikhe's role in mass repressions the conclusion is inescapable: Pospelov and Khrushchev did their best to cover up any evidence that tended to suggest Eikhe's guilt. By doing this they forestalled any serious investigation into Eikhe's case, and by extension into Ezhov's conspiracy.

Eikhe also claims that Stalin had said all CC members were permitted to "acquaint themselves with the special files of the Politburo". Exactly what was in these *osobye papki* was probably not clear to the CC members of 1956. But they would have asked whether **they** themselves had such permission!

It would have made it impossible for Khrushchev to deny to the CC members the right to review the investigation materials on these and other persons – if they had believed they were entitled to do so. And we can be confident that they did not have this right, because even Politburo members like Molotov and Kaganovich had not seen these investigative materials. Presumably this was because Khrushchev denied them access. It is impossible to imagine otherwise how Khrushchev and his supporters could have gotten away with some of the false accusations they made against the "anti-party group" in 1957.

In sum: Eikhe's letter **as a whole** was very damaging to Khrushchev's case. Its contents tend to exculpate both Stalin and Beria and to confirm the existence of a serious conspiracy among at least some CC members, as well as among others. Khrushchev could only cite it if he had made certain beforehand that nobody but his own supporters could see it.

* * * * *

Our examination of these three rehabilitation reports leads us to some conclusions that are important for our study of Khrushchev's Speech.

- The reports ignore a great deal of evidence against
  the persons "rehabilitated."

- They do not subject any of the evidence to a close analysis. Any contradictions among different confessions are considered sufficient to dismiss all of them.

- Until all the investigative materials are made available to researchers we can't know exactly what happened. For our present purposes this isn't necessary. What we can tell is this:

- The rehabilitation reports do not establish the innocence of the persons "rehabilitated."

- These reports did not attempt to determine the truth, but to provide a documentary basis to declare the persons "innocent".

- We have what Khrushchev had; what Pospelov had; and what Rudenko reported to them. The inescapable conclusion of our analysis of this material is that Khrushchev had instructed Rudenko to prepare "whitewashes" – documents that declared the accused innocent, tricked out with as much air of plausibility as necessary.

- When juxtaposed to what else we know about the charges against the defendants, the rehabilitation reports of Postyshev, Kosarev, and Rudzutak cannot stand up to scrutiny. Such a conclusion is consistent with the fact that Khrushchev lied in many other instances in his Speech, as we can now prove.

Eikhe's Letter to Stalin
of October 27, 1939

Text from *Doklad Khrushcheva o Kul'te Lichnosti Stalina na XX S"ezde KPSS. Dokumenty.* Ed. K. Aimermakher et al. Moscow: ROSSPEN, 2002, pp. 225-228.

Bold - Khrushchev's Speech

Italics - Pospelov Report

Bold Italics - both Khrushchev's Speech and the Pospelov Report

Regular Text - omitted from both.

Letfter of R.I. Eikhe to J.V. Stalin

October 27 1939

Top Secret

To Secretary of the CC ACP(b) J.V. Stalin

On October 25 of this year I was informed that the investigation in my case has been concluded and I was given access to the materials of this investigation. Had I been guilty of only one hundredth of the crimes with which I am charged, I would not have dared to send you this pre-execution declaration; however, I have not been guilty of even one of the things with which I am charged and my heart is clean of even the shadow of baseness. I have never in my life told you a word of falsehood, and now, finding my two feet in the grave, I am also not lying. My whole case is a typical example of provocation, slander and violation of the elementary basis of revolutionary legality. I realized as early as September or October 1937 that some kind of foul provocation was being organized against me. In official transcripts of an interrogation of accused persons sent from Krasnoyarsk region in the course of exchange with other regions, including the Novosibirsk NKVD (in the transcript of the accused Shirshov or Orlov) the following clearly provocational question was written: "Haven't you heard about Eikhe's connection to the conspiratorial organization?" and the answer: "The person who recruited me told me that as a youth you were already a member of a counterrevolutionary organization and you'll find out about that later."

This foul provocational trick seemed to me so stupid and clumsy that I did not even consider it necessary to inform the CC CPSU and you about it. But if I had been an enemy, I really could have used this stupid provocation to construct a pretty good coverup for myself. What this provocation meant in my own case only became clear to me long after my arrest, and I have written Commissar Beria about it.

The second source of this provocation is the Novosibirsk prison where, since there is no isolation, enemies who have been exposed and who were arrested at my order remained together, and made plans to spite me and openly agreed that "now we must incriminate those who are incriminating us." According to Gorbach, chief of the NKVD office, this was said by Van'ian, whose arrest I actively pursued in the Commissariat of Transportation. *The confessions which were made part of my file are not only absurd but contain a number of instances of slander toward the Central Committee of the All-Union Communist Party (Bolsheviks) and toward the Council of People's Commissars, because correct resolutions of the Central Committee of the All-Union Communist Party (Bolsheviks) and of the Council of People's Commissars which were not made on my initiative and without my participation are presented as hostile acts of counterrevolutionary organizations made at my suggestion.* This is the case with the confessions of Printsev, Liashenko, Neliubin, Levits and others. In addition during the investigation there was full opportunity to establish the provocational nature of this slander on the spot with documents and facts.

All this is most clear from the confessions about my alleged sabotage in kolkhoz building, specifically that at regional conferences and at plenums of the regional committee of the ACP(b) I argued for the creation of gigantic kolkhozy. All these speeches of mine were transcribed and published, but not a single concrete fact or a single quotation was cited in accusation against me. And no one ever will be able to prove it, because the whole time I worked in Siberia I promulgated the Party's line with determination and without mercy. The kolkhozy in W. Siberia were strong and, when compared to the other grain-producing regions of the Soviet Union, were the best kolkhozy.

You and the CC ACP(b) know how Syrtsov and his cadres who remained in Siberia warred against me. They formed in 1930 a group that the CC ACP(b) smashed and condemned as an unprincipled gang, yet I am accused of supporting this group and of being in the leadership of it after Syrtsov's departure from Siberia. Especially striking is the material about my founding a c.r. Latvian nat. organization in Siberia. One of my principal accusers is the Lithuanian, not Latvian (as far as I know, since I can neither speak nor read Latvian) Turlo, who came to Siberia to work in 1935. But Turlo's confessions about the existence of a c.r. nationalist organization start with 1924 (this is very important if one is to see with what provocational methods the investigation into my case was conducted). In addition to which Turlo does not even state from whom he heard of the existence of the Lat nat counterrevolutionary organization since 1924. According to Turlo's transcript he is a Lithuanian and joined the Latvian nation. c.r. organization with the goal of separating territory from the USSR and uniting it to Latvia. In the confessions of Turlo and Tredzen it is said that a Latvian newspaper in Siberia praised bourgeois Latvia but did not give a single quotation nor identify a single issue. I must speak separately about the accusations of ties with the German consul and of espionage.

The confessions concerning banquets at the consul's and my supposed moral corruption of the Party activists are given by the accused Vaganov, who arrived in Siberia in 1932 or 1933. They begin with 1923 (this is the result of the same provocation as in Turlo's confessions), the description of banquetmania, moral corruption, etc., again without indication of anyone from whom he learned this. The truth is this: when I was chairman of the area executive committee and there was no representative of the Commissariat of Foreign Affairs, I would attend receptions at the consul's twice a year (on the day of ratification of the Weimar constitution and on the day the Treaty of Rapallo was signed). But I did this on the recommendation of the Commissariat of Foreign Affairs. I did not host banquets in return and the inappropriateness and incorrectness of such behavior was even indicated to me. I never went hunting with the consul and permitted no moral corruption of the activists. The housekeeper who lived with us, the workers of the economic section of the area executive committee, and the chauffeurs who drove with me in my auto can confirm the accuracy of my words. The clumsiness of these accusations is also obvious from the fact that, if I had been a German spy, then German intelligence would have been obliged to categorically forbid any public association with the consul, in order to maintain my cover. But I have never been either a c.r. or a spy. Every spy, naturally, must strive to acquaint himself with the most secret decisions and directives. You have told the members of the Central Committee many times in my presence that every CC member has the right to acquaint himself with the special files ["osobye papki" – GF] of the P.B., but I have never consulted the special files, and Poskrebyshev can confirm that.

In his own confessions Gailit, former commander of the Siberian Military District, confirms the provocation about my spying, and I am forced to describe to you how these confessions were fabricated.

In May 1938 Major Ushakov was reading me an excerpt from Gailit's confessions that on a free day Gailit had seen me walking together with the German consul and he, Gailit, understood that I was transmitting to the consul sec information I had received from him. When I pointed out to Ushakov that beginning in 1935 a commissar and NKVD intelligence accompanied me, they tried to add in that I had escaped them by car. But when it was made clear to them that I do not know how to drive, they left me alone. Now in my case file a transcript of Gailit has been inserted from which that part has been excised.

Pramnek confesses that he established c.r. ties with me during the January 1938 plenum of the CC ACP(b). This is a bald-faced lie. I have never spoken with Pramnek about anything, and during the January plenum of the CC ACP(b), after he finished his report right there in front of the tribunal in a group of secretaries of regional committees, who demanded to be given a time when they could come to the PCA to decide a number of questions, the following conversation took place. Pramnek asked me when he could come to the PCA and I gave him an appointment for the next day after 12 o'clock at night, but he did not come. Pramnek lies that I was sick then, it can be established through the secretaries and the commissar of the NKVD that, starting the 11th of January, the day I got out of the hospital, I was in the Commissariat every day until 3-4 o'clock in the morning. The monstrous nature of this slander is also clear from the fact that an experienced conspirator such as I fearlessly established contact through Mezhlauk's word a month after Mezhlauk's arrest.

N.I. Pakhomov confesses that even at the time of the June 1937 plenum of the CC ACP(b) he and Pramnek were discussing how to make use of me as Commissar of Agriculture for the c.r. organization. I only learned of my proposed appointment from you at the end of the October 1937 plenum and after the end of the plenum I remember that not all members of the Pb knew about this proposal. How is it possible to believe the kind of provocational slander that is in Pakhomov's and Pramnek's confessions?

Evdokimov says he found out about my participation in the conspiracy in August 1938 and that Ezhov told him he was taking steps to preserve my life.

In June 1938 Ushakov inflicted cruel torment on me so that I would confess to an attempt to kill Ezhov, and these confessions of mine were formulated by Nikolaev with Ezhov's knowledge. Could Ezhov have acted in this way if there were even one word of truth in what Evdokimov says?

I was at Ezhov's dacha together with Evdokimov, but Ezhov never called me either friend or supporter and did not embrace me. Malenkov and Poskrebyshev, who were there too, can confirm this.

In his confessions Frinovskii opens yet another source of provocation in my case. He confesses that, supposedly, he found out about my participation in the conspiracy from Ezhov in April 1937, and that Mironov (chief of the NKVD in Novosibirsk) was asking Ezhov in a letter at that time that he, Mironov, "could come out on Eikhe" concerning the conspiracy, as a participant in the conspiratorial organization. Mironov only arrived in Siberia at the end of March 1937, and without any materials had already received Ezhov's preliminary sanction on whom to conduct a provocation. Anybody can understand that what Frinovskii confesses is no attempt to protect me, but is rather the organization of a provocation against me. Above I have stressed, in the confessions of Turlo and Vaganov, the year with which they begin their confessions regardless of the clumsiness. *It should have been pointed out to Ushakov, who was chief investigator on my case, that the false confessions beaten out of me were contradicted by the confessions in Siberia, and my confessions were being transmitted by telephone to Novosibirsk.*

This was done with blatant cynicism and in my presence Lieutenant Prokof'ev ordered a telephone call to Novosibirsk. **Now I have come to the most disgraceful part of my life and to my really grave guilt against the party and against you. This is my confession of counterrevolutionary activity.** *Commissar Kobulov told me that no one could just think all of this up and really I never could have thought it up.* **Here is what happened: Not being able to endure the tortures to which I was submitted by Ushakov and Nikolaev and especially by the former who utilized the knowledge that my broken vertebra have not properly mended and have caused me great pain, I have been forced to accuse myself and others.**

The greater part of my confession has been suggested or dictated by Ushakov, and the remainder is my reconstruction of NKVD materials from Western Siberia for which I assumed all responsibility. If some part of the story which Ushakov fabricated and which I signed did not properly hang together, I was forced to sign another variation. The same thing was done to Rukhimovich, who was at first designated as a member of the reserve net and whose name later was re-

moved without telling me anything about it; the same was also done with the leader of the reserve net, supposedly created by Bukharin in 1935. At first I wrote my name in and then I was instructed to insert V.I. Mezhlauk. There were other similar incidents.

I must pause especially on the provocational legend of the treason of the Latvian SPC in 1918. This legend was wholly invented by Ushakov and Nikolaev. There never was any tendancy favoring separation from Russia among the Latv Soc Dems and I and the whole generation of workers of my age were educated in Russian literature and in revolutionary and Bolshevik legal and underground publications. The question of a separate state soviet body such as a Latvian soviet soc. republic seemed so wild to me as to many others that at the first congress of soviets in Riga I took a stand against it and I was not alone. The decision concerning the establishment of a soviet republic was only taken after it had been announced that that was the decision of the CC RCP(b).

I only worked for about two weeks in soviet Latvia and at the end of November of 1918 I left to do provision work in the Ukraine and was there until the collapse of soviet power in Latvia. Riga fell because it was in fact almost surrounded by the Whites. In Estonia the Whites were victorious and occupied Balk. The Whites also took Vil'no and Mitava and were advancing on Dvinsk. In this connection it had already been proposed in March 1919 to evacuate Riga, but it held out until May 15 1919.

I have never been at any c.r. meetings with either Kosior or Mezhlauk. Those meetings indicated in my confessions took place in the presence of a number of other people who could also be questioned. My confession of c.r. ties with Ezhov is the blackest spot on my conscience. *I gave these false confessions when the investigator had reduced me to the point of losing consciousness by interrogating me for 16 hours. When he stated, as an ultimatum, that I should choose between two handles (one of a pen and the other of a rubber truncheon) then I, believing they had brought me to the new prison in order to shoot me, once again demonstrated the greatest cowardice and gave slanderous confessions. I did not care what crimes I took upon myself as long as they shot me as soon as possible. But to subject myself again to* beatings for that arrested and exposed c.r. Ezhov, who had doomed me who had never done anything criminal, *was beyond my strength.*

This is the truth about my case and about myself. Each step of my life and work can be verified and no on will ever find anything other than devotion to the Party and to you.

I am asking and begging you that you again examine my case, and this not for the purpose of sparing me but in order to unmask the vile provocation which, like a snake, has wound itself around many persons in part also because of my cowardice and criminal slander. I have never betrayed you or the party. I know that I perish because of the vile, base work of the enemies of the party and of the people, who have fabricated the provocation against me. My dream has been and remains the wish to die for the party and for you.

Eikhe

The genuine statement is located
in Eikhe's archival investigative file

"Rehabilitation by List"

MEMORANDUM OF I.A. SEROV AND R.A. RUDENKO TO THE
CC CPSU CONCERINING THE REVIEW OF THE CASES AND
THE REHABILITATION OF MEMBERS AND CANDIDATE
MEMBERS OF THE CC AUCP(b) CHOSEN AT THE 17TH CON-
GRESS OF THE AUCP(b)

March 2 1956

CC CPSU

Having reviewed the cases of those members and candidate members of
the CC AUCP(b) elected at the 17th Party Congress who were convicted,
the Committee for State Security [KGB] of the Council of Ministers of
the USSR and the Procuracy of the USSR have determined that the majority of these cases were falsified by the investigative organs, and that the
so-called confessions of guilt of the persons arrested were obtained as the
result of serious beatings and provocations.

Having reported this, we believe it expedient to propose that the Military
Collegium of the Supreme Court of the USSR review and posthumously
rehabilitate the illegally condemned persons listed below:

1. Kosior Stanislav Vikent'evich – former vice-chairman of the Council
of People's Commissars of the USSR, member of the CPSU from 1907.

2. Eikhe Robert Indrikovich – former People's Commissar for Agriculture of the USSR, member of the CPSU from 1905.

3. Bubnov Andrei Sergeevich – former People's Commissar for Education of the RSFSR [the Russian Republic], member of the CPSU from
1903.

4. Evdokimov Efim Georgievich – former secretary of the Azov-Black
Sea Regional Committee of the Party, member of the CPSU from 1918.

…

6. Kabakov Ivan Dmitrievich – former secretary of the Sverdlovsk *oblast'*
committee of the Party, member of the CPSU from 1914.

…

14. Rukhimovich Moisei L'vovich – former People's Commissar for the
Defense Industry of the RSFSR, member of the CPSU from 1913.

…

The cases concerning the accusations of other members and candidate members of the CC AUCP(b), members of the Commission of Party Control, of Soviet Control, and of the Central Review Commission, who were elected at the 17ᵗʰ Party Congress, will also be reviewed and reported to the CC CPSU.

We request a decision.

Chairman of the Committee for State Security
Of the Council of Ministers of the USSR
I. Serov
The General Procuror [Prosecutor] of the USSR
R. Rudenko

The rehabilitation decree from the Presidium of the CC CPSU followed without delay:

"March 5 1956

No. 3.II.54 – Concerning the Posthumous rehabilitation of illegally condemned members of the CC AUCP(b) elected at the 17th Party Congress.

To confirm the proposal of the Chairman of the Committee for State Security of the Council of Ministers of the USSR com. Serov and the General Procuror of the USSR com. Rudenko concerning the review of the cases and posthumous rehabilitation of the illegally condemned members of the CC AUCP(b) and candidate members of the CC AUCP(b), elected at the 17ᵗʰ Congress of the Party: Kosior S.V., Eikhe R.I., Bubnov A.S., Evdokimov E.G., ...Kabakov I.D., ...Rukhimovich M.

Chapter 12.

Conclusion: The Enduring Legacy

of Khrushchev's Deception

For decades it's been assumed that Khrushchev attacked Stalin for the reasons he set forth in the "Secret Speech." But now that we have established that Khrushchev's accusations, or "revelations", against Stalin in the Speech are false, the question returns with even greater force: What was really going on?

Why Did Khrushchev Attack Stalin?

Why **did** Khrushchev attack Stalin? What were his real motives? The reasons he stated cannot be the true ones. The "revelations" Khrushchev made are false, and Khrushchev either knew this (in most cases), or did not care.

Khrushchev had some kind of real motives, but it was precisely those that he remained silent about in his Speech at the 20th Party Congress and, for that matter, for the rest of his life. In other words, "behind" the "Secret Speech" known to the world there is a **second,** and real "secret speech" – one that **remained** "secret," undelivered. My purpose in this essay is to raise this question rather than to answer it. I'll simply mention a few possibilities and areas for further inquiry, some obvious, others less so.

Surely Khrushchev wanted to forestall anybody's dragging up his own role in the unjustified mass repressions of the 1930s by shifting the blame onto Stalin and initiating "rehabilitations." He probably surmised that the "rehabilitations' would make him popular in much of the Party elite, irrespective of whether those "rehabilitated" had been guilty or not. Even, perhaps, in Moscow and the Ukraine, where his reputation as architect of mass repressions was well earned and widely known, shifting the blame onto the dead Stalin while vindicating those repressed and, just as importantly, their surviving families, would mitigate the animosity many must have held for him.

Khrushchev's Speech has hitherto been taken at face value. The research published here proves that it is an error to do so. That leaves us with a number of questions. Why did Khrushchev give his speech? Why did he go to such lengths – phony research, hiding genuine documents, – and make such political sacrifices, in order to deliver a speech that was, for all practical purposes, nothing **but** falsehoods?

The Chinese Communist Party came up with one answer. They believed that Khrushchev and his allies wanted to lead the USSR onto a sharply different political trajectory than they believed it had taken under Stalin. We have briefly alluded to some economic and political policies instituted under Khrushchev that the CCP leadership saw as an abandonment of basic Marxist-Leninist principles.

There has to be some truth in this theory. But a base for such ideas already existed in the USSR. The origins of these policies, now identified with Khrushchev and his epigones Brezhnev and the rest, lie in the immediate post-Stalin period, long before Khrushchev came to dominate the Soviet leadership. In fact, many of them can be traced back to the late 1940s and early 1950s, the "late Stalin" period.

It is difficult to discern to what extent Stalin himself supported or opposed these policies. **In his last years he was less and less active politically.** Periodically it seems as though Stalin did try to assert a different path towards communism, – in his last book *Economic Problems of Socialism in the USSR* (1952), for example, and at the 19th Party Congress in October 1952. Later, Mikoian wrote that Stalin's late views were "an incredibly leftist deviation".[211] But immediately after Stalin died the "collective leadership" all agreed on dropping all mention of Stalin's book and on dumping the new system of Party governance.

Khrushchev used his attack on Stalin and Beria as a weapon against the others in the "collective leadership", especially Malenkov, Molotov, and Kaganovich. This course was fraught with risk, however. How could he have known that they would not accuse him equally, or even more so? Part of the reason must have been that Khrushchev was able to rely on allies like Pospelov, who helped him "purge" the archives of documentation of his own participation in mass repressions

Khrushchev may have also realized that with Beria gone he alone had a

---

[211] "Neveroiatno levatskii zagib." Mikoian, *Tak Bylo*, Ch. 46: "On the Eve of and During the 19th Party Congress: Stalin's Last Days."

"program": a plan and the initiative to carry it out. We can see in retro-
spect that the other Presidium members were amazingly passive during
this period. Perhaps they had always relied on Stalin to take the initiative,
to make important decisions. Or perhaps that seeming passivity hid a
struggle of political ideas confined to the leadership body.

Historian Iuri Zhukov has set forth a third theory. In his view Khrushchev's aim was to decisively close the door on democratic reforms with
which Stalin was associated and which Stalin's former allies in the Presidium (until October 1952 called the Politburo), especially Malenkov,
were still trying to promote. Those reforms aimed at removing the Party
from control over politics, the economy and culture and putting these in
the hands of the elected Soviets. This would have been a virtual
"perestroika", or "restructuring", but within the limits of socialism as
opposed to the full-blown restoration of predatory capitalism to which
Gorbachev's later "perestroika" led.

Zhukov details a number of moments in the struggle between Stalin and
his allies, who wanted to remove the party from the levers of power, and
the rest of the Politburo, who firmly opposed this. In May 1953, shortly
after Stalin's death, the executive branch of the Soviet government, the
Council (Soviet) of Ministers, passed resolutions depriving leading Party
figures of their "envelopes", or extra pay, **reducing their income to a
level or two lower than their corresponding government figures.**
According to Zhukov, Malenkov promoted this reform. It is consistent
with the project of turning power over to the Soviet government and
downgrading the role of the Party, getting the Party out of the running of
the country, economy and culture. Significantly, it was done before the
illegal repression of Lavrentii Beria who, we now know, supported this
same project.

In late June 1953 Beria was repressed, either by arrest and imprisonment
or by outright murder. In August Khrushchev managed – how, we do
not know – to reinstate the "envelopes" of special bonuses to high-
ranking Party functionaries and even to get them the three months back
pay they had missed. Three weeks later, at the very end of a Central
Committee Plenum, the post of First Secretary of the Party was reinstated (until 1934 it had been called 'General Secretary') and Khrushchev was elected to it. It is hard not to see this as the Party *nomenklatura's*
reward for "their man."

Zhukov concludes:

> It is my firm conviction that the true meaning of the 20th Congress lies precisely in this return of the Party apparatus to power. It was the necessity to hide this fact ... that necessitated distracting attention from contemporary events and concentrating them on the past with the aid of the "secret report" [Secret Speech – GF][212]

The first two explanations, the anti-revisionist or "Chinese" and the "power struggle" explanations, surely contain elements of truth. In my view, however, Zhukov's theory best accounts for the facts at hand while also remaining consistent with the contents of the Secret Speech and the fact that, as we have discovered, it is virtually entirely false.

Stalin and his supporters had championed a plan of democratization of the USSR through contested elections. Their plan seems to have been to move the locus of power in the USSR from Party leaders like Khrushchev to elected government representatives. Doing this would also have laid the groundwork for restoring the Party as an organization of dedicated persons struggling for communism rather than for careers or personal gain.[213] Khrushchev appears to have had the support of the Party First Secretaries, who were determined to sabotage this project and perpetuate their own positions of privilege.

Khrushchev pursued policies, both internal and external, that contemporary observers recognized as a sharp break from those identified with Stalin's leadership. In fact similar policy changes not identical to those initiated or championed later by Khrushchev but broadly congruent with them were begun immediately after Stalin's death, when Khrushchev himself was still just another member, and not the most important one, of the Presidium of the Central Committee.[214] Among the "reforms"

---

[212] IU. N. Zhukov, "Krutoi povorot...nazad" ("A sharp turn ... backwards"), *XX S"ezd. Materialy konferentsii k 40-letiiu XX s"ezda KPSS. Gorbachev-Fond, 22 fevralia 1996 goda.* Moscow: April-85, 1996, pp. 31-39; quotation on p. 39. This was the only presentation to which Gorbachev himself personally responded in sharp disagreement. Also at http://www.gorby.ru/activity/conference/show_553/view_24755/

[213] I have outlined this hypothesis at some length in "Stalin and the Struggle for Democratic Reform", *Cultural Logic* 2005. At http://clogic.eserver.org/2005/2005.html

[214] Indeed the "post-Stalin 'Thaw'" can be said to have begun during Stalin's lifetime, at least as far as culture was concerned. This idea is developed by the late historian Vadim Kozhinov, in Chapter 8 of *Rossiia: Vek XX (1939-1964)*. (Moscow: EKSMO / Algoritm, 2005), "On the so-called 'Thaw'", pp. 309-344.

most often cited that went directly contrary to Stalin's long-held policies
were

- A shift towards "market"-oriented reforms;
- A concomitant shift away from heavy industry and
  the manufacture of the means of production, towards
  consumer-goods production;
- In international politics, a shift away from the
  traditional Marxist-Leninist concept that war with
  imperialism was inevitable as long as imperialism
  exists, to the avoidance of any direct warfare with
  imperialism at all costs;
- A de-emphasis on the working class as the vanguard
  of social revolution in order to emphasize building
  alliances with other classes;
- A new notion that capitalism itself could be
  overcome without revolution by "peaceful
  competition" and through parliamentary means;
- An abandonment of Stalin's plans for moving on to
  the next stage of socialism and towards true
  communism.

Khrushchev could not have taken power, nor his "Secret Speech" been
conceived, researched, delivered and had the success it did, without profound changes in Soviet society and the Communist Party of the Soviet
Union.[215]

The Khrushchev Conspiracy?

Elsewhere Zhukov has argued that it was the First Secretaries, led by
Robert Eikhe, who seem to have initiated the mass repressions of 1937-
1938.[216] Khrushchev, one of these powerful First Secretaries, was himself
very heavily involved in large-scale repression, including the execution of
thousands of people.

Many of these First Secretaries were themselves later tried and executed.

---

[215] Before 1952 the party's name was the All-Union Communist Party (Bolsheviks).

[216] I have briefly summarized and discussed Zhukov's theory, citing all his relevant books
and articles, in the two-part series "Stalin and the Struggle for Democratic Reform", in
Cultural Logic for 2005. At http://clogic.eserver.org/2005/2005.html

Some of them, like Kabakov, were accused of being part of a conspiracy. Others, like Postyshev, were accused, at least initially, of mass, unwarranted repression of Party members. Eikhe also seems to fall into this group. Later many of these men were also charged with being part of various conspiracies themselves. Khrushchev was one of the few First Secretaries during the years 1937-38 not only to escape such charges, but to have been promoted.   *Stalin liked him*

Might it be that Khrushchev **was** part of such a conspiracy – but was one of the highest-ranking members to have remained undetected? We can't prove or disprove this hypothesis. But it would explain all the evidence we now have.

Khrushchev's Speech has been described as aiming at the rehabilitation of Bukharin. Some of the figures in the 1938 "Bukharin" Moscow Trial were in fact rehabilitated. So it would have been logical to include Bukharin. But this was not done. Khrushchev himself wrote that he wanted to rehabilitate Bukharin, but did not because of opposition from some of the foreign communist leaders. Mikoian wrote that the documents had already been signed, but that it was Khrushchev who reneged.[217]

Of all the figures in the three big Moscow Trials, why would Khrushchev want to rehabilitate Bukharin specifically? He must have felt strong loyalty towards Bukharin more than he did towards others. Perhaps this loyalty was only to Bukharin's ideas. But it is not the only possible explanation.

Since Khrushchev's day, but especially since the formal rehabilitation under Gorbachev in 1988, Bukharin's "innocence" has been taken for granted. In a recently published article Vladimir L. Bobrov and I have shown that there is no reason to think this is true.[218] The evidence we have – only a small fraction of what the Soviet government had in the 1930s – overwhelmingly suggests that Bukharin was in fact involved in a

---

[217] Khrushchev, N.S., *Vremia, Liudi, Vlast'. Vospominania.* ("Times, People, Power: Memoirs"). (Moscow, 1999), Book 2, Part 3, p. 192. Anastas Mikoian, *Tak Bylo* ("That's How It Was"). Moscow: Vagrius, 1999. Chapter 49, "Khrushchev u Vlasti" (Khrushchev in power) , print version p. 611.

[218] Grover Furr and Vladimir L. Bobrov, "Nikolai Bukharin's First Statement of Confession in the Lubianka". *Cultural Logic* 2007. At

http://clogic.eserver.org/2007/Furr_Bobrov.pdf This article was first published in the Russian historical journal *Klio* 1 (36), 2005, 38-52. I have put the Russian version online at http://chss.montclair.edu/english/furr/research/furrnbobrov_bukharin_klio07.pdf

wide-ranging conspiracy. In another study recently published in Russian[219] we have demonstrated that the Gorbachev-era decree of rehabilitation of Bukharin by the Plenum of the Soviet Supreme Court, issued on February 4, 1988, contains deliberate falsifications.

According to this theory Bukharin told the truth in his confession at the March 1938 Moscow Trial. But we know that Bukharin did not tell the **whole** truth. Getty has suggested that Bukharin did not begin to confess until after Tukhachevsky had confessed, and the imprisoned Bukharin could have reasonably known about that – at which time he named Tukhachevsky.

Evidence exists that Bukharin knew of other conspirators whom he did not name. Frinovskii claimed Ezhov himself was one of them.[220] This appears credible in the light of the evidence about Ezhov that we now have at our disposal. Could Khrushchev also have been one of these – whether known to Bukharin or not? If he had been, he would have been a highly-placed conspirator, and therefore very secret.

From what we can tell now, Khrushchev "repressed" a huge number of people – perhaps more than any other individual aside from Ezhov and his men, and perhaps Robert Eikhe. Perhaps that was because he was First Secretary in Moscow (city and province) until January 1938, and thereafter First Secretary in the Ukraine. These are two large areas. Given a party-based conspiracy, or suspicion of one, it would be logical that it would have been strong in Moscow, while the Ukraine had always had its share of nationalist opposition.

Frinovskii stated flatly that he and Ezhov "repressed" – tortured, fabricated phony confessions of, and judicially murdered – a great many people in order to appear more loyal than the loyal and thereby to cover up their own conspiratorial activities. This admission by Frinovskii is not only credible; it is the only explanation that makes any sense. Ezhov himself cited the additional motive of spreading dissatisfaction with the Soviet system in order to facilitate rebellions in the event of foreign invastion.[221]

[219] "Reabilitatsionnoe moshenichestvo", in Grover Furr and Vladimir Bobrov, *1937. Pravosudie Stalina. Obzhalovaniiu ne podlezhit!* (Moscow: Eksmo, 2010). Glava 2, 64-84.

[220] *Lubianka 3*, p. 47.

[221] See Ezhov's interrogation-confession of August 4 1939 in Nikita Petrov, Mark Jansen. *"Stalinskii pitomets" – Nikolai Ezhov.* Moscow: ROSSPEN, 2008, pp. 367-379. English translation at http://chss.montclair.edu/english/furr/research/ezhov080439eng.html

It appears that Postyshev and Eikhe, two First Secretaries who repressed many innocent people, acted from like motives, and we know Eikhe, at least, worked closely with Ezhov in so doing. May not other First Secretaries have also acted in this way? Specifically, may not Khrushchev have organized massive frameups, kangaroo trials, and executions, in order to cover up his own participation?

Alternative explanations are: (1) several hundred thousand people were in fact guilty of conspiracy; or (2) these people were simply massacred because "Stalin was paranoid" – i.e. wanted to kill anyone who *might* be a danger sometime in the future. But we know that it was **Khrushchev,** not Stalin and the Politburo, who took the initiative in demanding higher "limits" of numbers of persons to be repressed. And no one has ever claimed Khrushchev was "paranoid."

Anti-communists, Trotskyites, and adherents to the "totalitarian" paradigm have normally embraced the "paranoid" explanation, even though it really "explains" nothing but is, rather, an excuse for a lack of an explanation. But we know now that this is not so. Not Stalin, but the CC members – and, specifically, the First Secretaries – initiated the mass repressions and executions.

Frinovskii explicitly claims that Bukharin knew Ezhov was a part of the "Right-Trotskyite" conspiracy but refused to name Ezhov in his confessions or at trial. Frinovskii claims this was because Ezhov had told Bukharin that he would be spared in return for his silence. This is possible – though it is an explanation that does no credit to Bukharin who was, after all, a Bolshevik, veteran of the very bloody days of the October revolution of 1917 in Moscow.

Underground revolutionaries sometimes went to execution rather than inform on all their comrades. Why not concede that Bukharin might have refused to name Ezhov for this reason alone? We know that Bukharin had not, in fact, told the "whole truth" in **any** of his statements previous to his trial. Why not – unless he were still not "disarmed", were still fighting against Stalin? Bukharin's cringing professions to "love" Stalin "wisely"[222] are embarrassing to read. They cannot have been sincere, and

---

[222] Bukharin's letter to Stalin of December 10, 1937, was published in **two** major Russian historical journals in the same year. For the passage cited, see "Poslednoe pis'mo," *Rodina* 2, 1993, p. 52 col. 2; "'Prosti menia, Koba…' Neizvestnoe pis'mo N. Bukharina," *Istochnik* 0, 1993, p. 23 col. 2. It is translated in Getty & Naumov, *Road to Terror*, pp. 556 ff; quoted passage on p. 557.

Stalin could hardly have believed them any more than we can today.

We have seen that Bukharin only named Tukhachevsky **after** he could have known the latter was under arrest and had confessed. If Bukharin, for whatever motive, went to his execution without naming Ezhov as a co-conspirator – as Frinovskii later claimed – why should he not have protected other co-conspirators as well?

We can't know for certain whether Khrushchev were one of these hidden conspirators, or that Bukharin knew about him. But we do know that anti-government conspirators continued to exist in the USSR **after** 1937-38,[223] and that some of them were in high positions. We know too that Khrushchev remained loyal to Bukharin even long after the latter was dead.

The hypothesis that Khrushchev may have been a secret member of one branch of the many-branched "Right-Trotskyite conspiracy" is enhanced by the fact that he was certainly involved in a number of **other** conspiracies that we do know of.

- On March 5 1953, with Stalin not yet dead, the old Politburo members met and abolished the enlarged Presidium which had been approved at the 19th Party Congress the previous October. This was virtually a *coup d'état* within the Party, neither voted on, nor even discussed, by the Presidium or Central Committee.

- Khrushchev was the moving force behind the conspiracy to "repress" – to arrest, perhaps murder – Lavrentii Beria. We know that this arrest was not planned much in advance, because Malenkov's draft speech for the Presidium meeting at which the arrest (or murder) occurred has been published. That draft speech calls only for Beria's removal as head of the combined MVD-MGB and as Vice-Chairman of the Council of Ministers, and Beria's appointment as Minister of the Petroleum Industry.

- Since Khrushchev was able to deny other members of the Presidium access to the documents studied by the Pospelov Report and rehabilitation commissions,

[223] For one example see Grigory Tokaev, *Comrade X*. London: Harvill Press, 1956.

> he had to head another conspiracy of persons who
> would feed information to him but not to others.

This conspiracy had to include Pospelov, who wrote the Report. It had to include Rudenko as well, because he signed all the major rehabilitation reports. Research on how the rehabilitation and Pospelov Commission reports were prepared has yet to be done. Presumably the other members of the rehabilitation commissions, plus the researchers and archivists who located the documents for these reports and for Pospelov, were sworn to silence, or were in fact part of the conspiracy too.

We do know the names and a little about some of the people who, supposedly, reviewed the investigation materials. For example we know a certain Boris Viktorov was one of the jurists involved in the rehabilitations. Viktorov at least one article about his work, in *Pravda* on April 29, 1988, the purpose of which was to reaffirm the innocence of Marshal Tukhachevsky and the other military commanders convicted with him on June 11, 1937. In 1990 Viktorov published a book claiming to give details about many other repressions.

His account is certainly a dishonest coverup. Viktorov **asserts** their innocence, but cannot **demonstrate** it. He quotes a disputed document and ignores some damning evidence that he himself certainly would have seen and that had not been made public when he wrote but which we now have. So Viktorov at least was part of the "conspiracy" to provide Khrushchev with phony evidence that those discussed in the Speech were, in fact, innocent.

There is general agreement that after he took power Khrushchev had the archives searched and many documents removed and doubtless destroyed.[224] The same scholars agree that these documents probably had to do with Khrushchev's own role in the massive repressions of the late 1930s. Now that we know Khrushchev falsified virtually every statement in his Secret Speech, and that the rehabilitation reports and Pospelov Report are heavily falsified too, it seems likely that Khrushchev had other documents removed as well.

---

[224] IU. N. Zhukov, "Zhupel Stalina… Chast' 3". *Komsomol'skaia Pravda* Nov. 12 2002; Nikita Petrov, *Pervyi predsedatel' KGB Ivan Serov*. Moscow: Materik, 2005, pp. 157-162; Mark IUnge and R. Binner, *Kak terror stal "Bal'shim". Sekretnyi prikaz No. 00447 i tekhnologiia eto ispolneniia*. Moscow: AIRO-XX, 2003, p. 16. For convenience I have repeated these references in my discussion of No. 28, the "Torture Telegram".

This is a big job, and would have taken a lot of archivists, who would have to have been supervised. It seems too big a job to have been supervised by Rudenko and Pospelov alone. A large number of researchers and officials, including of course Party officials loyal to Khrushchev but as yet unknown to us, would have had to be involved. Naturally **those** people would have known what evidence Khrushchev was hiding or destroying.

Aleksandr S. Shcherbakov

In January 1938 Khrushchev had been removed as First Secretary of the Moscow City and Oblast' Party and sent to be First Secretary in the Ukraine. Replacing him in Moscow was Alexandr Sergeevich Shcherbakov.

In his memoirs Khrushchev shows real hatred for Shcherbakov, though the reasons Khrushchev cites are vague ones. The recent biography of Shcherbakov by A.N. Ponomarev published by the Central Moscow Archive examines Khrushchev's hostility in some detail. According to this study Khrushchev's hatred for Shcherbakov can be traced to the latter's refusal to permit Khrushchev to inflate harvest figures by double-counting seed grain as harvest grain.[225]

More threatening to Khrushchev was Shcherbakov's role in the appeals process whereby 90% of appeals by Party members expelled by Khrushchev in 1937-38, when Khrushchev headed the Moscow Oblast' and City Committees, were reinstated, more than 12,000 for the year 1937 alone. What Ponomarev leaves unsaid is that a great many of those Party members had been executed, their appeals brought forward by their families.[226]

Khrushchev was, of course, a member of the *troika* that decided upon these massive repressions, though he was sometimes represented by a deputy. **All** of the other Moscow *troika* members were executed for illegal repressions. It's logical to conclude that Khrushchev himself felt extremely vulnerable. Few, if any, other First Secretaries (Khrushchev was by 1939 in the Ukraine) had been responsible for as many expulsions and

---

[225] A.N. Ponomarev. *Aleksandr Shcherbakov. Stranitsy biografii.* M: Izd. Glavarkhiva Moskvy, 2004, p. 49.

[226] Ponomarev specifically gives the example of "troika" NKVD decisions appealed and heard in April 1939. Of the 690 protests, the judges reviewed 130 in April 1939 and reinstated all but 14 – about 90%.

executions – as much "repression" – as he had been.

Ponomarev cites other evidence of Shcherbakov's coolness towards Khrushchev as well. At the 18th Party Congress in 1939 Shcherbakov gave a report in which he pointedly failed to mention his predecessor Khrushchev even once. Georgii Popov, second secretary under both Khrushchev and Shcherbakov, pointedly did praise Khrushchev in his speech – a fact that highlighted Shcherbakov's silence.[227]

Using testimony from Shcherbakov's family as well as evidence from Moscow archives Ponomarev takes pains to refute a number of accusations against Shcherbakov that Khrushchev made in his memoirs – for example, his allegation that Shcherbakov was a serious alcoholic.[228] According to his children, Shcherbakov seldom drank at all.[229] Ponomarev details Khrushchev's two-faced behavior towards Shcherbakov's family after the latter's death. Khrushchev was friendly to them while Stalin lived. But once in power Khrushchev deprived them of their *dacha* and cancelled all memorials to Shcherbakov.

Certainly, Khrushchev was a snake; to use the language Khrushchev himself used against the dead Shcherbakov, he had a "poisonous, serpent-like character."[230] Anastas Mikoian, though a close political ally, denounced Khrushchev as very dishonest and disloyal towards people, and also dishonest in his recounting of historical facts.[231] But why was Khrushchev so vindictive towards Shcherbakov and his family? Why did he clearly hate Shcherbakov so much?

In his memoirs Khrushchev does not mention that Shcherbakov had been instrumental in unmasking A.V. Snegov as a conspirator in 1937. Khrushchev later became very friendly with Snegov, got him released

---

[227] Ponomarev, pp. 51-2. Popov was not spared Khrushchev's wrath in later years and wrote about Khrushchev in strongly negative terms in his memoir. See Taranov, *"Partiinii gubernator Moskvy Georgii Popov.* Moscow: Izd. Glavarkhiva Moskvy, 2004.

[228] Khrushchev, N.S. *Vremia. Liudy. Vlast'.* Kn. 2. Chast' III, p. 41.

[229] Ponomarev, pp. 204-5. The allegation seems dubious on other grounds as well. During the war Shcherbakov was a candidate member of the Politburo, acted as Stalin's replacement on the Defense Committee, was Political Commissar of the Red Army, and in charge of all the organs of war propaganda. Under Stalin's eye he had to work long hours. Impairment of his abilities through drink would simply not have been tolerated.

[230] These are the words Khrushchev uses about Shcherbakov at *op.cit.* p. 39.

[231] Ponomarev, p. 207 n. 32, citing Mikoian, *Tak Bylo.* I have verified these quotations with the digital version of Mikoian's memoirs.

from a labor camp, gave him an important post, consulted with Snegov and cited him in his Secret Speech. According to Khrushchev's son-in-law Alexei Adzhubei Snegov became a friend and confidant of Khrushchev's.[232]

Why would Khrushchev have been so partial to Snegov that he personally interceded to get Snegov released from a camp in 1954 and then promoted and favored him so much? A good guess might be that Khrushchev must have been a friend of Snegov's long ago, before Snegov was arrested. Perhaps Khrushchev managed things so that Snegov avoided execution, even though there seems to have been much evidence against him, and he was in "Category One."

Given that Khrushchev and Snegov must have been close, that Snegov was convicted of being involved in a conspiracy, and that Khrushchev went to the trouble of "rescuing" and favoring Snegov – never a high-ranking Party member, certainly never a powerful person – is it not logical to suppose that Snegov knew something about Khrushchev? Of course, Khrushchev could have had Snegov killed, no doubt. But if they were old comrades it would make sense for Khrushchev to do what he did, and honor Snegov.

Contemporary scholars have established that Khrushchev rushed to cover up evidence of his own role in massive repressions. During Stalin's time many Party leaders and NKVD men were tried and even executed for such abuses. It follows that Khrushchev would have lived in fear for many years lest his role in massive unjustified repressions become known. His fear would have been all the greater if, as we suspect, he was involved in some kind of Right-Trotskyite conspiracy himself and had simply avoided discovery.

Shcherbakov was not only in a position to know about Khrushchev's role in mass repressions better than almost anyone else.[233] He was also influential enough that his word would carry weight with Stalin and the Polit-

---

[232] Shcherbakov discusses confessions against Snegov in a letter to Zhdanov of June 18, 1937. See No. 206, p. 363 in *Sovetskoe Rukovodstvo. Perepiska. 1928-1941*. Moscow: ROSSPEN, 1999. Adzhubei, *Krushenie Illiuzii* (Moscow: Interbuk, 1991), pp. 162-167. After Khrushchev's ouster Snegov was in fact disciplined by the Party for spreading Trotskyist ideas. See *RKEB* 2, Section 6, No. 23, pp. 521-525.

[233] As First Secretary in the Ukraine Khrushchev had carried out mass repression in the Ukraine as well as in Moscow. But he remained for 12 years, until 1949. He had plenty of time to cover his tracks there, and to leave the Ukrainian party in safe hands.

buro. In May 1941 Shcherbakov was made one of the secretaries of the Central Committee, a position more powerful than Khrushchev's own.

Shcherbakov died in May 1945 at the age of only 44 years. He had suffered a heart attack on December 10, 1944, and since then had been convalescing at home. On May 9, 1945 his doctors permitted him to get out of bed to go to Moscow to rejoice in the hard-won victory over Nazi Germany. This brought on a final heart attack from which he died on May 10.

Why did Shcherbakov's doctors let a man with a heart condition out of bed at all, when the basic treatment is complete bed rest? [234] One of Shcherbakov's doctors, Etinger, confessed to his interrogator M.T. Likhachev that he had "done everything he could to shorten Shcherbakov's life" as he considered Shcherbakov to be an anti-Semite.[235] Under questioning by Abakumov, Minister of State Security (head of the MGB), Etinger withdrew his confession, but thereafter repeated them again. Not long thereafter he died in prison.

This was all part of what later became the "Doctors' Plot," a very murky business elements of which were certainly fabricated. Etinger's confession may have been forced, and he may have been innocent of causing Shcherbakov's death from mistreatment. Still, even the doctors in the "Doctors' Plot" who had actually treated Andrei Zhdanov in 1948 agreed that they had mistreated him and by so doing caused his death. They had not only permitted their patient to get out of bed and walk around; they called in a cardiologist to take his EKG and, when she reported that

---

[234] Ponomarev, p. 275 and p. 277 n. 20, states that the doctors "did not object" to Shcherbakov making the trip that killed him. That is, Ponomarev raises, and so acknowledges, the question of the doctors' decision, incompetent if not criminal. But he does not pursue it.

[235] IA.IA. Etinger, *Eto nevozmozhno zabyt'. Vospominaniia.* Moscow: Ves' Mir, 2001, p. 87. At http://www.sakharov-center.ru/asfcd/auth/auth_pages.xtmpl?Key=10153&page=78&print=yes Riumin's letter to Stalin of July 2 1951, from which these details ultimately come, is printed in translation in Jonathan Brent and Vladimir P. Naumov, *Stalin's Last Crime: The Plot Against the Jewish Doctors, 1948-1953.* NY: Harper Collins, 2003, pp. 115-118. The book itself is terribly unreliable. But the **documents** may well be genuine, as they come from Naumov who, as a prominent archivist, could certainly have had access to them. He has never made available the Russian originals. Ponomarev examines the accusations of anti-Semitism against Shcherbakov and concludes that they are all false; see pp. 212-3; 218 ff.; 227-8.

Zhdanov had had a heart attack, told her she was wrong and refused either to believe her or even to let her enter her findings into the report on
Zhdanov's health. Some "mistake"! In fact, their behavior meets all the
requirements of a "conspiracy" – though whether their conspiracy was to
kill Party leaders, as later charged, or simply to "cover up" for one another, is far from clear.

Moreover, there was a history of this kind of thing. At the March 1938
Moscow Trial of Bukharin, Rykov and others two medical doctors, Pletnev and Levin, had confessed to a conspiracy to bring about the deaths
of the writer Maxim Gorkii, Valerian V. Kuibyshev, a Politburo member,
and Vyacheslav Menzhinsky, head of the OGPU, to whom Iagoda was
second-in-command and whom Iagoda wanted out of the way as soon as
possible. We now have confirmation of these charges from previously
unpublished pretrial interrogations of Iagoda as well as from several
"face-to-face confrontations", or *ochnye stavki,* between Iagoda and doctors Levin and Pletnev, as well as between Kriuchkov and Levin.

We now also have two pretrial interrogations of Avel' Enukidze. They
confirm Iagoda's confessions generally. Dr. Levin even admits to direct
contact with Enukidze. The present author has done a study of Dr. Pletnev's "rehabilitation" and the so-called "research" based on it. This study
concludes that Pletnev's "rehabilitation" too was falsified. Pletnev admitted guilt and never retracted that admission.[236]

In June 1957 one of the defendants in the "Bukharin Trial", Akbal Ikramov, was "rehabilitated." The only evidence cited that Ikramov had been
wrongly accused was the fact that those who accused him, including
Bukharin, had also accused others who had previously also been declared
"rehabilitated."[237] No claim was made that either Ikramov, who had confessed at trial, nor any of those who had accused him, acted under com-
pulsion.

---

[236] The materials from Iagoda's interrogations and face-to-face controntations are in
*Genrikh Iagoda. Narkom vnutrennikhdel SSSR, General'niy komissar gosudarstvennoi bezopasnosti.
Sbornik dokumentov.* Kazan', 1997, pp. 218-223. The first of the two transcripts of
interrogations of Enukidze, that of May 30, 1937, is published here too (pp. 508-517). In
it the NKVD investigator refers to an earlier interrogation of Enukidze from April 27,
1937, which has now been published in Lubianka 2 No. 60, pp. 144-156. This last
publication, by the Iakovlev fund, has a semi-official status and therefore confirms the
genuine nature of the first publication. On contacts between Levin and Enukidze see *ibid.*
p. 222.

[237] *RKEB* 2, p. 135.

By December 1957 several other defendants had been similarly "rehabilitated." Though the rest of the defendants were not "rehabilitated" until 1988, under Gorbachev, this was only a formality. At a national convention of historians held in 1962 Pospelov was asked what should be said in the schools about the accused. He replied that "neither Bukharin nor Rykov, of course, were spies or terrorists."[238] However, Pospelov also refused the inquiring historians in the audience any access to the documentary evidence they had asked for!

Bukharin had confessed to being a terrorist, but not personally to espionage, only through his co-conspirators, while Rykov had refused to admit he was a spy but agreed that he had tried to overthrow the government. In effect, therefore, Pospelov made explicit in 1962 what Khrushchev had only implied earlier: the claim – false, as we can now prove -- that the Moscow Trials were a frameup, the testimony false.

In his Secret Speech Khrushchev declared the "Doctors' Plot" a fabrication. But he lied about it completely. He claimed it had been faked by Beria when in fact it was Beria's investigation that had discovered it was a fake in the first place. He also blamed Dr. Timashuk for starting the "plot". But Timashuk had nothing whatsoever to do with it. All the primary evidence we have attests to these facts.

In any case, Shcherbakov's death could not have been but welcome to Khrushchev. So much of what Khrushchev claimed to have revealed about the Stalin years has proven false that it would be imprudent to simply "believe" him in this case. In the light of the evidence we now have concerning the "doctors' plots" alleged in the 1938 Moscow Trial it would be a mistake to foreclose the possibility that some, at least, of the postwar "doctors' plots" might have had some basis in reality.

---

[238] *Vsesoiuznoe soveshchanie o merakh uluchsheniia podgotovki nauchno-pedagogicheskikh kadrov po istoricheskim naukam, 18-21 dekabria 1962 g.* Moscow: Nauka, 1964, p. 298. IUri Fel'shtinskii, a well-known Russian Trotskyist scholar, claims that Pospelov said this "summarized the official results of the secret researches undertaken by the appropriate organs of the CC CPSU." See IU. G. Fel'shtinskii, *Razgovory s Bukharinym. Kommentarii k vospominaniem A.M. Larinoi (Bukharinoi 'Nezabyvaemoe' s prelozheniami.* Moscow: Izd. Gumanitarnoi literatury, 1993, p. 92. There is no reason to think this is true, since the full context of Pospelov's statement is this: "I can state that it is sufficient to study carefully the documents of the 22nd Party Congress to say that neither Bukharin nor Rykov, of course, were spies or terrorists." We know that utter fabrications were stated as fact at the 22nd Party Congress – Shelepin's misreading of Iona IAkir's letter, discussed below, is an example – so there is no reason to think Pospelov was telling the truth here.

Finally, there is a long-recognized mystery of why medical care was not summoned for the gravely ill Stalin until a day or more after it had been discovered that he had had a stroke. Whatever the details of this affair Khrushchev was involved in it.

＊

＊   ＊

Implications: The influence on Soviet society

Khrushchev's personal motives aside, of greater interest and importance are the implications for Soviet society and politics suggested by the Speech.

The fact that the "Secret Speech" is not just untruthful in spots but rather is composed of falsehoods from beginning to end requires a profound readjustment of our historical and political frameworks.

The fact that the research and "rehabilitation" commission that provided Khrushchev with the information he used in his speech, the Pospelov Commission, did not carry out honest research has implications for any and all other commissions of historical investigation set up under Khrushchev and answerable to him.

For example, many commissions of "rehabilitation" were set up under Khrushchev in order to "study" the cases of individuals, overwhelmingly communists, who had been convicted and either executed or imprisoned in the GULAG for long periods. In almost all the cases we know of these commissions exculpated the accused and declared them "rehabilitated" – innocent, for all practical purposes. Those so "rehabilitated" were declared to have been "victims of Stalinist repression."

However, in few cases was any evidence presented sufficient to establish the innocence of the "rehabilitated" person. On the contrary: in some cases there is good reason to believe that the "rehabilitated" persons may not have been innocent at all.

For example, at the June 1957 Central Committee Plenum at which Khrushchev and his supporters expelled the "Stalinists" Malenkov,

Molotov, and Kaganovich for having plotted to have Khrushchev removed as First Secretary, Marshal Zhukov read from a falsified letter
from Komandarm (General) Iona Iakir. Iakir had been tried and executed
with Marshal Tukhachevskii in June 1937 for plotting with the Germans
and oppositionists within the USSR, for a *coup d'etat*.

Marshal Zhukov quoted it as follows:

> On June 29 1937 on the eve of his own death he [Iakir –
> GF] wrote a letter to Stalin in which he says: 'Dear, close
> comrade Stalin! I dare address you in this way because I
> have told everything and it seems to me that I am that
> honorable warrior, devoted to Party, state and people,
> that I was for many years. All my conscious life has been
> passed in selfless, honorable work in the sight of the
> Party and its leaders. I die with words of love to you, the
> Party, the country, with a fervent belief in the victory of
> communism.'
>
> On this declaration we find the following resolution:
> "Into my archive. St. A scoundrel and prostitute. Stalin.
> A precisely accurate description. Molotov. For a villain,
> swine, and b***, there is only one punishment – the
> death penalty. Kaganovich.
>
> - Molotov, Malenkov, Kaganovich. 1957. Moscow, 1998,
> p. 39. [239]

This text was falsified by the omission of the part of Iakir's letter in
which he confirms his guilt and repents. Here is the text from the
"Shvernik Report" on the Tukhachevskii case given to Khrushchev in
1964, shortly before his ouster, but not published until 1994. The sentences omitted in Zhukov's 1957 reading are in boldface here:

> "Dear, close com. Stalin. I dare address you in this way
> because I have told everything and and it seems to me
> that I am **once more** that honorable warrior, devoted to
> Party, state and people, that I was for many years. All my
> conscious life has been passed in selfless, honorable
> work in the sight of the Party and its leaders. – **then I
> fell into a nightmare, into the irreparable horror of**

---

[239] *Molotov, Malenkov, Kaganovich. 1957.* Moscow, 1998, p. 39

> treason… The investigation is finished. The
> indictment of treason to the state has been
> presented to me, I have admitted my guilt, I have
> repented completely. I have unlimited faith in the
> justice and appropriateness of the decision of the
> court and the government. Now each of my words is
> honest, I die with words of love to you, the Party, the
> country, with a fervent belief in the victory of
> communism.'
>
> On Iakir's declaration we find the following resolution:
> "Into my archive. St." "A scoundrel and prostitute. I.
> St[alin]". "A precisely accurate description. K.
> Voroshilov." "Molotov". "For a villain, swine, and
> bastard there is only one punishment – the death penalty.
> Kaganovich."[240]

Aside from relatively inconsequential errors in Zhukov's account – Iakir's
letter was written on June 9 1937, not June 29 – there are important falsifications. In this letter Iakir repeatedly **confirmed** his guilt. Voroshilov,
as well as Stalin, Molotov, and Kaganovich wrote on the letter, a detail
Zhukov omitted. In 1957 Voroshilov had backed away from the plot to
remove Khrushchev. The latter, though criticizing the old Marshal severely, spared him the punishment meted out to the others. This same
falsified letter was read out at the 22nd Party Congress in November 1961
by Alexander Shelepin. [241]

---

[240] *RKEB* 2 (2003), 688; *Voenno-Istoricheskii Arkhiv*, Vypusk 1. Moscow, 1997, p. 194. Also
in *Voennye Arkhivy Rossi* No. 1, 1993, p. 50. This was the first publication of the "Shvernik
Report." But this journal, whose sole issue is surrounded in mystery, is very hard to find.
There was evidently never another issue, and this one, while dated 1993, may not have
actually been published until the following year.

[241] At the 22nd Party Congress in 1961, during which Khrushchev and his supporters
leveled an even more virulent attack on Stalin than in 1956, Alexander Shelepin repeated
this same distortion, reading aloud Iakir's letter while omitting the parts in which Iakir
confirmed his guilt (Sokolov, B.V. *Mikhail Tukhachevskii. Zhizn' I Smert' 'Krasnogo Marshala'*.
Smolensk, 1999; also at http://militera.lib.ru/bio/sokolov/09.html ; Leskov, Valentin.
Stalin i Zagovor Tukhachevskogo. Moscow: Veche, 2003, n. 171 p. 461. The actual transcript
of Shelepin's Speech to the 22nd Party Congress of the CPSU is printed in Pravda,
October 27, 1961. Shelepin's dishonest misquotation of Iakir's letter is at p. 10, cols 3-4.
It is also in the official transcript: *XXII s"ezd Kommunisticheskoi Partii Sovetskogo Soiuza. 17-
31 oktiabria 1961 goda. Stenograficheskii otchiot.* Moscow: Gos. Izd. Politicheskoi Literatury,
1962, 399-409.

In 1957 none of the accused – Malenkov, Molotov, and Kaganovich – complained about Zhukov's falsification of Iakir's letter. Therefore we must assume that they did not have access to it, even though they were Presidium members themselves. It is possible that Zhukov himself may not have known that he was reading a falsified document. But Khrushchev's "researchers" had to have known – they provided the text! They would never have dared do this behind Khrushchev's back. Therefore Khrushchev knew too.[242]

(We should note too that even in the version of Iakir's letter published in 1997 there is an ellipsis – the three dots, in Russian a *troetochie* – after the word "treason." Something is still omitted from Iakir's letter, of which therefore the genuine and complete text is still being withheld from us by the Russian government.)

Therefore, none of the "rehabilitation" decisions, in which a great many repressed communists were declared innocent, can be taken at face value. But therefore the same is true of other documents created for Khrushchev's use.

One such set of documents is known as the "Colonel Pavlov" reports. A recent work by Oleg Khlevniuk calls them "the main source of our knowledge about the scale of repression."[243] These have provided the main sources for estimating the number of people "repressed" during the 1930s.[244] But since they were prepared for Khrushchev we cannot assume they were honestly done. Maybe it was in Khrushchev's interest to exaggerate – or, for that matter, minimize – the number of those executed? Or maybe Pavlov, like Pospelov, thought he should do one or the other? Given the fraudulent nature of other studies done for Khrushchev we can no longer simply assume that the "Colonel Pavlov" reports are accurate.

In terms of scholarship, almost all research on the Stalin years published during the past half-century relies heavily on Khrushchev-era Soviet pub-

---

[242] Matthew Lenoe too concludes that Khrushchev kept important documents secret from Molotov and others. See *The Kirov Murder and Soviet History* (New Haven: Yale U.P. 2010) 592. I am preparing a detailed review of this extremely flawed book.

[243] *The History of the Gulag.* Yale U.P. 2004, p. 287.

[244] They are a main source in the now-famous article by Getty, Rittersporn and Zemskov, "Victims of the Soviet Penal System in the Prewar Years: A First Approach on the Basis of Archival Evidence," *AHR* October 1993, 1017-1049.

lications.[245] It also includes many or most of the non-émigré sources cited in the numerous works by Robert Conquest such as *The Great Terror*, Stephen Cohen's famous biography of Bukharin[246], and many other works. Cohen drew his evidence for his final chapter on the 1930s from Khrushchev-era sources and the Speech itself, with the result that almost every statement of fact in this chapter has turned out to be false. No such works can be accepted unless and until the assertions made in them can be verified independently.

This goes for the supposedly "primary-source" documents as well. Khrushchev and others cited dishonestly from many such sources. Unless and until scholars can see the originals, and their whole texts, it is invalid to assume that Khrushchev, or a Khrushchev-era book, article, or speaker, quoted them honestly.[247]

Political Implications

The "Secret Speech" threw the world communist movement into crisis. But the **claim** was that all the damage done was necessary, prophylactic. An evil part of the past, largely unknown to the communists of the world and even of the USSR, had to be exposed, a potentially fatal cancer in the body of world communism had to be mercilessly excised, so that the movement could correct itself and once again move towards its ultimate goal.

In the years that followed it became more and more apparent that the USSR was not moving towards a classless society, but rather in the opposite direction. Even so, those who stuck with the Soviet-led movement did so because they still held to the original ideal. Millions of people around the world hoped and believed that a movement that could afford

---

[245] Careful students have long questioned the historical worth of some of these works, like that of Roi Medvedev's *Let History Judge* (Russian title: *K sudu istorii*) or Alexander Solzhenitsyn's *The GULAG Archipelago*.

[246] Bukharin and the Bolshevik Revolution (1973).

[247] An article by myself and Vladimir Bobrov proves, by citing documents from the formerly secret Soviet archives, that every statement made by Cohen in the final chapter of his biography of Bukharin is false. All were based on Khrushchev-era sources, with a few émigré rumors thrown in. See "V krivoi zerkale «antistalinskoi paradigvy»" in *1937. Pravosudie Stalin. Obzhalovaniiu ne podlezhit'*. (Moscow: Eksmo 2010) 195-333. An English version of this article is scheduled to appear in the 2010 issue of *Cultural Logic,* which is scheduled to appear in 2011.

to take such huge losses, to admit such crimes had been committed in its name, to ruthlessly expose them – as Khrushchev claimed to have done – might have the integrity and fortitude to correct itself and move, with whatever political zigs and zags necessary, towards a communist future. This picture is no longer tenable.

Khrushchev was **not** trying to "right the ship of communism." A total trashing of the truth like the "Secret Speech" is incompatible with Marxism, or with idealistic motives of any kind. Nothing positive, democratic, or liberating can be built on a foundation of falsehood. Instead of reviving a communist movement, and Bolshevik Party, that had strayed from its true course through grievous errors, Khrushchev was killing it off.

Khrushchev himself is "revealed" not as an honest communist but instead as a political leader seeking personal advantage while hiding behind an official persona of idealism and probity, a type familiar in capitalist countries. Taking into account his murder of Beria and the men executed as "Beria's gang" in 1953, he seems worse still – a political thug. Khrushchev was guilty *in reality* of the kinds of crimes he *deliberately and falsely* accused Stalin of in the "Secret Speech."

The fraudulent nature of Khrushchev's Speech forces us to revise our view of those "Stalinists" who tried and failed to have Khrushchev removed from leadership in 1957 and who were dismissed and, at length, expelled from the Party. With all their sins and failings the interviews of the aged Molotov and Kaganovich (as retold by Felix Chuev) reveal men devoted to Lenin, Stalin, and the ideal of communism to the end who often commented incisively on the capitalist developments within the late USSR. Molotov predicted the overthrow of socialism by capitalist forces within the Party even as, in his 80s and 90s, he sought reinstatement in it.

Yet their acceptance of the main outlines of Khrushchev's attack on Stalin suggests that they had their own doubts about some of the policies followed during Stalin's time. To one degree or another they shared Khrushchev's political views. Furthermore, they did not know the details of the repressions of the 1930s and thereafter, and were utterly unprepared to refute anything Khrushchev and his supporters said about them – until it was far too late.

Perhaps the only positive step the post-Stalin Soviet leadership made was in criticizing, and partially dismantling, the disgusting "cult of personality" they themselves had built up around the figure of Stalin. Even here Khrushchev himself deserves no credit. He had opposed Malenkov's much earlier attempts – within days of Stalin's death – to criticize the "cult." And Malenkov had the honesty to blame, not Stalin, but those around him, himself included, for being too weak to stop the "cult", which Stalin finally grew accustomed to but never endorsed and viewed with distaste.

Khrushchev himself lost no time in attempting to build up around himself an even bigger "cult" than that around Stalin. He was criticized for doing so even by his supporters in 1956 and 1957, and his self-aggrandizement and arrogance was the main accusation made by the Presidium leadership that unseated him in October 1964.[248]

The fraudulent nature of Khrushchev's Speech demands that we rethink the Stalin years and Stalin himself. Stripped both of the idol-worshipping "cult" around him and of Khrushchev's calumnies the figure of Stalin, and the shape of the policies he tried to put into practice, reassert themselves as the central issue, the greatest question mark in Soviet and Comintern history. Stalin's successes and failures must be not just re-studied; they have yet to be discovered and acknowledged.

Trotsky

It also demands a reconsideration of Trotsky and of Trotskyism. In its essentials Khrushchev's denunciation of Stalin in the "Secret Speech" echoed Trotsky's earlier demonization of Stalin. But in 1956 Trotskyism was a marginal force, its murdered leader most often dismissed as a megalomaniacal failure.

Khrushchev's speech breathed new life into Trotsky's all-but-dead caricature of Stalin. Communists and anti-communists alike began to view Trotsky as a "prophet". Had he not said things very similar to what Khrushchev had just "revealed" to be true? They dusted off Trotsky's little-read works. Trotsky's reputation, and that of his followers, soared. That the "Secret Speech" constituted an unacknowledged "rehabilitation" of Trotsky was recognized by Trotsky's widow Sedova who, within a day of the Speech, applied to the Presidium of the 20th Party Congress for full rehabilitation for both her late husband and her son.[249] But now, no

---

[248] The transcript of the October 1964 Plenum at which Khrushchev was removed has been published in *Istoricheskii Arkhiv* 1, 1993, pp. 3-19.

[249] *Doklad Khrushcheva*, p. 610. I have put a facsimile of Sedova's letter on the web at http://chss.montclair.edu/english/furr/research/sedovaltr022856.jpg

longer "confirmed" by Khrushchev's testimony, Trotsky's highly partisan portrait of Stalin and Soviet society and politics during his time needs to be revisited with a critical eye.

Unresolved weaknesses in the Soviet system of socialism

It is easy and of course justified to criticize Khrushchev himself. He chose to undermine the CPSU and the international communist movement by deliberately lying about Stalin and Soviet history. Whatever we conclude about the historical conditions that produced Khrushchev and his era, nothing can absolve him of the responsibility for his own acts.

But Khrushchev could not have been promoted to the Politburo/Presidium if his concept of socialism had been worlds different from that shared by many other Party leaders. Khrushchev's rise is no doubt partly explained by his extraordinary energy and initiative, qualities that the rest of the Presidium members showed little of. But he could not have triumphed if he had been seen by Stalin and the Party elite as a rightist, or bad, communist. The concept of what was meant in the Bolshevik Party by "socialism" had evolved since the Revolution.

Malenkov, Molotov, and Kaganovich, the major figures associated with Stalin for decades, did acquiesce, however grudgingly, to Khrushchev's "Secret Speech". It is clear that they themselves did not have access to the documents prepared for Khrushchev by his allies. Their remarks at the time and afterwards show that they did not suspect that what Khrushchev said was false. Moreover, they accepted the political implications of the Speech.

Had Malenkov managed somehow to fend off Khrushchev and kept the leadership of the CPSU, the "Secret Speech" would never have been delivered, and the history of the Communist movement, and therefore much of the history of the world, might have developed very differently. In like manner many people have reasoned that the Soviet Union might well still exist if Iurii Andropov had lived a normal life span as its leader and Mikhail Gorbachev never taken office. But the "role of the individual in history" does not grant unlimited choice even to the strongest leaders. Andropov's USSR was just as much in crisis as was Gorbachev's – or as was the USSR in 1953.

Khrushchev was able to take power, deliver the bombshell of the "Secret

Speech" with all its fabrications, and then "make it stick": to win over the Soviet elite, along with most of the Soviet population and – though not after huge losses – most of the communists around the world. These facts themselves demand explanation. And the roots of that outcome have to be sought in the previous period of Soviet history, the period of Stalin's leadership, and of Lenin's before him, and in the very conditions that led to the Russian Revolution and Bolshevik victory.

There are historical and ideological roots to Khrushchev's Speech, and these must also be sought in Soviet history. Stalin tried hard to apply Lenin's analysis to the conditions he found in Russia and the world communist movement. Lenin, in turn, had tried to apply the insights of Marx and Engels. Lenin had tried to find answers to the critical problems of building socialism in Russia in the works of the founders of modern communism.

Stalin, never claiming any innovations for himself, had tried to follow Lenin's guidelines as closely as he could. Meanwhile Trotsky and Bukharin, as well as other oppositionists, found support for their proposed policies in Lenin's works too. And Khrushchev, like his epigones up to and including Gorbachev, cited Lenin's words to justify, and give a Leninist or "left" cover to, every policy he chose.

Therefore, something in Lenin's works, and in those of Lenin's great teachers Marx and Engels, facilitated the errors that his honest successor Stalin honestly made, and that his dishonest successor Khrushchev was able to use to cover up his own betrayal.

But that is a subject for further research and a different book.

January 2005 – February 2007. Revised December 2010.

Appendix – Quotations from Primary and Other Sources

1. Cult.

Khrushchev:

> "Comrades! In the report of the Central Committee of the party at the 20th Congress, in a number of speeches by delegates to the Congress, as also formerly during the plenary CC/CPSU [Central Committee of the Communist Party of the Soviet Union] sessions, quite a lot has been said about the cult of the individual and about its harmful consequences. After Stalin's death the Central Committee of the party began to implement a policy of explaining concisely and consistently that it is impermissible and foreign to the spirit of Marxism-Leninism to elevate one person, to transform him into a superman possessing supernatural characteristics, akin to those of a god. Such a man supposedly knows everything, sees everything, thinks for everyone, can do anything, is infallible in his behavior. Such a belief about a man, and specifically about Stalin, was cultivated among us for many years.

> The objective of the present report is not a thorough evaluation of Stalin's life and activity. …

> At present, we are concerned with a question which has immense importance for the party now and for the future – with how the cult of the person of Stalin has been gradually growing, the cult which became at a certain specific stage the source of a whole series of exceedingly serious and grave perversions of party principles, of party democracy, of revolutionary legality."

1. Stalin's Opposition to the Cult

June 1926:

"I must say in all conscience, comrades, that I do not deserve a good half of the flattering things that have been said here about me. I am, it appears, a hero of the October Revolution, the leader of the Communist Party of the Soviet Union, the leader of the Communist International, a legendary warrior-knight and all the rest of it. This is absurd, comrades, and quite unnecessary exaggeration. It is the sort of thing that is usually said at the graveside of a departed revolutionary. But I have no intention of dying yet...

"I really was, and still am, one of the pupils of the advanced workers of the Tiflis railway workshops." (J. V. Stalin: *Works*, Volume 8; Moscow; 1954; p. 182).

October 1927:

"And what is Stalin? Stalin is only a minor figure." (J. V. Stalin: *Works*, Volume 10; Moscow; 1954; p. 177).

December 1929:

"Your congratulations and greetings I place to the credit of the great Party of the working class which bore me and reared me in its own image and likeness. And just because I place them to the credit of our glorious Leninist Party, I make bold to tender you my Bolshevik thanks." (J. V. Stalin: *Works*, Volume 12; Moscow; 1955; p. 146).

April 1930:

"There are some who think that the article 'Dizzy with Success' was the result of Stalin's personal initiative. That, of course, is nonsense. It is not in order that personal initiative in a matter like this be taken by anyone, whoever he might be, that we have a Central Committee." (J. V. Stalin: *Works*, ibid.; p. 218).

August 1930:

"You speak of your 'devotion' to me. Perhaps this is a phrase that came out accidentally. Perhaps... But if it is not a chance phrase, I would advise you to discard the 'principle' of devotion to persons. It is not the Bolshevik way. Be devoted to the working class, its Party, its state.

That is a fine and useful thing. But do not confuse it
with devotion to persons, this vain and useless bauble of
weak-minded intellectuals." ("Letter to Comrade
Shatunovsky." *Works*, Volume 13; Moscow; 1955; p. 20).

December 1931:

"As for myself, I am just a pupil of Lenin's, and the aim
of my life is to be a worthy pupil of his...

"Marxism does not deny at all the role played by
outstanding individuals or that history is made by people.
But... great people are worth anything at all only to the
extent that they are able correctly to understand these
conditions, to understand how to change them. If they
fail to understand these conditions and want to alter
them according to the promptings of their imagination,
they will find themselves in the situation of Don
Quixote...

applies to Gorbachev

"Individual persons cannot decide. Decisions of
individuals are always, or nearly always, one-sided
decisions... In every collective body, there are people
whose opinion must be reckoned with... From the
experience of three revolutions we know that out of
every 100 decisions taken by individual persons without
being tested and corrected collectively, approximately 90
are one-sided...

"Never under any circumstances would our workers now
tolerate power in the hands of one person. With us
personages of the greatest authority are reduced to
nonentities, become mere ciphers, as soon as the masses
of the workers lose confidence in them." (J. V. Stalin:
ibid.; p. 107-08, 109, 113).

February 1933:

"I have received your letter ceding me your second
Order as a reward for my work.

"I thank you very much for your warm words and
comradely present. I know what you are depriving
yourself of in my favour and appreciate your sentiments.

"Nevertheless, I cannot accept your second Order. I cannot and must not accept it, not only because it can only belong to you, as you alone have earned it, but also because I have been amply rewarded as it is by the attention and respect of comrades and, consequently, have no right to rob you.

"Orders were instituted not for those who are well known as it is, but mainly for heroic people who are little known and who need to be made known to all.

"Besides, I must tell you that I already have two Orders. That is more than one needs, I assure you." (J. V. Stalin: ibid.; p. 241).

May 1933:

"Robins: I consider it a great honour to have an opportunity of paying you a visit.

"Stalin: There is nothing particular in that. You are exaggerating.

"Robins: What is most interesting to me is that throughout Russia I have found the names Lenin-Stalin, Lenin-Stalin, Lenin-Stalin, linked together.

"Stalin: That, too, is an exaggeration. How can I be compared to Lenin?" (J. V. Stalin: ibid.; p. 267)

February 1938:

"I am absolutely against the publication of 'Stories of the Childhood of Stalin'.

"The book abounds with a mass of inexactitudes of fact, of alterations, of exaggerations and of unmerited praise...

"But... the important thing resides in the fact that the book has a tendency to engrave on the minds of Soviet children (and people in general) the personality cult of leaders, of infallible heroes. This is dangerous and detrimental. The theory of 'heroes' and the 'crowd' is not a Bolshevik, but a Social-Revolutionary theory...

"I suggest we burn this book." (J. V. Stalin: ibid.; p. 327).

February 1946:

"The ear is pained too by the sound of the dithyrambs in Stalin's honor – it is simply embarrassing to read." ("Answer to Comrade Razin", Works Vol. 16).

Dimitrov's diary

Dimitrov: [Proposes toast with fulsome praise of Stalin, ending with the words] There can be no speaking of Lenin without linking him with Stalin!

Stalin: I respect Comrade Dimitrov very much. We are friends and will remain friends. But I must disagree with him. He has even expressed himself here in an un-Marxist fashion. What the victory of the cause requires is the correct conditions, and then leaders will always be found. (p. 66; November 7, 1937)

Dimitrov: …This is a collective work, with Com[rade] Man[uilsky] as chief editor.

Stalin (regarding the passage in the appeal praising Stalin, especially:

"Long live our Stalin!

Stalin means peace!

Stalin means Communism!

Stalin is our victory!")

– Manuilsky is a toady!

He was a Trotskyite! We criticized him for keeping quiet and not speaking out when the purges of Trotskyite bandits were going on, and now he has started toadying!

There is something suspicious here.

– That article of his is *Pravda* – "Stalin and the World Communist Movement" – is harmful and provocative.

J.V. [Stalin] would not allow "under the banner of Marx-Engels-Lenin-*Stalin*" to remain in the appeal, but insisted on simply "Marx-Engels-Lenin." (pp. 104-105, April 26 1939)

Stalin refused to permit an exhibition about him in honor of his 55th birthday, December 1934:

"spiritual director"
or "guru"?

> "... on a letter from the All-Union Society of Old
> Bolsheviks, in which it was proposed to conduct a
> campaign of propaganda dedicated to his 55th birthday,
> he wrote the following resolution: 'I am opposed, since
> such undertakings lead to the strengthening of a 'cult of
> personality', which is harmful and incompatible with the
> spirit of our party.'"

- Rogovin, *1937*, Chapter 41, citing *Voprosy Istorii KPSS.* No. 3, 1990, p.
104.

Stalin criticized playwrite Afinogenov for using the term "Vozhd'" (leader) about him:

> "Having read, in 1933, the MS of the play *The Lie* by
> A.N. Afinogenov Stalin wrote an extensive letter to the
> playwrite, in the notes to which he remarked: 'P.S. Your
> going on about "the leader" (*vozhd'*) is not helpful. This is
> bad and, if you will permit me, indecent. It's not a
> question of "a leader", but of the collective leader – the
> C.C. of the Party. I.St[alin]" What did Stalin have in
> mind. One of the heroes of the play, the assistant
> Commissar Riadovoy, while arguing with the former
> oppositionist Nakatov affirmed with feeling: 'I speak of
> our Central Committee.. I speak of the leader who leads
> us, who has torn away the masks from many highly-
> educated leaders who had unlimited possibilites and yet
> showed themselves to be bankrupt. I speak of the person
> whose strength is composed of the granite-like trust of
> hundreds of millions. His name on the tongues of men
> the world over sounds like a symbol of the fortress of
> the Bolshevik cause. And this leader is
> unconquerable..." Stalin edited and corrected this tirade
> with his own hand, making this key correction: 'I speak
> of our Central Committee which leads us, having torn
> away the mask from many highly-educated leaders who
> had unlimited possibilities and yet showed themselves to
> be bankrupt. I speak of the Central Committee of the
> party of communists of the land of the Soviets, the
> strength of which is composed of the granite-like trust of
> hundreds of millions. Its banner on the tongues of men
> the world over sounds like a symbol of the fortress of

the Bolshevik cause. And this collective leader is unconquerable...."

On January 27 1937 having seen a screening of the film "The Great Citizen" (the subject of this film by director F.M. Ermler resembles the story of the murder of S.M. Kirov), Stalin wrote a letter to B.Z. Shumiatskii, director of Soviet cinematography, in which he gave the following well-known specific directive: "You must exclude any mention of Stalin. Instead of Stalin should be substituted the CC of the party." (*Surovaia drama naroda. Uchenye i publitsisty o prirode stalinizma*. Sost. IU. P. Senokosov. Moscow: Politizdat, 1989.).

"In 1936 was published a biographical sketch of the life of Sergo Ordzhonikidze compiled by M.D. Orakhelashvili. Stalin read this book and left many notatonis on its pages. In the sketch, for example, the July crisis of 1917 is retold like this: 'In this difficult period for the proletarian, when many faltered in the face of the approaching danger, comrade Stalin stood firmly at his post of the leadership of the CC and the Petrograd party organization. [Lenin was in hiding – L.M.]. Com. Ordzhonikidze was constantly with him, leading an energetic, wholehearted struggle for the Leninist slogans of the party.' (*ibid*, p. 33). These words were underlined by Stalin, and at the edge of the pages he wrote with a red pencil: 'And what about the CC? and the party?' In another place the VI Congress of the RSDLP (summer of 1917) was discussed, about how Lenin, in hiding in Razliv, 'gave directives on the questions that stood on the Congress' agenda. In order to receive Lenin's directives com. Ordzhonikidze, on Stalin's orders, twice went to Lenin's hut.' Stalin again posed his question: 'And the CC – where is it?'"

- L. Maksimenkov, in *Al'manakh 'Vostok'* 12 (24), December 2004. Also quoted in Iulia Ivanova, *The Dreaming Doors*.

Stalin refused Hero of the Soviet Union (May 1945):

On the day after the parade, by order of the Presidium of the Supreme Soviet of the USSR J.V. Stalin was awarded the title of Hero of the Soviet Union. Malenkov took the initiative in this affair, but Stalin refused this high honor and even spoke sharply with Kalinin, who had signed the order: "I", he said, "took no part in military actions, did no heroic deeds; I am only a leader."

V.F. Alliluev, 'Chronicle of a family': Alliluev – Stalin. Moscow, 1995, p. 195.

Other accounts confirm this:

...A conversation followed concerning the awarding to Stalin of the Hero of the Soviet Union after the war. Stalin said that he did not fit the criteria of Hero of the Soviet Union, which was awarded only for the demonstration of personal courage.

'I did not demonstrate such courage' – said Stalin. And he did not accept the Star. They only drew him with this star in portraits. When he died, the leader of the awards section gave him the Gold Star of the Hero of the Soviet Union. They pinned it on a pillow and carried it at the funeral."

NB Stalin wore only one little star: Hero of Socialist Labor – added Molotov.

- Felix Chuev, p.140; *Conversations with Molotov. From the Diary of F. Chuev.* Moscow, 1994, p. 254.

Khrushchev quote "hero vs masses" – exactly what Stalin had written

Khrushchev:

"While ascribing great importance to the role of the leaders and organizers of the masses, Lenin at the same time mercilessly stigmatized every manifestation of the cult of the individual, inexorably combated the foreign-to-Marxism views about a "hero" and a "crowd," and countered all efforts to oppose a "hero" to the masses and to the people." (p. 2)

See Stalin's quotes above.

QED

2. Malenkov's Attempt To Call a CC Plenum Concerning the "Cult" April 1953

Zhukov, *Tainy Kremlia*. 617-621, in April 1953 Malenkov had wanted to call an extraordinary session of the Central Committee to discuss the cult of personality of Stalin. On pp. 618-9 Zhukov quotes from Malenkov's draft report and draft resolution

> "Guided by these principled considerations the Presidium of the CC CPSU submits to the Plenum of the CC CPSU the following draft resolution for its consideration:
>
> 'The Central Committee of the CPSU considers that in our printed and oral propaganda there exists an abnormal situation that expresses itself in that our propagandists stray into an un-Marxist understanding of the role of the individual in history, and into the propagating of a cult of the individual.
>
> [It is well known that comrade Stalin firmly condemned such a cult of the individual, and called it a Socialist Revolutionary error.] In this connection the Central Committee of the CPSU considers it obligatory to condemn and to definitively put an end to the un-Marxist, essentially Socialist-Revolutionary tendencies in our propaganda, which flow from the line of the cult of the individual and of diminishing the significance and role of the political line worked out by the party, diminishing the significance and role of a consolidated, monolithic, united, collective leadership of the party and government.'
>
> Many of those present know that com. Stalin often spoke out in this spirit and firmly condemned the un-Marxist, Socialist-Revolutionary understanding of the role of the individual in history."

- Zhukov, *Taini Kremlia*, pp. 618-9; sentence in brackets is quoted as part of this same draft resolution in M.P. Odesskii, D.M Fel'dman, "Cult of the Individual (Materials for a Hyper-reference)", in *Osvoboditel'noe Dvizhe-niie v Rossii,* 2003 (Saratov University), at http://www.sgu.ru/files/nodes/9873/09.pdf

According to these two scholars these remarks are from Pospelov's notes on the March 10 1953 Presidium discussion, less than a week after Stalin's death (March 5).

Malenkov was not permitted to call a CC Plenum, though it is not known who voted for and against it. Zhukov believes Khrushchev was most likely opposed.

QED

3. July 1953 Plenum – Beria Attacked for Allegedly Opposing "Cult"

At the July 1953 Central Committee Plenum attacking Beria Mikoian, later a major ally of Khrushchev's, strongly blamed Beria for beginning the attack on Stalin's 'cult':

> Another question is his [Beria's] two-facedness. In the first days [after Stalin's death – GF] he spoke up strongly about the cult of personality. We understood that there were excesses in this matter even during comrade Stalin's lifetime. Comrade Stalin sharply criticized us. The fact that they have created a cult around me, said Comrade Stalin, the SRs have done that. We could not correct this matter at that time, and so it went on. We must approach the question of the individual in a Marxist fashion. But Beria spoke up strongly. It turned out that he wanted to destroy the cult of Comrade Stalin and create his own cult.

- *Lavrentii Beria. 1953*, p. 168

Andreev (p. 207) also spoke up to blame Beria for raising the issue of the "cult", claiming it was simply not a problem. Kaganovich did likewise (*ibid.* p. 283).

Clearly they all knew that it had really been Malenkov!

Maksimenkov too discusses Malenkov's March 1953 attack on "cults of personality" as "self-criticism," since Malenkov himself had engaged in it. In the dishonest criticisms leveled at Beria during the July 1953 Central Committee Plenum devoted to attacking him, Andreev blamed Beria for raising the issue of the "cult"!

4. Who fostered the "Cult"?

Roi Medvedev points out that

"The first issue of 'Pravda' for 1934 carried a huge two-page article by Radek, heaping orgiastic praise on Stalin. The former Trotskyite, who had led the opposition to Stalin for many years, now called him 'Lenin's best pupil, the model of the Leninist Party, bone of its bone, blood of its blood'... He 'is as far-sighted as Lenin', and so on and on. This seems to have been the first large article in the press specifically devoted to the adulation of Stalin, and it was quickly reissued as a pamphlet in 225,000 copies, an enormous figure for the time."

- R. A. Medvedev: *Let History Judge: The Origins and Consequences of Stalinism.* London; 1972; p. 148. Quoted from Bland, pp. 8-9.) Radek's article was published as a 32-page pamphlet: *Zodchii sotsialisticheskogo obshchestva.*(Architect of socialist society) Moscow: Partiinoe izdatel'stvo, 1934).

BUKHARIN: I recall one such incident. Following the instructions of Kliment Efremovich [Voroshilov] I wrote an article on the exhibition about the Red Army. There Voroshilov, Stalin and others were discussed. When Stalin said, "What are you writing there?" Someone retorted: "How could he not write something of the kind?" I explained all these things very simply. I knew that there's no reason to create a cult of Stalin, but as far as I am concerned, it is expedient.

SOSNOVSKY: And in my case you thought it essential.

BUKHARIN: For the very simple reason that you are a former Oppositionist. I see nothing wrong in this.

– *Voprosy Istorii* No. 3, 2002, p. 28

5. Khrushchev and Mikoian

Khrushchev himself was one of those most guilty of building up the "cult." (Bland, 9-11)

"It was Khrushchev who introduced the term 'vozhd' ('leader', corresponding to the German word 'Führer'). At the Moscow Party Conference in January 1932, Khrushchev finished his speech by saying:

"The Moscow Bolsheviks, rallied around the Leninist Central Committee as never before, and around the *vozhd* of our Party, Comrade Stalin, are cheerfully and confidently marching toward new victories in the battles for socialism, for world proletarian revolution." (*Rabochaia Moskva*, 26 January 1932, cited in: L. Pistrak: *The Grand Tactician: Khrushchev's Rise to Power*, London; 1961; p. 159).

At the 17th Party Conference in January 1934 it was Khrushchev, and Khrushchev alone, who called Stalin "… 'vozhd' of genius." ("nashego geneal'nogo vozhdia tovarishcha Stalina") (XVII S'ezd Vsesoiuznoi Kommunisticheskoi Partii (B.); p. 145, cited in: L. Pistrak: ibid.; p. 160). Transcript of Khrushchev's speech at http://www.hrono.ru/vkpb_17/6_4.html

In August 1936 during the treason trial of Lev Kamenev and Grigorii Zinoviev Khrushchev, in his capacity as Moscow Party Secretary, said:

"Miserable pygmies! They lifted their hands against the greatest of all men,… our wise 'vozhd', Comrade Stalin!… Thou, Comrade Stalin, hast raised the great banner of Marxism-Leninism high over the entire world and carried it forward. We assure thee, Comrade Stalin, that the Moscow Bolshevik organisation – the faithful supporter of the Stalinist Central Committee – will increase Stalinist vigilance still more, will extirpate the Trotskyite-Zinovievite remnants, and close the ranks of the Party and non-Party Bolsheviks even more around the Stalinist Central Committee and the great Stalin." (Pravda, 23 August 1936, cited in: L. Pistrak: ibid.; p. 162. The entire speech is reprinted in N. G. Tomilina, ed. *Nikita Sergeevich Khrushchev. Dva Tsveta Vremeni. Dokumenty iz lichnogo fonda N.S. Khrushchev. Tom 1* (Moscow: Mezhdunarodnyi Fond «Demokratiia», 2009), pp. 440-456.)

At the Eighth All-Union Congress of Soviets in November 1936 it was again Khrushchev who proposed that the new Soviet Constitution, which was before the Congress for approval, should be called the 'Stalinist Constitution' because

"…it was written from beginning to end by Comrade Stalin himself." (Pravda, 30 November 1936, cited in: L. Pistrak: ibid.; p. 161).

It has to be noted that Vyacheslav Molotov, then Prime Minister, and Andrey Zhdanov, then Party Secretary in Leningrad, did not mention any special role by Stalin in the drafting of the Constitution.

In the same speech Khrushchev coined the term 'Stalinism':

"Our Constitution is the Marxism-Leninism-Stalinism that has conquered one sixth of the globe." (Ibid.).

Khrushchev's speech in Moscow to an audience of 200,000 at the time of the treason trial of Georgii Piatakov(23) and Karl Radek in January 1937 was in a similar vein:

"By lifting their hands against comrade Stalin they lifted them against all the best that humanity possesses. For *Stalin* is hope; he is expectation; he is the beacon that guides all progressive mankind. Stalin is our banner! Stalin is our will! Stalin is our victory!" (Pravda, 31 January 1937), cited in: L. Pistrak: ibid.; p. 162. Entire speech at Tomilina ed., *Nikita Sergeevich Khrushchev T. 1* pp. 465-8; this exact passage at top of p. 467).

Stalin was described by Khrushchev in March 1939 as "...our great genius, our beloved Stalin," (*Visti VTsVK*, 3 March 1939, cited in: L. Pistrak: ibid.;p. 164).

at the 18th Congress of the Party in March 1939 as

"...the greatest genius of humanity, teacher and 'vozhd', who leads us towards Communism, our very own Stalin" (*XVIII S'ezd Vsesoiuznoi Kommunisticheskoi Partii (b.)*), p. 174, cited in: L. Pistrak: ibid., p. 164).

and in May 1945 as "...great Marshal of the Victory." (*Pravda Ukrainy*, 13 May 1945, cited in: L. Pistrak: ibid.; p. 164)."

Mikoian

On the occasion of the celebration of Stalin's fiftieth birthday in December 1929, Anastas Mikoian accompanied his congratulations with the demand

"...that we, meeting the rightful demand of the masses, begin finally to work on his biography and make it available to the Party and to all working people in our country." (*Izvestia*, 21 December 1929, cited in: L. Pistrak: ibid.; p. 164).

Ten years later, on the occasion of Stalin's sixtieth birthday in December 1939, Mikoian was still urging the creation of a "...scientific biography" of Stalin. (*Pravda*, 21 December 1939, cited in: L. Pistrak: ibid.; p. 158)."

Stalin's suspicions of cult – Tuominen, Feuchtwanger (Bland, 12)

That Stalin himself was not unaware of the fact that concealed revisionists were the main force behind the 'cult of personality' was reported by the Finnish revisionist Tuominen in 1935, who describes how, when he was informed that busts of him had been given prominent places in Moscow's leading art gallery, the Tretyakov, Stalin exclaimed:

"That's downright sabotage!" (A. Tuominen: op. cit.; p. 164).

Bland, 12-13 (fm Tuominen) – Bill Bland, "The Cult of the Individual," http://www.mltranslations.org/Britain/StalinBB.htm Bland has collected much more evidence of Stalin's opposition to the "cult."

The German writer Leon Feuchtwanger (24) in 1936 confirms that Stalin suspected that the 'cult of personality' was being fostered by 'wreckers' with the aim of discrediting him:

"It is manifestly irksome to Stalin to be worshipped as he is, and from time to time he makes fun of it... Of all the men I know who have power, Stalin is the most unpretentious. I spoke frankly to him about the vulgar and excessive cult made of him, and he replied with equal candour... He thinks it is possible even that 'wreckers' may be behind it in an attempt to discredit him." (L. Feuchtwanger: *Moscow 1937*; London; 1937; p. 93, 94-95).

Stalin refused to allow the establishment of an Order of Stalin, which was proposed first in 1945 by five Politburo members, and again on his 70th birthday in 1949. It was established only after his death.

> In the Politburo of the CC ACP(b)
>
> We present for consideration by the Politburo the following resolutions:
>
> 1. To award com. Stalin with the order of "Victory";
>
> 2. To award com. Stalin the title of "Hero of the Soviet Union."
>
> 3. To establish an Order of Stalin;
>
> 4. To erect a Stalin Arch of Victory on the autoroute Moscow-Minsk at the entrance to Moscow.
>
> We propose that the corresponding decrees be taken at the XII session of the Supreme Soviet.
>
> 22.VI.45
>
> V. Molotov
>
> L. Beria
>
> G. Malenkov
>
> K. Voroshilov
>
> A. Mikoian

When was Stalingrad named?

- V.A. Durov, "Orden Stalina Stalin ne utverdil", *Rodina* No. 4, 2005. At http://chss.montclair.edu/english/furr/research/durovorden.pdf

The last two proposals were not taken. Writing in pencil on the left-hand corner reads "My archive. J. Stalin."

Stalin rejected renaming Moscow after himself

In 1937-38 a proposal was made to rename Moscow "Stalinodar" ("gift of Stalin").

> However, this renaming never happened. M.I. Kalinin informed the Presidium of the Supreme Soviet of the USSR and RSFSR that J.V. Stalin expressed his categorical opposition to this proposal…
>
> Moscow remained Moscow.

- B.A. Starkov, "Kak Moskva chut' ne stala Stalinodarom." *Izvestiia TsK KPSS.* 1990, No.12, pp. 126-127. At http://chss.montclair.edu/english/furr/research/stalinodar.pdf

2. Lenin's "Testament"

Khrushchev:

"In December 1922, in a letter to the Party Congress, Vladimir Il'ich wrote: "After taking over the position of Secretary General, Comrade Stalin accumulated in his hands immeasurable power and I am not certain whether he will be always able to use this power with the required care."

This letter – a political document of tremendous importance, known in the party history as Lenin's "testament" – was distributed among the delegates to the 20th Party Congress. You have read it and will undoubtedly read it again more than once. You might reflect on Lenin's plain words, in which expression is given to Vladimir Il'ich's anxiety concerning the party, the people, the state, and the future direction of party policy.

Vladimir Il'ich said:

> "Stalin is excessively rude, and this defect, which can be freely tolerated in our midst and in contacts among us Communists, becomes a defect which cannot be tolerated in one holding the position of the Secretary General. Because of this, I propose that

the comrades consider the method by which Stalin would be removed from this position and by which another man would be selected for it, a man who, above all, would differ from Stalin in only one quality, namely, greater tolerance, greater loyalty, greater kindness and more considerate attitude toward the comrades, a less capricious temper, etc."

This document of Lenin's was made known to the delegates at the 13th Party Congress, who discussed the question of transferring Stalin from the position of Secretary General. The delegates declared themselves in favor of retaining Stalin in this post, hoping that he would heed the critical remarks of Vladimir Il'ich and would be able to overcome the defects which caused Lenin serious anxiety.

Comrades! The Party Congress should become acquainted with two new documents, which confirm Stalin's character as already outlined by Vladimir Il'ich Lenin in his "testament." These documents are a letter from Nadezhda Konstantinovna Krupskaia to [Leo B.] Kamenev, who was at that time head of the Political Bureau, and a personal letter from Vladimir Il'ich Lenin to Stalin.

I will now read these documents:

"LEV BORISOVICH!

"Because of a short letter which I had written in words dictated to me by Vladimir Il'ich by permission of the doctors, Stalin allowed himself yesterday an unusually rude outburst directed at me. This is not my first day in the party. During all these 30 years I have never heard from any comrade one word of rudeness. The business of the party and of Il'ich are not less dear to me than to Stalin. I need at present the maximum of self-control. What one can and what one cannot discuss with Il'ich I know better than any doctor, because I know what makes him nervous and what does not, in any case I know better than Stalin. I am turning to you and to Grigorii [E. Zinoviev] as much closer comrades of V. I. and I beg you to protect me from rude interference with my private life and from vile invectives and threats. I have no doubt as to what will be the unanimous decision of the Control Commission, with which Stalin sees fit to threaten me; however, I have neither the strength nor the time to waste on this foolish quarrel. And I am a living person and my nerves are strained to the utmost.

"N. KRUPSKAIA"

Nadezhda Konstantinovna wrote this letter on December 23, 1922. After two and a half months, in March 1923, Vladimir Il'ich Lenin sent Stalin the following letter:

"TO COMRADE STALIN:

"COPIES FOR: KAMENEV AND ZINOVIEV."

"Dear Comrade Stalin!

"You permitted yourself a rude summons of my wife to the telephone and a rude reprimand of her. Despite the fact that she told you that she agreed to forget what was said, nevertheless Zinoviev and Kamenev heard about it from her. I have no intention to forget so easily that which is being done against me; and I need not stress here that I consider as directed against me that which is being done against my wife. I ask you, therefore, that you weigh carefully whether you are agreeable to retracting your words and apologizing or whether you prefer the severance of relations between us.

"SINCERELY: LENIN

"MARCH 5, 1923"

(Commotion in the hall.) *These asides not in speech. Added later.*

Comrades! I will not comment on these documents. They speak eloquently for themselves. Since Stalin could behave in this manner during Lenin's life, could thus behave toward Nadezhda Konstantinovna Krupskaia – whom the party knows well and values highly as a loyal friend of Lenin and as an active fighter for the cause of the party since its creation – we can easily imagine how Stalin treated other people. These negative characteristics of his developed steadily and during the last years acquired an absolutely insufferable character."

Trotsky denies Lenin wrote a "Testament", 1925

"In several parts of his book Eastman says that the Central Committee concealed' from the Party a number of exceptionally important documents written by Lenin in the last period of his life (it is a matter of letters on the national question, the so-called 'will', and others); there can be no other name for this than slander against the Central Comriitee of our Party. From what Eastman says it may be inferred that Vladimir Il'ich intended those letters, which bore the character of advice on internal organisation, for the press. In point of fact, that is absolutely untrue ... .It goes without saying that all those letters and proposals ... were brought to the knowledge of the delegates at the 12th and 13th Congresses, and always, of course, exercised due influence upon the Party's decisions; and if not all of those letters were published, it was because the author did not intend them for the press. **Vladimir Il'ich did not leave any 'will', and the very character of his attitude towards the Party, as well as the character of the Party itself, precluded any possibility of such a 'will'. What is usually referred to as a 'will' in the émigré and foreign bourgeois and Menshevik press (in a manner garbled beyond recognition) is one of Vladimir Il'ich's letters containing advice on organizational matters.** The 13th Congress of the Party paid the closest attention to that letter, as to all of the others, and drew from it the conclusions appropriate to the conditions and circumstances of the time. **All talk about concealing or violating a 'will' is a malicious invention and is wholly directed against the actual desires of Vladimir Il'ich and the interests of the Party he founded"**.

- L.D.Trotsky: 'Concerning Eastman's Book *Since Lenin Died*', in: *Bolshevik*, 16; 1 Sep, 1925; p. 68, my translation; emphasis GF. Cf. the text in Trotsky, Leon, "Two Statements 'By Trotsky'".*The Challenge of the Left Opposition (1923-25)*, p. 310.[250]

In December 1922 the Plenum of the Central Committee took the decision to entrust to Stalin the responsibility to isolate Lenin, 1922:

DECISION OF THE PLENUM OF THE CENTRAL COMMITTEE OF THE RUSSIAN COMMUNIST PARTY (Bolshevik)
18 December 1922

---

[250] The Trotskyist editors of this volume put quotation marks around Trotsky's name here to indicate that he wrote and signed these documents even though they did not express his true thoughts. The editors do not seem to realize that this makes Trotsky look like the kind of unprincipled self-promoter his political opponents accused him of being!

In the case of the request of c(omrade) Lenin about the Plenum's decision on the question of foreign trade, with the agreement of Stalin and the doctors, to communicate to him [Lenin] the text of the resolution with the addition that both the resolution and the makeup of the commission were taken unanimously.

Not in any event to transmit [to Lenin] c(omrade) Yaroslavsky's report and to keep it in order to transmit it when permitted by the doctors, in agreement with c(omrade) Stalin.

To entrust c(omrade) Stalin with personal responsibility for the isolation of Vladimir Il'ich [Lenin] with respect both to personal contact with workers and to correspondence.

- *Izvestiia TsK KPSS* No. 12, 1989, p. 191. Also at
http://www.hrono.ru/libris/stalin/16-62.html

According to Volkogonov (and others),

"On the morning of December 24 (1922) Stalin, Kamenev and Bukharin discussed the situation. They decided they did not have the right to enforce silence upon their Leader [Lenin]. But care, precautions, the maximum possible quiet were essential. They took the following decision:

'1. Vladimir Ilich has the right to dictate 5-10 minutes every day, but not to conduct a correspondence, and Vladimir Ilich must not expect answers from these notes. Meetings are forbidden.

2. Neither friends nor domestic persons must communicate to Vladimir Ilich anything political, so as not to give him cause for reflections and upset."

- Volkogonov, Dmitri. *Stalin.* Vol. I. M., 1992, Ch. 2, par. 156; cited at
http://militera.lib.ru/bio/volkogonov_dv/02.html

Stalin's reply to Lenin concerning Krupskaia

"March 7, 1923.

Comrade Lenin!

About five weeks ago I had a talk with com. N. Konst.
[Natalia Konstantinova – Krupskaia's name and
patronymic], whom I consider not only your wife, but
also my old Party comrade, and told her (on the
telephone) approximately the following:

'The doctors have forbidden us to give Il'ich polit.
information, and consider this regimen the most
important means of treating him. Meanwhile you, N.K.,
as it turns out, are violating this regime. We must not
play with Il'ich's life', etc.

My explanations with N.K. have confirmed that there is
nothing in this but empty misunderstandings, and indeed
there could not have been.

However, if you consider that I must "take back" the
above words which I spoke for the sake of keeping our
"relationship," I can take then back. But I do not
understand what the problem here is, what my "fault" is,
and what precisely is expected of me."

- *ibid.*, p. 193. Also at http://www.hrono.ru/libris/stalin/16-47.html I
have made a facsimile of the original letter handwritten by Stalin on
March 7, 1923 available on the internet at

http://chss.montclair.edu/english/furr/research/staltolenin03071923.jpg

According to Lenin's sister, Stalin's letter was not given to Lenin because
his health was getting worse, and Lenin never knew that Stalin had written it:

"…and so V.I. never did know of his letter, in which
Stalin excused himself."

- M. Ul'ianova. *Izvestiia TsK KPSS*. No. 12, 1989, p. 195.

According to M. Volodicheva, one of Lenin's secretaries during his final
illness, when given Lenin's letter Stalin acted like this:

"I handed the letter to him personally. I asked Stalin to
write a letter to Vladimir Ilich right away, as he was
awaiting his answer and was upset. Stalin read through
the letter while standing, right there, in my presence. His
face remained calm. He was silent a time, thought a bit,
and then said the following words, pronouncing each

word clearly, pausing between them: 'It is not Lenin but his illness that is speaking. I am not a medical doctor, I am a political person. I am Stalin. If my wife, who is a Party member, acted wrongly and was disciplined, I would not consider it right for me to interfere in the matter. And Krupskaia is a Party member. But since Vladimir Il'ich insists, I am prepared to excuse myself to Krupskaia for rudeness."

- M. Volodicheva, cited by A. Bek, *Moskovskie Novosti* April 23, 1989.

In one of his talks with the writer Felix Chuev L.M. Kaganovich touched upon the subject of the mutual relations between Stalin and Lenin:

"Well, in Lenin's time there were some things that were very unpleasant. Concerning Lenin's letter, Stalin once told me: 'But what could I do in this situation? The Politburo assigned me to make sure that he [Lenin] was not burdened, that the doctors' orders were carried out, not to give him paper, not to give him newspapers, and what could I do – violate the Politburo's decision? I just couldn't do that. And they attacked me.' He told me this personally with great bitterness, great bitterness. With such heartfelt bitterness."

- Chuev, F. *Tak govoril Kaganovich*. Moscow, 1992, p. 191. Also in Felix I. Chuev, *Kaganovich, Shepilov*. Moscow: OLMA-PRESS, 2001, p. 263.

For Maria Il'inichn Ul'ianova's letters, published in *Izvestiia TsK KPSS* No. 12, 1989, pp. 195-199, see

http://chss.montclair.edu/english/furr/research/ulianova.html

Another of Lenin's assistants, Lidia Fotieva, remarked:

Nadezhda Konstantinova did not always conduct herself as she ought to have done. She could have discussed this with Vladimir Il'ich. She was accustomed to share everything with him. And even in those cases when she ought not to have done so … For example, why did she tell Vladimir Il'ich that Stalin was crude to her on the phone?

- Cited by A. Bek, *Moskovskie Novosti* April 23, 1989.

Lenin asked Stalin to give him poison on demand:

On Saturday March 17 c. Ul'ianova (N.K.) communicated to me in a very conspiratorial manner the request of Vl. Il'ich to Stalin that I, Stalin, should assume the duty of obtaining and giving to Vl. Il'ich an amount of sodium cyanide. In this conversation with me N.K. said, among other things, that "Vl. Il'ich is suffering unimaginable pain", that "it is unthinkable to go on living like this", and she stubbornly insisted that I "not refuse Il'ich's request". In view of N.K.'s especial insistence and the fact that V. Il'ich demanded my agreement (during this conversation with me V.I. twice called N.K. to come to see him, demanding with great emotion Stalin's agreement), I considered it impossible to refuse and replied: "I ask V. Il'ich to calm himself and be assured that, when it becomes necessary, I will carry out his demand without hesitation." V. Il'ich did in fact become calm.

However, I must state that I do not have the strength to carry out V. Il'ich's request, and am forced to reject this commission, regardless of how humanitarian and necessary it may be. I will so inform the meeting of the members of the P.Buro of the CC.

J. Stalin

Remark: The note is on an official form of Secretary of the Central Committee of the RCP(b) J.V. Stalin and is dated March 21, 1923. In the upper part of the sheet are the signatures of those who read it: G. Zinoviev, V. Molotov, N. Bukharin, L. Kamenev, L. Trotsky, M. Tomsky. The last considered it essential to express his opinion: "Read. I consider St's 'indecision' correct. We must discuss this strictly among the members of the Pol. Buro. Without secretaries (I mean the technical ones).

- DmitriiVolkogonov, *Stalin*. Russian edition, vol. 2, between pages 384 and 385. I have put an exact facsimile of the originals of these documents at

http://chss.montclair.edu/english/furr/research/stalinleninpoison23.pdf

3. "Collegiality" In Work.

At several points in his speech Khrushchev complains about Stalin's lack of collegiality and violation of collective leadership.

"We have to consider seriously and analyze correctly this matter in order that we may preclude any possibility of a repetition in any form whatever of what took place during the life of Stalin, who absolutely did not tolerate collegiality in leadership and in work, and who practiced brutal violence, not only toward everything which opposed him, but also toward that which seemed, to his capricious and despotic character, contrary to his concepts.

Stalin acted not through persuasion, explanation and patient cooperation with people, but by imposing his concepts and demanding absolute submission to his opinion. Whoever opposed this concept or tried to prove his viewpoint and the correctness of his position was doomed to removal from the leading collective and to subsequent moral and physical annihilation." (5-6)

"In practice, Stalin ignored the norms of party life and trampled on the Leninist principle of collective party leadership."

Marshal Zhukov:

> "After J.V. Stalin's death appeared the tale about how he used to take military and strategic decisions unilaterally. This was not the case at all. I have already said above that if you reported questions to the Supreme Commander with a knowledge of your business, he took them into account. And I know of cases when he turned against his own previous opinion and changed decisions he had taken previously."

- Zhukov, G.K. *Vospominaniia i razmyshleniia*. V. 2 tt. Moscow: OLMA-PRESS, 2002, p. 163. Also at http://militera.lib.ru/memo/russian/zhukov1/17.html

> "By the way, as I was convinced during the war, J.V. Stalin was not at all the kind of man before whom one could not post sharp questions and with whom one could not argue, and even firmly defend one's own point of view. If someone says differently [e.g. Khrushchev – GF] then I tell you directly – their affirmations are not truthful."

- *ibid.* p. 229. Also at
http://militera.lib.ru/memo/russian/zhukov1/09.html
Zhukov again:

> "His style of work, as a rule, was businesslike. Everyone could express his own opinion without being nervous. The Supreme Commander treated everyone the same way – strictly and officially. He knew how to listen attentively when you reported to him with knowledge of your topic. He himself was laconic, and did not like verbosity in others."

- *ibid.* p. 338. Also at
http://militera.lib.ru/memo/russian/zhukov1/11.html

Anastas Mikoian:

> "I must say that each one of us had the full ability to express himself and defend his opinion or proposal. We frankly discussed the most complicated and contested questions (as for myself, I can speak on this point with the fullest responsibility), and met on Stalin's part in most cases with understanding, a reasoned and patient attitude even when our statements were obviously disagreeable to him.
>
> He was also attentive to the proposals by the generals. Stalin listened carefully to what was said to him and to counsel, listened to disagreements with interest, extracting intelligently from them that bit of truth that helped him later to formulate his final, most appropriate decisions which were born in this way, as a result of collective discussion. More than this: it commonly happened that, convinced by our evidence, Stalin changed his own preliminary viewpoint on one or another question."

- Mikoian, *Tak bylo.* Moscow: Vagrius, 1999. Chapter 37, p. 464.

> … the companionable atmosphere of management work did not lessen Stalin's role. On the contrary, we almost always attributed out own proposals, formalized under Stalin's signature, entirely to Stalin, without revealing that

> their author was not Stalin but some other comrade. And he [Stalin] signed, sometimes making amendments, sometimes not, sometimes not even reading it, since he trusted us.

- Mikoian, *Tak bylo*, Chapter 41.

Benediktov, long-time high official in Agriculture:

> Contrary to a widespread view, all questions in those years, including those involving the transfer of leading party, state and military figures, were decided in a collegial manner in the Politburo. At the Politburo sessions themselves arguments and discussions often flared up, different, sometimes contradictory opinions were expressed within the framework, naturally, of party directives. There was no quiet, untroubled unanimity – Stalin and his colleagues could not abide that. I am quite justified in saying this because I was present at Politburo sessions many times. Yes, as a rule Stalin's viewpoint came out on top. But this occurred because he was more objective, thought through problems in a more all-round way, saw further and deeper than others.

- I.A. Benediktov, "O Staline I Khrushcheve", *Molodaia Gvardiia* No. 4, 1989. At http://stalinism.newmail.ru/benedikt.htm

Marshal Shtemenko:

> "General of the army S.M. Shtemenko who was closely associated by his work with J.V. Stalin during the war years, writes: 'I must say that Stalin did not decide, and in general did not like to decide, important military questions unilaterally. He well understood the necessity of collective work in this complex field. He recognized the authorities in this or that military problem, took their opinions into account, and gave each man his due. In December 1943 after the Teheran Conference, when we needed to work out plans for future military actions, the report at the joint session of the Politburo of the CC of the AUCP(b), the Supreme Defense Committee, and the General Staff concerning the course of the war at the front and its future course was made by A.M. Vasilevskii and A.I. Antonov, while N. A Voznesenskii reported on

question of the war economy, and J. V. Stalin took upon himself the analysis of problems of an international character."

- S.M. Shtemenko, *The General Staff During the War Years*. Book 2. Moscow, 1981, p. 275. Cited from B. Solov'ev and V. Sukhdeev, *Polkovodets Stalin*. M 2003, at http://militera.lib.ru/research/suhodeev_vv/04.html

Dmitri Shepilov:

> "Stalin looked very good and for some reason was very cheerful. He joked, laughed, and was very democratic.
>
> – Shepilov has just told me that it is hard to lead *Pravda*. Of course it's hard. I thought, maybe we should nominate two editors?
>
> Here everyone began to disagree noisily:
>
> – No, there'll be a dual leadership… There'll be no order, no one will know whom to ask.
>
> – Well, I see that the people do not support me. Where the people go, there too go I."

-*Neprimknuvshii*, M. 2001, pp. 236-7. Also at http://www.pseudology.org/ShepilovDT/11.htm

Khrushchev himself admitted this quality in Stalin:

> "I remained in my opinion. And here was something interesting (which was also characteristic of Stalin): this man, in a flairup of anger, could do a lot of harm. But when you demonstrated to him that you were right and if you adduced good facts, he would understand in the end that this was a man who was defending a useful cause, and would support you. … Yes, there were cases when you could firmly disagree with him and if he was convinced you were right, then he would yield his own point of view and take the point of view of his interlocutor. Of course this is a positive quality.

But then Khrushchev hastened to add:

> "But, unfortunately, you could count the number of times this happened on your fingers."

(Khrushchev had evidently already forgotten that he had just called this quality of Stalin's "characteristic.")

- Khrushchev, N.S. *Vrenia, Liudi, Vlast'*. Book 2, Part 3. Moscow: Moskovskie novosti, 1999, Chapter 3, pp. 43-4 (Russian edition). Also at
http://hronos.km.ru/libris/lib_h/hrush34.html

In fact it was Khrushchev himself who refused to lead collectively and
was removed in large part for that in 1964.

> [From Suslov's speech]"Com. Khrushchev, having
> concentrated in his hands the posts of First secretary of
> the CC of the party and Chairman of the Council of
> Ministers, has by no means always correctly used the
> rights and obligations entrusted to him. Breaking with
> the Leninist principles of collectivity in leadership, he has
> begun to strive towards unilaterally deciding the most
> important questions of party and state work, has begun
> to neglect the opinions of the collective of party and
> government leaders, has stopped considering the views
> and advice of his comrades. More recently he has
> decided even the most important questions in an
> essentially individual manner, crudely insisting upon his
> own subjective, often completely incorrect point of view.
> He believes himself to be without error, has appropriated
> to himself a monopolistic claim to the truth. To all
> comrades who have expressed their opinions and made
> remarks unpleasing to com. Khrushchev, he has
> arrogantly given all kinds of demeaning and insulting
> nicknames that lower their personal dignity…. As a
> result of com. Khrushchev's incorrect behavior the
> Presidium of the CC has become less and less an organ
> of collective, creative discussion and decision-making.
> Collective leadership has in fact become impossible.
>
> It has become more and more clear that com.
> Khrushchev is striving for an exaltation of his own
> personality and the ignoring of the Presidium and the CC
> CPSU. These incorrect actions of com. Khrushchev can
> be interpreted as his striving to advance a cult of his own
> personality…"

- "Kak snimali N.S. Khrushcheva." *Istoricheskii Arkhiv* No. 1, 1993, pp.7-
10.

Stalin's Four Attempts to Resign as First Secretary, then as Secretary, of the Party

August 19, 1924

To the Plenum of the CC RCP

One and a half years of working in the Politburo with comrades Zinoviev and Kamanev after the retirement and then the death of Lenin have made perfectly clear to me the impossibility of honest, sincere political work with these comrades within the framework of one small collective. In view of which I request to be considered as having resigned from the Pol[itical] Buro of the CC.

I request a medical leave for about two months.

At the expiration of this period I request to be sent to Turukhansk region or to the Iakutsk oblast', or to somewhere abroad in any kind of work that will attract little attention.

I would ask the Plenum [of the C.C. – GF] to decide all these questions in my absence and without explanations from my side, because I consider it harmful for our work to give explanations aside from those remarks that I have already made in the first paragraph of this letter.

I would ask comrade Kuibyshev to distribute copies of this letter to the members of the CC.

With com[munist] greet[ings], J.Stalin.

19.VIII.24

- *Rodina.* 1994. 7. . 72   -73.

December 27, 1926

To the Plenum of the CC (to com. Rykov). I ask that I be relieved of the post of GenSec [General Secretary] of the CC. I declare that I can work no longer in this position, I do not have the strength to work any more in this position. J. Stalin.

27.XII.26

- *Rodina*. 1994. 7. . 72   -73.

December 19, 1927

Fragment of the transcript of the CC Plenum.

> Stalin: Comrades! For three years I have been asking the CC to free me from the obligations of General Secretary of the CC. Each time the Plenum has refused me. I admit that until recently conditions did exist such that the Party had need of me in this post as a person more or less severe, one who acted as a certain kind of antidote to the dangers posed by the Opposition. I admit that this necessity existed, despite comrade Lenin's well-known letter, to keep me at the post of General Secretary. But those conditions exist no longer. They have vanished, since the Opposition is now smashed. It seems that the Opposition has never before suffered such a defeat since they have not only been smashed, but have been expelled from the Party. It follows that now no bases exist any longer that could be considered correct when the Plenum refused to honor my request and free me of the duties of General Secretary. Meanwhile you have comrade Lenin's directive which we are obliged to consider and which, in my opinion, it is necessary to put into effect. I admit that the Party was compelled to disregard this directive until recently, compelled by well-known conditions of inter-Party development. But I repeat that these conditions have now vanished and it is time, in my view, to take comrade Lenin's directive to the leadership. Therefore I request the Plenum to free me of the post of General Secretary of the CC. I assure you, comrades, that the Party can only gain from doing this.

> Dogadov: Vote without discussion.

> Voroshilov: I propose that we reject the announcement we just heard.

> Rykov: We will vote without discussion. ... We vote now on Stalin's proposal that he be freed from the General

Secretaryship. Who is for this proposal? Who is against?
Who abstains? One.

The proposal of comrade Stalin is rejected with one
abstention.

Stalin: Then I introduce another proposal. Perhaps the
CC will consider it expedient to abolish the position of
Gensec. In our Party's history there have been times
when no such post existed.

Voroshilov: We had Lenin with us then.

Stalin: We had no post of Gensec before the 10th
Congress.

Voice: Until the 11th Congress.

Stalin: Yes, it seems that until the 11th Congress we did
not have this position. That was before Lenin stopped
working. If Lenin concluded that it was necessary to put
forward the question of founding the position of
Gensec, then I assume he was prompted by the special
circumstances that appeared with us bfore the 10th
Congress, when a more or less strong, well-organized
Opposition within the Party was founded. But now we
no longer have these conditions in the Party, because the
Opposition is smashed to a man. Therefore we could
proceed to the abolition of this position. Many people
associate a conception of some kind of special rights of
the Gensec with this position. I must say from my
experience, and comrades will confirm this, that there
ought not to be any special rights distinguishing the
Gensec from the rights of other members of the
Secretariat.

Voice: And the duties?

Stalin: And there are no more duties than other members
of the Secretariat have. I see it this way: There's the
Politburo, the highest organ of the CC; there's the
Secretariat, the executive organ consisting of five
persons, and all these five members of the Secretariat are
equal. That's the way the work has been carried out in
practice, and the Gensec has not had any special rights

or obligations. The result, therefore, is that the position of Gensec, in the sense of special rights, has never existed with us in practice, there has been only a collegium called the Secretariat of the CC. I do not know why we need to keep this dead position any longer. I don't even mention the fact that this position, called Gensec, has occasioned in some places a series of distortions. At the same time that at the top no special rights or duties are associated with the position of Gensec, in some places there have been some distortions, and in all the oblasts there is now a struggle over that position among comrades who call themselves secretaries, for example, in the national CCs. Quite a few Gensecs have developed, and with them in the localities special rights have been associated. Why is this necessary?

Shmidt: We can dismiss them in these localities.

Stalin. I think the Party would benefit if we did away with the post of Gensec, and that would give me the chance to be free from this post. This would be all the easier to do since according to the Party's constitution there is no post of Gensec.

Rykov: I propose not to give comrade Stalin the possibility of being free from this position. As concerns the Gensecs in the oblast and local organs, that should be changed, but without changing the situation in the CC. The position of General Secretary was created by the proposal of Vladimir Il'ich. In all the time since, during Vladimir Il'ich's life and since, this position has justified itself politically and completely in both the organizational and political sense. In the creation of this organ and in naming comrade Stalin to the post of Gensec the whole Opposition also took part, all those whom we have now expelled from the Party. That is how completely without doubt it was for everyone in the Party (whether the position of Gensec was needed and who should be the General Secretary). By which has been exhausted, in my opinion, both the question of the "testament" (for that point has been decided) and exhausted by the Opposition at the same time just as it has been decided by us as well. The whole Party knows this. What has changed now after the 15ᵗʰ Congress and why is it necessary to set aside the position of Gensec?

Stalin. The Opposition has been smashed.

(A long discussion followed, after which:)

Voices: Correct! Vote!

Rykov: There is a proposal to vote.

Voices: Yes, yes!

Rykov: We are voting. Who is for comrade Stalin's proposal to abolish the post of General Secretary? Who is opposed? Who abstains? No.

Stalin: Comrades, during the first vote about freeing me from the duties of secretary I did not vote, I forgot to vote. I ask that my vote be counted as "Against."

Voice from a seat. That does not mean much.

- Quoted from G. Cherniavskii. "Prizhok iz partiinykh dzhunglei." *Kaskad* (Baltimore, MD) at http://kackad.com/kackad/?p=855

October 16, 1952

In the memoirs of Akakii Mgeladze we read:

... At the first Plenum of the CC of the CPSU called after the XIX Congress of the Party (I had been elected member of the CC and took part in the work of this Plenum), Stalin really did present the question that he should be freed either of the post of General Secretary of the CC CPSU, or of the post of Chairman of the Council of Ministers of the USSR. He referred to his age, overwork, said that other cadres had cropped up there were and people to replace him, for example, N.I. Bulganin could be appointed as Chairman of the Council of Ministers, but the CC members did not grant his request, all insisted that comrade Stalin remain at both positions.

- A.I. Mgeladze, *Stalin. Kakim ia ego znal. Strannitsy nedavnogo proshlogo*. N.pl., 2001, p. 118. Also see Chapter 9, where Stalin's speech to this Plenum as recalled by L.N. Efremov is discussed.

4. Stalin "Morally and Physically Annihilated" Leaders Who Opposed Him.

Khrushchev:

> "Stalin acted not through persuasion, explanation and patient cooperation with people, but by imposing his concepts and demanding absolute submission to his opinion. Whoever opposed this concept or tried to prove his viewpoint and the correctness of his position was doomed to removal from the leading collective and to subsequent moral and physical annihilation."

5. Mass Repressions generally

Khrushchev:

"It was precisely during this period (1935-1937-1938) that the practice of mass repression through the Government apparatus was born, first against the enemies of Leninism – Trotskyites, Zinovievites, Bukharinites, long since politically defeated by the party – and subsequently also against many honest Communists,..."

Khrushchev killed more than others:

From the Interview of V.P. Pronin, Chairman of the Moscow Soviet in 1939-45, from *Voenno-Istoricheskii Zhurnal* No. 10, 1991.

> "Question: And Khrushchev? What memories remain with you about him?
>
> Answer: [...] He actively aided the repressions. A sword of Damocles hung above his head. In 1920 Khrushchev had voted for the Trotskyist position. And therefore, obviously, he feared the consequences, and he himself 'battled' with especial zeal against carelessness, loss of political alertness, political blindness, etc. Khrushchev sanctioned the repressions of a large number of Party and Soviet workers. Under him almost all of the 23 secretaries of the raikoms of the city were arrested. And

almost all the secretaries of the raikoms of the [Moscow] province [oblast']. All the secretaries of the Moscow Committee and the Moscow City Committee of the party were repressed: Katsenelenbogen, Margolin, Kogan, Korytniy. All the managers of the sections, including Khrushchev's own assistant. Even after he was in the Ukraine Khrushchev insisted, in the Politburo in 1938, upon the repression of the second tier of leadership of the Moscow City Committee of the Party.

We, at that time young [Party] workers, were astonished. How could Khrushchev instruct us about 'alertness', if everybody around him turned out to be enemies of the people? He was the only one in the Moscow Committee who remained unharmed.

Question: Do you believe that the scale of repressions in Moscow was Khrushchev's personal "contribution"?

Answer: To a significant degree. After the autumn of 1938, the arrival of Shcherbakov to the leadership of the [Moscow] City Committee, not one of the [Party] workers of the Moscow Soviet, the Moscow [Party] Committee, the Moscow City [Party] Committee, or the regional committees was repressed. I know that in July 1940, when the question arose of removing Shcherbakov from work for the poor work of the aviation factories, they accused him also of very rarely, and even then very unwillingly, giving his agreement to repressions. On the contrary; in my presence at a meeting of the secretaries of the City Committee and on Shcherbakov's motion the head of the investigative section of the NKVD was expelled from the Party for unfounded arrests.

- Cited in Vladimir Alliluev, *Khronika odnoi sem'i: Alliluevy, Stalin.* Moscow, Molodaia gvardiia, 2002, p. 172.

Khrushchev promoted repression:

"We must annihilate all these scoundrels. In annihilating one, two, dozens, we do the work for millions. Therefore our hand must not tremble, we must walk across the corpses of the enemy for the people's benefit."

- Khrushchev, August 14, 1937. Vadim Kozhinov, *Russia. 20th Century. 1939-1964.* Ch. 8, at http://www.hrono.ru/libris/lib_k/kozhin20v11.php Mark IUnge and S.A. Kokin state that Khrushchev made this remark to a plenum of the Moscow City Soviet; *"Cherez trupy vraga na blago naroda"... T. 1.* Moscow: ROSSPEN 2010), p. 13.

Historian IUrii Zhukov claims he has seen the document in which Khrushchev asks for permission to raise "Category one" to 20,000 – a number, with no names.

> "Iuri Nikolaevich, we have Zoria Leonidovna Serebriakova on the line. Why do you, when you evaluate Stalin, not take into account the "lists to be shot", in which are documented, by the mark of his own pencil, the thousands of people sent off to their deaths?
>
> Zoria Leonidovna, and how is one to take into account those lists, where there are not even names, but simply the words: 'Permit me to shoot 20,000 people.' And the signature: 'Khrushchev, Nikita Sergeevich.' I will tell you where this document is."

- *Komsomolskaia Pravda* December 3 2002.

> "...Half of the first harvest took place in the Moscow province [oblast'], by no means the largest in the country. On the 'troika' formed here were, as specified, the first secretary of the Moscow obkom of the Party N.S. Khrushchev. Next to his name and signature we always find the name and signature of Redens, head of the UNKVD for the Moscow oblast' and relative of N. Allilueva, Stalin's second wife. Today Redens is numbered among the lists of 'victims of Stalin's willfulness.' And here is what Khrushchev and Redens represented... well, it's better if I cite their request to the Politburo: 'To shoot: 2,000 kulaks, 6,500 criminals, and to exile: 5869 kulaks, 26,936 criminals.' And this was only one swing of the sickle!"

- Zhukov, *Komsomolskaia Pravda* Nov. 19, 2002:

Khrushchev asked for authority to repress huge numbers of people in Moscow, including killing thousands.

> "CC ACP(b) – to comrade Stalin J.V.

I report that we have counted a total of 41,305 criminal and kulak elements who have served their sentences and settled in Moscow city and province.

Of those there are 33,436 criminal elements. Materials at hand give us the basis to put 6,500 criminals in Category 1 [to be shot – GF], and 26,396 in Category 2 [to be exiled- GF]. Of this number, for orientation purposes in the city of Moscow there are 1,500 in Category 1 and 5,272 in Category 2.

We have calculated there are 7,869 kulaks who have served their sentences and settled in Moscow city and oblast' Materials at hand give us the basis to put 2,000 from this group into Category 1 and 5,869 in Category 2.

We request that a commission be confirmed, consisting of comrades Redens, head of the UNKVD for the Moscow oblast'; Maslov, assistant prosecutory of the Moscow oblast', and Khrushchev, N.S. – Secretary of the Moscow Committee and Moscow City Committee, with the right, when necessary, to be replaced by A.A. Volkov – second secretary of the Moscow City Committee.

Secretary of the M[oscow] C[ommittee] of the ACP(b) –

(N. Khrushchev)". July 10, 1937.

- *Trud* June 4, 1992; republished in *Molotov, Malenkov, Kaganovich. 1957.* p. 747, n. 22.

Getty (Excesses, 127) cites Khrushchev's request for 41,000 people in both categories:

> In Moscow, First Secretary Nikita Khrushchev knew that he needed to repress exactly 41,805 kulaks and criminals. Nearly all of the submissions from the forty provinces and republics responding to Stalin's telegram were in such exact figures."

[Note: from Zhukov, totals are 41305; Getty writes 41,805. This must be from the same document cited above, so Getty copied wrong – GF]

According to Getty, after conferences in Moscow, the categories of people subject to this repression were greatly expanded, and "the target numbers submitted previously by the local authorities were revised, most

often downward." (p.128) That is, the "Center" – Stalin and the Politburo – tried to limit these repressions.

Taubman's large (876 pp.) work *Khrushchev: The Main and His Era* (NY:
Norton, 2003), does not even mention Khrushchev's repressions in Moscow, though they were greater in number than those in any other region.

As for the Ukrainian repression directed personally by Khrushchev, here
is what he says:

> "Yet the same Khrushchev presided over the purges,
> which apparently accelerated after his arrival. In 1938
> alone, 106,119 people are said to have been arrested;
> between 1938 and 1940 the total was 165,565. According
> to Molotov, hardly objective but extremely well
> informed, Khrushchev 'sent 54,000 people to the next
> world as a member of the [Ukrainian] troika.'
> Khrushchev's speeches dripped venom, and at least one
> case has come to light in which he scrawled, 'Arrest,'
> across the top of a document that doomed a high official
> of the Ukrainian Komsomol."

-Taubman, 116.

An example of Khrushchev's complaining to Stalin about "Moscow's" –
that is, Stalin and the Politburo's – lowering the numbers of people for
repression is this note from Khrushchev to Stalin:

> "Dear Iosif Vissarionovich! The Ukraine sends [requests
> for] 17,000 – 18,000 [persons to be] represed every
> month. And Moscow confirms no more than 2,000 –
> 3,000. I request that you take prompt measures. Your
> devoted N. Khrushchev."

- cited from Kosolapov, *Slovo Tovarishchu Stalinu*. M: Eksmo, 2002, p. 355
Although this note is widely quoted, I have not been able to find an archival citation for this statement.

> Khrushchev's appointment to the post of First Secretary
> of the CC of the Communist Party (b) of the Ukraine
> brought a qualitative increase in repression, testimony of
> which we find in a fragment from his speech at the 14th
> Congress of the Communist Party of the republic. "We
> will do everything, he said, in order to fulfill with honor
> the task and commands of the CC ACP(b) and of

comrade Stalin – to make the Ukraine an impregnable
fortress for enemies [of the people – GF].

... In his speech to the 20th Congress of the Party N.S.
Khrushchev deliberately avoided any mention of events
in the Ukraine and cited facts concerning the repressions
in other regions. But as they say, "You can't hide a
needle in a sack." We must consider as purely objective
the evaluation of his role in organizing mass repressions
in the Ukraine given, for example, in the speech of the
People's Commissar of Internal Affairs of the republic
Uspensky at the 14th Congress of the CP(b)U: "I, like
many other comrades speaking here – said the
Commissar – must acknowledge that the rout of enemies
of the people in the Ukraine began for real just a few
months ago, when we received to lead us that
experienced Bolshevik, pupil and comrade-in-arms of
great Stalin, Nikita Sergeevich Khrushchev."

- S. Kuz'min. "K repressiiam prichasten. Strikhi k politicheskomu por-
tretu N.S. Khrushchev. *Vozrozhdenie Nadezhdy.* No. 2, 1997. At
http://memory.irkutsk.ru/pub/fr2.htm Also quoted in N.F. Bugai,
Narody Ukrainy v 'Osoboi papke' Stalina. Moscow: Nauka, 2006, pp. 252-3.

More details about the huge number of persons "repressed" by Khrushchev in Moscow, 1936-37:

"N.S. Khrushchev, working as first secretary of the
M[oscow] C[ommittee] and the M[oscow] C[ity]
C[ommittee] of the ACP(b) in 1936-1937, and from 1937
as first secretary of the CC of the CP(b)U (Communist
Party of the Ukraine, Bolshevik), personally gave his as-
sent to the arrests of a significant number of Party and
Soviet workers. In the archive of the KGB there are
documentary materials that attest to Khrushchev's
participation in carrying out massive repressions in
Moscow, Moscow oblast', and in the Ukraine in the
prewar years. In particular he personally sent documents
with proposals for the arrests of leading workers of the
Moscow Soviet and Moscow Oblast' Committee of the
Party. In all, during 1936-1937 55,741 persons were

repressed by the organs of the Moscow and Moscow oblast' NKVD.

From January 1938 Khrushchev headed the Party organization of the Ukraine. In 1938 106,119 persons were arrested in the Ukraine. Repressions did not stop during the following years. In 1939 about 12,000 persons were arrested, and in 1940 – about 50,000 persons. In all, during the years 1938-1940 167,565 persons were arrested in the Ukraine.

The NKVD explained the increase in repressions in 1938 in the Ukraine in that, in connection with the arrival of Khrushchev, counter-revolutionary activity of the Right-Trotskyite underground grew especially quickly. Khrushchev personally sanctioned the repression of several hundred persons who were suspected of organizing terrorist acts [= assassination attempts] against himself.

In the summer of 1938 with Khrushchev's sanction a large group of leading Party, Soviet, and economic workers were arrested, among them the vice-chair of the Council of People's Commissars of the Ukrainian SSR, government ministers [*narkomy*], assistant ministers, secretaries of the oblast' committees of the Party. All were sentenced to execution or to long terms of imprisonment. According to lists sent by the NKVD of the USSR to the Politburo, for 1938 alone permission was given for the repression of 2,140 persons of the republican Party and Soviet cadre."

- "Massovye repressii opravdany byt' ne mogut." *Istochnik* No. 1, 1995, 126-7; *Reabilitatsia. Kak Eto Bylo*. III (Moscow, 2004), 146-7.

Khrushchev, February 1, 1956:

Question of com. Khrushchev [to Rodos]: Tell us in relation to coms. Postyshev, Kosior, you declared them enemies.

Com. Khrushchev:

The guilty parties are higher. Semi-criminal elements were brought into leading these investigations. Stalin is to blame.

Aristov: Comrade Khrushchev, do we have the courage to tell the truth?

Aristov: Eikhe refused to confess to the last, and they shot him nevertheless.

Com. Khrushchev: Ezhov, in all probability, was innocent, an honest man.

Com. Mikoian: The Decree about the struggle against terror was taken on December 1 1934.

[...]

Com. Khrushchev: Iagoda, in all probability, was an innocent [*chistiy* = 'clean'] man. Ezhov [also].

- *RKEB 1* 308-9, p. 308-9.

6. "Enemy of the people".

Khrushchev:

> Stalin originated the concept "enemy of the people." This term automatically rendered it unnecessary that the ideological errors of a man or men engaged in a controversy be proven; this term made possible the usage of the most cruel repression, violating all norms of revolutionary legality, against anyone who in any way disagreed with Stalin, against those who were only suspected of hostile intent, against those who had bad reputations. This concept "enemy of the people" actually eliminated the possibility of any kind of ideological fight or the making of one's views known on this or that issue, even those of a practical character. In the main, and in actuality, the only proof of guilt used, against all norms of current legal science, was the "confession" of the accused himself; and, as subsequent probing proved, "confessions" were acquired through physical pressures against the accused. This led to glaring violations of revolutionary legality and to the fact that many entirely innocent persons, who in the past had defended the party line, became victims.

> We must assert that, in regard to those persons who in their time had opposed the party line, there were often no sufficiently seri-

ous reasons for their physical annihilation. The formula "enemy of the people" was specifically introduced for the purpose of physically annihilating such individuals."

Jean-Paul Marat used the term "l'ennemi du people" in the first issue of his journal *L'Ami du Peuple* of 1793. See
http://membres.multimania.fr/jpmarat/amidpaf.html#ennemi

It is also famously the name of a play by Ibsen.

Maxim Gorky, in the story "Khersones Tavricheskii",1897.

> "…and in the conspiracy I will not act against the community, nor against any of the citizens who has not been declared an enemy of the people."

– Text at http://www.archaeology.ru/ONLINE/Gorki/gorky.html. S. Lifshits, "Preslovutiy Doklad Khrushcheva", at

http:// www.m-s-k.newmail.ru/pub/1.htm (retrieved July 5, 2004) gives the print citation as Gor'kii, M. *Sobranie sochinenii. V 30-ti t.* 23, p. 266.

Used by Lenin:

Lenin, "The land campaign and 'Iskra"s plan", 1903:

> "Serious support by the workers of the Zemstvo appeals should consist not in agreement about the conditions on which the Zemstvo representatives can speak in the name of the people, but by striking a blow at the enemies of the people."

- http://www.marxists.org/russkij/lenin/works/9-19.htm

Lenin, "The beginning of the revolution in Russia," 1905.

> "We Social-Democrats can and must proceed independently of the revolutionaries of the bourgeois democracy, guaranteeing the class independence of the proletariat, but we must go hand in hand with them during the uprising, while striking direct blows against Tsarism, in opposing the army, in attacking the Bastilles of the cursed enemy of the whole Russian people."

- http://www.marxists.org/russkij/lenin/1905/01/12a.htm

Lenin, May 9, 1918:

> "To declare all owners of grain who have surpluses and do not bring them to the export points, and also all the

grain supplies of all those who raise it for distilling
spirits, as enemies of the people; to turn them over to
the Revolutionary court and submit them from now on
to prison sentences of not less than 10 years,
confiscation of all property, and exile from their
community [obshchina] for life, and in addition to
subject distillers to forced social labor."

- Lenin, *Complete Works* v. 36, p. 318 (Russian edition). Quoted at
http://www.kursach.com/biblio/0010024/103_1.htm The Decree was
taken with minor changes. *Dekrety Sovetskoi vlasti.* Ed. G.D. Obichina et al.
T. 2: 17 marta – 10 iulia 1918 g. Moscow: Gospolitizdat, 1959, p. 265.

Decree of the Central Executive Committee and the Soviet of People's
Commissars of August 7, 1932:

"…People who infringe upon social property must be
considered enemies of the people, in view of which a
determined struggle against plunderers of social
possessions is the first duty of the organs of Soviet
power."

- *Tragediia Sovetskoi Derevni. Kollektivizatsia I raskulachivanie. Dokumenty I
materialy. 1927-1939. Tom 3. Konets 1930-1933.* Moscow: ROSSPEN, 2001.
No. 160, p. 453. Also at the Russian Wikisource page
http://tinyurl.com/law-of-aug-7-32

Khrushchev's use of the term:

"3. Enemies of the people have managed to do a lot of
damage in the area of assignment of cadres. The military
soviet has set as the main task to uproot completely the
remenants of hostile elements by carefully studying each
commander and political worker at the time of
promotion, and to boldly promote verified, devoted and
upcoming cadres…"

- quoted by Volkogonov, *Stalin*. Vol. 1, Ch. 7, at note 608. . For full text
and context, see below, under "Commanders Killed."

Trotskyites, Bukharinists, bourgeois nationalists and
other evil enemies of the people, suborners of the
restoration of capitalism, have made desperate attempts
to destroy from within the Leninist unity of the Party's

ranks – and they have all broken their heads on this unity.

- cited by IU.V. Emel'ianov. *Khrushchev. Smut'ian v Kremle*. Moscow: Veche, 2005, p. 32.

6a. "Convincing and Educating".

Khrushchev:

> "An entirely different relationship with people characterized Stalin. Lenin's traits – patient work with people, stubborn and painstaking education of them, the ability to induce people to follow him without using compulsion, but rather through the ideological influence on them of the whole collective -were entirely foreign to Stalin. He discarded the Leninist method of convincing and educating, he abandoned the method of ideological struggle for that of administrative violence, mass repressions and terror. " (pp. 7-8)

See below.

7. Zinoviev & Kamenev.

Khrushchev:

> "In his "testament" Lenin warned that "Zinoviev's and Kamenev's October episode was of course not an accident." But Lenin did not pose the question of their arrest and certainly not their shooting." (p. 9)

Stalin to Kaganovich, about testimony at the Zinoviev-Kamenev "Trial of the 16", August 1936.

> ... Second. From Reingol'd's confessions it is clear that Kamenev, through his wife Glebova, was feeling out the French ambassador [Hervé] Alphand concerning possible relations of the French government with / a future "government" of the Trotskyite-Zinovievite bloc. I think that Kamenev also felt out the English, German and American ambassadors. That means that Kamenev must have disclosed to these foreigners the plans of the plot and of the murders of the leaders of the Bolshevik Party. That also means that Kamenev had already

disclosed to them these plans, or else the foreigners
would not have agreed to have discussions with him
about a future Zinoviev-Trotskyite "government." This
is the attempt of Kamenev and his friends to conclude a
direct bloc with the bourgeois governments against the
Soviet government. This explains the secret of the well-
known advance obituaries of the American
correspondents. Obviously, Glebova is well informed
about all this sordid material. We must bring Glebova to
Moscow and submit her to a series of meticulous
interrogations. She might reveal many interesting things.

- Stalin i Kaganovich, *Perepiska 1931-1936 gg.* [Stalin-Kaganovich Correspondence, 1931-1936] (Russian), No. 763, pp. 642-3

D.M. Dmitriev's confession, concerning this event:

I remember the following cases:

1. The case of Tat'iana KAMENEVA. She was the wife
of L.E. KAMENEV. We had information that Tat'iana
KAMENEVA, on instructions from L.B. KAMENEV,
went to the French ambassador in Moscow AL'FAND
with a proposal to set up a meeting with L.B.
KAMENEV for countrevolutionary discussions
concerning help by the French government to
underground Trotskyites inside the USSR.

I and CHERTOK interrogated Tat'iana KAMENEVA
"steered away" from this accusation, making it possible
for her to avoid testimony about this fact during the
investigation.

- *Lubianka* 2, Doc. 356, p. 586. "L.E. Kamenev" is a typographical error
for L.B. Kamenev. The Kameneva referred to here is the same person as
the Glebova of the previous quotation.

8. Trotskyites

Khrushchev:

"Or, let us take the example of the Trotskyites. At
present, after a sufficiently long historical period, we can
speak about the fight with the Trotskyites with complete
calm and can analyze this matter with sufficient

objectivity. After all, around Trotsky were people whose origin cannot by any means be traced to bourgeois society. Part of them belonged to the party intelligentsia and a certain part were recruited from among the workers. We can name many individuals who, in their time, joined the Trotskyites; however, these same individuals took an active part in the workers' movement before the Revolution, during the Socialist October Revolution itself, and also in the consolidation of the victory of this greatest of revolutions. Many of them broke with Trotskyism and returned to Leninist positions. Was it necessary to annihilate such people?"

Stalin on Trotskyites at February-March 1937 C.C. Plenum, March 3:

"5. It should be explained to our Party comrades that the Trotskyites, who represent the active elements in the diversionist, wrecking and espionage work of the foreign intelligence services, have already long ceased to be a political trend in the working class, that they have already long ceased to serve any idea compatible with the interests of the working class, that they have turned into a gang of wreckers, diversionists, spies, assassins, without principles and ideas, working for the foreign intelligence services.

It should be explained that in the struggle against contemporary Trotskyism, not the old methods, the methods of discussion, must be used, but new methods, methods for smashing and uprooting it."

- J.V. Stalin, *Mastering Bolshevism*. NY: Workers Library Publishers, 1937, pp. 26-7; cited from http://www.marx2mao/Stalin/MB37.html

Stalin, concluding speech of Plenum on March 5:

"But here is the question – how to carry out in practice the task of smashing and uprooting the German-Japanese agents of Trotskyism. Does this mean that we should strike and uproot not only the real Trotskyites, but also those who wavered at some time toward Trotskyism, and then long ago came away from Trotskyism; not only those who are really Trotskyite agents for wrecking, but also those who happened once upon a time to go along a street where some Trotskyite or other had once passed? At any rate, such voices were heard here at the plenum. Can we consider such an interpretation of the resolution to be correct? No, we cannot consider it to be correct.

On this question, as on all other questions, there must be an individual, differentiated approach. You must not measure everyone with the same yardstick. Such a sweeping approach can only harm the cause of struggle against the real Trotskyite wreckers and spies.

Among our responsible comrades there are a certain number of former Trotskyites who left Trotskyism long ago, and now fight against Trotskyism not worse but better than some of our respected comrades who never chanced to waver toward Trotskyism. It would be foolish to vilify such comrades now.

Among our comrades there are also those who always stood against Trotskyism ideologically, but in spite of this kept up personal contacts with individual Trotskyites, which they did not delay in liquidating as soon as the actual visage of Trotskyism became clear to them. It is, of course, not a good thing that they did not break off their personal friendly connections with individual Trotskyites at once, but belatedly. But it would be silly to lump such comrades together with the Trotskyites."

- ibid., pp. 43-4.

Recall Khrushchev's own words – exactly what Stalin advocated at the Feb.-March 1937 Plenum:

"After all, around Trotsky were people whose origin cannot by any means be traced to bourgeois society. Part of them belonged to the party intelligentsia and a certain part were recruited from among the workers. We can name many individuals who, in their time, joined the Trotskyites; however, these same individuals took an active part in the workers' movement before the Revolution, during the Socialist October Revolution itself, and also in the consolidation of the victory of this greatest of revolutions. Many of them broke with Trotskyism and returned to Leninist positions." (p. 9; see above)

Further on in the "Secret Speech, in a passage it will be convenient to consider here, Khrushchev returned to the question of Trotskyites in the USSR in the 1930s.

> "We should recall that in 1927, on the eve of the 15th Party Congress, only some 4,000 votes were cast for the Trotskyite-Zinovievite opposition while there were 724,000 for the party line. During the 10 years which passed between the 15th Party Congress and the February-March Central Committee plenum, Trotskyism was completely disarmed; many former Trotskyites had changed their former views and worked in the various sectors building socialism. It is clear that in the situation of socialist victory there was no basis for mass terror in the country."

Stalin, at the February- March 1937 Central Committee Plenum:

> "Call to mind the last discussion on Trotskyism in our Party in 1927… Out of 854,000 Party members, 730,000 members voted at that time. Among them, 724,000 Party members voted for the Bolsheviks, for the Central Committee of the Party, against the Trotskyites, and 4,000 Party members, or about one-half of one per cent, voted for the Trotskyites, while 2,600 members of the Party refrained from voting…. Add to this the fact that many out of this number became disillusioned with Trotskyism and left it, and you get a conception of the insignificance of the Trotskyite forces."

- J.V. Stalin, *Mastering Bolshevism*. NY: Workers Library Publishers, 1937, pp. 59-60. At http://www.marx2mao.com/Stalin/MB37.html (Emphasis added in both cases – GF)

Khrushchev may very well have copied this passage out of Stalin's very speech!

Sudoplatov on guilt of Trotskyites:

> "In the interests of the political conjuncture the activities of Trotsky and his supporters abroad in the 1930s are

said to have been propaganda only. But this is not so. The Trotskyites were also involved in actions. Making use of the support of persons with ties to German military intelligence [the 'Abwehr'] they organized a revolt against the Republican government in Barcelona in 1937. From Trotskyist circles in the French and German special intelligence services came "indicative" information concerning the actions of the Communist Parties in supporting the Soviet Union. Concerning the connections of the leaders of the Trotskyist revolt in Barcelona in 1937 we were informed by Schulze-Boysen... Afterward, after his arrest, the Gestapo accused him of transmitting this information to us, and this fact figured in his death sentence by the Hitlerite court in his case.

Concerning other examples of the Abwehr's use of their ties to the Trotskyites for searching out leaders of the Communist Party of France who were in hiding in 1941 our resident in Paris, Vasilevsky, appointed in 1940 to the post of plenipotentiary for the Executive Committee of the Comintern, reported to us."

- English translation from Gen. Pavel Sudoplatov, *The Intelligence Service and the Kremlin*, Moscow 1996, p. 58:

The relevant paragraph from the Nazi military court, verifying Sudoplatov's contention:

Anfang 1938, während des Spanienkrieges, erfuhr der Angeklagte dienstlich, daß unter Mitwirkung des deutschen Geheimdienstes im Gebiet von Barcelona ein Austand gegen die dortige rote Regierung vorbereitet werde. Diese Nachricht wurde von ihm gemeinsam mit der von Pöllnitz der sowjetrussischen Botschaft in Paris zugeleitet.

English translation:

"At the beginning of 1938, during the Spanish Civil War, the accused learned in his official capacity that a rebellion against the local red government in the territory of Barcelona was being prepared with the co-operation of the German Secret Service. This information, together

with that of Pöllnitz, was transmitted by him to the
Soviet Russian embassy in Paris."

("Pöllnitz" was Gisella von Pöllnitz, a recent recruit to the "Red Orchestra" (Rote Kapelle) anti-Nazi Soviet spy ring who worked for United
Press and who "shoved the report through the mailbox of the Soviet
embassy." Shareen Blair Brysac, *Resisting Hitler: Mildred Harnack and the
Red Orchestra*. Oxford University Press, 2000, p. 237).

- Haase, N. *Das Reichskriegsgericht und der Widerstand gegen nationalsozialistische
Herrschaft*. Berlin, 1993, S. 105. See also Grover Furr. "Evidence of Leon
Trotsky's Collaboration with Germany and Japan." *Cultural Logic* 2009. At
http://clogic.eserver.org/2009/Furr.pdf

9. Stalin neglected Party

Khrushchev:

"Was it a normal situation when over 13 years elapsed between the 18th
and 19th Party Congresses, years during which our party and our country
had experienced so many important events?"

> "At the February (1947) Plenum of the CC A[ndrei]
> Zhdanov spoke about the decision to convoke a regular,
> 19th Congress of the ACP(b) at the end of 1947 or in any
> case during 1948. Besides that, in the interests of
> enlivening inner-party life, he proposed adopting a
> simplified order of convoking party conferences,
> carrying them out every year with compulsory renewal of
> the totals of the membership of the Plenum of the CC
> not less than by one-sixth."

- Pyzhikov, A.V. "Leningradskaia gruppa: Put' vo vlasti (1946-1949)."
Svobodnaia Mysl' 3, 2001, p. 96.

Khrushchev:

> "It should be sufficient to mention that during all the
> years of the Patriotic War not a single Central
> Committee plenum took place. It is true that there was
> an attempt to call a Central Committee plenum in
> October 1941, when Central Committee members from
> the whole country were called to Moscow. They waited
> two days for the opening of the plenum, but in vain.
> Stalin did not even want to meet and talk to the Central

Committee members. This fact shows how demoralized
Stalin was in the first months of the war and how
haughtily and disdainfully he treated the Central
Committee members."

Boris Nikolaevsky's note to the original *New Leader* edition of this speech:

"If one were to trust official Soviet sources, this
statement by Khrushchev would not be true: According
to the collection, The Communist Party of the Soviet
Union in the Resolutions and Decisions of Congresses,
Conferences and Central Committee Plenums (published
by the MarxEngels-Lenin-Stalin Institute of the Party
Central Committee in 1954), one Central Committee
plenum was held during the war (January 27, 1944),
when it was decided to give the various Union Republics
the right to have their own foreign ministries and it was
also decided to replace the Internationale by the new
Soviet national anthem."

Nikolaevsky goes on to add: "But it is likely that Khrushchev is correct,
that there was no Central Committee plenum in 1944 and a fraud was
perpetrated: The plenum was announced as having occurred although it
never had." (note 10)

But Nikolaevsky was wrong. It was Khrushchev, not Stalin, who "perpetrated a fraud."

1989 Russian edition of Khrushchev's Speech, note 8:

By a decree of the Politburo of the CC ACP(b) of
October 2, 1941 there was given the notice of the
convocation of a Plenum of the CC ACP(b) on October
10, 1941, with the agenda: "1. The military situation of
our country. 2. Party and state work for the defense of
the country." By a decree of the Politburo of the CC
ACP9(b) of October 9, 1941 the convocation of the
Plenum was put off "in view of the recently declared
state of emergency at the fronts and the inexpediency of
recalling leading comrades from the fronts ." During the
war years there was only one Plenum of the CC, which
took place on January 27, 1944.

Decisions of the January 1944 Plenum of the CC are described in a 1985
Soviet textbook. See P.N. Bobylev et al., *Velikiaia Otechestvennaia Voina*.

Voprosy i Otvety. Moscow: Politizdat, 1985, at
http://www.biografia.ru/cgi-
bin/quotes.pl?oaction=show&name=voyna083

10. Ref. to "a party commission under the control of the Central Committee Presidium"; fabrication of materials during repressions

Khrushchev:

> "The commission has become acquainted with a large quantity of materials in the NKVD archives and with other documents and has established many facts pertaining to the fabrication of cases against Communists, to false accusations, to glaring abuses of socialist legality, which resulted in the death of innocent people. It became apparent that many party, Soviet and economic activists, who were branded in 1937-1938 as "enemies," were actually never enemies, spies, wreckers, etc., but were always honest Communists; they were only so stigmatized and, often, no longer able to bear barbaric tortures, they charged themselves (at the order of the investigative judges -falsifiers) with all kinds of grave and unlikely crimes."
>
> ...
>
> "It was determined that of the 139 members and candidates of the party's Central Committee who were elected at the 17th Congress, 98 persons, i.e., 70 per cent, were arrested and shot (mostly in 1937-1938). (Indignation in the hall.) ... The same fate met not only the Central Committee members but also the majority of the delegates to the 17th Party Congress. Of 1,966 delegates with either voting or advisory rights, 1,108 persons were arrested on charges of anti-revolutionary crimes, i.e., decidedly more than a majority."

– See under Ezhov, below (#17).

11. December 1, 1934 "directive" signed by Enukidze

Khrushchev:

> "On the evening of December 1, 1934 on Stalin's initiative (without the approval of the Political Bureau - which was passed two days later, casually)..."

The 1989 critical edition of the Russian text of Khrushchev's speech (ed. Ayermakher, K., ed. *Doklad N.S. Khrushcheva o Kul'te Lichnosti Stalina na XX s"ezde KPSS. Dokumenty.* Moscow: ROSSPEN 2002) states, in n. 11:

> This concerns the decree of the Central Executive Committee of the Soviet Union of December 1, 1934 "On the correct method of handling cases concerning the preparation or commission of acts of terrorism," which was later called "the Law of December 1, 1934" and was in force until 1956. The Decree in question was not introduced for confirmation by a session of the Central Executive Committee of the USSR, as demanded in the Soviet Constitution.

See reproduction of the original copy from the Volkogonov Papers online at:
http://chss.montclair.edu/english/furr/research/12_01_34_law.pdf

12. Khrushchev Implies Stalin's involvement in Kirov's murder

Khrushchev:

> "It must be asserted that to this day the circumstances surrounding Kirov's murder hide many things which are inexplicable and mysterious and demand a most careful examination. There are reasons for the suspicion that the killer of Kirov, Nikolayev was assisted by someone from among the people whose duty it was to protect the person of Kirov. A month and a half before the killing, Nikolayev was arrested on the grounds of suspicious behavior but he was released and not even searched. It is an unusually suspicious circumstance that when the Chekist assigned to protect Kirov was being brought for

an interrogation, on December 2, 1934, he was killed in a
car "accident" in which no other occupants of the car
were harmed. After the murder of Kirov, top
functionaries of the Leningrad NKVD were given very
light sentences, but in 1937 they were shot. We can
assume that they were shot in order to cover the traces
of the organizers of Kirov's killing."

Sudoplatov:

"No documents or evidence exist to support the theory
of the participation of Stalin or of the apparat of the
NKVD in Kirov's assassination.... Kirov was not an
alternative to Stalin. He was one of the staunchest
Stalinists. Khrushchev's version was later approved and
used by Gorbachev as a part of his anti-Stalin
campaign."

- *Razvedka i Kreml'* Moscow, 1996, pp. 60-61.

Alla Kirilina:

"...Today under the conditions of 'all is permitted' and
so-called pluralism articles appear whose authors do not
bother with searching out documents and are not
burdened by the effort of arriving at an objective
understanding of what happened on December 1, 1934.
Their main goal is to declare yet again that 'Stalin
murdered Kirov,' though they have neither primary nor
secondary evidence for this statement, but instead make
broad use of myths, legends, and rumor."

- *Neizvestniy Kirov.* Moscow, 2001, p. 304. On p. 335 of this work Kirilia
reveals that Trotsky was the origin of the rumors that Stalin had had Kirov killed. This in turn implies that Khrushchev and Pospelov were copy-
ing from Trotsky here.

Arch Getty:

"On Kirov, and in no particular order:

1. Over the years, there were three, and perhaps four,
"blue ribbon" investigations of the Kirov killing. Each
was commissioned by the Politburo's General Secretary
and each, in true Soviet fashion, started with a desired
conclusion in advance. Stalin wanted to pin it on

Zinoviev and Trotsky; Khrushchev and Gorbachev
wanted to pin it on Stalin and all of them handpicked
their investigators accordingly. Having been able to
acquaint myself with archival materials from these
efforts, it is clear that none of the three investigations
produced the desired conclusions. In particular, the
Khrushchev and Gorbachev-era efforts involved massive
combing of archives and interviews and failed to
conclude that Stalin was behind the killing. Stalin's effort,
of course, concluded that the opposition did it and was
the basis for the Moscow trials. But aside from the
incredible confessions of the accused, there was no
evidence to support this a priori conclusion either."

on the H-RUSSIA disussion list, August 24, 2000. See
http://tinyurl.com/hjput

13. Stalin's and Zhdanov's telegram to the Politburo of September 25 1936.

Khrushchev:

> Mass repressions grew tremendously from the end of
> 1936 after a telegram from Stalin and [Andrei] Zhdanov,
> dated from Sochi on September 25, 1936, was addressed
> to Kaganovich, Molotov and other members of the
> Political Bureau. The content of the telegram was as
> follows:

>> We deem it absolutely necessary and urgent that
>> Comrade Yezhov be nominated to the post of
>> People's Commissar for Internal Affairs. Yagoda has
>> definitely proved himself to be incapable of
>> unmasking the Trotskyite-Zinovievite bloc. The
>> OGPU is four years behind in this matter. This is
>> noted by all party workers and by the majority of the
>> representatives of the NKVD.

> This Stalinist formulation that the "NKVD is four years
> behind" in applying mass repression and that there is a
> necessity for "catching up" with the neglected work

directly pushed the NKVD workers on the path of mass arrests and executions."

Here is the full text of the telegram, a small fragment of which Khrushchev read out in the "Secret Speech."

CC of the VKP(b). Moscow.

To Comrades Kaganovich, Molotov, and other members of the Politburo.

First, We consider it absolutely essential and urgent that com. Ezhov be appointed to the post of People's Commissar of Internal Affairs. Iagoda has clearly not turned out to be up to his job in the matter of exposing the Trotskyite-Zinvoievite bloc. The OGPU was four years late in this matter. All the party workers and most of the oblast' representatives of the NKVD say this. Agranov can remain as Ezhov's deputy at the NKVD.

Second. We consider it essential and urgent that Rykov be removed as People's Commissar of Communications and Iagoda be appointed to the post as People's Commissar of Communications. We do not think this matter requires any explanation, since it is clear as it is.

Third. We consider it absolutely urgent that Lobov be removed and com. Ivanov, secretary of the Northern Region committee, be appointed to the post of People's Commissar of the Timber Industry. Ivanov knowls forestry, he is an efficient man. Lobov as People's Commissar is not up to the job and every year fails in it. We propose to leave Lobov as first assistant to Ivanov as People's Commissar for the Timber Industry.

Fourth. As concerns the PCC (Party Control Commission), Ezhov can remain as Chairman of the PCC at the same time provided that he devotes nine-tenths of his time to the NKVD, and Iakov A. Iakovlev could be promoted to Ezhov's first assistant at the PCC.

Fifth. Ezhov is in agreement with our proposals.

Stalin, Zhdanov

No. 44. 25/IX.36

- *Stalin i Kaganovich. Perepiska 1931-1936 gg.* Moscow: ROSSPEN, 2001, No. 827, pp. 682-3. Also at http://www.hrono.ru/dokum/193_dok/19360925stal.html and http://www.alexanderyakovlev.org/almanah/inside/almanah-doc/56532 A slightly different translation is in the English version of this book, *The Stalin-Kaganovich Correspondence.* Ed. R.W. Davies, Oleg V. Khlevniuk, and E.A. Rees. New Haven, CT: Yale University Press, 2003. No. 169, pp. 359-60.

Thurston:

> What did the four years refer to? Western writers usually answer that the phrase meant the Riutin Memorandum. But in December 1936 Ezhov mentioned, once again in a speech to a Central Committee plenum, 'the formation at the end of 1932 of a Zinovievite-Trotskyite bloc on the basis of terror.'" [n. 83, p. 244 to this passages cites an archival document. The partial transcript of the December 1936 CC Plenum printed in VI 1/95, pp. 5-6 mentions these same points, but without the word "bloc", and without the direct quotation here.]. (p. 35)

Jansen & Petrov:

> The "four years" referred to the formation in 1932 of a Trotskiist-Zinovievist bloc, which had been discovered no earlier than in June–July 1936… (p. 54)

14. Stalin's report at the February-March 1937 CC Plenum.

Khrushchev:

> Stalin's report at the February-March Central Committee plenum in 1937, "Deficiencies of party work and methods for the liquidation of the Trotskyites and of other two-facers," contained an attempt at theoretical justification of the mass terror policy under the pretext that as we march forward toward socialism class war must allegedly sharpen. Stalin asserted that both history and Lenin taught him this.

Lenin, saying something like what Stalin said:

The annihilation of classes is a matter of long, hard, and
stubborn class struggle, that after the overthrow of the
power of capital, after the smashing of the bourgeois
state, after the establishment of the dictatorship of the
proletariat does not disappear (as the Philistines of the
old socialism and old social-democracy imagine), but
only changes its forms, becoming, in many respects, even
more ferocious.

- Lenin,V.I. "Privet vengerskim rabochim. 27 maia 1919 g." *Complete
Works* (Russian: *Polnoe Sobranie Sochinenii,* v. 38, p. 387. Stalin quoted this
passage in his April 1929 speech "On the Right Deviation in the Bolshevik Party." At http://www.hrono.ru/libris/stalin/12-9.html

At the February-March 1937 Plenum of the CC of the ACP(b) Stalin did
make the report with the title Khrushchev cited. But there is nothing in
that report that alleges that the class struggle **must** sharpen "as we march
forward toward socialism."

Concerning this distortion by Khrushchev in his Secret Speech Richard
Kosolapov writes:

> In reality the aforesaid thesis, endlessly repeated as
> "Stalinist", is neither in Stalin's report nor in his
> concluding speech. It is true that Stalin pointed out the
> need to "destroy and cast aside the rotten theory that
> with every advance we make the class struggle here of
> necessity would die down more and more, and that in
> proportion as we achieve successes the class enemy
> would become more and more tractable." Stalin also
> stressed that "while one end of the class struggle has its
> operation within the bounds of the U.S.S.R., its other
> stretches to the bounds of the bourgeois states
> surrounding us." But he never set forth any "theory of
> sharpening" in the second half of the 1930s, that is when
> in the USSR the absolute predominance of socialist
> forms of the economy had been guaranteed and the
> Constitution of victorious socialism had been passed…"

- R.K. Kosolapov, "Uverenno torit' tropy v budushchee. Doklad 'O
resheniiakh XX i XXII s"ezdov KPSS po voprosu 'O kul'te lichnosti i
ego posledstviiakh'". (2003). At
http://www.cea.ru/~shenin/news/news20.htm

Point 7 of Stalin's report of March 3, 1937, and published in *Pravda* on March 29, 1937.

> 7. We must destroy and cast aside the rotten theory that with every advance we make the class struggle here of necessity would die down more and more, and that in proportion as we achieve successes the class enemy would become more and more tractable.
>
> This is not only a rotten theory but a dangerous one for it lulls our people, leads them into a trap, and makes it possible for the class enemy to rally for the struggle against the Soviet government.
>
> On the contrary, the further forward we advance, the greater the successes we achieve, the greater will be the fury of the remnants of the broken exploiting classes,
>
> / page 30 /
>
> the sooner will they resort to sharper forms of struggle, the more will they seek to harm the Soviet state and the more will they clutch at the most desperate means of struggle, as the last resort of doomed people.
>
> It should be borne in mind that the remnants of the broken classes in the U.S.S.R. are not alone. They have the direct support of our enemies beyond the bounds of the U.S.S.R. It would be a mistake to think that the sphere of the class struggle is limited to the bounds of the U.S.S.R. While one end of the class struggle has its operation within the bounds of the U.S.S.R., its other stretches to the bounds of the bourgeois states surrounding us. The remnants of the broken classes cannot but be aware of this. And precisely because they are, they will continue their desperate assaults in the future.
>
> This is what history teaches us. This is what Leninism teaches us.
>
> We must remember all this and be on our guard."

- Joseph Stalin, *Mastering Bolshevism*. NY: Workers Library Pubs, 1937, pp.1-40. http://www.marx2mao.com/Stalin/MB37.html.

Stalin's proposal for political education, and for each higher Party official choosing replacements for himself:

> The task is to raise the ideological level and political vigor of these command cadres and to introduce among them fresh forces awaiting promotion, and thus expand the ranks of our leading forces.
>
> What does this require?
>
> First and foremost, we must make the proposal to our Party leaders beginning with secretaries of our Party units to the secretaries of regional and republican Party organizations to select, during a definite period, two individuals, two Party functionaries each capable of being able to act as their effective deputies.
>
> The question may be asked: Where are we to get these two deputies for each one, if we have no such people, no workers who correspond to these requirements? This is incorrect, comrades. We have tens of thousands of capable and talented people. It only needs to know them and to promote them in time so that they should not remain in their old places too long and begin to rot. Seek and ye shall find.
>
> Further, four-month Party courses must be established in each regional center to give secretaries of units Party training and to re-equip them. The secretaries of all primary Party organizations (units) should be sent to these courses and then when they finish them and return home their deputies and the most capable members of the primary Party organizations should be sent to these courses.
>
> Further, to re-equip politically the first secretaries of the district organizations, eight-month Lenin courses must be established in the U.S.S.R., in, say, ten of the most important centers.
>
> The first secretaries of district and regional Party organizations should be sent to these courses, and then when they finish them and return home their deputies and the most capable members of the district and regional organizations sent there.

Further, six-month courses for the study of history and the Party's policy under the Central Committee of the Communist Party of the Soviet Union must be set up to achieve the ideological re-equipment and political improvement of secretaries of the town Party organizations. The first and second secretaries of town Party organizations should be sent to these courses and then when they have finished them and return home the most capable members of the town Party organizations should be sent there.

Finally, a six-month conference on questions of internal and international policy under the Central Committee of the C.P.S.U. must be established.

The first secretaries of divisional and provincial organizations and the Central Committees of the national Communist Parties should be sent here. These comrades should provide not one but several persons really capable of replacing the leaders of the Central Committee of our Party. This should and must be done.

- Joseph Stalin, *Mastering Bolshevism*. NY: Workers Library Pubs, 1937, pp.36-38. At http://www.marx2mao.com/Stalin/MB37.html

Stalin also made another report at the February-March CC Plenum. It was the concluding report, on March 5.

> "But here is the question: how to carry out in practice the task of smashing and uprooting the German-Japanese agents of Trotskyism. Does this mean that we should strike and uproot not only the real Trotskyites, but also those who wavered at some time toward Trotskyism, and then long ago came away from Trotskyism; not only those who are really Trotskyite agents for wrecking, but also those who happened once upon a time to go along a street where some Trotskyite or other had once passed? At any rate, such voices were heard here at the plenum. Can we consider such an interpretation of the resolution to be correct?
>
> No, we cannot consider it to be correct. On this question, as on all other questions, **there must be an individual, differentiated approach.** You must not

measure everyone with the same yardstick. Such a sweeping approach can only harm the cause of struggle against the real Trotskyite wreckers and spies.

Among our responsible comrades there are a certain number of former Trotskyites who left Trotskyism long ago, and now fight against Trotskyism not worse but better than some of our respected comrades who never chanced to waver toward Trotskyism. It would be foolish to vilify such comrades now.

Among our comrades there are also those who always stood against Trotskyism ideologically, but in spite of this kept up personal contacts with individual Trotsky

/page 44 /

-ites, which they did not delay in liquidating as soon as the actual visage of Trotskyism became clear to them. It is, of course, not a good thing that they did not break off their personal friendly connections with individual Trotskyites at once, but belatedly. But it would be silly to lump such comrades together with the Trotskyites." [Emphasis added, GF]

Further on in the report Stalin made the same point again, explicitly arguing **against** a mass approach (pp. 58-9):

"7. Finally, still another question. I have in view the question of the formal and heartless bureaucratic attitude of some of our Party comrades toward the fate of individual Party members, toward the question of expelling members from the Party, or the question of restoring the rights of Party membership to those who have been expelled.

The fact is that some of our Party leaders suffer from lack of attention to people, to Party members, to workers. Furthermore, they do not study the Party members, do not know what is close to their hearts, and how they are growing, do not know workers in general. They have, therefore, not an individual approach to Party members,

/page 59 /

to Party workers. And just because they have not an individual approach when appraising Party members and Party workers, they usually act at random, either praising them wholesale, without measure, or crushing them, also wholesale, and without measure, expelling thousands and tens of thousands from the Party.

Such leaders try, in general, to think in tens of thousands, not to worry about "units", about individual Party members, about their fate. They think it a mere bagatelle to expel thousands and tens of thousands of people from the Party, comforting themselves by the fact that our Party is 2,000,000 strong, and that tens of thousands of people expelled cannot change anything in the position of the Party.

But, only people who in essence are profoundly anti-Party can have such an approach to members of the Party."

- Joseph Stalin, *Mastering Bolshevism*. NY: Workers Library Pubs, 1937, pp.40-63. At http://www.marx2mao.com/Stalin/MB37.html Note that in this edition it is erroneously dated March 3, not March 5, but is correctly titled "Concluding Speech."

Stalin's report of the commission on the investigation of Bukharin and Rykov, February 27, 1937. (See Getty & Naumov, 409-11; Russian text in *Voprosy Istorii* 1/94, 12-13, for whole text).

Getty & Naumov on this report:

> "It was quite unusual for Stalin himself to give such reports; this is the first and only time in party history that he did so. This text was truly a hidden transcript; it was never published with any of the versions of the stenographic report and was never transferred to the party archives with other materials of the plenum... The transcript of this ambiguous and contradictory decision on Bukharin never even found its way into the heavily edited and limited-circulation stenographic report, which showed the plenum beginning on 27 Feburary – four days after it actually started." (411)

In his pathbreaking study of archival sources historian IUrii Zhukov cites the unpublished resolution of the February-March 1937 CC Plenum and comments on it.

> Just as far from a 'witch-hunt' as were Stalin's final words was the resolution based upon Stalin's report. The Plenum's participants voted in favor of it unanimously and without any comment, as had become customary during the previous few years. The words "treasonous and espionage-sabotage activity of Trotskyist fascists" were mentioned only once and only in the preamble. They served only as a pretext for the presentation of serious shortcomings in the work of Party organizations and of their leaders. The resolution specified the following:
>
> 1. Party organizations had been carried away with economic activity and had retreated in their Party-political leading activity, 'had subordinated to themselves and had effaced the local organs of the People's Commissariat for Agriculture, replacing them with themselves, and had turned themselves into narrow economic chiefs.'
>
> 2. 'Our Party leaders have turned themselves away from Party-political work toward economic and especially agricultural campaigns, thereby gradually transferring the main base of their work from the city to the oblast. They have begun to look upon the city with its working class not as the leading political and cultural strength of the oblast, but as one of many sectors of the oblast.'
>
> 3. 'Our Party leaders have begun to lose the taste for ideological work, for work on the Party-political upbringing of the Party and non-Party masses.'
>
> 4. 'They have also begun to lose the taste for criticism of our shortcomings and of self-criticism of Party leaders...'
>
> 5. 'They have also also begun to retreat from direct responsibility to the masses of Party members ... they have taken upon themselves to replace elections with co-

optation… in this manner a bureaucratic centralism has resulted.'

6. In cadre work, which the resolution also focused on, 'it is necessary to deal with workers not in a formal, bureaucratic manner, but according to the real situation, that is, first of all, from the political point of view (whether they are politically trustworthy) and, second, from the point of view of their work (whether they are suitable for the work they have been assigned).'

7. Leaders of Party organizations 'suffer from a lack of the necessary attention to people, to Party members, to workers …As a result of such a soulless relationship to people, Party members, and Party workers dissatisfaction and hostility is artificially created in one part of the Party.'

8. Finally the resolution mentions that, despite their lack of education, Party leaders do not want to raise their educational level, to study, to retrain themselves.

Naturally, the resolution echoes with the demand for the immediate removal of the real shortcomings in Party work outlined in this manner. In points one through eight, to condemn the practice of usurpation and effacement of the local organs; to immediately return exclusively to Party-political work and transfer it above all to the city; to give more attention to the press. In points nine through fourteen, to reject decisively 'the practice of turning the Plenums of the oblast committees, regional committees, Party conferences, city activists, etc., into means for parades and demonstrations, and of vociferous praise for Party leaders'; to restore the accountability of Party organs to the Plenums, to stop the practice of co-optation in Party organizations. In points fifteen through eighteen the fundamentally new approach to cadre work is discussed, and in points nineteen through twenty-five the instruction and retraining of Party leaders.'

- IUrii Zhukov. *Inoi Stalin. Politicheskie reformy v SSSR v 1933-1937 gg.* Moscow: Vagrius, 2003, pp. 360-363 and notes on p. 506, referring to the archives at RGASPI F.17 Op. 2 D. 612. Vyp. III L. 49 ob.-50.

15. "Many Members questioned mass repression". Especially Postyshev.

Khrushchev:

> "At the February-March Central Committee plenum in 1937 many members actually questioned the rightness of the established course regarding mass repressions under the pretext of combating "two-facedness."

> Comrade Postyshev most ably expressed these doubts. He said:

> "I have philosophized that the severe years of fighting have passed. Party members who have lost their backbones have broken down or have joined the camp of the enemy; healthy elements have fought for the party. These were the years of industrialization and collectivization. I never thought it possible that after this severe era had passed Karpov and people like him would find themselves in the camp of the enemy. (Karpov was a worker in the Ukrainian Central Committee whom Postyshev knew well.) And now, according to the testimony, it appears that Karpov was recruited in 1934 by the Trotskyites. I personally do not believe that in 1934 an honest party member who had trod the long road of unrelenting fight against enemies for the party and for socialism would now be in the camp of the enemies. I do not believe it… **I cannot imagine how it would be possible to travel with the party during the difficult years and then, in 1934, join the Trotskyites. It is an odd thing…**"

Khrushchev seriously and deliberately distorted what Postyshev actually said in his speech to the February-March CC Plenum. The text of Postyshev's remarks has now been published in *Voprosy Istorii* nos. 5-6, 1995, pp. 3-8. This part is on p. 4.

I will now pause for a bit on my errors in the Kiev oblast Party committee. How is it that I did not personally notice people who sat very close to me . Why could I not notice them, since I worked with them for a fairly long period?

…Here is Karpov. I trusted him very much. Karpov was in Party work continuously for ten years. I took him with me to the Ukraine because he was an old Ukrainian worker, spoke Ukrainian, knows the Ukraine, had lived all the time in the Ukraine and was born in the Ukraine. And not only I myself, but a great many comrades knew him as a decent person.

What led me astray? In 1923-24 Karpov fought with the Trotskyites before my eyes. He also fought them in Kiev. …**I have philosophized** in this manner: **that the severe years of fighting have passed**, in which there were such developments that people either **have broken down**, or remained firmly on their feet, or **have joined the camp of the enemy – the years of industrialization and collectivization**, there was a fierce struggle between the Party and the enemies in this period. I never thought it possible that after this severe era had passed one would then go to the camp of the enemy. And now it turns out that from 1934 he has fallen into the hands of the enemies and has become an enemy. Of course one can either believe or not believe this. **I personally** think that it would be terribly hard after all these years for a person **who had trod the long road of unrelenting fight against enemies for the party and for socialism would now be in the camp of the enemies. It is very difficult to believe this.** (Molotov. Hard to believe that he only became an enemy in 1934? Most likely he became one earlier.) Of course, earlier. **I cannot imagine how it would be possible to travel with the party during the difficult years and then, in 1934, join the Trotskyites. It is an odd thing.** There was some kind of worm inside him all the time. When this worm appeared – in 1926 or 1924, or 1930, it's hard to say, but obviously some kind of worm there

> was, something that did some kind of work on him so
> that he at length fell into the herd of enemies.

The words Khrushchev quoted in his "Secret Speech" are in **boldface** here. Postyshev's whole speech from the text of *Voprosy Istorii* No. 5, 1995, is here:

http://chss.montclair.edu/english/furr/research/postyshevspmar0437.pdf

Khrushchev's own harsh speech is in *VI* no.8, 1995, pp. 19-25. It is available at

http://chss.montclair.edu/english/furr/research/khrushchevspmar0537.pdf

Postyshev was the harshest in mass expulsions, and was expelled for this at the January 1938 CC. Getty & Naumov discuss this at length on pp. 498-512. Getty quotes at length how Postyshev was raked over the coals at this Plenum for excessive repression.

Zhukov's analysis:

> At the January 1938 Plenum the main report was done
> by Malenkov. He said that the first secretaries were
> brandishing not even lists of those condemned by the
> "troikas", but just two lines with an indication of the
> number of those condemned. He openly accused the
> first secretary of the Kuibyshev *obkom* of the party P.P.
> Postyshev: you have imprisoned the entire Party and
> Soviet apparatus of the *oblast*! At which Postyshev
> replied in the same vein, that "I arrested, am arresting,
> and will arrest, until I annihilate all enemies and spies!
> But he was in a dangerous solitude: two hours after this
> polemic he was demonstratively dismissed from his post
> as candidate member of the Politburo, and none of the
> members of the Plenum stood up to defend him.

- *Komsomolskaia Pravda* Nov. 19, 2002.

The document confirming Postyshev's expulsion and arrest is reprinted in Getty & Naumov, pp. 514-6. Khrushchev was one of those who spoke up forcefully against Postyshev (G&N 512). For Khrushchev's appointment to replace Postyshev as candidate member of Politburo, *Stalinskoe Politbiuro*...p. 167.

Rogovin's excerpt from January 1938 CC Plenum on Postyshev:

On the character of Postyshev's speech, which was in fact converted into his interrogation, the following fragment of the transcript will give an idea:

Postyshev: The leadership there (in the Kuybyshev oblast), both that of the party and of the Soviets, was enemies, beginning from the oblast leadership and ending with that of the raions.

Mikoian: Everybody?

Postyshev: How can you be surprised? …. I added it up and it comes out that enemies have been sitting there for 12 years. On the Soviet side the same enemy leadership has been sitting there. There they sat and selected their cadres. For example, in our oblast executive committee we had the most obdurate enemies right down to the technical workers, enemies who confessed to their wrecking activity and behaved insolently, beginning with the chairman of the oblast executive committee, with his assistant, consultants, secretaries – all were enemies. Absolutely all the sections of the oblast executive committee were soiled with enemies. … Now take the chairmen of the raion executive committees – all were enemies. Sixty chairmen of raiispolkoms – all enemies. The overwhelming majority of second secretaries – I'm not even speaking of first secretaries – are enemies, and not only enemies, but there were also many spies among them: Poles, Latvians, they selected all kinds of died-in-the-wool swine…

Bulganin: Were there at least some honest people there… It turned out that there was not a single honest person.

Postyshev: I am talking abut the leadership, the heads. From the leading body, of the secretaries of the raion committees, the chairmen of the raiispolkoms, there was almost not a single honest man. And how can you be surprised?

Molotov: Aren't you exaggerating, comrade Postyshev?

Postyshev: No, I'm not exaggerating. Here, take the oblast executive committee. People are in prison. We have investigative materials, and they confess, they themselves confess their enemy and espionage work.

Molotov: We must verify the materials.

Mikoian: It turns out that there are enemies below, in every raion committee.

Beria: Is it possible that all members of the plenums of the raion committees were enemies?

Kaganovich: There is no basis to say that they are all swindlers.

Stalin evaluated Postyshev's methods this way: "This is the massacre of the organization. They are very easy on themselves, but they're shooting everybody in the raion organizations.... This means stirring up the party masses against the CC, it can't be understood any other way."

- Rogovin, *Partiia rasstreliannykh*. Ch. 2, Section III: "The January Plenum: The Case of Postyshev." At http://trst.narod.ru/rogovin/t5/iii.htm. Fuller text at *Stalinskoe Politbiuro v 30-e gody*, pp. 161-4. See the text of this session with Postyshev from *Stalinskoe Politbiuro...* at http://chss.montclair.edu/english/furr/research/postyshev0138.pdf

According to Russian historian, writer, and military figure Vladimir Karpov, Postyshev confirmed his confession to Molotov:

In my conversations with Molotov at his dacha we had a conversation about the repressions. Once I asked:

– Is it possible that you never had any doubts? After all, they were arresting people whom you knew well by their work even before the revolution, and then also in the Civil War.

– Doubts did arise, once I spoke to Stalin about this, and he answered: "Go to the *Lubianka* and check on this yourself, take Voroshilov here with you. Voroshilov was then in the office. We both went right away. Those were exactly the days when we had fresh doubts about the arrest of Postyshev. We drove to Ezhov. He ordered Postyshev's file to be brought out. We looked through the transcripts of interrogations. Postyshev admitted his guilt. I said to Ezhov: "I want to have a talk with Postyshev himself." He was brought. He was pale, had lost weight, and generally looked depressed. I asked him: Were his confessions written down accurately in the transcripts of interrogation? He answered: They are written correctly. I asked again – "That means, you admit that you are guilty?" He was silent, and somehow reluctantly answered: "Since I signed them, that means, I admit it, what is there to say…" That's how it was. How could we not believe it, when the man himself said it?"

- Karpov, Vladimir Vasil'evich. *Marshal Zhukov, ego soratnikii i protivniki v goty voiny I mira. Book 1.* Chapter 6, "The Tukhachevsky Affair.". At http://militera.lib.ru/bio/karpov/06.html

Letter from Andreev to Stalin of January 31, 1938 about Postyshev's lawless and arbitrary repressions:

2) Since August about 3,000 members have been expelled from the party, a significant part of whom were expelled without any basis whatsoever as "enemies of the people" or their confederates. At the plenum of the oblast committee the secretaries of the raion committees brought forward facts, when Postyshev became arbitrary and demanded the expulsion and arrest of honest party members either for the slightest criticism at party meetings of the leadership of the oblast committee [i.e. Postyshev himself] or even without any basis at all. In general this whole tone came from the oblast committee.

3) Since all these matters look like a provocation, we had to arrest a few of the most suspicious, zealout deviationists from the oblast and city committees, the former second secretary Filimonov, the obcom workers Sirotinskii, Alakin, Fomenko, and others. At the very first interrogations they all confessed that they were members of a Right-Trotskyite organization up to the present. Surrounding Postyshev and enjoying his full confidence, they developed their disorganizational and procational work of dissolving the party organizations and mass expulsions of party members. We also had to arrest Pashkovskii, Postyshev's assistant. He confessed that he had concealed the fact that he had been a Social-Revolutionary in the past, had been recruited to the

Right-Trotskyite organization in 1933 in Kiev, and
obviously was a Polish spy. He was one of the most
active of those in Postyshev's circle in the matter of
arbitrariness and disorganization in Kuybyshev. We are
untangling matters further, in order to unmask this gang.

4) The oblast committee plenum has not met a single
time since the elections in June, the oblast committee
directly forbade plenums of the raion committees in
Kuybyshev to meet, there were also no activists.

- *Sovetskoe rukovodstvo. Perepiska. 1928-1941.* ed. A.V. Koshonkin et al.,
Moscow: ROSSPEN, 1999, p. 387. Full text at
http://chss.montclair.edu/english/furr/research/andreevrepostyshev013
8.pdf

16. Eikhe

Khrushchev:

The Central Committee considers it absolutely necessary
to inform the Congress of many such fabricated "cases"
against the members of the party's Central Committee
elected at the 17th Party Congress. An example of vile
provocation, of odious falsification and of criminal
violation of revolutionary legality is the case of the
former candidate for the Central Committee Political
Bureau, one of the most eminent workers of the party
and of the Soviet Government, Comrade Eikhe, who
was a party member since 1905."

- Eikhe's letter to Stalin of October 27 1939: selections in the Pospelov
report, at http://www.alexanderyakovlev.org/almanah/inside/almanah-
doc/55752. Published in full in Ayermakher, K., ed. *Doklad N.S. Khrushcheva o Kul'te Lichnosti Stalina na XX s"ezde KPSS. Dokumenty.* Moscow:
ROSSPEN 2002, pp. 225-229.

We now have a statement by Frinovskii, Ezhov's right-hand man, from
April 1939, in which he discusses Ezhov's and Evdokimov's involvement
in the Rightist conspiracy. He mentions Eikhe in this connection.

Evdokimov mentioned Eikhe in 1935 to Frinovskii:

At one of our meetings in 1935 Evdokimov, in his
apartment, told me about a number of people who had

been invited to work in Piatigorsk by him. He named
Pivovarov, and a large group of Chekists: Boiar, Diatkin,
and Shatsky. Here too he told me about his connections
with Khataevich, praising him as someone who knew the
countryside well; with Eikhe, and about a part of the
Leningrad group...

- *Lubianka* 3, p. 40

After one of the sessions of the [October 1937 Central
Committee] Plenum, in the evening, Evdokimov, I and
Ezhov were at Ezhov's dacha. When we arrived there,
Eikhe was already there, but Eikhe did not have any
conversations with us. What took place with Eikhe
before our arrival at Ezhov's – Ezhov did not tell me.
After dinner Eikhe went away, and we remained and
talked almost till morning."

- *Lubianka* 3, p. 44

Iurii Zhukov:

It was June 29 [1937 – GF], the Plenum was already
concluding, when a note arrived at the Politburo from
the first secretary of the Novosibirsk oblast committee
R. I. Eikhe, in which he applied to the Politburo with a
request to give him extraordinary powers on a temporary
basis in his territory. He wrote that in Novosibirsk oblast
a mighty anti-Soviet counter-revolutionary organization,
huge in numbers, had been uncovered, one which the
organs of the NKVD had not succeeded in completely
liquidating. It was, he said, necessary to create a "troika"
with the following composition: the First Secretary of
the Party obkom [i.e. Eikhe himself – GF], the oblast
procurator [prosecutor – GF], and the head of the oblast
directorate of the NKVD, with the powers to take
operational decisions about the exile of anti-Soviet
elements and the carrying out of death sentences on the
more dangerous of the numbers of these people. That is,
in fact, a military field court, without defense, without
witnesses, with the right of immediate execution of
sentences. Eikhe's request was rationalized by the fact
that, in the face of such a powerful counterrevolutionary

organization elections to the Supreme Soviet could bring about an undesirable political result.

- IUrii Zhukov. "Stalin. Inoi Vzgliad. Beseda s avtorom knigi 'Inoi Stalin'". *Nash sovremennik.* 2004, No. 12. Text at

http://nash-sovremennik.ru/p.php?y=2004&n=12&id=4

Zhukov first developed these ideas in his now-famous series "Zhupel Stalina" ("The scarecrow of Stalin") in *Komsomolskaia Pravda* in November 2002. This subject is covered in the article of November 16, 2002.

This series is now widely reprinted on the Internet; for example, at http://www.x-libri.ru/elib/smi__958/00000001.htm (emphasis added GF).

Zhukov again:

> Well, Ezhov received the first [meeting with Stalin] with happiness: it was his appointment in April 1938."concurrently" as the People's Commissar of Water Transportation. The second warning was in August: for four hours Stalin and Molotov tried to convince Ezhov to agree to the candidacy of L.P. Beria as his first assistant [see *Lubianka 2*, 545, for this decree – GF]. And the third, final act of this long procedure was on November 23. Ezhov was again summoned to Stalin, where Molotov and Voroshilov were already present. I have held in my hands the document which Ezhov wrote, obviously at their dictation. It is written on three pages, all of different sizes, that is they snatched up the first sheets of paper they could find at hand and shoved them at Ezhov, just so that he wouldn't stop writing. The following rationale for his dismissal was arrived at: obviously, he resisted, protested. But it was necessary to somehow wrest from him a decision to leave "according to his own wishes." There was written a draft of a decree, which sounds like a guarantee: "To keep comrade Ezhov in the position of secretary of the CC ACP(b), Chairman of the Commission of Party Control and People's Commissar for Water Transportation." Finally the announcement was written and signed: "N. Ezhov." With this the ending of the "Ezhovshchina" began. The Politburo sent on the spot telegrams with the

direct text: Stop repressions, dissolve the "troikas."
Having seized the initiative, the Stalin group had already
at the end of 1938 achieved the promulgation of the first
judicial processes against NKVD workers accused of
falsification and fabrication of cases, according to which
they tried, exiled, and executed thousands of people for
almost a whole year. That is how they managed to stop
the Great Terror."

Contradiction

- *KP* Nov. 20, 2002.

Jansen & Petrov, p. 91:

"Consider the objections raised at the time of the July
1937 Moscow conference by the Western Siberian
NKVD chief, Mironov, to Ezhov against the First Party
secretary, Robert Eikhe. Mironov reported to Ezhov—
according to his testimony after arrest —that Eikhe
"interfered in NKVD affairs." **He had ordered the
chiefs of the Kuzbass NKVD town branches to
arrest Party members, although in most cases
evidence was missing. Mironov thought his position
difficult: either he had to liberate part of the
prisoners and clash with Eikhe, or the NKVD
organs were forced to "create fictitious cases."** When
Mironov suggested to orally instruct the NKVD organs
concerned only to carry out orders approved by him,
Ezhov answered: "Eikhe knows what he is doing. He is
responsible for the Party organization; it is useless to
fight with him. You better report to me the moot points
arising, and I will settle them… Comply with Eikhe's
instructions, and don't strain your relations with him."
Mironov added that it was Eikhe's habit to "suddenly
come to the NKVD apparatus, attend interrogations,
interfere in the investigation, and then exert pres/ 92 /
sure in this or that direction, thereby muddling the
investigation."

But Ezhov stuck to his opinion.[38] [n. 38, p. 237, is to
archival documents no longer available: 38. Ibid., [fm
previous note – "TsA FSB, f. 3-os, op. 4, d. 6, l. 61."]

Archival investigation case of Frinovskii, N-15301, t. 7,
ll. 36–37.]

p. 107:

Regional Party leaders feared that class enemies would
take advantage of the freedom offered at the elections.
At the June 1937 Plenum the Kazakh government leader,
U. D. Isaev, warned: "We will clash here with a situation
of direct class struggle. Even now, mullahs, Trotskiist,
and every kind of other counterrevolutionary elements
are preparing for the elections." [108] At the October 1937
Plenum the Moscow Party leader, A. I. Ugarov, again
pointed to intensifying utterances of hostile activity. By
now, however, his Western Siberian colleague R. I. Eikhe
was able to establish that, on the contrary, thanks to the
crushing of the organized counterrevolutionary base the
situation had much improved. Stalin agreed: "People are
glad to have freed themselves of the wreckers." [109] For
safety's sake, during the same month it was decided to
ban contested elections and introduce uncontested single
candidacies.

[both nn. 108 and 109 are to archival documents no
longer available: "108. RTsKhIDNI, f. 17, op. 2, d. 617,
l. 167. 109. Ibid., d. 626, ll. 40–41, 62."]

17. Ezhov

Although it breaks the order of the original somewhat, it is convenient to
examine what Khrushchev says about Ezhov here, since it is closely
linked to Eikhe.

Khrushchev:

> We are justly accusing Yezhov for the degenerate
> practices of 1937. But we have to answer these
> questions: Could Yezhov have arrested Kossior, for
> instance, without the knowledge of Stalin? Was there an
> exchange of opinions or a Political Bureau decision
> concerning this? No, there was not, as there was none
> regarding other cases of this type. Could Yezhov have
> decided such important matters as the fate of such
> eminent party figures? No, it would be a display of

naiveté to consider this the work of Yezhov alone. It is
clear that these matters were decided by Stalin, and that
without his orders and his sanction Yezhov could not
have done this.

Frinovskii's statement of April 11 1939:

Before the arrest of Bukharin and Rykov Ezhov,
speaking with me openly, started to talk about the plans
for Chekist work in connection with the current situation
and the imminent arrests of Bukharin and Rykov. Ezhov
said that this would be a great loss to the Rights, after
that regardless of our own wishes, upon the instructions
of the Central Committee large-scale measures might be
taken against the cadres of the Right, and that in
connection with this his and my main task must be to
direct the investigation in such a way so that, as much as
possible, to preserve the Rightist cadre. Then he outlined
his plan for this matter. Basically this plan consisted of
the following: "We must put our own men, in the main,
in the apparatus of the Secret Political department (SPO)
and to select as investigators those who might be either
completely tied to us or in whose records there are some
kind of sins and they would know that they had these
sins in their records, and on the basis of these sins we
can hold them completely in our hands. We must
connect them ourselves to the investigation and direct
them." "And this consists in the following", said Ezhov,
"not to write down everything that a person under arrest
says, but the investigator must bring all the outlines, the
rough drafts to the chief of the department, and in
relation to those arrested persons who in the past
occupied an important position and those who occupy a
leading position in the organization of the Rights, it is
necessary to write these people down in a special list and
to report to him each time. It would be good, said
Ezhov, to take into the apparatus people who have
already been tied to the organization. "Here, for
example, Evdokimov spoke to you about people, and I
know some of them. It will be necessary in the first place
to draw them into the central apparatus. In general it will

be necessary to familiarize ourselves with capable people and from a businesslike point of view among those who are already working in the central apparatus, to somehow bring them close to ourselves and then to recruit them, because without these people it will be impossible for us to arrange our work, and it is necessary to somehow show the Central Committee some work."

In carrying out this suggestion of Ezhov's we chose a firm course in preserving Yagoda's cadres in leading posts in the NKVD. It is essential to mention that we only managed to do this with difficulty, since in various local organs [of the NKVD] there were materials on the majority of these people about their participation in the conspiracy and in anti-Soviet work generally. – p. 42

After the October 1937 Central Committee Plenum I and Evdokimov met for the first time at Ezhov's dacha. At that time Evdokimov started the conversation. Turning to Ezhov he asked: "What's the matter with you, you promised to straighten out Yagoda's position and instead the case is getting more and more serious and now is coming very close to us. Obviously, you are leading this affair poorly." Ezhov was silent at first, and then stated that "really, the situation is difficult, so now we will take steps to reduce the scope of the operations, but obviously, we have to deal with the head of the Rights." Evdokimov swore, spit, and said: "Can't you get me into the NKVD, I'll be able to help more than the rest." Ezhov said: "It would be good, but the Central Committee will scarcely agree to transfer you to the NKVD. I think that the situation is not altogether hopeless, but you need to have a talk with Dagin, you have influence on him, it's necessary for him to develop the work in the operations department, and we need to be prepared to carry out terrorist acts." – p. 43

… And here Evdokimov and Ezhov together talks about the possible limiting of the operations but, as this was considered impossible, they agreed to deflect the blow from their own cadre and to try to direct to against

honest cadres who were devoted to the Central
Committee. That was Ezhov's instruction. -- p. 44

After the arrests of the members of the center of Rights
Ezhov and Evdokimov in essence became the center,
and organized:

1) the preservation, as far as possible, of the anti-Soviet
cadre of the Rights from destruction; 2) the direction of
the blows against honest party cadre who were dedicated
to the Central Committee of the ACP(b); 3) preservation
of the rebel cadre in the North Caucasus and in other
krais and oblasts of the USSR, with the plan to use them
at the time of international complications; 4) a reinforced
preparation of terrorist acts against the leaders of the
party and government; 5) the assumption of power of
the Rights with Ezhov at their head. – p. 45

- *Lubianka 3*, also at:
http://chss.montclair.edu/english/furr/research/frinovskyeng.html

Investigative Work

The investigative apparatus in all departments of the
NKVD was divided into "investigator-bonebreakers",
"bonebreakers", and "ordinary" investigators.

[NOTE: Jansen & Petrov translate this word,
kolol'shchiki, as 'butchers'. 'Thugs' would be a modern
English equivalent, meaning someone whose job is to
beat people up.- GF]

What did these groups represent and who were they?

"Investigator-bonebreakers" were chosen basically from
among the conspirators or persons who were
compromised. They had unsupervised recourse to
beating arrested persons and in a very short time
obtained "confessions" and knew how to write up
transcripts in a grammatical and elegant fashion.

In this category belong: Nikolayev, Agas, Ushakov,
Listengurt, Evgen'ev, Zhupakhin, Minaev, Davydov,

Al'tman, Geiman, Litvin, Leplevsky, Karelin, Kerzon, Iamnitsky, and others.

Since the quantity of those under arrest who confessed due to such methods grew daily and there was a great need for investigators who knew how to compose interrogations, the so-called "investigator-bonebreakers" began, each on his own, to create groups of simple "bonebreakers."

The group of "bonebreakers" consisted of technical workers. These men did not know the evidence concerning the suspect, but were sent to the Lefortovo [prison in Moscow], summoned the accused, and set to beating him. The beatings continued up to the moment that the accused agreed to give a confession.

The remaining group of investigators took care of interrogations of those accused of less serious crimes and were left to themselves, without leadership from anyone.

The further process of investigation was as follows: the investigator conducted the interrogation and instead of a transcript put together notes. After several such inter-

/ 46 /

rogations a draft transcript was put together by the investigator. The draft went for "correction" to the chief of the appropriate department, and from him, still unsigned, for "review" to former People's Commissar Ezhov and in rare cases to myself. Ezhov looked through the transcript, made changes and additions. In most cases those under arrest did not agree with the editing of the transcript and stated that they had not said that during the investigation and refused to sign it.

Then the investigators would remind the arrested party about the "bonebreakers", and the person under investigation would sign the transcript. Ezhov produced the "correction" and "editing" of transcripts, in most cases, never having seen with his own eyes the person under arrest and if he did see him, then only during a

momentary inspection of the cells or investigative
rooms.

With such methods the investigations supplied the
names.

In my opinion I would speak the truth if I declared, in
general, that very often the confessions were given by
the investigators, and not by those under investigation.

Did the leadership of the People's Commissariat, that is I
and Ezhov, know about this? We knew.

How did we react? Honestly speaking – not at all, and
Ezhov even encouraged it. No one bothered to find out
to which of the accused physical pressure was applied.
And since the majority of the persons who were
employing these methods were themselves enemies of
the people and conspirators, then clearly false
accusations too place, we took false accusations and
arrested and shot innocent people who had been
slandered by enemies of the people from among those
under arrest and by enemies of the people among the
investigators. Real investigation was wiped out– pp. 45-6.

The preparation of the trial of Rykov, Bukharin,
Krestinsky, Yagoda and others

An active participant in investigations generally, Ezhov
kept himself aloof from the preparation of this trial.
Before the trial the face-to-face confrontations of the
suspects, interrogations, and refining, in which Ezhov
did not participate. He spoke for a long time with
Yagoda, and that talk concerned, in the main, of assuring
Yagoda that he would not be shot.

Ezhov had conversations several times with Bukharin
and Rykov and also in order to calm them assured them
that under no circumstances would they be shot.....
Here Ezhov unquestionably was ruled by the necessity of
covering up his own ties with the arrested leaders of the
Right who were going into the public trial."– pp. 47-8.

Deceiving the party and government

When Ezhov arrived in the NKVD, in all meetings, in
conversations with operational workers, he rightly
criticized the institutional narrow-mindedness and
isolation from the party, stressed that he would instill a
party spirit into the workers, that he did not hide and
would never hide anything, ever from the party and from
Stalin. In reality he was deceiving the party both in
serious, major matters and in small things. Ezhov had
these talks for no other purpose than to put to sleep any
sense of watchfulness in the honest NKVD workers. –
p. 49

- Original at
http://chss.montclair.edu/english/furr/research/frinovskyeng.html

Ezhov's interrogation of April 26 1939:

ANSWER: I must admit that, although I gave a truthful
confession about my espionage work on behalf of
Poland, in fact I hid from the investigation my espionage
ties with the Germans. – p. 52

Having discussed with EGOROV the current situation,
we came to the conclusion that the Party and the popular
masses were going with the leadership of the ACP(b)
and the soil for the *coup* had not been prepared.
Therefore we decided that it was necessary to remove
STALIN or MOLOTOV, under the flag of some kind of
anti-Soviet organization or other, with the purpose of
creating the conditions for my future accession to power.
After that, once I had assumed a position of more
power, the possibility of further, more decisive changes
in the policies of the Party and the Soviet government, in
conformity to the interests of Germany, would be
created.

I asked EGOROV to transmit to the Germans, through
KÖSTRING, our plans and to ask the opinion of
government circles in Germany about this.

QUESTION: What kind of answer did you receive?

ANSWER: Soon afterwards, from the words of KÖSTRING, EGOROV reported to me that government circles in Germany agreed with our suggestion.

QUESTION: What did you undertake in order to effect your traitorous plans?

ANSWER: I decided to organize a conspiracy in the NKVD and to attract into it people through whom I would be able to carry out terrorist acts against the leaders of the Party and government.

QUESTION: Was it only after the conversation with EGOROV that you decided to put together a conspiratorial organization within the NKVD?

ANSWER: No. In fact the matter was like this. Long before this conversation with EGOROV, at the time of my being named Commissar of Internal Affairs, I took with me into the NKVD a group of workers who were closely tied to me through counterrevolutionary work. In this way my confession that I set about organizing a conspiracy should be understood only in the sense that in connection with my conversations with GAMMERSHTEIN and my establishing contact with the military conspirators it became necessary to develop more widely, to accelerate, within the NKVD the setting up of the conspiratorial organization within the NKVD itself. – p. 64

As concerning EVDOKIMOV and FRINOVSKII, the latter was completed introduced to the details of the conspiracy by me, and knew absolutely everything, incluing about my ties with the group of military conspirators in the Red Army and in military circles in Germany. – p. 65

… I informed KÖSTRING about the further arrests among the military workers and declared to him that it was beyond my ability to prevent these arrests. In particular I reported about the arrest of EGOROV, which could cause the collapse of the whole conspiracy. KÖSTRING was very much upset by this situation. He put to me sharply the question of whether it was not at this time essential to undertake some kind of measures towards a seizure of power, or you would be smashed one at a time. – p. 67.

ANSWER: I did not meet any more personally with KÖSTRING. After that communications between us were realized through KHOZIAINOV.

QUESTION: Did KHOZIAINOV know about the terrorist acts you were preparing against the leaders of the Party and government?

ANSWER: Yes, he knew. Concerning them KHOZIAINOV had been informed not only by me, but by German intelligence, since during the first meeting after the establishment of contact between us KHOZIAINOV transmitted to me a directive from the Germans: to accelerate as quickly as possible the completion of terrorist acts.

Besides that KHOZIAINOV transmitted to me the directives of German intelligence that, in connection with my dismissal from work in the NKVD and the naming of BERIA as People's Commissar for Internal Affairs German intelligence considered it essential to effect the murder of some one of the members of the Politburo and, in this way, to provoke a new leadership in the NKVD [i.e., Beria's dismissal – GF].

In this same period within the NKVD itself there began arrests of the active participants of the conspiracy I was heading, and there and then we arrived at the conclusion that it was essential to organize an action on November 7 1938.

QUESTION: Who is "we"?

ANSWER: I – EZHOV, FRINOVSKII, DAGIN and EVDOKIMOV. – p. 67.

…In one of the meetings in my office in the Commissariat of Water I communicated to LAZEBNY that there were compromising materials on him in the NKVD, that his arrest and doom was threatening.

> I told LAZEBNY: "There's no way out for you, you're
> doomed, but you can save a large group of people by
> sacrificing yourself." During the corresponding
> questiong of LAZEBNY I informed him that the
> murder of STALIN would save the situation in the
> country. LAZEBNY gave me his consent. – p. 69

- Original at
http://chss.montclair.edu/english/furr/research/ezhov042639.html

Reason for Ezhov's indictment: Jansen & Petrov, p. 108 ff.

> p. 108:

> Legality was of no concern to Ezhov's NKVD. In
> January 1939, after his fall, a commission consisting of
> Andreev, Beriia, and Malenkov accused Ezhov of having
> used illegal investigation methods: "In a most flagrant
> way, investigation methods were distorted, mass beatings
> were indiscriminately applied to prisoners, in order to
> extort false testimony and 'confessions.' " During
> twenty-four hours an investigator often had to obtain
> several dozen confessions, and investigators kept each
> other informed about the the testimony obtained so that
> corresponding facts, circumstances, or names could be
> suggested to other prisoners. "As a result, this sort of
> investigation very often led to organized slander of
> totally innocent people." Very often, confessions were
> obtained by means of "straight provocation"; prisoners
> were persuaded to give false testimony about their
> "espionage activity" in order to help the Party and the
> government to "discredit foreign states" and in exchange
> for the promise of release. According to Andreev et al.,
> "the NKVD leadership in the person of comrade Ezhov
> not only did not cut short such arbitrariness and excesses
> in arresting and conducting investigation, but sometimes
> themselves encouraged it." All opposition was
> suppressed.[112]

> [note 112, p. 241, is to archival documents no longer
> available: "112. TsA FSB, f. 3-os, op. 6, d. 1, ll. 1–2."]

pp. 109-110:

The functioning of the troikas was also sharply criticized. Andreev et al. reported that there had been "serious slips" in their work, as well as in that of the so-called Grand Collegium [bol'shaia kollegiia], where during a single evening session from 600 to 2,000 cases were often examined. (They were referring to the examination in Moscow of albums in the national operations; before being signed by the People's Commissar of Internal Affairs and the Procurator, the albums were examined by a number of department chiefs of the central NKVD apparatus.) The work of the regional troikas was not controlled by the NKVD at all. Approximately 200,000 people were sentenced to two years by the so-called militia troikas, "the existence of which was not legal." The NKVD Special Board "did not meet in its legal composition even once."[113]

As an executive of the Tiumen' operational sector of the NKVD testified later, arrests were usually made arbitrarily— people were arrested for belonging to groups that did not actually exist—and the troika duly fell in line with the operational group:

At a troika meeting, the crimes of the defendants were not examined. In some days during an hour I reported to the troika cases involving 50–60 persons." In a later interview the Tiumen' executive gave a more detailed account of how the operational group carried out the troika's "first category" sentences. Those sentenced to death were executed in the basement in a special room with covered walls, with a shot in the back of the head, followed by a second shot in the temple. The corpses were then taken away to a cemetery outside town. In Tobol'sk, to which the person involved was transferred in 1938, they executed and buried right in prison; for lack of space, the corpses were piled up.[114] The assistant chief of the Saratov police administration gave similar testimony: "The basic instruction was to produce as many cases as possible, to formulate them as quickly as possible, with maximum simplification of investigation. As for the quota of cases, [the NKVD chief] demanded [the inclusion of] all those sentenced and all those that had been picked up, even if at the moment of their seizure they had not committed any sort of concrete crime.[115]

/ 110 /

After arrest, Ezhov's deputy, Frinovskii, explained that the main NKVD investigators had been the "butchers" [sledovatelikolol'shchiki], mainly selected from "conspirators or compromised people." "Unchecked, they applied beatings to prisoners, obtained 'testimony' in the shortest possible time." With Ezhov approving, it was the investigator rather than the prisoner who determined the testimony. Afterward, the protocols were "edited" by Ezhov and Frinovskii, usually without seeing the prisoner or only in passing. According to Frinovskii, Ezhov encouraged the use of physical force during interrogations: he personally supervised the interrogations and instructed the investigators to use "methods of physical influencing" if the results were unsatisfactory. During interrogations he was sometimes drunk.[116]

As one of the investigators later explained, if somebody was arrested on Ezhov's orders, they were convinced of his guilt in advance, even if all evidence was lacking. They "tried to obtain a confession from that individual using all possible means."[117] Under arrest, the former Moscow NKVD deputy chief A. P. Radzivilovskii quoted Ezhov as saying that if evidence was lacking, one should "beat the necessary testimony out of [the prisoners]." According to Radzivilovskii, testimony "as a rule was obtained as a result of the torturing of prisoners, which was widely practiced both in the central and the provincial NKVD apparatuses."[118]

After arrest both the chief of the Moscow Lefortovo investigation prison and his deputy testified that Ezhov had personally participated in beating prisoners during interrogation.[119] His deputy, Frinovskii, had done the same thing.[120] Shepilov recollects how after Stalin's death

Khrushchev told his colleagues that one day, while visiting Ezhov's Central Committee office, he saw spots of clotted blood on the skirt and cuffs of Ezhov's blouse. When asked what was up, Ezhov answered, with a shade of ecstasy, that one might be proud of such spots, for it was the blood of enemies of the revolution.[121]"

[Notes are on p. 241:

113. Ibid., ll. 2–3. [TsA FSB, f. 3-os, op. 6, d. 1, ll. 1–2.]

114. Gol'dberg, "Slovo i delo po-sovetski."

115. Hagenloh, "Socially Harmful Elements," p. 301.

116. TsA FSB, Archival investigation case of Frinovskii , N-15301, t. 2, ll. 32–35.

117. B. A. Starkov, "Narkom Ezhov," in J. A. Getty and R. T. Manning, eds., *Stalinist Terror: New Perspectives* (Cambridge, Eng., 1993), pp. 21–39, esp. p. 33; Pravda, 29 April 1988.

118. "M. N. Tukhachevskii i 'voenno-fashistskii zagovor,' " *Voenno-istoricheskii arkhiv*, no. 2 (Moscow, 1998): 3–81, esp. pp. 55–56.

119. Ibid., p. 50; see also, V. Shentalinskii, "Okhota v revzapovednike," *Novyi mir* 1998, no. 12: 170–96, esp. p. 180.

120. Papkov, Stalinskii terror v Sibiri, p. 269; "Tukhachevskii," *Voenno-istoricheskii arkhiv*, no. 1 (Moscow, 1997): 149–255, esp. p. 179.

121. D. Shepilov, "Vospominaniia," *Voprosy istorii* 1998, no. 4: 3–25, esp. p. 6. [NB: This passage is in Shepilov's memoirs in book format, *Neprimknuvshiy*, M. Vagrius, 2001, p. 43 - GF]

Stalin blamed Ezhov

Jansen & Petrov, p. 210:

Only months after his fall, Stalin explained to the aircraft designer A. Iakovlev: Ezhov was a scoundrel! He ruined our best cadres. He had morally degenerated. You call him at the People's Commissariat, and you are told that

he went out to the Central Committee. You call him at
the Central Committee, and you are told that he went
out for work. You send for him at home, and it turns out
that he is lying in bed, dead drunk. He ruined many
innocent people. That is why we have shot him.[42]

From Iakovlev's memoirs:

[Stalin] – Well, how is Balandin?

– [Iakovlev] He's working, comrade Stalin, as if nothing
had happened.

– Yes, they imprisoned him for nothing.

Evidently Stalin read astonishment in my look – how
then could innocent people be imprisoned? – and
without any questions on my part he said:

– Yes, it happens that way. A sensible man, one who
works hard, is envied, and they undermine him. And if,
in addition, he is bold, speaks his mind – this evokes
unease and attracts to him the attention of suspicious
Chekists, who do not understand their business, but who
willingly make use of all kinds of rumors and gossip....
(Chapter 20).

- Iakovlev, A.S. *The Purpose of Life*. Moscow, 1973, Ch. 20.

Jansen & Petrov:

Because he especially referred to 1938, Stalin suggested
that in his opinion in that year, unlike 1937, the terror
had gotten out of control and endangered the country's
stability.[43] At the end of his life, Stalin told his bodyguard
that "the drunkard Ezhov" had been recommended for
the NKVD by Malenkov: "While in a state of
intoxication, he signed lists for the arrest of often
innocent people that had been palmed off on him."[44]

In interviews in the 1970s, Molotov reasoned along
similar lines. According to him, Ezhov had enjoyed a
good reputation, until he "morally degenerated." Stalin
had ordered him to "reinforce the pressure," and Ezhov
"was given strong instructions." He "began to chop
according to plan," but he "overdid it": "Stopping him
was impossible." Extremely selective in his memory,

Molotov gave the impression that Ezhov had fixed the quotas on his own and that therefore he had been shot. He did not agree that Ezhov had only carried out Stalin's instructions: "It is absurd to say that Stalin did not know about it, but of course it is also incorrect to say that he is responsible for it all."[45] Another former Stalin adjutant who justified the purges was Kaganovich. There was sabotage and all that, he admitted, and "to go against the public opinion was impossible then." Only Ezhov "overdid it"; he even "organized competitions to see who could unmask the most enemies of the people." As a result, "many innocent people perished, and nobody will justify this."[46]

[nn. 42-46, p. 261:

42. A. Iakovlev, *Tsel' zhizni*, 2d ed. (Moscow, 1970), p. 509.

43. Reference to 1938 in A. Iakovlev, *Tsel' zhizni: Zapiski aviakonstruktora* (Moscow, 1966), p. 179.

44. RTsKhIDNI, f. 558, op. 4, d. 672, l. 10.

45. F. Chuev, *Sto sorok besed s Molotovym* (Moscow, 1991), pp. 398–400, 402, 438.

46. F. Chuev, *Tak govoril Kaganovich* (Moscow, 1992), p. 89.]

18. Rudzutak

Khrushchev:

"Comrade Rudzutak, candidate-member of the Political Bureau, member of the party since 1905, who spent 10 years in a Tsarist hard-labor camp, completely retracted in court the confession which was forced from him. ... After careful examination of the case in 1955, it was established that the accusation against Rudzutak was false and that it was based on slanderous materials. Rudzutak has been rehabilitated posthumously."

The arrests of Rudzutak and Tukhachevsky were ordered in the same Politburo decision of May 24 1937.

No. 136

Resolution of the Politburo concerning Rudzutak and Tukachevsky

May 24, 1937

309. On Rudzutak and Tukhachevsky.

Set for a vote of the members and candidate members of the CC ACP(b) the following resolution:

'The CC ACP(b) has received information that exposes member of the CC ACP(b) Rudzutak and candidate member of the CC ACP(b) Tukhachevsky in participation in an anti-Soviet Trotskyist-Right conspiratorial bloc and in espionage work against the USSR in the interest of fascist Germany. In connection with this the Politburo of the CC ACP(b) presents for vote of the members and candidates of the CC ACP(b) a resolution concerning the expulsion from the Party of Rudzutak and Tukhachevsky and giving their cases over to the People's Commissariat for Internal Affairs.

- *Stalinskoe Politbiuro v 30-e gody.* Ed. O.V. Khlevniuk et al. Moscow: AIRO-XX, 1995, p. 156.

Rudzutak named by Stalin in Speech to Expanded Session of the Military Council attached to the People's Commisar for Defense June 2, 1937:

"Trotsky, Rykov, Bukharin – these are, so to speak, the political leadership. To them I also add Rudzutak, who also stood at the head and worked very craftily, confused everything, but all in all turned out to be a German spy; Karakhan; Enukidze."

"Let us continue. I have enumerated 13 people, and repeat their names: Trotsky, Rykov, Bukharin, Enukidze, Karakhan, Rudzutak, Iagoda, Tukhachevsky, Iakir, Uborevich, Kork, Eideman, Gamarnik."

"Bukharin. We do not have evidence that he informed [the Germans] himself, but he had very close connections with Enukidze, Karakhan, and Rudzutak, they advised him…"

"Rudzutak. I have already said that he does not admit he is a spy, but we have all the evidence. We know to whom he gave his information. There is a certain experienced female intelligence agent in Germany, in Berlin. When

> you may happen to visit Berlin, Josephina Genzi, maybe
> one of you knows her. She is a beautiful woman. An
> experienced intelligence agent. She recruited Karakhan.
> Recruited through sexual encounters [lit. 'on the female
> side' – GF]. She recruited Enukidze. She helped recruit
> Tukhachevsky. And she holds Rudzutak in her hands."
>
> "This is the nucleus, and what does it show? Did any of
> these men vote for Trotsky. Rudzutak never voted for
> Trotsky, and yet he turned out to be a secret agent. ...
> There's the worth of your point of view of 'who voted
> for whom.'"

Rudzutak is named many times by defendants at the March 1938 "Bukharin" Trial, many times by Krestinsky alone. According to Krestinsky Rudzutak was one of the central figures of the antigovernment conspiracy.

> KRESTINSKY: I learnt from Pyatakov, when he spoke
> to me about this in February 1935, that an organization
> had been formed, which united the Rights, Trotskyites
> and military men, and which set itself the aim of
> preparing for a military coup. I also knew that the
> leading centre included Rykov, Bukharin, Rudzutak and
> Yagoda from the Rights, Tukhachevsky and Gamarnik
> from the military, and Pyatakov from the Trotskyites....
>
> In the beginning of 1935 Pyatakov informed me that an
> understanding had been reached, named the composition
> of the centre of which I spoke yesterday, and told me
> that myself and Rosengoltz, while not joining the centre,
> would work under its direction, mainly in connection
> with the planning and preparing of the future
> government machinery. Here was a division of labour.
> We were told that we would be connected in this work
> with Rudzutak from the Rights, and with Tukhachevsky.
> My impression was that only Rudzutak was mentioned.
> But Rosengol'ts took an active part in this and he
> subsequently spoke to me of his meetings with Rykov. In
> general, it was Rykov and Rudzutak from the Rights, and
> Tukhachevsky from the military group. There was no
> such thing as my knowing of the connections with

Tukhachevsky and Rosengol'ts's not knowing of them; but, as part of the division of labour, he took upon himself mainly the connections with the Rights, although I was the one who used to see Rudzutak, and, as far as Tukhachevsky was concerned, it was mainly I, but he also.

Report of Court Proceedings in the Case of the Anti-Soviet"Bloc of Rights and Trotskyites" Heard Before the Military Collegium of the Supreme Court of the U.S.S.R. Moscow, March 2-13, 1938…Verbatim Report. (Moscow: People's Commissariat of Justice of the U.S.S.R., 1938) , pp. 184; 279-80. (1938 Trial)

Rudzutak is named in that Trial several times by Rozengol'ts, who is himself named by Ezhov:

Question: What did you undertake to do in order to accomplish the Germans' task?

Answer: I promised Kandelaki my support and in fact I did negotiate with Rozengol'ts about the desirability of concluding such an agreement. As a re-/ 64 /sult the People's Commissariat for Foreign Trade rendered a positive decision concerning this agreement.

- "Transcript of the Interrogation of the Prisoner Ezhov Nikolai Ivanovich of April 26 1939," *Lubianka. Stalin i NKVD – NKGB – GUKR "SMERSH". 1939 – mart 1946.* Moscow, 2006, pp. 63-4. Translation at http://chss.montclair.edu/english/furr/research/ezhov042639eng.html

This also confirms his association with the Tukhachevsky military conspirators, with whom Rudzutak was accused of being involved with. Rozengol'ts is named many times as a major Rightist conspirator, and as the person who personally recruited him, by Tamarin, in a recently published interrogation-confession.

Rudzutak was named by Rukhimovich in the latter's confession of January 31, 1938:

Question: What do you know about the activities of this Latvian organization?

Answer: I have already confessed that it was BAUMAN and MEZHLAUK who maintained contact with the Latvians. Therefore they are the ones who should give you the details about the personnel and activities of this organization. All I know is that RUDZUTAK and ALKSNIS headed this organization. The organization

was firmly connected with the Latvian and German
intelligence services and had a rather large number of
counterrevolutionary cadre. In particular the armed units
of the military Latvian organization were to have been
used in the plan for the 'palace coup.'

- *Lubianka* 3, No. 290, p.484.

19. Rozenblium

Khrushchev:

> The way in which the former NKVD workers
> manufactured various fictitious "anti-Soviet centers" and
> "blocs" with the help of provocatory methods is seen
> from the confession of Comrade Rozenblum, party
> member since 1906, who was arrested in 1937 by the
> Leningrad NKVD.

> During the examination in 1955 of the Komarov case
> Rozenblum revealed the following fact: When
> Rozenblum was arrested in 1937, he was subjected to
> terrible torture during which he was ordered to confess
> false information concerning himself and other persons.
> He was then brought to the office of Zakovskii, who
> offered him freedom on condition that he make before
> the court a false confession fabricated in 1937 by the
> NKVD concerning "sabotage, espionage and diversion
> in a terroristic center in Leningrad." (Movement in the
> hall.) With unbelievable cynicism, Zakovskii told about
> the vile "mechanism" for the crafty creation of
> fabricated "anti- Soviet plots."

>> "In order to illustrate it to me," stated Rozenblum,
>> "Zakovskii gave me several possible variants of the
>> organization of this center and of its branches. After
>> he detailed the organization to me, Zakovskii told
>> me that the NKVD would prepare the case of this
>> center, remarking that the trial would be public.
>> Before the court were to be brought 4 or 5 members
>> of this center: Chudov, Ugarov, Smorodin, Pozern,
>> Shaposhnikova (Chudov's wife) and others together

with 2 or 3 members from the branches of this
center…

"…The case of the Leningrad center has to be built
solidly, and for this reason witnesses are needed.
Social origin (of course, in the past) and the party
standing of the witness will play more than a small
role.

"'You, yourself,' said Zakovskii, 'will not need to
invent anything. The NKVD will prepare for you a
ready outline for every branch of the center; you will
have to study it carefully and to remember well all
questions and answers which the Court might ask.
This case will be ready in four-five months, or
perhaps a half year. During all this time you will be
preparing yourself so that you will not compromise
the investigation and yourself. Your future will
depend on how the trial goes and on its results. If
you begin to lie and to testify falsely, blame yourself.
If you manage to endure it, you will save your head
and we will feed and clothe you at the Government's
cost until your death.'"

This is the kind of vile things which were then
practiced."

For the whole method of beating confessions out of people, innocent or
guilty, see part 16. above, on Ezhov, and quotations from Frinovskii's
statement.

Jansen and Petrov quote Ezhov as having Zakovskii shot in August 1938
to get him out of the way, so he could not testify against him (Ezhov).

Frinovskii had returned to Moscow on 25 August, just
after Beriia's appointment, and he was invited straight to
the NKVD and stayed with Ezhov for more than an
hour. After arrest he testified: "I had never seen Ezhov
in such a depressed state. 'Things are rotten,' he said,
passing right away to the question that Beriia had been
appointed contrary to his wish." On 27–28 August
Frinovskii met with Evdokimov, who insisted that
before Beriia arrived he must take care of any unfinished
cases (nedodelki) that might compromise them. He told

> Frinovskii: "Check to see whether Zakovskii and all
> Iagoda people have been executed, because after Beriia's
> arrival the investigation of these cases may be renewed
> and they may turn against us." Frinovskii then
> ascertained that a group of Chekists, including Zakovskii
> and Mironov, had been shot on 26–27 August (actually
> they were shot on 29 August).

- Jansen & Petrov, p. 151. This is the same document as the Frinovskii statement published recently (2006) and which I put on the Internet at http://chss.montclair.edu/english/furr/research/frinovskyeng.html

Zakovskii was part of Ezhov's conspiracy, along with Frinovskii and others.

Zakovskii was explicitly blamed for torturing people "as a rule" in Stalin's telegram of Jan. 10, 1939. See below for the discussion of this document and the reference to Zakovskii. Khrushchev had this, because he quoted it. But he didn't quote the part involving Zakovskii, no doubt because it would have undermined his insinuation here that Zakovskii was acting in accordance with Stalin's wishes.

20. Kabakov

Khrushchev:

> "Even more widely was the falsification of cases
> practiced in the provinces. The NKVD headquarters of
> the Sverdlov Oblast "discovered" the so-called "Ural
> uprising staff" -an organ of the bloc of rightists,
> Trotskyites, Socialist Revolutionaries, church leaders -
> whose chief supposedly was the Secretary of the
> Sverdlov Oblast Party Committee and member of the
> Central Committee, All-Union Communist Party
> (Bolsheviks), Kabakov, who had been a party member
> since 1914. The investigative materials of that time show
> that in almost all krais, oblasts [provinces] and republics
> there supposedly existed "rightist Trotskyite, espionage-
> terror and diversionary-sabotage organizations and
> centers" and that the heads of such organizations as a
> rule -for no known reason -were first secretaries of
> oblast or republic Communist party committees or
> central committees."

From Mirzoian rehabilitation materials, 1955:

> Mirzoian further confessed that in 1930-1933, while he
> was in the Urals, he was supposedly in touch with one of
> the leaders of the Rights – Kabakov – and continued his
> counterrevolutionary activity, and in 1933-1938, on the
> orders of Rykov and Bukharin, he supposedly headed
> the Right-Trotskyite underground in Kazakhstan.

-*RKEB* 1, No. 52, p. 280.

Kabakov was dismissed from both the CC and the Party itself by a resolution circulated to the CC on May 17-19, 1937 and confirmed at the
June 1937 on June 29th.

Kabakov figured in Ezhov's report to the June 1937 CC Plenum on the
widespread nature of the conspiracy:

> In his report Ezhov sketched an all-embracing
> conspiracy against Stalin. Allegedly, already in 1933 on
> the initiative of various opposition groups a united
> "Center of Centers" had been created with Rykov,
> Tomskii, and Bukharin on behalf of the Rightists, SRs,
> and Mensheviks; Enukidze on behalf of the Red Army
> and NKVD conspirators; Kamenev and Sokol'nikov on
> behalf of the Zinovievists; and Piatakov on behalf of the
> Trotskiists. The main task of the "Center of Centers" or
> "United Center" had been the overthrow of Soviet
> power and the restoration of capitalism in the USSR.
> Reportedly, the military conspirators led by
> Tukhachevskii, as well as Iagoda and his NKVD people,
> had also been subordinated to the Center. New in
> Ezhov's scheme was that in the leadership of every
> republic or province there were conspirators too. He
> mentioned the regional Party leaders Sheboldaev from
> Kursk, Razumov from Irkutsk, Kabakov from
> Sverdlovsk, and Rumiantsev from Smolensk—all of
> them Central Committee members who had already been
> arrested before the Plenum.[104]
>
> 104. TsA FSB, f. 3, op. 4, d. 20, ll. 117–22.

- Jansen & Petrov, p. 75 & 233.

Kabakov was named as head of a counterrevolutionary organization in Urals in a note to the Politburo signed by Obkom Secretary, Stoliar.

> On the basis of evidence at hand in the obkom and the confessions of five arrested workers of the apparatus specially designated by the CPC [Commission of Party Control – GF] for this oblast the plenipotentiary of the CPC Bukharin [note: not the famous Bukharin – GF] and the secretary of the Party college Nosov have been exposed as enemies of the people, as active participants in the counterrevolutionary organization headed in the Urals by Kabakov.

- *Lubianka* 2, No. 276, 7 Jan. 1938.

Kabakov was named by Zubarev, one of the defendants in the March 1938 "Bukharin" Moscow Trial, as known by him to be a member of the Rightist conspiracy in the Urals as early as 1929. Rykov, one of the main defendants along with Bukharin, also named Kabakov as an important member of the Rightist conspiracy.

> ZUBAREV: …When I consented he at once told me that I would not be the only one working in the Urals, that there was already an active member of the counter-revolutionary organization there, very influential, that he was already directly connected with the Union centre through Rykov. He mentioned Kabakov.

> ZUBAREV: Rykov referred to A.P. Smirnov and stated that he had heard from him that I was an active member of the Right organization. I described to him the general situation in the Urals, the state of our organization and told him that already at the end of 1929, in December, Kabakov and I had organized a regional leading group which co-ordinated the whole work. I told him who belonged to this group: Kabakov, myself Sovetnikov and others. I told him of the work I had done on Smirnov's instructions and on his, Rykov's, instructions conveyed by Kabakov.

> RYKOV: … There were a number of members of our organization in various places, as has been enumerated, including peole like Kabakov, secretary…

-1938 Trial pp. 139; 160.

Kabakov was named in the Pospelov report, Section II.

> The UNKVD of the Sverdlovsk oblast 'discovered' a so-
> called 'Ural rebellion staff – an organ of the bloc of
> Rights, Trotskyites, SRs, Orthodox believers, and the
> agency of the ROVS [a White Russian Émigré military
> organization – GF], led by the secretary of the
> Sverdlovsk obkom Kabakov, member of the CPSU since
> 1914. This staff supposedly united 200 subgroups,
> formed along military lines, 15 rebellion organizations
> and 56 groups.

- *RKEB* 1, p. 323; *Doklad Khrushcheva* p. 192.

John D. Littlepage discusses sabotage in Urals (See Chapters 9, 10 and 25
generally on sabotage, or "wrecking.")

On Kabakov specifically:

> p. 99:

> "It seemed clear to me at the time that the selection of
> this commission and their conduct at Kalata traced
> straight back to the Communist high command in
> Sverdlovsk, whose members must be charged either with
> criminal negligence or actual participation in the events
> which had occurred in these mines. / 100 /

> However, the chief secretary of the Communist Party in
> the Urals, a man named Kabakoff, had occupied this
> post since 1922, all through the period of great activity in
> developing the mines and industries of the Urals. For
> some reason which was never clear to me he had always
> commanded the complete confidence of the Kremlin,
> and was considered so powerful that he was privately
> described as the 'Bolshevik Viceroy of the Urals.'

> If this man's record was examined, there was nothing to
> justify the reputation he appeared to have. Under his
> long rule, the Ural area, which is one of the richest
> mineral regions in Russia and which was given almost
> unlimited capital for exploitation, never did produce
> anything like what it should have done.

> … I told some of my Russian acquaintances at the time
> that it seemed to me there was a lot more going on in the

Urals than had yet been revealed, and that it came from somewhere high up.

All these incidents became clearer, so far as I was concerned, after the conspiracy trial in January, 1937, when Piatkoff, together with several of his associates, confessed in open court that they had engaged in organized sabotage of mines, railways, and other industrial enterprises since the beginning of 1931. A few weeks after this trial had ended and Piatakoff had been sentenced to be shot, the chief Party Secretary in the Urals, Kabakoff, who had been a close associate of Piatakoff's, was arrestd on charges of complicity in this same conspiracy."

- Littlepage, with Demaree Bess. *In Search of Soviet Gold* NY: Harcourt, Brace & Co., 1938 (1937).

John R. Harris gained access to Kabakov's investigative file. He states:

As Kabakov put it, "A large number of party leaders were imperceptably enveloped into the clique [by means of illegal gifts] such that within a year or two when they understood the criminal nature of what they were involved in, they were already beholden to us."

The Great Urals: regionalism and the evolution of the Soviet system. Ithaca: Cornell U.P. 1999, p. 163.

21. Kosior; 22. Chubar'; 23. Postyshev; 24. Kosarev

Khrushchev:

"Many thousands of honest and innocent Communists have died as a result of this monstrous falsification of such "cases," as a result of the fact that all kinds of slanderous "confessions" were accepted, and as a result of the practice of forcing accusations against oneself and others. In the same manner were fabricated the "cases" against eminent party and state workers -Kossior, Chubar, Postyshev, Kosarev and others."

Kosior and Chubar':

Ezhov's recently-published interrogation-confession of April 26 1939 names both Kosior and Chubar' as among those who "visited" the German intelligence agent Norden who also recruited Ezhov:

> Of the large number of people whom NORDEN consulted, I specifically remember GAMARNIK, IAKIR, CHUBAR', PETROVSKY, KOSIOR, VEINBERG, and METALIKOV. Norden also consulted me. – p. 57

- Ezhov interrogation-confession of April 26 1939; see http://chss.montclair.edu/english/furr/research/ezhov042639eng.html

According to the Rehabilitation materials of Postyshev prepared for Khrushchev, Kosior implicated Postyshev, then withdrew his confessions, but then reiterated them again.

Kosior implicated him; then withdrew it; then repeated it. In his own confessions Postyshev implicated Kosior, as well as Iakir, Chubar', and others.

> Kosior S.V. at the outset of the investigation named Postyshev among the number of the participants in the military conspiracy in the Ukraine. Then he recanted his confessions, but thereafter he confirmed them again. In Kosior's file there is a statement by Antipov N.K. in which he asserts that there were completely abnormal personal relations between Kosior and Postyshev, and that Postyshev was not in the general center of the counterrevolutionary organizations in the Ukraine. In this situation Kosior's confessions about Postyshev give serious cause for doubting their truthfulness.

- *RKEB* 1, 219 – rehab of Postyshev.

Postyshev implicated Kosior:

> Postyshev confessed he was guilty in that since 1934 he had been a member of the counterrevolutionary Right-Trotskyite organization in the Ukraine, and that together with Kosior and other particpants in the organization he carried out sabotage and subversive work.

Postyshev confessed he was guilty also in that since 1920 he had been an agent of Japanese intelligence, to which he gave information constituting state secrets of the USSR right up to the day of his arrest.

At the preliminary investigation and at trial Postyshev said that he was guilty. However the facts set forth in the transcripts of Postyshev's interrogation were not confirmed during the process of verification.

In the "confessions" of Postyshev it is stated that he was personally tied, in his counterrevolutionary work, to Balitsky V.A., Kosior S.V., Iakir I. E., Chubar' V.Ia., Popov N.N., Musul'bas I.A., and other participants of the anti-Soviet organization in the Ukraine.

- *RKEB* 1, 218.

p. 251 – in rehabilitation documents about Chubar'

The accusations against Chubar' of membership in the Right-Trotskyite organization were based on the indirect confessions of the arrested persons Antipov, Kosior, Pramnek, Sukhomlin, Postyshev, Boldyrev, and others, who, in identifying him as a member of the counterrevolutionary organization, referred to Rykov, Grin'ko, Bubnov and other persons, whose confessions do not mention Chubar'.

p. 252: same, continued:

The accusation against Sukhomlin of membership in the Right-Trotskyite organization and in Japanese intelligence were based on the confessions of the arrested persons Tiagnibeda, Marchak, Shumiatsky, Ermolenko, and others, who referred to Kosior, Postyshev, Iakir, and other persons.

Chubar' was implicated in the Right-Trotskyite conspiracy by Antipov, Kosior, Pramnek, Sukhomlin, Postyshev, Boldyrev, and others.

Kaganovich, interviewed by Felix Chuev:

"The general situation, social opinion was such, that it was not possible. I defended Kosior and Chubar', but when I was shown a whole notebook written by Chubar', his confessions in his own handwriting, I yielded [lit. "spread my arms," a sign of acquiescence].

Chuev, *Tak govoril Kaganovich*, pp. 68-9.

Molotov told Chuev that he himself was present when Antipov, Chubar's friend, accused Chubar'. Chubar' denied it heatedly and got very angry at Antipov. Molotov knew both of them very well. (Chuev, *Molotov: Po-luderzhavnyi Vlastelin*, pp. 486-7)

According to the Pospelov Report prepared for Khrushchev, Kosior was arrested on May 3, 1938 – that is, under Ezhov, long before Beria arrived at the NKVD – and both tortured (no details are given) and subjected to prolonged interrogations of up to 14 hours at a stretch. Of 54 interrogations of Kosior only 4 were preserved. This is consistent with the recently-revealed statement by Frinovskii.

No. 139

June 16, 1938

60. Concerning com. Chubar V.IA.

1. In view of the fact that **the confessions of Kosior, Eikhe, Tr. Chubar'**, and beside that, **the confessions of Rudzutak and Antipov, throw suspicion upon com. V. IA. Chubar'**, the Politburo of the CC considers it impossible for him to remain as a member of the Politburo of the CC and Deputy Chairman of the Council of People's Commissars of the SSR and considers it possible to give him work only in the provinces on a trial basis.

2. To decide the question of concrete work of com. Chubar' in the course of the next two days.

- *Stalinskoe Politbiuro v 30-e gody*, p. 167. (emphasis added, GF)

Dmitriev's confession:

LIUSHKOV told me that LEPLEVSKII came to the Ukraine and made a big fuss over rooting out all of BALITSKII's people. He arrested a series of leading workers of the Ukrainian NKVD and accused them of carrying out counterrevolutionary activity on BALITSKII's orders, and at the same time conspired with a number of plotters who were supposed to act under his instructions. LEPLEVSKII carried out the

fight against the Rights in such a way that he always
protected the leadership of the organization from
exposure by any means.

In this case the person in question was KOSIOR S.V.
He, according to LIUSHKOV's words, was in fact in
command of the operative work of the Ukrainian
NKVD…

One time I had the impression and BALITSKII and
LEPLEVSKII were at war with one another and were
personal enemies. LEPLEVSKII told me that all this was
for show only and that in reality he and BALITSKII
were in the same counterrevolutionary underground, led
by **KOSIOR, who was one of the most clandestine of
the Rights in the Ukraine.**

- *Lubianka* 2, No. 356, pp. 577-602., at 590-1 (emphasis added, GF).

Kosarev

Kosarev is named by Babulin, Ezhov's live-in nephew, fellow conspirator, and witness to Ezhov's and Ezhov's wife Evgeniia's "moral degeneration," as someone who visited them frequent, along with other conspirators such as Piatakov:

Answer. EZHOV and his wife Evgenia Solomonovna
had a wide circle of acquaintances which whom they
were on friendly relations and simply accepted into their
house. The most frequent guests in EZHOV's home
were PIATAKOV, the former director of the State Bank
of the USSR MAR'IASIN, the former manager of the
foreign section of the State Bank SVANIDZE, the
former trade representative in England BOGOMOLOV,
the editor of the *Peasant Gazette* URITSKY Semion,
KOL'TSOV Mikhail, KOSAREV A.V., RYZHOV and
his wife, Ziniaida GLIKINA and Ziniaida KORIMAN.

- Babulin confession, p. 75. At
http://chss.montclair.edu/english/furr/research/babulinru.html

Working, it seems, with this same confession by Babulin plus other archival materials no longer available to researchers, Jansen and Petrov hy-
pothesized some kind of similar relationship between Kosarev & Ezhov's
wife.

Viktor Babulin added Aleksandr Kosarev and a student
of the Industrial Academy, Nikolai Baryshnikov, as
persons she had had intimate relations with.27 Former
Komsomol leader Kosarev (who had been editor in chief
of Evgeniia's USSR in Construction) had already been
arrested on 28 November 1938 and was shot on 23
February of the following year. He was arrested as a
participant in an alleged Komsomol conspiracy,
however, and there is no evidence that his case was in
any way intertwined with Ezhov's.

- Jansen & Petrov, 185.

Rogovin:

"The Plenum [of the CC of the Komsomol] dismissed
Kosarev from his position, as well as four other
secretaries of the CC of the Komsomol, for "callous,
bureaucratic and hostile behavior towards honest
Komsomol workers who had tried to disclose
weaknesses in the work of the CC of the Komsomol,
and for taking revenge on one of the best Komsomol
workers (the case of comrade Mishakova)."

-Rogovin, *Partiia rasstreliannykh*. Ch. 26, at
http://trst.narod.ru/rogovin/t5/xxvi.htm

According to Akakii Mgeladze, *Stalin. Kakim Ia Ego Znal*. N.p. (Tbilisi?),
n.pub. 2001, Mgeladze, later First Secretary of the Georgian Party but in
the 1930s a leading Komsomol figure, discussed Kosarev with Stalin in
1947 (p. 165). During this discussion Stalin told him:

...The question of Kosarev was discussed twice in the
Politburo. Zhdanov and Andreev were assigned to verify
the evidence. They confirmed that the declarations of
Mishakova and others corresponded to reality, and the
materials gathered by the NKVD gave no cause for
doubt.

Mgeladze, who clearly believed that Kosarev was either entirely innocent
and had been framed by Beria for personal reasons, or had simply made
some mistake or other, replied:

I read the transcript of the Plenum of the Central
Committee of the VLKSM [abbreviation for the

Komsomol, "All-Union Leninist Communist Soviet of Youth"- GF], at which Kosarev was removed. In the speeches of both Zhdanov and Andreev, and in Shkiriatov's report everything was so thorough that it was not possible to doubt anything.

According to Mgeladze, Stalin went on to explain that everybody made mistakes, and that many mistakes were made in 1937. But Stalin did not apply this to Kosarev's case. (p.172)

25. The Lists

See citations in the text of Chapter Four.

26. Resolutions of the January 1938 CC Plenum

Khrushchev:

"Resolutions of the January plenum of the Central Committee, All-Union Communist Party (Bolsheviks), in 1938 had brought some measure of improvement to the party organizations. However, widespread repression also existed in 1938."

Getty & Naumov:

"Thus the mass depredations in the party were to be blamed (not without some justification) on former party secretaries who for the most part had already been removed." (496)

"In the months that followed [the January 1938 Plenum], mass expulsions from the party ceased, large numbers of expelled members were readmitted, and recruitment of new members began for the first time since 1933." (497)

Robert Thurston:

Vyshinskii "questioned the whole course of the Terror." (109) "Without the Gensec's [Stalin's] approval, the Procuracy would never have taken the steps it did to protest and curb the Terror."

"Chuianov's account demonstrates that the NKVD had been out of control at the regional level, if not nationally. ... But all the evidence assembled here suggests that the

> / Terror had two tracks: on one, Stalin pushed events forward personally, arranging the show trials and demanding, in a muddled way, that hundreds of thousands be arrested in 1937. **On another level the police fabricated cases, tortured people not targeted in Stalin's directives, and became a power unto themselves.**" (112; see Ch. 4 passim. Emphasis added, GF)

See also Zhukov, *Tainy Kremlia*, Ch. 2; Getty & Naumov 501-2; Postyshev's insistence on mass expulsions, *Tainy* pp. 50-51. For Malenkov's report, see *Tainy* pp. 48- 9. See decree (*postanovlenie*) "Ob oshibkakh…".)

Benediktov:

> Stalin, undoubtedly, knew about the capriciousness and illegalities that took place during the course of the repressions, regretted them, and took concrete measures towards correcting the excesses that had taken place and the liberation of honest people who had been imprisoned. I mention by the way that in those days we had little tolerance for slanderers and denouncers. Many of them, after they were uncovered, were hosted in the same camps to which they had sent their victims. The paradox is that some of them, released during the period of Khrushchev's "thaw", started to trumpet about Stalinist illegalities louder than anyone else, and even had the gall to published their memoirs about them!…
>
> The January Plenum of the CC ACP(b) in 1938 openly admitted the illegalities committed towards honest communists and non-party people, and to this end adopted a special resolution which, by the way, was published in all the central newspapers. Just as openly, to the whole country, occurred the discussions at the 18th Party Congress in 1939 concerning the harm done by unfounded repressions. Right after the January 1938 CC Plenum thousands of illegally repressed persons, including prominent military leaders, began to return from their places of imprisonment. They were all officially rehabilitated, and Stalin personally apologized to some of them."

- I.A. Benediktov, "O Staline I Khrushcheve", *Molodaia Gvardiia* No. 4, 1998, 12-65; cited at http://rksmb.ru/print.php?143 Benediktov was either Minister or First Deputy Minister of Agriculture from 1938 to 1953 (http://www.hrono.ru/biograf/benediktov.html)

Lev Balaian:

> All together in 1938 there were adopted six resolutions of the CC ACB(b) concerning the facts of violations of socialist legality. Besides those discussed above, they were … [the six are then enumerated]. The "troikas" and "dvoikas" attached to the NKVD were abolished by order of the People's Commissar of Internal Affairs (L.P. Beria) on November 26, 1938.

- Balaian, *Stalin i Khrushchev*, 28-9/237. All but the first (28 March) are in *Lubianka* 2. The date of abolition of *troikas* was Nov. 17, 1938, by "Ob arestakh…"

> On February 1, 1938 Procurator of the USSR A. Ia. Vyshinsky reported to J.V. Stalin and V.M. Molotov that the Main Military Procuracy had heard, on the request of the secretary of the Vologodskii obkom facts concerning especially dangerous crimes committed by a series of employees of the Vologoskii UNKVD. It was established that falsifiers of criminal cases compiled fabricated transcripts of interrogations of accused people, who had supposedly confessed to the commission of the most serious state crimes…. The cases fabricated in this way were handed over to the troika attached to the UNKVD of the Vologodskii oblast, and more than 100 people were shot. … During the interrogations atrocities were committed, all kinds of tortures were applied to those interrogated. It got to the point that during interrogations by these individuals four of the persons under interrogation had been killed.

> The aforesaid case concerning the most serious crimes against socialist legality was held in closed session of the Military tribunal of the Leningrad Military District in the presence of a small group of operative workers of the Vologoskii directorate of the NKVD and the Vologodskii procuracy. The accused Vlasov, Lebedev

and Roskuriakov, as the initiators and organizers of the
aforesaid outrageous crimes were sentenced to the
supreme penalty – shooting, and the other seven of their
collaborators were sentenced to lengthy terms of
imprisonment. (L. Mlechin, *Smert' Stalina*, p. 215).
Throughout the whole country there were 11,842 such
Vlasovs, Lebedevs and Roskuriakovs, repressed
scoundrels who even during the period of careless
Gorbachev-era pardoning of almost everyone the
infamous Iakovlev Commission did not consider it
possible to rehabilitate. (I. Rashkovets. "Nesudebnye
Organy", in *Rasprava. Prokurorskie sud'by*, p. 317). It is
precisely on the consciences of these falsifiers of criminal
cases, accused of the commission of baseless massive
arrests and the application of illegal methods of
investigation (i.e. tortures – L.B.), to whom even a half-
century later rehabilitation by the Decree of the Supreme
Court of the USSR of January 16, 1989 had been refused
– on them lies the responsibility for those same
"thousands and thousands of innocently repressed
people" whom Khrushchev, and then his creation and
student Gorbachev generously "hung" on the dead J.V.
Stalin."

- Balaian, *Stalin i Khrushchev*, Ch. 2. at
http://www.stalin.su/book.php?action=header&id=6 Balaian refers to
the collection *Rasprava. Prokurorskie sud'by* (Moscow: Iuridicheskaia literature, 1990), p. 314 for the disbanding of the "troikas" and gives the incorrect date of November 26, 1938. In fact the decree is dated November 17, 1938 (cf. *Lubianka 2*. No. 362, pp. 607-11.)

Vyshinsky's letter to Stalin is in *Sovetskoe Rukovodstvo: Perepiska 1928-1939*.
M, 1999, No. 239, pp. 398-400 and is online at
http://chss.montclair.edu/english/furr/research/vyshinsky_stalinfeb013
9.html

Jansen & Petrov, on Uspensky about Ezhov's directions for massive falsification of cases:

> … the notion that the regional NKVD chiefs silently
> opposed Ezhov's plans and that Ezhov forced them to
> conduct mass operations under threats of arrest is

contradicted by the testimony of another conference
participant, the Orenburg NKVD chief, A. I. Uspenskii
(given during investigation in April 1939). In his words,
they "tried to surpass each other with reports about
gigantic numbers of people arrested." Uspenskii is of
course incorrect in speaking of "people arrested," since
the conference dealt with quotas of future arrests in each
region. According to him, Ezhov's instruction amounted
to, "Beat, destroy without sorting out," and he quotes
Ezhov as saying that in connection with the destroying
of the enemies "a certain number of innocent people will
be annihilated too," but this was "inevitable."[15] Two
other sources offer similar wording: Ezhov announced
that "if during this operation an extra thousand people
will be shot, that is not such a big / 85 / deal.

During the conference, Ezhov and Frinovskii talked with
each of the attending NKVD chiefs, discussing the
quotas for arrest and execution put forward by them and
giving instructions for the necessary measures in view of
the preparation and the conduct of the operation.
Mironov informed Ezhov about a "Rightist-Trotskiist
bloc" that had been discovered within the Western
Siberian leadership. When he called the evidence against
some of those arrested unconvincing, Ezhov answered:
"Why don't you arrest them? We are not going to work
for you, imprison them, and then sort it out afterward,
dropping those against whom there is no evidence. Act
more boldly, I have already told you repeatedly." He
added that in certain cases, with Mironov agreeing,
department chiefs could also apply "physical methods of
influencing."[17] When Uspenskii asked Ezhov what to do
with prisoners older than age seventy, he ordered them
to be shot.

Ezhov approved of the activity of those NKVD chiefs,
who cited "astronomic" numbers of persons repressed,
such as, for instance, the NKVD chief of Western
Siberia, citing a number of 55,000 people arrested,
Dmitriev of Sverdlovsk province— 40,000, Berman of
Belorussia—60,000, Uspenskii of Orenburg —40,000,

Liushkov of the Far East—70,000, Redens of Moscow province—50,000.* The Ukrainian NKVD chiefs each cited numbers of people arrested from 30,000 to 40,000. Having listened to the numbers, Ezhov in his concluding remarks praised those who had "excelled" and announced that, undoubtedly, excesses had taken place here and there, such as, for instance, in Kuibyshev, where on Postyshev's instruction Zhuravlev had transplanted all active Party members of the province. But he immediately added that "in such a large-scale operation mistakes are inevitable." (Jansen & Petrov, 131).

Uspenskii was astonished and alarmed by his drunken table talk. During the trip, Ezhov drank uninterruptedly, boasting to Uspenskii that he had the Politburo "in his hands" and could do literally anything, arrest anyone, including Politburo members. (J&P 133)

* Redens was on the Moscow "troika" with Khrushchev himself.

27. "Beria's gang"

Khrushchev:

Meanwhile, Beria's gang, which ran the organs of state security, outdid itself in proving the guilt of the arrested and the truth of materials which it falsified.

Thurston, p. 118:

"Khrushchev then suggested that police torture continued freely and even increased under Beria. Because part of Khrushchev's purpose in the speech was to show his archenemy and political opponent after Stalin's death in the worst possible light, this claim must not be taken as a definitive statement.

Beria's negative image… has…wrongly overridden the firsthand evidence of what happened when he replaced Ezhov. Boris Men'shagin, a defense attorney in Smolensk, commented that Beria "right away displayed astonishing liberalism." Arrests "fell away practically to nothing," as the inmate Alexander Weissberg put it. … a

new and much improved policy was in place. / 119 /
Political repression declined acutely in 1939-41....

In late 1938 prison and camp inmates regained the rights,
allowed under Iagoda but lost with Ezhov, to have
books and play chess and other games... Investigators
now addressed them using the polite term "vy" instead
of the condescendingly familiar "ty." ... torture once
again became the exception, contrary to Khrushchev's
assertion... prisoners like R.V. Ivanov-Razumnik, Mariia
Ioffe, and Abdurakman Avtorkhanov, among others,
reported that physical methods ceased where they were
being held when Beria assumed control of the police.

Under Beria, a purge swept through the NKVD,
removing most of Ezhov's lieutenants and many in the
lower ranks as well"

According to the Pospelov report, arrests dropped hugely, by over 90%,
in 1939 and 1940 in comparison to 1937 and 1938

Year	1935	1936	1937	1938	1939	1940
Arrests	114,456	88,873	918,671	629,695	41,627	127,313
Of whom were executed	1,229	1,118	353,074	328,618	2,601	1,863

http://www.alexanderyakovlev.org/almanah/inside/almanah-
doc/55752; published in many places, including *Doklad Khrushcheva*, p.
185).

Executions in 1939 and 1940 dropped to **far less than 1%** of the levels
of mass executions in 1937 and 1938. Beria took over as head of the
NKVD in December, 1938, so this corresponds precisely with Beria's
period in command.

28. "Torture telegram"

Khrushchev:

When the wave of mass arrests began to recede in 1939, and the leaders of territorial party organizations began to accuse the NKVD workers of using methods of physical pressure on the arrested, Stalin dispatched a coded telegram on January 10, 1939 to the committee secretaries of oblasts and krais, to the central committees of republic Communist parties, to the People's Commissars of Internal Affairs and to the heads of NKVD organizations. This telegram stated:

> "The Central Committee of the All-Union Communist Party (Bolsheviks) explains that the application of methods of physical pressure in NKVD practice is permissible from 1937 on in accordance with permission of the Central Committee of the All-Union Communist Party (Bolsheviks) ...It is known that all bourgeois intelligence services use methods of physical influence against the representatives of the socialist proletariat and that they use them in their most scandalous forms.
>
> The question arises as to why the socialist intelligence service should be more humanitarian against the mad agents of the bourgeoisie, against the deadly enemies of the working class and of the kolkhoz workers. The Central Committee of the All-Union Communist Party (Bolsheviks) considers that physical pressure should still be used obligatorily, as an exception applicable to known and obstinate enemies of the people, as a method both justifiable and appropriate."

Thus, Stalin had sanctioned in the name of the Central Committee of the All-Union Communist Party (Bolsheviks) the most brutal violation of socialist legality, torture and oppression, which led as we have seen to the slandering and self-accusation of innocent people.

Getty on the original of this telegram, or a similar one.

In the course of this research, we have located the famous 1939 Stalin directive on "physical methods" of

interrogation mentioned by Khruschev in his 1956 Secret
Speech (See I.V.Kurilov, N.N.Mikhailov and
V.P.Naumov, eds., Reabititatsia: Politicheskie protsessy
30-50-kh godov [Moscow, 1991], 40). It is in TsA FSB,
f.100, op.1, por. 6, ll. 1-2 (second series). **Dated 27 July
(not 10 July [this is an error for 10 January – GF]
according to Khruschev),** it is a telegram from Stalin to
party secretaries in all regions. It refers to a still unfound
1937 Central Committee directive authorizing physical
methods in exceptional circumstances. Interestingly, the
1939 telegram was written after N.I. Ezhov's fall, and **in
a passage not mentioned by Khruschev it accuses
Ezhov's men of excessive torture, "converting an
exception into a rule."**

- Getty, "Excesses Are Not Permitted." *The Russian Review* 61 (January
2002): 113-38, at p.114, n. 45.

I have put a photocopy of the only known text of the "Torture Telegram
of January 10, 1939" at
http://chss.montclair.edu/english/furr/research/ShT_10_01_39.pdf

Full Text of the "Torture Telegram"

Bold - parts Khrushchev quoted;

Italics - section omitted by Khrushchev that proves his intent to deceive
his audience.

BY CODE CC VKP(b)

TO THE SECRETARIES OF OBLAST AND
REGIONAL PARTY COMMITTEES, CCS OF
NATIONAL COMMUNIST PARTIES, PEOPLE'S
COMMISSARS OF INTERNAL AFFAIRS, HEADS
OF NKVD DIRECTORATES

The CC [Central Committee] of the VKP [All-Union Communist Party]
has learned that in checking up on employees of NKVD directorates secretaries of oblast and regional party committees have blamed them for
using physical pressure against persons who have been arrested, as something criminal. **The CC of the VKP explains that use of physical
pressure in the practice of the NKVD has been permitted since**

1937 in accordance with permission of the CC of the VKP. *At the same time it was stated that physical pressure is permitted as an exception and, in addition, only in relation to blatant enemies of the people who, taking advantage of the humane method of interrogation, stubbornly refuse to give up their co-conspirators; who refuse to confess for months; and who strive to slow down the discovery of conspirators who are still at large; and so continue their struggle against Soviet power even from prison. Experience has shown that this policy has produced results by greatly speeding up the exposure of enemies of the people. It is true that subsequently in practice the method of physical pressure was sullied by the scum Zakovsky, Litvin, Uspensky, and others, because they turned it from an exception into a rule and employed it against honest people who had been accidentally arrested. For these abuses, they have been duly punished. But this does not invalidate the method itself, insofar as it is employed correctly in practice.* **It is well known that all bourgeois intelligence services use physical pressure against representatives of the socialist proletariat and in its most disgraceful forms at that. One won- / page break / ders why a socialist intelligence service is obliged to be humane in relation to inveterate agents of the bourgeoisie and implacable enemies of the working class and collective farmers. The CC of the VKP considers that the method of physical pressure must necessarily be continued in future in exceptional cases in relation to manifest and unrepentant enemies of the people, as a completely correct and expedient method.** The CC of the VKP demands that the secretaries of oblast and regional committees [and] of the CCs of national communist party [evidently a misprint for "parties" - GF] act in accordance with this clarification when checking up on employees of the NKVD.

SECRETARY OF THE CC VKP(b) I. STALIN [typed, not signed- GF]

[Dated by hand - GF] 10/I.-39 g. 15 hrs]

Additionally printed
two cop. 8.II.1956 g.[251]

---

[251] My translation; that by Mark Kramer on the H-HOAC list Feb. 27 2005, at http://tinyurl.com/bqp6j, and widely reprinted – for example, at the Marxist Internet Archive -- is inaccurate.

The question of such a telegram was discussed at the June 1957 CC Plenum, more than a year after Khrushchev's "Secret Speech." The entire discussion is a mystery, for there is no reference at all to the document now identified as the "torture telegram" (above). Instead a different, or two different, documents are under discussion here. The copy from the Dagestan Obkom (oblast' committee) of the Party that Aristov refers to here is not the copy we now have. This whole question has never been satisfactorally resolved.

> Kaganovich: If I'm not mistaken, I seem to remember
> that a document like that was officially sent around to
> the Party *obkoms* [oblast', or province, committees – GF].
> Let's search for it.
>
> Khrushchev: A telegram like that was really sent around.
> But I am talking about another document. ...
>
> Kaganovich:... There's a document that was sent around
> to all the Party *obkoms*.
>
> Voices: That's another document, we all know it.
>
> Khrushchev: But the original is destroyed?
>
> Molotov: The telegram about the use of physical
> measures of action against spies and the like, about
> which we are now speaking, was sent around to all
> members of the Central Committee and to all *obkoms*.
>
> Malin: The original is not in the archive of the Central
> Committee, it has been destroyed. The telegram exists in
> the copy that was sent around to the *obkoms*.
>
> Aristov: We found it in only one *obkom* of the Party, in
> Dagestan.

- *Molotov, Malenkov, Kaganovich, 1957. Stenogramma iiun'skogo plenuma TsK KPSS I drugie dokumenty.* Ed. A.N. Iakovlev, N. Kovaleva, A. Korotkov, et al. Moscow: MDF, 1998, pp. 121-2.)

Both Iurii Zhukov ("Zhupel Stalina", Part 3. *Komsomol'skaia Pravda*, Nov. 12, 2002) and Mark Junge and Rolf Binner (*Kak Terror Stal Bol'shim*. Moscow, 2003, p. 16, n. 14) attest to the fact that Khrushchev seems to have destroyed more documents than anyone else. Benediktov had also heard of this destruction:

Benediktov:

> Competent people have told me that Khrushchev gave
> orders to destroy a number of important documents
> related to the repressions of the 30s and 40s. In the first
> place, of course, he wanted to hide his own part in the
> illegalities in Moscow and the Ukraine where, currying
> favor with the Center, he condemned many innocent
> people. At the same time were destroyed documents of
> another sort, documents that indisputably proved that
> the repressive actions undertaken at the end of the 1930s
> against some prominent party and military figures were
> justified. It's an understandable tactic: having sheltered
> himself, he tried to shift the whole blame for the
> illegalities onto Stalin and the "Stalinists", from whom
> Khrushchev expected the fundamental threat to his own
> power.

- *Molodaia Gvardiia* No. 4, 1989, cited at http://rksmb.ru/print.php?143

29. Rodos tortured Chubar' & Kosior on Beria' orders

Khrushchev:

> Not long ago – only several days before the present
> Congress – we called to the Central Committee
> Presidium session and interrogated the investigative
> judge Rodos, who in his time investigated and
> interrogated Kossior, Chubar and Kosarev. He is a vile
> person, with the brain of a bird, and morally completely
> degenerate. And it was this man who was deciding the
> fate of prominent party workers; he was making
> judgments also concerning the politics in these matters,
> because, having established their "crime," he provided
> therewith materials from which important political
> implications could be drawn.

> The question arises whether a man with such an intellect
> could alone make the investigation in a manner to prove
> the guilt of people such as Kossior and others. No, he
> could not have done it without proper directives. At the
> Central Committee Presidium session he told us: "I was
> told that Kossior and Chubar were people's enemies and

> for this reason I, as an investigative judge, had to make them confess that they are enemies."

(Indignation in the hall.)

> He would do this only through long tortures, which he did, receiving detailed instructions from Beria. We must say that at the Central Committee Presidium session he cynically declared: "I thought that I was executing the orders of the party." In this manner, Stalin's orders concerning the use of methods of physical pressure against the arrested were in practice executed.

> These and many other facts show that all norms of correct party solution of problems were invalidated and everything was dependent upon the willfulness of one man."

Rodos' interrogations, confessions, and case file have never been made available to researchers. As we note in the text, Rodos and other former NKVD men appear to have been scapegoats. If in fact they had followed CC directives, as the "torture telegram" above states, then they had broken no laws even if they did beat or otherwise torture some defendants.

30. Stalin didn't heed warnings about war

Khrushchev:

> The power accumulated in the hands of one person, Stalin, led to serious consequences during the Great Patriotic War...During the war and after the war, Stalin put forward the thesis that the tragedy which our nation experienced in the first part of the war was the result of the "unexpected" attack of the Germans against the Soviet Union.... Stalin took no heed of these warnings. What is more, Stalin ordered that no credence be given to information of this sort, in order not to provoke the initiation of military operations....everything was ignored: warnings of certain Army commanders, declarations of deserters from the enemy army, and even the open hostility of the enemy.

...Is this an example of the alertness of the chief of the party and of the state at this particularly significant historical moment?"

Marshal Golovanov:

> We normally lay all responsibility for the suddenness of Hitler's attack on our country, which was unexpected as to time, on J.V. Stalin, since he was the head of state, although S.K. Timoshenko, as People's Commissar of Defense, and G.K. Zhukov, as Head of the General Staff, as well as a number of other comrades, also had direct responsibility. But no one does this. It's just as proper both to speak of the strategic victories that had worldwide significance, and also to credit them to those people who stood at the head of those or other campaigns or of the war as a whole and who were responsible for their fulfillment. This is logical. The great, world-historical victory in the Second World War was won by the country, the party, and the army, all led by Stalin.

- Andrew Kazantsev, in *Nakanune*, June 22, 2005, at http://www.nakanune.ru/articles/22_ijunja__dva_blickriga

Vadim Kozhinov.

> But if considered dispassionately, both Stalin's and Roosevelt's miscalculations have a completely convincing explanation. The communications of intelligence services are always contradictory to a greater or lesser degrees, because they derive from the most varied, and often deliberately misinformed – sources. Not long ago a collection of documents titled 'Hitler's Secrets on Stalin's Table. Intelligence and Counter-intelligence on the Preparation of German Aggression against the USSR. March-June 1941' was published. This work makes it clear that during this period Stalin received extremely varied intelligence, including disinformation, particularly, information according to which Germany (as Stalin also believed) intended to occupy England before invading the USSR. One of the leaders of the intelligence services of that time, General P. A. Sudoplatov, later remarked: "The information of

Enemy massed at Russ border should have made Barbarossa N. evident

three *reliable* (my emphasis – V.K.) sources from within
Germany deserved special attention, [that] the leadership
of the Wehrmacht decisively protested against any war
on two fronts.'

Lack of trust of the intelligence information about a
German invasion was also caused by the disagreements
they contained about the dating of the beginning of the
war. 'They specified May 14 and 15, May 20 and 21, June
15 and, at last, June 22… Once the first May periods had
passed, Stalin… finally came to believe that Germany
would not invade the USSR in 1941…'

In the 1960s and later many authors wrote, with great
indignation, for example, that no one believed the
information that arrived about a week before the
beginning of the war and which was obtained by the spy
Richard Sorge, who later became world famous, and
which gave the accurate date of the German invasion –
June 22. However, it was impossible to simply believe it
after a series of inaccurate dates that had been
communicated through sources considered 'reliable.' (by
the way, Sorge himself at first reported that the invasion
would take place in May). And contemporary 'analysts',
knowing – as does the whole world – that the war began
precisely on June 22, and therefore waxing indignant at
Stalin because he had neglected Sorge's precise
information sent out on June 15, seem naïve at the very
least…"

- Vadim Kozhinov, *Rossiia. Vek XX. (1939-1964). Opyt bespristrastnogo is-
sledovaniia.* Moscow: Algoritm, 1999, pp. 73-4 (His chapter 2 is entitled
"Suddenness and Lack of Preparation"). Also at
http://www.hrono.ru/libris/lib_k/kozhin20v03.php

In the "Secret Speech" Khrushchev said (p. 26):

This pertained, alas, not only to tanks, artillery and
planes. At the outbreak of the war we did not even have
sufficient numbers of rifles to arm the mobilized
manpower. I recall that in those days I telephoned to
Comrade Malenkov from Kiev and told him, "People

have volunteered for the new Army and demand arms. You must send us arms."

Malenkov answered me, "We cannot send you arms. We are sending all our rifles to Leningrad and you have to arm yourselves."

According to Marshal Vasilevskii what really happened was quite different:

In conclusion the Supreme Commander said that he would take all measures to help the Southwestern Front, but at the same time asked them to reply more on themselves in this matter.

– It would be unreasonable to think – he said – that we will give you everything already prepared on the side. Learn to supply and resupply yourselves. Create supply sections with each army, prepare several factories for the production of rifles and machine guns, pull all the strings you need to pull, and you will see that you can create a great deal for the front in the Ukraine itself. That's the way Leningrad is acting at the present time, using its own machine manufacturing bases, and they are to a great extent successful, already have had some success. The Ukraine can do the same. Leningrad has already arranged for the production of RS's. This is a very effective weapon like a minesweeper, which literally crushes the enemy. Why not do this yourselves?

Kirponos and Khrushchev replied:

– Comrade Stalin, we will put all your orders into practice. Unfortunately, we are not acquainted with the construction details of RSs. We request that you order to send us one example of an RS with diagrams, and we will organize construction here. – This answer followed:

– Your people already have the diagrams, and you have had samples for a long time. Your inattention in this serious matter is at fault. Good. I'll send you a battery of RSs, drawings, and instructors in their manufacture. All the best, I wish you success."

– Marshal A.M. Vasilevskii, *Delo vsei zhizni* ('My life's work'). 3rd ed. Moscow, Politizdat 1978, Chapter 11. Cited from the Russian at http://www.victory.mil.ru/lib/books/memo/vasilevsky/11.html

As Vadim Kozhinov points out,

> Khrushchev, who in 1956 was striving to discredit Malenkov, his competitor in the struggle for supreme power, unconsciously discredited himself. For by June 22 he had already been 'supreme boss' in Kiev and over the whole of the Ukraine for 3 ½ years, since January 1938 (which, by the way, had a common border with Germany since September 1939!) but, it turns out, had not taken the trouble even to provide himself with rifles! So either Khrushchev either did not pay attention to the 'eloquent evidence' that he cited in 1956, or else he did nothing with this 'evidence' in a practical way (for in fact the first secretary of the CC of the Ukraine and member of the Politburo could have prepared those rifles in plenty of time...)

- Kozhinov, V.V., *Rossiia: Vek XX (1939-1964)* Chapter 2, p. 50; also at http://www.hrono.ru/libris/lib_k/kozhin20v03.php

The German Army's disinformation plan to spread false rumors to the Soviet leadership, signed by Keitel, is dated February 15, 1941. It is on-line at http://chss.montclair.edu/english/furr/research/germandisinfo.html (in Russian only)

Marshal Meretskov, 1968

> I must say something else. Inasmuch as at the very beginning of the war England and the USA became our allies in the anti-Hitler coalition, most people who attempt to critical analyze the decisions made by our government at that time mechanically evaluate them only on the level of the Soviet-German war and thereby make a mistake. For the situation in the spring of 1941 was extremely complicated. At that time we could not be sure that an anti-Soviet coalition of capitalist countries including, let us say, Germany, Japan, England and the USA, would not arise. Hitler decided in 1940 against an invasion of England. Why? Did he not have the

strength? Did he decide to deal with England later? Or
were, perhaps, secret negotiations going on about a
⎩united anti-Soviet front? It would have been criminal
negligence not to weigh all the possibilities, because in
truth the well-being of the USSR depended on selecting
the correct political position. Where will the fronts be?
Where should our forces be concentrated? Only on the
Western borders? Or is a war on the southern border
⎛also possible? And what will be the situation in the Far
⎝East? This multiplicity of paths of possible action,
together with a lack of a firm guarantee that the correct
path could be immediately chosen in a given case, made
for a doubly complicated situation.

- K.A. Meretskov, *Na sluzhbe narodu* ("In Service to the People"). Moscow: Politizdat, 1968.

Marshal Zhukov:

I have thought for a long time about all this and here is
what I arrived at. It seems to me that the matter of the
defense of the country in its basic, broadest outlines and
directions was carried out correctly. During a period of
many years, in economic and social terms, everything, or
nearly everything, was done that was possible. As for the
period from 1939 to the middle of 1941, during that
period special efforts that demanded all our strength and
resources were made by the people and the party to
strengthen our defense.

- G.K. Zhukov, *Vospominaniia i razmyshleniia* ("Reminiscences and
Thoughts"). Vol. 1, Ch. 9. Moscow, 2002

Marshals Vasilevskii and Zhukov disagreed about whether Stalin should
have ordered all the troops to take positions along the border. Comment-
ing on Vasilevskii's article in 1965, Zhukov wrote:

⎛I think that the Soviet Union would have been smashed
if we had organized all our forces on the border. It's
good that this didn't happen, and if our main forces had
been smashed in the area of the state frontier, then the
Hiterlite armies would have had the possibility of
carrying out the war more successfully, and Moscow and

Leningrad would have been taken in 1941. G. Zhukov, ⟩
December 12, 1965.

- Shaptalov, B. *Ispytania voiny* ("The Trials of War"). Moscow: AST, 2002.
Russian edition at http://militera.lib.ru/research/shaptalov/02.html .The
same passage, with a longer quotation from Vasilevskii's unpublished MS,
is found in Gor'kov, IU.A. *Kremlin. Stavka. General Staff*. Tver' 1995,
Chapter 4, p. 68. Russian edition at
http://militera.lib.ru/research/gorkov2/04.html

Evidence of Betrayal by Gen. Dmitri Pavlov

Khrushchev does not explicitly name General Dmitri Pavlov, executed in
July 1941 for dereliction of duty in not preparing the Belorussian Front
for Hitler's invasion.

There is a good deal of evidence now, from former Soviet archives, that
Pavlov was indeed guilty, and a member of a military conspiracy to boot.
We omit this material here. Some of it and the references to it are con-
tained in the original Russian language edition of this book (p.368).

31. Vorontsov's Letter

Khrushchev:

> We must assert that information of this sort concerning
> the threat of German armed invasion of Soviet territory
> was coming in also from our own military and
> diplomatic sources; however, because the leadership was
> conditioned against such information, such data was
> dispatched with fear and assessed with reservation.
>
> Thus, for instance, information sent from Berlin on May
> 6, 1941 by the Soviet military attaché, Captain
> Vorontsov, stated: "Soviet citizen
> Bozer…communicated to the deputy naval attaché that,
> according to a statement of a certain German officer
> from Hitler's headquarters, Germany is preparing to
> invade the USSR on May 14 through Finland, the Baltic
> countries and Latvia. At the same time Moscow and
> Leningrad will be heavily raided and paratroopers landed
> in border cities…

In *Voenno-Istoricheskii Zhurnal* No. 2, 1992, pp. 39-40 we have the full text
of Captain Vorontsov's statement. It is contained in a letter of May 6,

1941 to Stalin from Admiral Kuznetsov. The crucial part omitted by Khrushchev is in **boldface**:

> Top secret
>
> May 6 1941
>
> No. 48582cc
>
> CC ACP(b)
>
> Com. STALIN J.V.
>
> Naval attaché in Berlin Captain 1 degree Vorontsov relates: Soviet citizen Bozer **(Jewish nationality, former Lithuanian subject)** communicated to the deputy naval attaché that, according to a statement of a certain German officer from Hitler's headquarters, Germany is preparing to invade the USSR on May 14 through Finland, the Baltic countries and Latvia. At the same time Moscow and Leningrad will be heavily raided and paratroopers landed in border cities.
>
> **Our attempts to clarify the primary source of this information and to amplify it have not as yet been successful, as bozer has declined to do this. Work with him and verification of the information continues.**
>
> **I believe that this information is false, specially directed through this channel with the object of reaching our government in order to find out how the USSR would react to it.**
>
> Admiral KUZNETSOV

32. German soldier

Khrushchev:

> The following fact is also known: On the eve of the invasion of the territory of the Soviet Union by the Hitlerite army, a certain German citizen crossed our border and stated that the German armies had received orders to start the offensive against the Soviet Union on the night of June 22 at 3 o'clock. Stalin was informed

about this immediately, but even this warning was ignored.

The soldier, (Alfred Liskow:)

> Many people know that on the night of June 22, 1941 a German soldier fled to our side and reported about the impending invasion of German forces. Beginning with the time of *perestroika* it became fashionable to state that this deserter was quickly shot as a provocateur. For example, here is what is stated on this matter in a biography of Stalin published in New York in 1990:
>
>> A German soldier and former communist bravely crossed the border in order to report the precise time of attack. Stalin ordered him to be shot immediately for disinformation.

This is completely false. It is a reference to Lewis Jonathan, Whitehead Phillip. *Stalin. A Time for Judgement.* New York, 1990. p. 121, cited from Zhores and Roi Medvedev, *Neizvestniy Stalin* , Russian ed. Moscow 2002, pp. 309-10. The English edition of this book, *The Unknown Stalin* (Woodstock and New York: The Overlook Press, 2004), fully refutes Khrushchev's tale on pp. 240-1.

Khrushchev's story is false as well.

We can do no better than to cite at some length from Igor' Pykhalov's eye-opening study *Velikaia Obolganniai Voina* ['The Great Calumniated War'] Moscow, 2005. Chapter 9: "The Fate of a Deserter."

> Many people know that on the night of June 22, 1941 a German soldier fled to our side and reported about the impending invasion of German forces. Beginning with the time of perestroika it became fashionable to state that this deserter was quickly shot as a provocateur. For example, here is what is stated on this matter in a biography of Stalin published in New York in 1990:
>
>> A German soldier and former communist bravely crossed the border in order to report the precise time of attack. Stalin ordered him to be shot immediately for disinformation. *

But is this so. Let's try to clarify the fate of this man.

German army soldier Alfred Liskow was detained on June 21 1941 at 2100 hours at a unit of the Sokalsk command of the 90th Border unit. At 310 on the night of June 22 the UNKVD of the L'vov oblast' transmitted by telephone to the NKGB of the Ukrainian SSR a message with the following contents:

> The German corporal who crossed the border in the region of Sokal' declared the following: His name is Liskow Alfred Germanovich, 30 years of age, a worker, carpenter in a furniture factory in the city of Kohlberg (Bavaria), where he left his wife, baby, mother and father.
>
> The corporal served in the 221st sapper regiment of the 15th division. The regiment is situated in the village of Tselenzh, 5 km north of Sokal'. He was drafted into the army from the reserves in 1939.
>
> He considers himself a communist, is a member of the Union of Red Front-line soldiers, and says that life is very hard for workers in Germany.
>
> Around evening his company commander Lieut. Schulz told them that tonight, after artillery preparation, their unit would begin the crossing of the Bug on rafts, boats and pontoons.
>
> As a supporter of Soviet power, once he learned of this he decided to flee to us and tell us.'

More details about this event are given in the report of the commander of the 90th border unit Major M.C. Bychkovskii:

> June 27 at 2100 in the area of the Sokal'sk command a soldier was detained who fled from the German Army, Liskow Alfred. Since there was no translator in the command station, I ordered the commander of the area Capt. Bershadsky to take the soldier by truck to the staff of the unite in the town of Vladimir.
>
> At 0030 June 22 1941 the soldier arrived in the town of Vladimir-Volynsk. Through an interpreter at

approximately 1:00 at night Liskow said that on June
22 at dawn the Germans were supposed to cross the
border. I immediately reported this to the
responsible duty officer of the army staff Brigade
Commissar Maslovsky. At the same time I reported
by telephone personally to the commander of the
5th army Major-General Potavpov, who regarded
my report with suspicious and did not pay attention
to it. I personally was not firmly convinced of the
truthfulness of the report of soldier Liskow, but all
the same I called out the commanders of the zones
and ordered them to reinforce the guard at the state
borders, to put special listening posts at the Bug
river and in the case of the Germans crossing the
river to fire upon and destroy them. At the same
time I ordered that if anything suspicious is noted
(any kind of movement on the opposite bank) to
report it to me personally and immediately. I
remained the whole time in the staff HQ.

At 100 on June 22 the commanders of the zones
reported to me that nothing suspicious was noted on
the opposite side of the river, all was calm. In view
of the fact that the translators in our unit are not
skilled, I summoned from the town a teacher of the
German language who has an excellent knowledge
of the German language, and Liskow again repeated
the same thing, that is, that the Germans are
prepared to invade the USSR at dawn on June 22
1941. He called himself a communist and declared
that he came over to us on his own initiative
especially to warn us. While the interrogation of the
soldier was not yet finished I heard from the
direction of Ustilug (the first command center)
strong artillery fire. I understood that this was the
Germans who had opened fire on our territory,
which the soldier under interrogation confirmed. I
immediately tried to call the commander by
telephone, but the connection had been destroyed.

It's perfectly natural that Soviet propaganda tried to
make use of Liskow's deed for its own purposes. Here is
what is said about this in the memoirs of Major-General
Burtsev, who headed the section (from August 1944
division) of special propaganda of the Main Political
Directorate of the Red Army:

> Already by June 27 the first leaflet of the German
> anti-fascist Alfred Liskow had appeared. Risking fire
> from both shores, he had swum the Bug in order to
> warn our border guards about the imminent invasion
> of the USSR. Liskow did this as soon as, in the
> 222nd regiment of the 75th division, where he
> served, they had been read the order for the
> invasion. We, of course, could not miss the chance
> to speak with this first deserter. Soon Liskow was
> brought to Moscow. A tall German "of working-
> class cut" serving as a field medic seemed
> sympathetic and trustworthy.

> " I am from a working-class family in the city of
> Kohlberg," he said. "My parents and I hate Hitler
> and his regime. For us the USSR is a friendly
> country, and we do not wish to fight with the Soviet
> people. There are many such working-class families
> in Germany. They do not want war with you."

> His story was published in *Pravda*, and it was that
> story that served as the initial leaflet, printed with his
> portrait, to inform the German soldiers that there
> are within the Wehrmacht opponents of the war and
> Hitlerism, friends of the Soviet Union.

Many participants in the war remember the agitational
materials in which Liskow's name appeared. For
example, the Leningrad writer Dmitry Shcheglov:

> June 28… In the newspapers pasted on the walls
> people are reading the announcement: 'German
> soldier Alfred Liskow, not wishing to fight against
> the Soviet people, has deserted to our side.

> Alfred Liskow has addressed German soldiers with
> a call to overthrow the Hitler regime.

And on a second sheet was Liskow's statement and portrait: 'Among the German soldiers a mood of depression reigns.

Unfortunately I have not yet been able to trace the further fate of Alfred Liskow. M.I. Burtsev writes:

After that A. Liskow perished, remaining to his last breath true to the idea of the fight against fascism.

However even if it should be that Liskow was later repressed, that did not happen during the first days of the war.

Pykhalov's whole chapter may be consulted (in Russian) at http://militera.lib.ru/research/pyhalov_i/09.html

In his memoirs Khrushchev repeats the story of the German soldier's desertion to warn the Soviets, but does **not** repeat his allegation that the soldier's warning was ignored. As with almost everything in Khrushchev's self-serving memoirs, his version is incorrect, either through design (i.e. a deliberate lie) or through faulty memory. At any rate, Khrushchev was not present and had no direct knowledge of the event.

A soldier fled to us from the forward area. He was interrogated, and all the details named by him and on which his story was based, were described logically and seemed trustworthy. He said that the invasion would start tomorrow at three o'clock. First, why specifically tomorrow? The soldier said that they had received dry provisions for three days. And why at three o'clock? Because the Germans always chose an early hour in such situations. I don't remember whether he said that the soldiers had been told about the three o'clock hour or whether they had heard it through the 'soldier's radio', which always learned the time of attack very accurately. What was left for us to do?

- Khrushchev's memoirs: *Vremia, Liudi, Vlast'*. Vol. 1, Part 2, p. 299.

The article featuring Liskow, with a photograph of him, from *Pravda*, June 27, 1941, p. 2 may be consulted here:

http://chss.montclair.edu/english/furr/research/liskowpravda062741.pdf

33. Commanders Killed

Khrushchev:

> Very grievous consequences, especially in reference to
> the beginning of the war, followed Stalin's annihilation
> of many military commanders and political workers
> during 1937-1941 because of his suspiciousness and
> through slanderous accusations. During these years
> repressions were instituted against certain parts of
> military cadres beginning literally at the company and
> battalion commander level and extending to the higher
> military centers; during this time the cadre of leaders
> who had gained military experience in Spain and in the
> Far East was almost completely liquidated.

No doubt Khrushchev is alluding to the Military Conspiracy and the so-
called "Tukhachevsky Affair." He doesn't mention them explicitly, and
completely avoids any question of their guilt or innocence. There is a
great deal of evidence that Tukhachevsky and the other high-ranking
officers tried and executed with him were indeed conspiring with the
Germans and Japanese, and with the Rightist forces in the Opposition to
overthrow the Soviet government.

Khrushchev would rehabilitate them before long. It is telling that in 1957
and again in 1961 expurgated versions of Komandarm Iona IAkir's letter
to Stalin of June 9, 1937, were used by Khrushchev's allies to smear Stalin and those who supported him. The real text of IAkir's letter makes it
clear that he is guilty.

None of this means that **all** military commanders who were imprisoned,
beaten, tortured, and executed were guilty. Ezhov and his henchmen no
doubt framed a good many of them, as he did hundreds of thousands of
other innocent persons.

Marshal Konev speaking in 1965 with writer Konstantin Simonov:

> To portray the matter as though, if these ten, twelve, five
> or seven men had not been killed in '37-'38, but had
> been leading the military at the start of the war, the war
> would have turned out differently – that is an
> exaggeration.

- Konstantin Simonov, *Glazami cheloveka moego pokoleniia* ("Through the
Eyes of a Man of My Generation"). Moscow: Novosti, 1988, 393.

To answer the question which of the men who were
killed then, how he would have fought the Germans,
how and how long it would have taken to beat the
Germans if these men were alive – all these questions,
unfortunately, are speculation. At the same time there
remains the undeniable fact that those men who
remained, who matured during the war and led the
armies, it was precisely they who won the war, at the
positions that they gradually came to occupy.

- *ibid.* . 401.

Khrushchev himself was directly responsible for "eradicating" most of
the commanders in the Kiev (Ukraine) Military District. Volkogonov
quotes a directive from Khrushchev, dated March 1938. The longer version, from the Russian edition, is translated below; a much shorter version is given in the English edition, Dmitrii A. Volkogonov, *Stalin: Triumph and Tragedy.* (NY: Grove Weidenfeld, 1991), p. 329.

Decree of the Military Soviet of the Kiev Military
District concerning the Situation of Cadres of the
Command, Operational Command, and Political Staff of
the District.

1. As a result of the great work carried out for the
cleansing of the forces of the Red Army of hostile
elements and of the promotion from below of
commanders, political workers, and operational
commanders, unquestionably devoted to the work of the
party of Lenin – Stalin, the cadre ... are firmly
consolidated around our party [and] around the leader of
peoples comrade Stalin, and guarantee political firmness
and success in the work of elevating the military power
of the units of the Red Army...

3. The enemies of the people [*vragi naroda* – here
Khrushchev is using the very term he attacked Stalin for
'inventing' and which Stalin virtually never used – GF]
succeeded in doing a lot of damage in the area of placing
cadres. The Military Council sets as its main task the
uprooting to the end of the remnants of hostile
elements, deeply studying every commander, operational
commander, [and] political worker upon his promotion,

boldly promoting proven cadres, devoted and developing…

The commander of the forces of the Kiev Military District, Army Commander second rank Timoshenko; Member of the Military Council Corps Commander Smirnov; Member of the Military Council, Secretary of the CC of the Communist Party of the Ukraine, Khrushchev."

Later Timoshenko, Smirnov and Khrushchev reported that 'in the total of mercilessly uprooting Trotskyite-Bukharinite and bourgeois nationalist elements' on March 28 1938 there was effected the following replacement of the leading staff of the District:

By rank:

Replaced corps commanders 9 9

Divisional commanders 25 24

Brigade commanders 9 5

Battalion commanders 137 87

Commanders of fortified areas 4 4

Heads of the staffs of Corps 9 b

Heads of divisional staffs 25 18

Heads of staff of the fortified areas 4 3

Heads of staff of battalions 135 78

Heads of sections of the staff of the District 24 19

- Volkogonov, *Stalin*. Vol. 1, Ch. 7, at note 608.

34. Stalin's "Demoralization after beginning of war

Khrushchev:

It would be incorrect to forget that, after the first severe disaster and de-feat at the front, Stalin thought that this was the end. In one of his speeches in those days he said:

All that which Lenin created we have lost forever.

The logbooks for June 21-28, 1941, were published in *Istoricheskii Arkhiv* No. 2, 1996, pp. 51-54. They have been reproduced here: http://www.hrono.ru/libris/stalin/16-13.html

Marshal Zhukov:

> They say that in the first days of the war J.V. Stalin was supposedly so distraught that he could not even give a radio speech and gave over his presentation to Molotov. ✓ This judgment does not comport with reality. Of course during the first hours J.V. Stalin was distraught. But he quickly returned to normal and worked with great energy, though it is true that he showed and excessive nervousness that often hampered our work.

- G.K. Zhukov, *Vospominaniia i razmyshleniia* ("Reminiscences and Thoughts"). Vol. 1, Ch. 9. Moscow, 2002, cited from the Russian at http://militera.lib.ru/memo/russian/zhukov1/10.html

In his very useful book *Velikaia Obolgannaia Voina* Igor' V. Pykhalov devotes Chapter 10 of his book, a whole chapter, to this question. It is on line in Russian at http://militera.lib.ru/research/pyhalov_i/10.html

Roi Medvedev:

> Stalin did not go to his Kremlin office on the Sunday; however, the assertion by two biographers, Radzinsky and Volkogonov, that this was the day Stalin fled and shut himself up in the dacha hardly corresponds to what actually happened. Both authors have rather unreliably based their conclusions on the fact that there are no ✓ entries in the Kremlin office visitors' book for 29 and 30 June. But according to Marshal Zhukov, 'on the 29th Stalin came to the Stavka at the Commissariat for Defense twice and on both occasions was scathing about the strategic situation that was unfolding in the west.' On 30 June Stalin convoked a meeting of the Politburo at the dacha at which it was decided to set up the State Defense Committee (GKO).

- Roi and Zhores Medvedev, *The Unknown Stalin* (Woodstock & New York: Overlook Press, 2004), pp. 242-3.

Concerning what occurred during these two days, June 29 and 30, 1941 when the register of visitors at Stalin's office show no visitors, we may turn to the work *KPSS v rezoliutsiiakh i resheniiakh s"ezdov, konferentsii I Plenumov TsK.* ("The Communist Party of the Soviet Union in resolutions and decisions of congresses, conferences, and Central Committee Plenums"), vol. 6 (Moscow: Politizdat, 1971), p. 19.

> June 29, 1941, that is one week after the beginning of the invasion was issued the Directive of the Council of People's Commissars of the USSR and the Central Committee of the All-Union Communist Party (b) to party and Soviet organizations of the oblasts at or near the front.
>
> In regions occupied by the enemy, form partisan units and diversionist groups to fight against the units of the enemy army, to ignite partisan warfare everywhere, to blow up bridges, roads, to ruin telephone and telegraph communications, to set fire to stores, etc. In occupied areas, create unbearable conditions for the enemy and for all those who collaborate with thim, pursue and destroy them at every step, break up all their undertakings.

- Cited by V.V. Kvachkov, *Spetsnaz Rossii.* Moscow: Voennaia literatura, 2004, at http://militera.lib.ru/science/kvachkov_vv/02.html . The full document is quoted at http://www.battlefield.ru/en/documents/87-orders-and-reports/314-order-to-soviet-organizations-frontline-1941.html

On June 20 1941 the decision to form the State Committee for Defense, headed by Stalin, was formed.

> Decree of the Presidium of the Supreme Soviet of the USSR, the Council of People's Commissars of the USSR, and the Central Committee of the ACP(b) of June 30, 1941:
>
> In view of the extraordinary situation that has arisen and in the interest of the rapid mobilization of all the forces of the peoples of the USSR for organizing resistance to the enemy that has treacherously invaded our Motherland, the Decree of the Presidium of the Supreme Soviet of the USSR, the Central Committee of the ACP(b), and the Council of People's Commissars of the USSR has determined it is necessary:

1. To establish the State Committee for Defense, with the following members:

com. Stalin J.V. (Chairman)

com. Molotov V.M. (Deputy Chairman)

com. Voroshilov K.E.

com. Malenkov G.M.

com. Beria L.P.

2. To concentrate all the fullness of the power of the state into the hands of the State Committee for Defense.

3. To obligate all citizens and all party, soviet, Young Communist League, and military organs to unconditionally carry out the decisions and measures taken by the State Committee for Defense.

Chairman of the Presidium

Of the Supreme Soviet of the USSR M.I. KALININ

Chairman of the Council of People's Commissars of the SSR

And Secretary of the CC of the ACP(b) J.V. STALIN

Moscow. The Kremlin. June 30, 1941.

- http://www.hrono.ru/libris/stalin/15-21.html

Volkogonov:

"No, Stalin suffered no great shock on the first day of) the war."

- *Stalin*, vol. 2, Ch. 8, cited from the Russian at http://militera.lib.ru/bio/volkogonov_dv/08.html

According to Pavel Sudoplatov in his memoirs:

In various books, and in particular in Khrushchev's memoirs we read of the panic that seized Stalin in the first days of the war. For my part I can state that I observed nothing of the sort.... The published notes of the Kremlin visitors [to Stalin's office – GF] prove that he received people regularly and personally, directly followed the situation as it worsened day by day.

- *Razvedka i Kreml'. Zapiski nezhelatel'nogo svidetelia.* Moscow, 1996, pp. 159-60.

35. Stalin A Bad Commander

Khrushchev:

> Stalin was very far from an understanding of the real situation which was developing at the front. This was natural because, during the whole Patriotic War, he never visited any section of the front or any liberated city except for one short ride on the Mozhaisk highway during a stabilized situation at the front. To this incident were dedicated many literary works full of fantasies of all sorts and so many paintings. Simultaneously, Stalin was interfering with operations and issuing orders which did not take into consideration the real situation at a given section of the front and which could not help but result in huge personnel losses.

Marshal Zhukov:

> In directing of military struggle as a whole J.V. Stalin was aided by his natural intelligence, experience of political leadership, wealth of intuition, [and] broad knowledge. He knew how to find the main link in a strategic situation and, by seizing it, to find the road for opposing the enemy, of successfully carrying out that or another offensive operation. Undoubtedly he was a worthy Supreme Commander...

> Besides that, in guaranteeing operations, the creation of strategic reserves, in the organizing of the production of military technology and in general in the creation of everything essential for waging war the Supreme Commander, I tell you directly, showed himself to be a superb organizer. And it would be unjust if we were not to give him his due in this manner."

- Zhukov, *Memoirs and Reflections*, Ch. 11, cited from the Russian at http://militera.lib.ru/memo/russian/zhukov1/11.html

Marshal Vasilevskii:

> I also had good relations with N.S. Khrushchev in the first postwar years. But they changed sharply after I refused to support his statements that J.V. Stalin was not able to understand operational-strategic questions and as

Supreme Commander led the movements of armies in an unqualified manner. To this day I cannot understand how he could have said that. Having been a member of the Politburo of the CC of the party and member of the Military Soviets of a series of fronts, N.S. Khrushchev could not be ignorant of how the authority of the Stavka and of Stalin was in questions of leading military actions. Neither could he have been ignorant of the fact that the commanders of the fronts and armies related to the Stavka and to Stalin with great respect and valued them for their exceptional competence in the leading of military struggles.

- Marshal A.M. Vasilevskii, *Delo vsei zhizni* ("My life's work"). 3rd ed. Moscow, Politizdat 1978, Chapter 11, cited from the Russian at http://victory.mil.ru/lib/books/memo/vasilevsky/16.html

Admiral N.G. Kuznetsov put it this way:

During the years of the war Marshal G.K. Zhukov met with the Supreme Commander on military matters more often than anyone else, and no one could give a better characterization of him, and Zhukov called him 'A worthy Supreme Commander.' As far as I know, all the military commanders who saw and met with Stalin are of the same opinion, as far as I know.

- N.G. Kuznetsov, cited from his memoirs in Russian at http://www.victory.mil.ru/lib/books/memo/kuznetsov_ng3/01.html Also in *Voenno-Istoricheskii Zhurnal*, 4 (1993), p. 51.

Marshal Golovanov:

Stalin's specific gravity [i.e. weight – GF] in the course of the war was very high both among commanders of the Red Army and among all soldiers and officers. This is an indisputable fact....

I was fortunate to work with a great man, one of the greatest, for whom nothing was more important than the interests of our state and people, who lived his whole life not for himself and strove to make our state the most progressive and powerful in the world. And I say this, I who also went through the year 1937!

- Felix Chuev, "Nespisochnyi marshal" ("An unscheduled [i.e. extraordinary] marshal"), cited from the Russian at
http://www.pseudology.org/Chuev/Golovanov_01.htm

Concerning Stalin's supposedly making all decisions instead of his generals Marshal Bagramian, to whom Khrushchev referred as someone who was present and who would confirm what he said, instead wrote the following:

> Aware of Stalin's immense power and truly iron will, I was amazed at his manner of leading. He could simply command: 'Commit the corps.' – period. But Stalin, with great tact and patience, tried to lead the person who had to carry out the order to arrive at the conclusion that this step was essential. Afterwards I myself, as front commander, had the opportunity to speak with the Supreme Commander rather often, and I became convinced that he knew how to listen attentively to the opinions of his subordinates. If the officer in charge firmly stood his ground and, in defense of his own opinion, set forth weighty arguments, Stalin almost always yielded.

I. Kh. Bagramian. *Tak nachinalas' voina.* Kiev: Politizdat Ukrainy, 1977. Online at http://militera.lib.ru/memo/russian/bagramyan1/index.html . This exact citation is in Part 4, "Krushenie mifa." Chapter 2: "Otkhod otkhodu rozn'",p. 404 (at
http://militera.lib.ru/memo/russian/bagramyan1/04.html)

36. Khar'kov 1942

Khrushchev:

> I will allow myself in this connection to bring out one characteristic fact which illustrates how Stalin directed operations at the fronts. There is present at this Congress Marshal Bagramian, who was once the chief of operations in the headquarters of the southwestern front and who can corroborate what I will tell you. When there developed an exceptionally serious situation for our Army in 1942 in the Kharkov region … And what was the result of this? The worst that we had expected. The Germans surrounded our Army concentrations and consequently we lost

hundreds of thousands of our soldiers. This is Stalin's military "genius"; this is what it cost us.

According to Sergei Konstantinov:

> It was not only many common people who were thunderstruck and upset by Khrushchev's de-Stalinization. How was it for those high-ranking military commanders sitting in the hall at the session of the 20th Congress, who knew all Stalin's strong and weak sides, to hear Khrushchev's bald-faced lie that in developing plans for military operations Stalin used only a globe? Khrushchev told an obvious lie in laying the whole responsibility for the Red Army's catastrophe at Khar'kov in 1942 exclusively on Stalin. Alexander Vasilevskii, Georgii Zhukov, [and] Sergei Shtemenko in their memoirs cite facts, fully confirmed by the latest archival publications, about how the main weight of responsibility for this catastrophe should fall on Khrushchev, on Semion Timoshenko, commander of the South-West front, and on Ivan Bagramian, member of the Military Council of that front. The majority of higher military leaders who had gone through the war with Stalin doubtless were very negative towards the de-Stalinization that Khrushchev carried out in the first place because Nikita Sergeevich crudely falsified historical facts. In addition some of these military commanders harbored the warmest feelings towards Stalin simply as a man. The Chief Marshal of aviation Alexander Golovanov told the writer Felix Chuev about the following episode. Once Khrushchev asked Marshal Rokossovsky to write an article about Stalin in the spirit of the 20th Congress. As answer Khrushchev heard: 'Nikita Sergeevich, for me comrade Stalin is a saint." On another occasion Rokossovsky together with Golovanov refused to drink a toast with Khrushchev at some banquet or other.

- Sergei Konstantinov. "Shokovaia terapia Nikity Khrushcheva." *Nezavisimaia Gazeta* February 14, 2001. At http://www.ng.ru/style/2001-02-14/16_therapy.html

According to Samsonov, Zhukov disagreed with Khrushchev's account:

> Concerning this situation Marshal of the Soviet Union
> Zhukov wrote that J.V. Stalin, relying on the reports of
> the Military Soviet of the Southwest front that said the
> offensive must be continued, rejected the General Staff's
> plans.

> / "The existing story about signals of alarm that
> supposedly came to Stavka (the General Staff) from the
> Military Soviets of the Southern and Southwestern
> fronts, does not conform to the facts. I can attest to this
> because I was personally present during the talks with
> (the Supreme Commander."

- Samsonov, A.M. *Stalingradskaia Bitva*. 4 izd. isp. i dop. ("The Battle of
Stalingrad, 4th corrected and enlarged edition"). Moscow, 1938, Ch. 2, at
note 50, cited from the Russian at
http://militera.lib.ru/h/samsonov1/02.html

In his memoirs Zhukov does blame Stalin in part.
http://militera.lib.ru/memo/russian/zhukov1/15.html (However,
Zhukov was very angry at Stalin – Stalin demoted him for stealing German
trophies. See *Voennie Arkhivy Rossii*, 1993, pp. 175 ff. Zhukov's confession,
241-44.) Khrushchev knew this, and had it all quashed, undoubtedly
to get Zhukov on his side.

The *Short History of the Great Patriotic War* carries this version, which
blames the front command, not Stalin and the GKO:

> The main reason of the failure of the Khar'kof
> operation was that the command of the Southwestern
> direction incorrectedly evaluated the situation, and when
> the forces of the Southwest front fell into a complex
> position, they failed to stop the offensive in time. What's
> more, they urged the General Staff to permit them to
> continue the offensive. The decision taken on May 19 to
> cease the offensive was taken too late. The command of
> the Southwest front did not take the essential steps to
> protect the flanks by shock groups, were weak in
> studying the opponent, and in part underestimated his
> possibility for maneuver during the course of the battle.

The staff of the front underestimated the forces of the }
enemy by 30%.

- *Velikaia Otechestvennaia Voina. Kratkaia istoriia* ("The Short History of the Great Patriotic War. Short edition."). Moscow: Voenizdat, 1970, 164-5.

This is consistent with Stalin's letter of June 26 1942 quoted by many sources, including Portugal'skii et al.'s biography of Timoshenko, and which blamed not only Bagramian, but also Timoshenko and – Khrushchev!

> The first to go was Bagramian. He was removed by the Stavka from the post he held for failing to fulfill his duties and 'being unsatisfactory to the Stavka as a simple bearer of information.' 'What is more', remarked Stalin, 'comrade Bagramian was incapable of learning the lesson from that catastrophe that developed on the Southwestern front. In the course of some three weeks the Southwest front, thanks to his carelessness, not only lost the Khar'kov operation, already have successful, but in addition succeeded in giving the enemy 18-20 divisions.' Having announced that Bagramian was being named the chief of staff of the 28th army and thus given a chance to redeem himself in practice, the Supreme Commander firmly underscored: 'It is to be understood that this is not simply a case of comrade Bagramian. The } issue is also the errors of all members of the Military } Soviet and above all of comrades Timoshenko and } Khrushchev. If we had announced to the country the full extent of this catastrophe – with the loss of 18-20 divisions, which the front suffered and from which it will still suffer, then I am afraid that it would have gone very hard with you. Therefore you must consider the errors you have made and take all necessary steps that they not take place in future.

- Portugal'skii, R.M., et al. *Marshal S.K. Timoshenko*, M. 1994, Ch. 5, from the Russian version at http://militera.lib.ru/bio/domank/05.html The same letter of Stalin's is also quoted by Beshanov, *1942 god – uchebnyi* . ("The "Year of Learning" 1942"), Minsk: Kharvest, 2003. Chapter 14: "How Bagramian Alone Doomed Two Fronts", at http://militera.lib.ru/research/beshanov_vv/14.html

Volkogonov:

> N.S. Khrushchev devoted a whole section of his report
> to the 20ᵗʰ Party Congress to the events at Kharkov,
> when he [Khrushchev] had been member of the Military
> Council of the Southwest front. According to
> Khrushchev, he phoned from the front to Stalin at the
> latter's dacha. However, Malenkov came to the phone.
> Khrushchev insisted on speaking personally with Stalin.
> But the Supreme Commander, who was 'only a few steps
> from the telephone' [this is a quote from Khrushchev's
> Secret Speech – GF], did not come to the phone and
> through Malenkov instructed Khrushchev to speak with
> Malenkov. After transmitting the request of the front
> about stopping the offensive through Malenkov – as he
> told the delegates of the 20ᵗʰ Congress, Stalin said 'Leave
> everything the way it is!' In other words, Khrushchev
> unmistakably declared that it was precisely Stalin who
> was at fault in the Khar'kov catastrophe.
>
> G.K. Zhukov sets forth another version, proposing that
> responsibility for the disaster should be born also by the
> commanders of the Military Councils of the South and
> Southwest fronts. In his book *Memoirs and Reflections*
> Zhukov writes that the danger was sensed at the General
> Staff before it was at the front. On May 18 the General
> Staff yet again spoke out for stopping our offensive
> operation at Khar'kov. … Towards the evening of May
> 18 the talk took place on this subject with the member of
> the Military Council of the front N.S. Khrushchev, who
> expressed the same views as did the command of the
> Southwest front: the danger from the side of the
> Kramator group of the enemy was seriously exaggerated,
> and there was no basis for stopping the operation.
> Relying on the reports of the Military Council of the
> Southwest front that it was essential to continue the
> offensive, the Supreme Commander rejected the views
> of the General Staff. The existing story about signals of
> alarm that supposedly came to Stavka (the General Staff)
> from the Military Soviets of the Southern and
> Southwestern fronts, does not conform to the facts. I

can attest to this because I was personally present during the talks with the Supreme Commander."

I think that in this case the Marshal [Zhukov] was closer to the truth. N.S. Khrushchev, conveying his personal memories in the report, gave after the passage of many years belated reaction to the disaster that he had had when it had already become clear to everyone that a catastrophe was in the making. Marshal Zhukov repeatedly emphasized that the decision of the Supreme Commander was based on the reports of Timoshenko and Khrushchev. It's one thing if this was simply forgetfulness on Khrushchev's part. But if this is an attempt to create for himself a historical alibi after the fact – that is something else again.

-   Volkogonov, *Stalin*, 2, Ch. 8, cited from the Russian at http://militera.lib.ru/bio/volkogonov_dv/08.html

37. Stalin Planned Military Operations on a Globe

Khrushchev:

I telephoned to Vasilevsky and begged him: "Alexander Mikhailovich, take a map" – Vasilevsky is present here – "and show Comrade Stalin the situation which has developed." We should note that Stalin planned operations on a globe. (Animation in the hall.) Yes, comrades, he used to take the globe and trace the front line on it. I said to Comrade Vasilevsky: "Show him the situation on a map…"

Marshal Meretskov:

In some of our books we find the story that J.V. Stalin led military operations on a globe. I have never read anything so ignorant.!

- K.A. Meretskov, *Na sluzhbe narodu* ("In Service to the People"). Moscow: Politizdat, 1968, cited from the Russian at

http://militera.lib.ru/memo/russian/meretskov/29.html

Solov'ev and Sukhodeev, citing General Gribkov:

> The lie about the "globe" is refuted by operational documents as well. General of the army A.I. Gribkov, who worked during the war years in the Operational directorate of the General Staff, testifies: "N.S. Khrushchev, in debunking the cult of personality around J.V. Stalin, asserted that, supposedly, Stalin led the fronts on a globe. Of course this is all a lie. The military archives hold maps of various scales with notes in the Supreme Commander's handwriting."

- B. Solov'ev and V. Sukhodeev, *Stalin the Military Leader.* Moscow, 2003, cited from the Russian at http://militera.lib.ru/research/solovyov_suhodeev/01.html

> Refutation of Khrushchev's slander on the 'globe' matter can also be found from Admiral N.G. Kuznetsov in his book *On the Eve.* 'It is a completely untrue, malicious assertion that, supposedly, he [Stalin] evaluated situations and took decisions with the use of a globe. I could cite many examples of how Stalin, verifying the position on the fronts with the military leaders, knew when it was necessary, even the position of each battalion.' In the book by K.S. Moskalenko *In the Southwestern direction*: 'When Nikolai Fiodorovich [Vatutin, front commander] told us about his talk with the Supreme Commander, I could not hide my amazement at the precision with which Stalin analyzed military activities, and despite myself I said 'What maps does the Supreme Commander use to follow our activities, if he sees more and deeper than we do?' Nikolai Fiodorovich smiled, and replied: "On maps of the scale of 1:2000 and 1:5000 on the fronts, and 1:100,000 for each army. The main thing – and this is why he is Supreme Commander – is to make suggestions, correct our errors…'
>
> But Marshal of the Air Force Novikov gave the best response to Khrushchev: 'What is the worth of Khrushchev's declaration that Stalin planed operations in wartime and directed them on a large globe in his office? This one assertion of the author of the report [Khrushchev – GF] evoked at that time a fairly broad,

> though silent, protest, especially among military men,
> and also among many rank-and-file veterans of the war."

- Balaian, *Stalin i Khrushchev*, Ch. 22: "Polkovodets Iosif Stalin", at
http://stalin.su/book.php?action=header&id=20

Molotov:

> Maps were on all the walls in the foyer. Khrushchev said
> that he gave leadership on a globe, – on the contrary, he
> loved geographical maps very much.

- Chuev, F. *Molotov: Poluderzhavnyi Vlastelin*, 361.

Marshal Zhukov:

> The story that has been disseminated that the Supreme
> Commander studied the situation and took decisions
> using a globe does not conform to reality... He
> understood the use of operational maps and the
> situations drawn upon them very well.

- G.K. Zhukov, *Vospominaniia i razmyshleniia* ("Reminiscences and
Thoughts"). Vol. 1, Ch. 9. Moscow, 2002, from the Russian at
http://militera.lib.ru/memo/russian/zhukov1/11.html

38. Stalin Downgraded Zhukov

Khrushchev:

> "Stalin was very much interested in the assessment of
> Comrade Zhukov as a military leader. He asked me often
> for my opinion of Zhukov. I told him then, "I have
> known Zhukov for a long time; he is a good general and
> a good military leader."

> After the war Stalin began to tell all kinds of nonsense
> about Zhukov, among others the following, "You
> praised Zhukov, but he does not deserve it. It is said that
> before each operation at the front Zhukov used to
> behave as follows: He used to take a handful of earth,
> smell it and say, 'We can begin the attack,' or the
> opposite, 'The planned operation cannot be carried
> out.'" I stated at that time, "Comrade Stalin, I do not
> know who invented this, but it is not true."

It is possible that Stalin himself invented these things for the purpose of minimizing the role and military talents of Marshal Zhukov."

According to Zhukov himself, Stalin never insulted him:

G.K. Zhukov stressed more than once that "Nowhere did Stalin say a single bad word about me", that "if anyone tried to insult me in his presence, Stalin would tear his head off on my behalf."

- B. Solov'ev and V. Sukhodeev. *Polkovodets Stalin* ("Stalin the General"). Moscow, EKSMO, 2003, Ch. 1, cited from the Russian at http://militera.lib.ru/research/solovyov_suhodeev/01.html

Zhukov was indeed demoted in 1948. But that was because he had been found guilty, and had admitted his guilt, in defrauding the Soviet government of very large sums by illegally keeping large amounts of looted German treasure for himself. This fact does not appear to be widely known even in Russia, although the relevant documents were published fifteen years ago. We have put these documents on line at

http://chss.montclair.edu/english/furr/research/zhukovtheft4648_var93.pdf

The quotations below give some idea of Zhukov's crime, and why Stalin demoted him.

Top Secret

THE COUNCIL OF MINISTERS OF THE USSR.

To comrade STALIN J.V.

…During the night of 8-9 January of this year a secret search was conducted of *Zhukov's* dacha, which is situated in the village of Rublevo near Moscow.

As a result of this search it was disclosed that two rooms of the dacha had been converted into storerooms in which a huge quantity of goods and valuables of various kinds are stored.

For example:

Woolen fabrics, silk, brocade, velvet, and other materials – in all, more than 4000 meters;

Furs – sable, monkey, fox, sealskin, Astrakhan [fine wool] – total 323 hides;

Kidskin of the best quality – 35 skins;

Valuable carpets and Gobelin rugs of very large size from the Potsdam and other palaces and homes of Germany – 44 pieces in all, some of which are laid or hung in various rooms, and the rest in the storeroom.

Especially worthy of note is a carpet of great size placed in one of the rooms of the dacha;

Valuable paintings of classical landscapes of very large sizes in artistic frames – 55 units in all, hung in various rooms of the dacha and a part of which remain in the storeroom;

Very expensive table and tea services (porcelain with artistic decoration, crystal) – 7 large chests;

Silver sets of table and tea place settings – 2 chests;

Accordeons with rich artistic decoration – 8 units;

Unique hunting rifles by the firm Gotland – Gotland and others – 20 units in all.

This property is kept in 51 trunks and suitcases, and also lies in heaps.

Besides that in all the rooms of the dacha, on the windows, staircase, tables and bedside tables are placed around great quantities of bronze and porcelain vases and statuettes of artistic work, and also all kinds of trinkets and knick-knacks of foreign origin.

I draw attention to the declaration by the workers who carried out the search that *Zhukov's* dacha is in essence an antique store or museum, with various valuable works of art hanging all around the interior...

There are so many valuable paintings that they could never be suitable for an apartment but should be transferred to the State fund and housed in a museum.

More than twenty large carpets cover the floors of almost all the rooms.

All the objects, beginning with the furniture, carpets, vessels, decorations, up to the curtains on the windows, are foreign, mainly German. There is literally not a single thing of Soviet origin in the dacha....

There is not a single Soviet book in the dacha, but on the other hand on the bookshelves stands a large quantity of books in beautiful bindings with gold embossing, all without exception in the German language.

When you go into the house it is hard to imagine that one is not in Germany but near Moscow...

Accompanying this letter please find photographs of some of the valuables, cloth and items we discovered in Zhukov's apartment and dacha.

ABAKUMOV.

January 10, 1948.

- *Voennie Arkhivy Rossii* (1993), pp. 189-191; also at the URL above.

39. Deportations of nationalities

Khrushchev:

Comrades, let us reach for some other facts. The Soviet Union is justly considered as a model of a multinational state because we have in practice assured the equality and friendship of all nations which live in our great Fatherland.

All the more monstrous are the acts whose initiator was Stalin and which are rude violations of the basic Leninist principles of the nationality policy of the Soviet state. We refer to the mass deportations from their native places of whole nations, together with all Communists and Komsomols without any exception; this deportation action was not dictated by any military considerations....

Not only a Marxist-Leninist but also no man of common sense can grasp how it is possible to make whole nations responsible for inimical activity, including women, children, old people, Communists and Komsomols, to use mass repression against them, and to expose them to

misery and suffering for the hostile acts of individual
persons or groups of persons.

1. Pykhalov, on exceptions to the deportations:

> According to the view generally held, all the Crimean
> Tatars without any exception were subject to
> deportation, including those who had fought honorably
> in the Red Army or in partisan ranks. In reality this was
> not the case. "Those who had taken part in the Crimean
> underground acting in the rear of the enemy were
> excepted from the status of 'special settler', as were
> members of their families. Thus the family of S. S.
> Useinov, who had been in Simferopol' during the period
> of the occupation of the Crimea and was a member of an
> underground patriotic group from December 1942 until
> March 1943, then was arrested by the Hitlerites and shot.
> Members of his family were permitted to remain living in
> Simferopol."

> ...Crimean-Tatar veterans of the front immediately
> applied with a request that their relatives be exempted
> from the status of 'special settler.' Such applications were
> sent from the commander of the second air squadron of
> the first fighter battalion of the Higher Officer School of
> air combat Captain E.U Chalbash, Major of armored
> forces Kh. Chalbash, and many others...Requests of this
> nature were granted in part, specifically, the family of E.
> Chalbash was permitted to live in Kherson oblast.'

- I. Pykhalov, *Vremia Stalina: Fakty protiv mifov.* 'Leningrad' (St. Peters-
burg), 2001, p. 84, citing N. Bugai, *L. Beria – I. Stalinu: "Soglasno Vashemu
Ukazaniiu"...* Moscow: AIRO-XX, 1995, pp. 156-7.

Chechen nationalist account of a pro-German anti-Soviet armed rebellion
in February 1943, when the German penetration towards the Caucasus
was at its greatest, from Radio Svoboda (Radio Liberty), Feb. 23, 2000:

> Here I would like to add an unknown fact of history that
> we have not yet touched on. The Chechens have always,
> permanently, fought for their freedom and self-
> determination, and in February 1943 a rebellion flared up
> in the mountains under the leadership of the lawyer
> Merbek Sheripov and the famous writer Khasan Israilov.

> Taking advantage of the fact that the Germans were
> fighting with the Russians the Chechens tried to separate
> from the USSR by armed struggle and to declare their
> independence. Their final goal was a union with the
> peoples of the Caucasus, in order to live freely in a
> confederation independently from the Soviet empire."

- http://www.svoboda.org/programs/LL/2000/ll.022300-3.shtml

"Freedom" flag of Caucasian nationalist groups, with Nazi swastika:
http://stalinism.narod.ru/foto/chech_1.jpg

Casualties among Chechen deportees during the deportation were low.

> Operation Chechevitsa, which began on 23 February
> [1944], was completed sometime during the third week
> of March. NKVD records attest to 180 convoy trains
> carrying 493,269 Chechen and Ingush nationals and
> members of other nationalities seized at the same time.
> Fifty people were killed in the course of the operation,
> and 1,272 died on the journey.

- Bugai and Gomov, *Russian Studies in History*, vol. 41, no. 2, Fall 2002, p.
56. This is 0.268% of those deported, about 2.5 deaths of every 1000 persons.

40. Leningrad Affair

Khrushchev:

> After the conclusion of the Patriotic War, the Soviet
> nation stressed with pride the magnificent victories
> gained through great sacrifices and tremendous efforts.
> The country experienced a period of political
> enthusiasm. ...

> And it was precisely at this time that the so-called
> "Leningrad affair" was born. As we have now proven,
> this case was fabricated. Those who innocently lost their
> lives included Comrades Voznesensky, Kuznetsov,
> Rodionov, Popkov, and others....

> How did it happen that these persons were branded as
> enemies of the people and liquidated?

> Facts prove that the "Leningrad affair" is also the result of will-
> fulness which Stalin exercised against party cadres.

Beria's letter to the Presidium of June 25, 1953 accused Riumin of falsifying the Leningrad Affair:

> Specifically RIUMIN took part in the falsification of the
> investigative materials in the so-called cases of the
> "Espionage center in the Jewish Anti-Fascist
> Committee" supposedly headed by LOZOVSKY,
> MIKHOELS, FEFER and others, and of the "Leningrad
> Affair," in the course of which, as is well known, were
> arrested and convicted the leading Party and Soviet
> workers of the city of Leningrad KUZNETSOV,
> POPKOV, KAPUSTIN, and others. In November 1950
> RIUMIN, on orders from ABAKUMOV, was assigned
> the investigation in the case of the arrested professor
> ETINGER. Knowing that ETINGER had been one of
> the doctors who treated A.S. SHCHERBAKOV as a
> consultant, RIUMIN adopted illegal means of
> investigation and forced ETINGER to give imaginary
> confessions about incorrect treatment of A.S.
> SHCHERBAKOV, that supposedly led to his death.

*Lavrentii Beriia. 1953. Stenogramma iul'skogo plenuma TsK KPSS I drugie do-
kumenty.* Moscow, 1999, pp. 64-66.

Having blamed Stalin's "willfulness" for the "Leningrad Affair" arrests,
convictions, and executions Khrushchev claimed in June 1957 claim that
Stalin had been **against** the arrests of Voznesenskii and the others!

> Khrushchev: Malenkov, you know – and this is well
> known to Molotov, Mikoian, Saburov, Pervykhin ... the
> comrades I have named know that **Stalin was against
> the arrests of Voznesenskii and Kuznetsov. He was
> against the arrests,** and those Jesuitical beasts, Beria
> and Malenkov, influenced Stalin and instigated the
> arrests and executions of Voznesenskii, Kuznetsov, [and]
> Popkov. Malenkov, your hands are bloody, your
> conscience unclean. You are a low-down person.
>
> Malenkov: You are slandering me.
>
> Khrushchev: Stalin said in my presence, and others heard
> it too, why isn't Voznesenskii named to a post in the
> State Bank, why are there no motions to this effect? But
> Beria and Malenkov presented the case to Stalin that

Voznesenskii, Kuznetsov, Popkov and others were
criminals. Why? Because at so*n*e time Stalin, deservedly
or not, promoted Kuznetsov instead of Malenkov, and
wanted to make Voznesenskii Chairman of the Soviet of
Ministers. That is why their heads rolled.

-Malenkov, Molotov, Kaganovich.1957. Stenogramma iun'skogo plenuma TsK KPSS I drugie dokumenty. Moscow, 1998, pp. 201-2, emph. added GF.

41. Mingrelian Affair

Khrushchev:

Instructive in the same way is the case of the Mingrelian
nationalist organization which supposedly existed in
Georgia. As is known, resolutions by the Central
Committee, Communist Party of the Soviet Union, were
made concerning this case in November 1951 and in
March 1952. These resolutions were made without prior
discussion with the Political Bureau. Stalin had
personally dictated them. They made serious accusations
against many loyal Communists. On the basis of falsified
documents, it was proven that there existed in Georgia a
supposedly nationalistic organization whose objective
was the liquidation of the Soviet power in that republic
with the help of imperialist powers.

In the notes to the critical edition of the decrees of the Politburo on
bribery in Georgia and "the anti-Party group of Baramia" of November
9, 1951 we read:

In the original of the transcript of the PB [Politburo]
sessions there is a copy of the decree written by
Poskrebyshev [Stalin's personal secretary – GF], and also
a typed copy of the draft with Stalin's corrections, …

There follow a number of Stalin's corrections to the decree. Another
note in the same critical edition, this time to the decree of the Politburo
about the situation in the Georgian Communist Party, from March 27,
1952, reads:

In the original transcript of the PB sessions Stalin wrote
in the title of the decree on the draft. **The decree**

**resulted from the Politburo sessions of March 25
and March 27 1952.** (emphasis added, GF)

These texts and the relevant context are from the work *Politbiuro TsK
VKP(b) i Soviet Ministrov SSSR 1945-1953*. Ed. Khlevniuk, O.V. et al.
Moscow: ROSSPEN, 2002, pp. 351 and 354. These pages and the relevant context (texts of decrees) are now at
http://chss.montclair.edu/english/furr/research/mingrelianres.pdf

Boris Sokolov, in *Rossiiskaia Gazeta* April 10 2003:

> On April 10 1953 was announced the decree of the CC
> of the CPSU "On the violation of Soviet laws by former
> ministers of state security of the USSR and the Georgian
> SSR." This decree annulled the previous decree of the
> CC of November 9, 1951 and March 27, 1952
> concerning the existence in Georgia of a Mingrelian
> nationalist organization. The Georgian leaders who were
> arrested earlier were liberated. However, soon thereafter
> many of them were arrested again under accusations of
> ties with Beria.

Boris Nikolaevsky's note to the *New Leader* edition:

> 51. "Khrushchev's statement on the "Mingrelian
> conspiracy" does explain the purges in Georgia in 1952.
> Though he implies that the "Mingrelian case," like the
> "Leningrad case," was also staged by Beria and
> Abakumov, this is a deliberate distortion. It was precisely
> in November 1951 that S. D. Ignatiev, one of Beria's
> bitterest enemies, was appointed Minister of State
> Security; the "Mingrelian case" was, therefore, trumped
> up as a blow at Beria. It and the purges which followed
> in Georgia (in April, September and November 1952)
> undermined Beria's position and cleared the way for the
> projected "second *Yezhovshchina*" which began, after the
> 19th Party Congress of November 1952, with the arrests
> in the "doctors' plot."

According to Khrushchev, Ignat'ev was among the listeners at the
Speech:

> "Present at this Congress as a delegate is the former
> Minister of State Security, Comrade Ignatiev." (p. 38)

Ignatiev was removed by the Presidium, of which Khrushchev was a
member, for gross misconduct in fabricating the Mingrelian Affair, the
Doctors' Plot, and other matters. See Beria's reports (in Russian) at
http://chss.montclair.edu/english/furr/research/mingrelianaff.pdf

42. Yugoslavia

Khrushchev:

> The July plenum of the Central Committee studied in
> detail the reasons for the development of conflict with
> Yugoslavia. It was a shameful role which Stalin played
> here. The "Yugoslav affair" contained no problems
> which could not have been solved through party
> discussions among comrades. There was no significant
> basis for the development of this "affair"; it was
> completely possible to have prevented the rupture of
> relations with that country. This does not mean,
> however, that the Yugoslav leaders did not make
> mistakes or did not have shortcomings. But these
> mistakes and shortcomings were magnified in a
> monstrous manner by Stalin, which resulted in a break of
> relations with a friendly country.

In July 1953 Khrushchev and other Presidium members attacked Beria
for trying to repair relations with Yugoslavia – that is, they did not want
relations as of one communist power to another.

> Molotov: I think, comrades, that this fact – comrade
> Malenkov read the draft letter to 'comrade Rankovic', for
> 'comrade Tito' – with this fact the traitor [Beria – GF]
> showed himself red-handed. He wrote it to them in his
> own hand and did not want the Presidium to discuss this
> question. What kind of man is this?
>
> True, we exchanged ambassadors.
>
> Malenkov: And we wanted a normalization of relations.
>
> Molotov: We wanted a normalization of relations, … we
> decided it was necessary to establish with Yugoslavia the
> same kind of relations as with other bourgeois
> governments… And what is this kind of thing: 'I make
> use of this opportunity to transmit to you, comrade

Rankovic, hearty greetings from comrade Beria and to inform comrade Tito that it would be expedient if comrade Tito shares this viewpoint....' Etc. etc. What kind of thing is this?

...

He might have found support among foreign capitalists – Titos, Rankoviches, these are capitalist agents, he learned from them. He went straight from them to us.

. . .

But isn't it clear what it means, this attempt by Beria to reach an agreement with Rankovich and Tito, who conduct themselves like enemies of the Soviet Union? Isn't it clear that this letter, composed by Beria in secret from the present Government, was still one more blatant attempt to strike the back of the Soviet Government and to render a direct service to the imperialist camp? This fact alone would be sufficient to conclude that Beria is the agent of a foreign camp, the agent of the class enemy.

Lavrentiii Beria. 1953. Stenogramma iul'skogo plenuma TsK KPSS I drugie dokumenty. Moscow, 1999. pp. 103-4; 246.

43. Doctors' Plot

Khrushchev:

Let us also recall the "affair of the doctor-plotters." (Animation in the hall.) Actually there was no "affair" outside of the declaration of the woman doctor Timashuk, who was probably influenced or ordered by someone (after all, she was an unofficial collaborator of the organs of state security) to write Stalin a letter in which she declared that doctors were applying supposedly improper methods of medical treatment.

Such a letter was sufficient for Stalin to reach an immediate conclusion that there are doctor-plotters in the Soviet Union. He issued orders to arrest a group of eminent Soviet medical specialists. He personally issued advice on the conduct of the investigation and the method of interrogation of the arrested persons. He said that the academician Vinogradov should be put in chains, another one should be beaten. Present at this Congress as a delegate is the former Minister of State Security, Comrade Ignatiev. Stalin told him curtly, "If you do not obtain confessions from the doctors we will shorten you by a head."

Stalin personally called the investigative judge, gave him instructions, advised him on which investigative methods should be used; these methods were simple: beat, beat and, once again, beat.

Shortly after the doctors were arrested, we members of the Political Bureau received protocols with the doctors' confessions of guilt. After distributing these protocols, Stalin told us, "You are blind like young kittens; what will happen without me? The country will perish because you do not know how to recognize enemies."

The case was so presented that no one could verify the facts on which the investigation was based. There was no possibility of trying to verify facts by contacting those who had made the confessions of guilt.

We felt, however, that the case of the arrested doctors was questionable. We knew some of these people personally because they had once treated us. When we examined this "case" after Stalin's death, we found it to be fabricated from beginning to end.

This ignominious "case" was set up by Stalin; he did not, however, have the time in which to bring it to an end (as he conceived that end), and for this reason the doctors are still alive. Now all have been rehabilitated; they are working in the same places they were working before; they treat top individuals, not excluding members of the Government; they have our full confidence; and they execute their duties honestly, as they did before.

In organizing the various dirty and shameful cases, a very base role was played by the rabid enemy of our party, an agent of a foreign intelligence service – Beria, who had stolen into Stalin's confidence."

Dr Timashuk's letters have all been published since the end of the USSR.[252] She had nothing whatsoever to do with the "Doctors' Plot" affair. Her letters solely concerned the treatment, or mistreatment, she witnessed of Politburo member Andrei Zhdanov in 1948.

In reality it was Beria – probably at Stalin's suggestion – who put a stop to the "Doctors' Plot" frameups.

Excerpts from Beria's report to the Presidium of April 1 1953:

> Former Minister of State Security [= the MGB , GF] of the USSR com. IGNAT'EV did not fulfill the obligations of his positions, did not guarantee the necessary control over the investigation, came to the aid of RIUMIN and of a few other MGB workers who, taking advantage of this, tortured the arrested persons brutally and falsified investigative materials with impunity.
>
> …
>
> 4) To review the question of the responsibility of former Minister of State Security of the USSR com. IGNAT'EV, S.D., the Ministry of Internal Affairs of the USSR has taken measures to prevent in future the possibility of a repetition of such violations of Soviet laws in the work of the organs of the MVD.

Excerpt from Presidium decision on Doctors' Plot case of April 3 1953:

> 3. To propose to the former Minister of State Security of the USSR com. Ignat'ev S.D. to present to the Presidium of the CC of the CPSU an explanation of the most crude violations of Soviet laws and the falsification of investigative materials permitted in the Ministry of State Security.

- *Lavrentii Beria. 1953.* pp. 21-25.

According to Soviet dissident Zhores Medvedev it must have been Stalin himself who put an end to the persecution of the "doctor-wreckers" in the press:

---

[252] "'Tsel' byla spasti zhizn' bol'nogo'. Pis'ma Lidii Timashuk v svoiu zashchitu." ['The goal was to save the patient's life.' Lidia Timashuk's letters in her own defense'] *Istochnik* 1997, No. 1, pp. 3-16.

> We can assume that Stalin called *Pravda* either on the
> evening of February 27 or in the morning of February 28
> and arranged for the cessation of publication of anti-
> Jewish materials and of all other articles dealing with the
> "Doctors' Plot."... In the Soviet Union at that time
> there was only one person who was able, with a single
> telephone call to the editor of *Pravda* or to the
> Department of Agitprop of the CC CPSU to change
> official policy. Only Stalin could do that...

Medvedev further stresses the following point:

> Stalin's anti-Semitism, about which one may read in
> almost all his biographies, was not religious, nor ethnic,
> nor cultural [*bytovym* = based on lifestyle or mores – GF].
> It was political, and expressed itself in anti-Zionism, not
> hatred of Jews [*iiudofobii*].

- ZH.A. Medvedev. *Stalin i evreiskaia problema. Noviy analiz.* Moscow: Prava
cheloveka, 2003, pp. 216-7.

In plain language, Medvedev confirmed that Stalin was not anti-Semitic at
all, since opposition to Zionism is common among both religious and
non-religious Jews, including in Israel itself.

Svetlana Allilueva:

> "The Doctors' Plot" took place during the last winter of
> his life. Valentina Vasil'evna told me later that father had
> been very saddened by the turn of events. She heard how
> it was discussed at the table, during meals. She served at
> table, as always. Father said that he did not believe in
> their "dishonorableness," that this could not be – after
> all, the "proof" were just the accusations of Dr.
> Timashuk.

- *Twenty Letters to a Friend*, Letter 18.

44. Beria

Khrushchev:

> In organizing the various dirty and shameful cases, a very
> base role was played by the rabid enemy of our party, an
> agent of a foreign intelligence service – Beria, who had
> stolen into Stalin's confidence.

Mikoian, at 1953 CC Plenum:

> We have no direct evidence that he was a spy [or])
> received assignments from foreign governments... /

- *Lavrentii Beria. 1953. Stenogramma iiul'skogo plenuma TsK KPSS i drugie do-kumenty.* Ed. Naumov, V., IU. Sigachev. Moscow: Mezhdunarodnyi Fond 'Demokratiia', 1999, p. 174.

Khrushchev:

> Beria showed himself more clearly as a provocateur and
> agent of the imperialists in the discussion of the German
> question, when he posed the question of renouncing the)
> construction of socialism in the GDR and yielding to the }
> West. That means yielding 18 million Germans to the
> rule of the American imperialists. He said: "We must
> create a neutral democratic Germany."

> The court has established that the beginning of L.P.
> Beria's criminal treasonous activity and the establishment
> by him of ties with foreign intelligence services relates to
> the period of the Civil War, when in 1919 L.P. Beria,
> being in Baku, committed treason when he accepted a
> position as a secret agent in the intelligence of the
> counterrevolutionary Mussavat government in
> Azerbaidjan, which acted under the control of English
> intelligence organs.

> In the active struggle against the revolutionary workers
> movement in Baku in 1919, when Beria entered his
> position as a secret agent in the intelligence of the
> counterrevolutionary Mussavat government in
> Azerbaidjan, he established ties with a foreign
> intelligence service, and thereafter supported and
> extended his secret criminal connections with foreign
> intelligence services until the moment of his exposure
> and arrest, ...

- *Lavrentii Beria*, pp. 238; 388; 390.

Kaganovich:

> I will say the following. They never gave us any
> documents establishing that Beria was connected to

imperialist powers, that he was a spy, and so on. Neither
I nor Molotov ever saw such documents.

(I [Chuev] asked Molotov: Was he a spy?" He said: "An
agent, not necessarily a spy."

I asked Molotov – said Kaganovich – did you have any
kind of documents concerning the charge that Beria was
an agent of imperialism? He said: There were none. They
gave us no such documents, and they did not exist.
That's how it was. They said that at the trial there were
[such] documents."

- Chuev, Feliks. *Tak govoril Kaganovich. Ispoved' Stalinskogo apostola.* Moscow:
"Otechestvo", 1992, p. 66. Same text in Chuev, *Kaganovich. Shepilov.* Moscow: OLMA-Press, 2001, pp. 83-4.

Molotov agreed, as he told Chuev:

"They argue to this day about Beria: was he an agent of
foreign intelligence, or not?

– I think, he was not, – said Molotov."

- Chuev, *Molotov: Poluderzhavniy Vlastelin.*Moscow: OLMA-Press, 2000, p.
409:

Even more striking is the rough draft of Malenkov's speech at the Presidium session where Beria was ultimately either arrested or killed, and
where Malenkov had planned to propose the following:

a) MVD – to give this post to another (Kr[uglov]) and
the CC....

b)To dismiss [Beria] from the post of deputy [Chairman]
of the Council of Ministers, to app[oint] him min[ister]
of petrol[eum] ind[ustry'.

- *Lavrentii Beria*, p. 70.

However, earlier in this draft speech Malenkov referred to "vragi" – enemies – trying to use the MVD. That denotes a lot of hostility towards
Beria.

It appears as though what really bothered the other members of the Presidium (or some of them, including Malenkov and Khrushchev) was that
the MVD was overseeing the activities of the Presidium members and
other Party leaders. This meant that the Soviet government was above

the Party, and Party leaders had to answer to the law. It would be similar ⟩
to the FBI investigating high-ranking government leaders in the USA.

> [Beria's] arrest took place at a session of the Plenum of
> the Central Committee on June 26 1953 [Note: This is an
> error; it was, supposedly, a session of the Presidium of
> the CC – GF], despite the fact that no concrete
> accusations at all had been leveled at Beria. His
> opponents understood this. At the outset even
> Khrushchev spoke only of "detaining" him in the
> interests of further investigation. "I said 'detain' him
> because we had no direct criminal accusations against
> him. I could have thought he was an agent of the
> Mussavat, but Kamensky had talked about that. And no
> one had verified these facts." It was proposed only to
> remove him from the post he held. Against this was,
> supposedly, Molotov, who was afraid to leave Beria at ⟩
> liberty: 'Beria is very dangerous, and I believe we must ⟩
> take more extreme measures.'
>
> n.16: "His Presidium comrades arrested him
> preventively. They feared him very much. In fact no
> 'Beria plot', about which so much was said afterwards,
> ever existed. They thought it up so as to be able to
> explain, somehow, to the masses why they had arrested
> Stalin's most faithful pupil." Interview with M.
> Smirtiukov, *Kommersant-Vlast* [a business newspaper]
> August 2, 2000 .

- Piotr Vagner, in *Arkhiv*. No. 20, 2002. At

http://history.machaon.ru/all/number_14/analiti4/vagner_print/index.
html; Smirtiukov article at

 http://www.kommersant.ru/doc.aspx?DocsID=16455

45. Kaminsky about Beria working with Mussavat

Khrushchev:

> Were there any signs that Beria was an enemy of the
> party? Yes, there were. Already in 1937, at a Central

Committee plenum, former People's Commissar of
Health Kaminsky said that Beria worked for the
Mussavat intelligence service. But the Central Committee
plenum had barely concluded when Kaminsky was
arrested and then shot. Had Stalin examined Kaminsky's
statement? No, because Stalin believed in Beria, and that
was enough for him.

Pavlunovsky's letter of June 1937, attesting to the fact that Beria had
done underground work for the Bolshevik Party among nationalists:

> To the Secretary of the CC ACP(b) com. Stalin
> concerning com. Beria. In 1926 I was assigned to
> Transcaucasia as the Chairman of the Transc. GPU.
> Before my departure for Tiflis com. Dzerzhinsky,
> Chairman of the OGPU, summoned me and informed
> me in a detailed way of the situation in Transcaucasia.
> Then com. Dzerzhinsky informed me that one of my
> aides in Transcaucasia, com. Beria, had worked for the
> Mussavat counterintelligence during the Mussavat
> regime. I was not to allow this situation to confuse me in
> any way or to bias me against com. Beria, as com. Beria
> had worked in their counterintelligence with the
> knowledge of responsible Transcaucasian comrades and
> that he, Dzerzhinsky, and com. Sergo Ordzhonikidze
> knew about this. Upon my arrival in Tiflis about two
> months later I dropped in to see com. Sergo and told me
> everything com. Dzerzhinsky had informed me about
> com. Beria.
>
> Com. Sergo Ordzhonikidze informed me that in fact
> com. Beria had worked in the Mussavat
> counterintelligence, that he carried out this work upon
> the assignment of party workers, and that he, com.
> Ordzhonikidze, com. Kirov, com. Mikoian, and com.
> Nazaretian were well informed about this. For this
> reason I should relate to com. Beria with full confidence
> and that he, Sergo Ordzhonikidze, completely trusted
> com. Beria.
>
> In the course of two years' work in Transcaucasia com.
> Ordzhonikidze told me several times that he prized com.

Beria very highly as a developing worker, that a staunch
worker

would be developed from com. Beria, and that he had
informed com. Stalin of his evaluation of com. Beria.

In the course of my two years of work in Transcaucasia I
knew that com. Sergo valued and supported com. Beria.
Two years ago com. Sergo for some reason said to me in
a conversation, do you know that Rightists and other
such trash were trying, in their struggle against com.
Beria, to use the fact that he had worked with the
Mussavat counterintelligence, but that they will not be at
all successful in this.

I asked com. Sergo whether com. Stalin was aware of
this. Com. Sergo Ordzhonikidze replied that this was
known to com. Stalin and that he had spoken to com.
Stalin about it.

25 June 1937 Candidate to the CC VKP(b) Pavlunovskii.

- Aleksei Toptygin, *Lavrentii Beria.* Moscow: Iauza, EKSMO, 2005, pp.
11-12).

Beria's own Party autobiography, including passages about his underground work among nationalists:

From February 1919 to April 1920 while I was chairman
of the comm. cell of technical workers, under the
direction of senior comrades I carried out several tasks
of the area committee, and handled other cells as
instructor. In the autumn of that same year 1919 I
entered service in counterintelligence from the
"Gummet" party, where I worked together with
comrade Mussevi. In about March 1920, after the
murder of com. Mussevi I left work in
counterintelligence and worked in the Baku customs
house.

- *Beria: Konets Kar'iery.* Ed. V.F. Nekrasov. Moscow: Politizdat, 1991, pp.
320-5, at page 323. Beria's whole autobiography is online at
http://chss.montclair.edu/english/furr/research/beriaautobiog.pdf

Zalessky, *Imperiia Stalina*:

> In April-May 1920 Beria was a plenipotentiary of the registration section of the Caucasus front attached to the Revolutionary Military Council of the 11th Army, and then was dispatched to underground work in Georgia. In June 1920 he was arrested, but was released at the demand of the Soviet plenipotentiary representative S.M. Kirov and was sent to Azerbaidjan.

- At http://www.hrono.ru/biograf/beria.html

Beria to Ordzhonikidze, letter of March 2, 1933.

> Dear Sergo!

> ...IV. Levan Gogoberidze is resting in Sukhumi. According to what com. Lakova and a number of other comrades say com. Gogoberidze is saying the vilest things about me and in general about the new Transcaucasian leadership. In particular, about my past work in the Mussavat counterintelligence, he is asserting that the Party supposedly did not know and does not know, about this.

> But you know very well that I was sent by the Party into the Mussavat intelligence service, and that this question was settled by the CC of the ACP(b) in 1920, in your presence, that of coms Stasova, Kaminsky, Mirza Davud Guseinov, Harimanov, Sarkis, Rukhull, Akhundov, Buniat-Zade, and others. (In 1925 I handed you the official note of the decision of the CC AKB(b) about this, in which I was completely rehabilitated, that is the fact of my work in counterintelligence *with the Party's knowledge* was confirmed by the declarations of coms. Mirza Davud Guseinov, Kasum Ismailov, and others). Com. Datiko, who will give you this letter, will tell you the details.

> Yours, Lavrentii Beria

> March 2, 1933

- in *Sovetskoe Rukovodstvo. Perepiska. 1928-1941.* Moscow: ROSSPEN, 2001. No. 116, p. 204. Letter online at http://chss.montclair.edu/english/furr/research/beriatoordzhon33.pdf

Even Khrushchev admitted in memoirs written in the late 1960s:

> ...We had no direct criminal accusations against him [Beria]. I might think he had been an agent of the Musavetists, like Kaminsky said. But no one ever verified this...

Khrushchev, *Vremia. Liudi. Vlast'.(Vospominaniia).* Kn. 2, Chast' 3. Moscow: Moskovskie Novosti, 1999. Chapter "Posle smerti Stalina", p. 168. Also in the online edition at http://hrono.ru/libris/lib_h/hrush48.html

46. Kartvelishvili (Lavrent'ev)

Khrushchev:

> The long, unfriendly relations between Kartvelishvili and Beria were widely known; they date back to the time when Comrade Sergo [Ordzhonikidze] was active in the Transcaucasus; Kartvelishvili was the closest assistant of Sergo. The unfriendly relationship impelled Beria to fabricate a "case" against Kartvelishvili. It is a characteristic thing that in this "case" Kartvelishvili was charged with a terroristic act against Beria.

Beria uncovered an underground Rightist group in Georgia, including Lavrent'ev-Kartvelishvili.

> 20 July 1937
>
> No. 1716/s
>
> Dear Koba!
>
> The investigation on the matter of the counterrevolutionaries in Georgia is developing further, uncovering new participants in the vilest crimes against the Party and Soviet power. The arrest of G. Mgaloblishvili, L. Lavrent'ev (Kartvelishvili), Sh. Eliava... shed a bright light on the traitorous work that they were carrying on as members of the counterrevolutionary organization of the Rights. ... In the Transcaucasian counterrevolutionary center of Rights are:
>
> From Georgia: Eliava Sh., Orakhelashvili M., Lavrent'ev L. and Enukidze A.

- *Lubianka: Stalin I GUGB NKVD. 1937-1938. Dokumenty.*Moscow: Materik, 2004. No. 142, p. 252. Hereafter Lubianka 2.

> SERGEEV was connected in espionage and diversionary work in Moscow with MUKLEVICH and STRELKOV, in the Far Eastern Region with the regional center, consisting of LAVRENT'EV, DERIBAS, KRUTOV, KOSIOR.

- *Lubianka* 2, No. 196, p. 347 of Sept. 11 1937 (Liushkov document)

> LIU-KU-SEN declared that there was one meeting at LAVRENT'EV's apartment, at which they distributed ministers' portfolios, etc.

- *ibid.*, No. 207 p. 370 of September 19 1937 (Liushkov document)

> Former regional procurator CHERNIN arrested in Khabarovsk admitted his participation in the plot, ties with LAVRENT'EV, KRUTOV, and other active conspirators.

- *ibid.*, No. 309, p. 507 of March 29, 1938 (Liushkov document)

Kartvelishvili named by Iakovlev (along with Kabakov and many others):

> Besides that, through VAREIKIS-BAUMAN we were connected with the group of Rights in Moscow – KAMINSKY, BUBNOV; … on the periphery with the leading workers of oblast and region Party organizations – Rights and Trotskyites who led anti-Soviet organizations, SHEBOLDAEV, KHATAEVICH, KABAKOV, IVANOV, LAVRENT'EV, SHUBRIKOV, PTUKHA, KRINITSKY.

- *ibid.*, No. 226, p. 392 of October 15-18 1937.

The Rehabilitation file on Kartvelishvili blames Beria for everything. Even if Kartvelishvili was framed, though, this cannot be the case. Most of the documents against him are by Liushkov or, in the case of Iakovlev's confession, have nothing to do with Beria at all.

47. Kedrov

Khrushchev:

> Here is what the old Communist, Comrade Kedrov, wrote to the Central Committee through Comrade

Andreyev (Comrade Andreyev was then a Central
Committee secretary): "I am calling to you for help from
a gloomy cell of the Lefortovsky prison. Let my cry of
horror reach your ears; do not remain deaf, take me
under your protection; please, help remove the
nightmare of interrogations and show that this is all a
mistake.

"I suffer innocently…"

The old Bolshevik, Comrade Kedrov, was found
innocent by the Military Collegium. But, despite this, he
was shot at Beria's order.

Kedrov was in fact shot by order of Chief Prosecutor, not of Beria:

"October 17 1941 a decision of the NKVD of the USSR
was taken concerning the necessity to execute by
shooting, according to the direction of 'the directing
organs of the USSR', 25 prisoners. It was signed by the
chief of the investigative section for especially important
matters of the NKVD USSR L. Vlodzimirsky, confirmed
by the Assistant People's Commissar for Internal Affairs
of the USSR B. Kobulov, and with the consent of the
Procurator [= Attorney General] of the USSR V.
Bochkov. On the basis of this decision Beria signed, on
October 18, 1941, the order to shoot the persons
indicated."

- *Organy gosudarstvennoi bezopasnosti SSSR v Velikoi Otechestvennoi Voine. T.2.
Nachalo, Kn.2. 1-sentiabria – 31 dekabria 1941 goda.* Moscow: Rus', 2000.
No. 617, p. 215, n. 1.

"Sentence", implying a judicial proceeding:

To Senior Lieutenant of State Security com. Seminikhin
D.E. Upon receipt of the present you are instructed to
proceed to the city of Kuibyshev and **to carry out the
sentence – the highest measure of punishment**
(shooting) in relation to the following prisoners…
[emph. added GF]

- *ibid.*, pp. 215-216.

Statement of the Prosecutor's conclusion (or, perhaps, a part of it) in
Kedrov's case (reprinted by Prudnikova p. 386):

"The condemned prisoners Afonskii, Kedrov I.M and Shilkin have fully confirmed their confessions about Kedrov M.S. both at the preliminary investigation and at the court.

On the basis of the aforementioned Kedrov Mikhael Sergeevich, born 1878, living in Moscow, of Russian nationality, citizen of the USSR, of higher education, former landowner, member of the Bolshevik Party, a pensioner before his arrest, is accused –

In that he is a participant in an anti-Soviet organization, shared the counterrevolutionary ideas of the Rights and has repeatedly conducted anti-Soviet and prevocational conversations.

In the interests of the British imperialists he engaged in traitorous behavior in the Northern fleet during the period of 1918 – that is in committing crimes covered by articles 58-1a, 58-10 and 58-11 of the Criminal Code of the Russian Federation.

Considering the preliminary investigation of the case of Kedrov M.S. closed and the charges laid against him proven, as laid down by a special order of the directive organs of the Union of SSR, –

Would propose:

That Kedrov Mikhail Sergeevich, born 1878 – to be shot.

(Signed) Vlodzimirsky."

- Sukhomlinov, A.V. *Kto vy, Lavrentii Beriia?* Moscow: Detektiv-Press, 2003, p. 216. Reprinted in Prudnikova, Elena. *Beriia. Prestupleniia, kotorykh ne bylo.* Spb: Neva, 2005, p.386. Sukhomlinov believes Vlodzimirsky's signature on the facsimile is forged, while Prudnikova accepts it as genuine.

The report on M.S. Kedrov is attached to one of the "Stalin shooting lists", that of March 28, 1941:

An active participant in the anti-Soviet organization disguised as the society "Association of Northerners" in Moscow.

Was connected to the leading participant in the Zinovievite-Trotskyist organization G.Safarov and approved his counterrevolutionary methods in struggle against the Party and Soviet power.

KEDROV is suspected of secret collaboration with the Tsarist secret police ["Okhrana"] on the basis of the following facts:

In 1912, after he had been arrested several times by the Okhrana, he journeyed to Switzerland under suspicious circumstances, where he established ties with the Menshevist organization, and in 1914 received the right to return to Russia as "politically reliable".

KEDROV was closely connected with the leading participant of the conspiratorial organization in the NKVD and active agent of German intelligence ARTUZOV (*condemned* to death), whom he recommended for work in the organs of the Cheka-OGPU.

The brother of KEDROV's wife – MAIZEL' – who has lived all this time in America, made contact with KEDROV during several visits to the USSR.

MAIZEL' is known to the NKVD of the USSR as an agent of American intelligence.

In addition it has been established that in 1918 KEDROV, in command of the Northern front, upon an offensive by the British forces left Arkhangel'sk of his own accord, disorganizing military action and opening the front to invasion by the enemy.

He is exposed in hostile work by the confessions of SHILKIN P.P. former worker of the People's Commissariat of Water (sentenced to death), AFONSKY V.A., former company commander (sentenced to death), SAFAROV G.I. (under arrest, undergoing investigation by the NKVD), in face-to-face confrontations with SAFAROV and AFONSKY, and also by the confessions of witness TAGUNOVA V.I. and by official documents about the treasonous work of KEDROV on the Northern front.

- http://stalin.memo.ru/spravki/13-184.HTM

But whatever the facts are about Kedrov's guilt or innocence, he was executed by an order signed by the Soviet Prosecutor.

48. Ordzhonikidze's brother

Khrushchev:

> Beria also handled cruelly the family of Comrade Ordzhonikidze. Why? Because Ordzhonikidze had tried to prevent Beria from realizing his shameful plans. Beria had cleared from his way all persons who could possibly interfere with him. Ordzhonikidze was always an opponent of Beria, which he told to Stalin. Instead of examining this affair and taking appropriate steps, Stalin allowed the liquidation of Ordzhonikidze's brother and brought Ordzhonikidze himself to such a state that he was forced to shoot himself.

Sergo Beria:

> I knew Papulia Ordzhonikidze well, because we lived in the same house. He always occupied prominent posts, but was better known as a carouser, a hunter, and generally as a lover of the good life. He never called his brother Sergo anything but, excuse me, shit. He cursed socialism all day long.

> Sergo was well informed about Papulia's riotous behavior. He resented him and, when he came to Tbilisi, made a show of staying with us. Maybe from today's point of view Papulia could be considered a 'democrat', but at that time abusing the existing social order was not forgiven even in the case of a brother of one who was leading and heading that social order...

- Raul Chilachava, *Syn Lavrentiia Beriia raskazyvaet...* Kiev, KITS Inkopress, 1992, p. 17.

Khlevniuk's fiercely anti-communist study still exonerates Beria:

> Valiko (Ivan) Ordzhonikidze worked as a budgetary inspector in the financial department of the Tbilisi Soviet. At the beginning of November 1936, one of his colleagues filed a statement with the party committee charging that Ivan Konstantinovich insisted upon the

innocence of Papulia Ordzhonikidze and denied he fraternized with Trotskyites. The party committee of the Tbilisi Soviet issued a denunciation. Valiko was called "on the carpet," and not only confirmed everything written in the statement, but added: "Papulia Ordzhonikidze couldn't go against his brother, Comrade Sergo Ordzhonikidze, nor the leader of our people, Comrade Stalin, whom he personally knows.... It's impossible to believe such accusations against Papulia Ordzhonikidze – they are all untrue." To the members of the party committee, Valiko protested: "You can be sure of the innocence not only of my brother, but of others who will be freed in a short time." For such impertinence, they expelled him from the group of party sympathizers, and fired him.

Sergo then got involved in the case. In the middle of December he phoned Beria and asked for help. Beria showed remarkable concern this time: He spoke with the accused and sought an explanation from the chairman of the Tbilisi Soviet. Sergo received a package within a week that contained an explanatory letter from Beria. Beria wrote: "Dear Comrade Sergo! After your call I quickly summoned Valiko; he told me the story of his dismissal and roughly confirmed that which is expounded upon in the enclosed explanation from the chairman of the Tbilisi Soviet, Comrade Nioradze. Today, Valiko was restored to his job. Yours, L. Beria."

Khlevniuk, Oleg V. *In Stalin's Shadow. The Career of 'Sergo' Ordzhonikidze.* (Armonk, London: M.E. Sharp, 1995), p. 108. The Russian edition of this book, *Stalin i Ordzhonikidze. Konflikty v Politbiuro v 30-e gody* (Moscow:; Izd. "Rossiia Molodaia", 1993) is not identical to the English translation.

49. Stalin, Short Biography

Khrushchev:

Comrades: The cult of the individual acquired such monstrous size chiefly because Stalin himself, using all conceivable methods, supported the glorification of his own person. This is supported by numerous facts. One of the most characteristic examples of Stalin's self-glorification and of his lack of even elementary modesty is the edition of his Short Biography, which was published in 1948.

This book is an expression of the most dissolute flattery, an example of making a man into a godhead, of transforming him into an infallible sage, "the greatest leader, sublime strategist of all times and nations." Finally, no other words could be found with which to lift Stalin up to the heavens.

We need not give here examples of the loathesome adulation filling this book. All we need to add is that they all were approved and edited by Stalin personally and some of them were added in his own handwriting to the draft text of the book.

What did Stalin consider essential to write into this book? Did he want to cool the ardor of his flatterers who were composing his Short Biography? No! He marked the very places where he thought that the praise of his services was insufficient. Here are some examples characterizing Stalin's activity, added in Stalin's own hand:

> "In this fight against the skeptics and capitulators, the Trotskyites, Zinovievites, Bukharinites and Kamenevites, there was definitely welded together, after Lenin's death, that leading core of the party... that upheld the great banner of Lenin, rallied the party behind Lenin's behests, and brought the Soviet people into the broad road of industrializing the country and collectivizing the rural economy. The leader of this core and the guiding force of the party and the state was Comrade Stalin." [(1) – see below for discussion, GF]

Thus writes Stalin himself! Then he adds:

> Although he performed his task as leader of the party and the people with consummate skill and enjoyed the unreserved support of the entire Soviet people, Stalin never allowed his work to be marred by the slightest

hint of vanity, conceit or self-adulation. [(2) – see below for discussion, GF]

Where and when could a leader so praise himself? Is this worthy of a leader of the Marxist- Leninist type? No. Precisely against this did Marx and Engels take such a strong position. This also was always sharply condemned by Vladimir Il'ich Lenin.

In the draft text of his book appeared the following sentence: "Stalin is the Lenin of today."

This sentence appeared to Stalin to be too weak, so, in his own handwriting, he changed it to read: "Stalin is the worthy continuer of Lenin's work, or, as it is said in our party, Stalin is the Lenin of today." [(3) - see below for discussion, GF] You see how well it is said, not by the nation but by Stalin himself.

It is possible to give many such self-praising appraisals written into the draft text of that book in Stalin's hand. Especially generously does he endow himself with praises pertaining to his military genius, to his talent for strategy.

I will cite one more insertion made by Stalin concerning the theme of the Stalinist military genius. "The advanced Soviet science of war received further development," he writes, "at Comrade Stalin's hands. Comrade Stalin elaborated the theory of the permanently operating factors that decide the issue of wars, of active defense and the laws of counteroffensive and offensive, of the cooperation of all services and arms in modern warfare, of the role of big tank masses and air forces in modern war, and of the artillery as the most formidable of the armed services. At the various stages of the war Stalin's genius found the correct solutions that took account of all the circumstances of the situation." [(4) – see below for discussion, GF]

And, further, writes Stalin: "Stalin's military mastership was displayed both in defense and offense. Comrade Stalin's genius enabled him to divine the enemy's plans and defeat them. The battles in which Comrade Stalin directed the Soviet armies are brilliant examples of operational military skill." [(5) – see below for discussion, GF]

In this manner was Stalin praised as a strategist. Who did this? Stalin himself, not in his role as a strategist but in the role of an author-editor, one of the main creators of his self-adulatory biography. Such, comrades, are the facts. We should rather say shameful facts.

V.A. Belianov, editor of Stalin's remarks:

His [Stalin's] supporters could even find confirmation of the Vozhd's modesty, since he crossed out numerous phrases praising him that had been included by the servile compilers (like "under Stalin's leadership," "genius", etc.)

Stalin's many changes included the addition of a paragraph stressing the importance of the role of women:

One of Stalin's great services has to be the fact that in this period, the period of the development of industrialization and collectivization, when it was essential to mobilize all our laboring forces to decide great tasks, he gave full attention to the woman question, the question of the position of women, of female labor, of the very important role of women, female workers, and women farmers in both the economic and the social-political life of society and, having raised this question to the necessary importance, gave it a correct resolution.

- *Izvestiia TsK KPSS* No. 9, 1990, pp. 113-129. Online at http://grachev62.narod.ru/stalin/t16/t16_17.htm

Maksimenkov's conclusion:

In contradiction to Khrushchev's thesis in these two examples what is obvious is the significant lowering of ideological expressions of the 'cult' by Stalin himself, and the exaltation of Leninist dogmas. All the formulations about "the teachings of Stalin" were removed. In the draft of the biography of Lenin, prepared in 1950 in accordance with Stalin's directives, the Vozhd [Leader, i.e. Stalin – GF] himself systematically lowered the high style of information connected with the depiction of the parallel "Lenin – Stalin." … For understandable reasons N.S. Khrushchev, P.N. Pospelov, M.A. Suslov, L.F. Il'ichev and other ideologists of "the Thaw" did not cite, in their own public statements and articles, examples of these corrections [by Stalin]. The present author is not aware of any mention of these primary sources even during the years of *perestroika*.

- Leonid Maksimenkov. "Kul't. Zametki o slovakh-simvolakh v sovetskoi politichesoi kul'ture" ("Cult. Remarks about word-symbols in Soviet political culture"). *Svobodnaia Mysl'* 10 (1993). Also at

http://www.situation.ru/app/j_art_677.htm

Excerpt from Mochalov's notes about Stalin's remarks:

There are very many errors. The tone is bad, Socialist-Revolutionary. I'm said to have all kinds of knowledge, including some kind of knowledge of constant factors of war. It appears that I have knowledge about communism, while Lenin, you see, spoke only about socialism and said nothing about communism. And I, you see, spoke about communism. Further, it is as though I have knowledge about the industrialization of the country, about the collectivization of agriculture, and so forth, etc. In fact it is to Lenin that the achievement of the posing of the question of industrializing our country, as well as concerning the question of collectivizing agriculture, etc. must be attributed.

There's a great deal of praise in this biography, the exaltation of the role of the individual. What is left for the reader to do after reading this biography? Get on his knees and pray to me…

Here, about Baku it is written that, supposedly, before my arrival the Bolsheviks had done nothing, and all I had to do was to arrive and suddenly everything changed at once. Believe it or not! In reality, how was it? We had to form our cadre. We did form cadre of Bolsheviks in Baku. I listed the names of these people in the corresponding place.

> The same about another period – people like
> Dzerzhinskii, Frunze, Kuibyshev, lived and worked, but
> nothing is written about them, they are absent...
>
> This has to do with the period of the Second World War.
> It was necessary to take capable people, gather them,
> forge them. Such people gathered around the main
> command of the Red Army.
>
> Nowhere is it said that I am a pupil of Lenin... In fact I
> considered myself, and still consider myself, a pupil of
> Lenin. I said this clearly in the well-known conversation
> with Ludwig... I am a pupil of Lenin's, Lenin taught me,
> not the other way around. He laid out the road, and we
> are proceeding along this cleared road.

- Richard Kosolapov, *Slovo tovarishchu Stalinu*. Moscow: EKSMO-Algoritm, 2002, pp. 470-472.

Elsewhere Kosolapov recounts a story – possibly apocryphal, though it is attested by many others as well – about Stalin's disdain for his "image:"

> Supposedly Joseph Vissarionovich had a conversation
> with his son Vasilii when, angered by the arrogance of
> his sons, he uttered this reproach: "Do you think that
> you are STALIN? Do you think I am STALIN? HE is
> Stalin – there!" he said, as he pointed at the pompous
> portrait.

- Speech on 122nd anniversary of Stalin's birth, *Solnce truda* No. 3 (2003), pp. 3-4. At http://www.cprf.info/analytics/10828.shtml

Non-Stalinist authors like IUrii Bogomolov, correspondent for *Izvestiia,* cite similar stories:

> A rumor has spread about a conversation between papa
> Iosif and his son Vasia. "You think you are Stalin? You
> think I am Stalin? THAT is Stalin!" said the Boss, as he
> finished his moral lesson and pointed at a portrait.

- "Stalin i TV", now at

http://web.archive.org/web/20050224073133/http://www.politcom.ru/2003/pvz74.php

50. The Short Course

Khrushchev:

> And when Stalin himself asserts that he himself wrote *The Short Course of the History of the All-Union Communist Party (Bolsheviks)*, this calls at least for amazement. Can a Marxist- Leninist thus write about himself, praising his own person to the heavens?

Molotov:

> Chuev: I have heard the assertion that it was Iaroslavskii who wrote *The Short Course*...
>
> Molotov: – That's impossible. But it wasn't written by Stalin. And he never said that he had written it. He read to us the only chapter of his – the philosophical one.

- Chuev, Molotov: *Poluderzhavnyi Vlastelin*, 302.

In reality, as Roi Medvedev has pointed out, Stalin's role in preparing the textbook was far more significant. In the chapter with the title "Stalin – main author of the *Short Course*", Medvedev notes:

> Stalin ... edited and wrote many of the pages of this *Short Course*. To Stalin belong not only the general plan of the book, but also the titles of each chater and paragraphs within these chapters. He wrote all the sections and pages of the book that related to theory....
>
> Already on November 28, 1938 Fiodr Samoilov, director of the State museum of the Revolution ... wrote a letter to A.N. Poskrebyshev, chief of Stalin's secretarial staff:
>
>> "To the CC of the ACP(b), com. Poskrebyshev. In connection with the necessary exposition in the Museum of the Revolution of the USSR of the *Short Course of the History of the ACP(b)* we must turn to comrade Stalin with a request to permit us to receive a few pages, written or corrected by him, of the *Short Course*, or page margins corrected by comrade Stalin's hand. If it is not possible to receive originals of the indicated materials, then could not the Museum be provided with photocopies of them? The exposition of these materials would be extremely valuable and interesting for visitors to the

Museum." Poskrebyshev showed this letter to Stalin
a few days later, and the latter wrote his answer
directly on the letter form of the Museum of the
Revolution: "Com. Samoilov. I would not think that
in your old age you would bother yourself with such
trifles. If the book has already been published in
millions of copies, why do you want the
manuscripts? With greetings. December 6, 1938. J.
Stalin." This letter with Stalin's resolution was taken
from the archives at the end of 1955 in preparation
for the XX Congress of the CPSU. On the basis of
this document N.S. Khrushchev virtually blamed
Stalin for plagiarism. *The Short Course*, as Khrushchev
said, was written by a collective of authors, and in
the *Short Biography of Stalin* published in 1948 in
Stalin's own hand was inserted the phrase "the book
History of the ACP(b). Short Course was written by
comrade Stalin and approved by a Commission of
the CC ACP(b)." "As you can see, – exclaimed N.S.
Khrushchev to the closed session of the Congress in
his secret report, – this constitutes a conversion of
the work created by a collective into a book written
by Stalin.

In this case N.S. Khrushchev was in error. As is known,
not all the manuscripts were burned. A part of the
typescript of the *Short Course* with corrections and
insertions of various kinds by Stalin has been retained,
and these materials were published in 2002-2003 in the
journal 'Voprosy Istorii'.

- R.A. Medvedev, *Liudi i Knigi. Chto chital Stalin?*. Moscow: Prava cheloveka, 2005, pp. 216-217.

51. Stalin Signed Order for Monument to Himself on July 2, 1951

Khrushchev:

It is a fact that Stalin himself had signed on July 2, 1951 a
resolution of the USSR Council of Ministers concerning
the erection on the Volga-Don Canal of an impressive

monument to Stalin; on September 4 of the same year he issued an order making 33 tons of copper available for the construction of this impressive monument.

February 16, 1951 the Politburo decision:

> The Chairmanship at the sessions of the Presidium of the Soviet of Ministers of the USSR and the Buro of the Presidium of the Soviet of Ministers of the USSR is to be assigned by turns to the Vice-Chairmen of the Presidium of the Soviet of Ministers of the USSR comrades Bulganin, Beria and Malenkov, to whom are [also] assigned the duties of considering and taking decisions upon current matters.

> Decrees and announcements of the Council of Ministers of the USSR will be issued under the signature of the Chairman of the Council of Ministers of the USSR comrade Stalin J.V.

- IU. Zhukov, *Tainy Kremlia. Stalin, Molotov, Beria, Malenkov.* Moscow: Terra-Knizhnyi Klub, 2000, pp. 544-5.

The original of this document:

http://www.rusarchives.ru/evants/exhibitions/stalin_exb/29.shtml

The rubber stamps of Stalin's signature used to sign documents in his name:

http://www.rusarchives.ru/evants/exhibitions/stalin_exb/31.shtml

Politburo members speaking in July 1953 concerning Stalin's political inactivity during final period of his life:

Khrushchev:

> We all respect comrade Stalin. But the years take their toll. During recent times comrade Stalin did not read papers, or receive people, because his health was weak.

- *Lavrentii Beria,* p. 236.

Kaganovich:

> It must be frankly said that in Stalin's day, since we had his general political leadership, we lived more calmly, although comrade Stalin, as has been accurately said, during recent times did not work very actively or take part in the work of the Politburo.

- *Lavrentii Beria*, p. 274.

Voroshilov:

> Together with the rest of us he knew that, as a result of
> hard work, during the past years he was often ill…

- *Lavrentii Beria*, p. 334.

Mikoian:

> Comrade Stalin at first took an active part in the
> formation of these organs, but during the past two years
> he stopped taking an interest in them.

- *Lavrentii Beria*, p170.

- All citations from *Lavrentii Beria. 1953.* Ed. Naumov and Sigachev.
Moscow 1999.

52. Palace of Soviets

Khrushchev:

> At the same time Stalin gave proofs of his lack of respect
> for Lenin's memory. It is not a coincidence that, despite
> the decision taken over 30 years ago to build a Palace of
> Soviets as a monument to Vladimir Il'ich, this palace was
> not built, its construction was always postponed and the
> project allowed to lapse.

Maksim Volchenkov's, "Dvorets Sovetov" ("The Palace of Soviets"):.

> Despite the stormy beginning of the construction, the
> realization of the project had to be frozen. More than
> this, the metallic carcass of the Palace of Soviets was
> taken down during the war: the capital needed metal for
> defense materials against fascist Germany. After the
> victory they did not resurrect the building, although the
> idea of the structure of this grandiose conception never
> left Stalin until his very death. The Vozhd wanted to
> underscore, with this building, the superiority of the
> Soviet system over the structure of capitalist states. "We
> won the war and are recognized throughout the world as
> great victors. We should be ready for the arrival of
> foreign tourists in our cities. What will they think if they
> go around Moscow and do not see any skyscrapers?

When they compare us to capitalist capitals, it may be to our detriment."

The resources set aside for the construction of the Palace of Soviets were used for the reconstruction of the state after this very severe war. In addition, the "Cold War" had begun, and many resources were needed to build the atom bomb. What was the sense of a grandiose building if the enemy, who had atomic weapons, could wipe the whole country off the face of the earth? Who would then admire the masterpiece of Soviet architecture? It was clear that the actualization of this magnificent conception was postponed for an indefinite time. Despite that, the directorate of construction of the Palace of Soviets attached to the Soviet of Ministers still remained in existence for several years. Then it was reassigned to the construction of other multistory buildings, using the experience of the designs of the Palace of Soviets that had been worked out with the years. A few more years passed, and the directorate would undertake the construction of the television tower in Ostankino.

…[Volchenkov quotes Khrushchev's attack on Stalin in the Secret Speech.] Despite Khrushchev's harsh criticism of the old project and its organizers, the new contest did not produce anything better, and the country never saw this building either during Khrushchev's time or later.

- Maksim Volchenkov. "Dvorets Sovetov."
http://www.4ygeca.com/dv_sovetov.html

53. Lenin Prize

Khrushchev:

We cannot forget to recall the Soviet Government resolution of August 14, 1925 concerning "the founding of Lenin prizes for educational work." This resolution was published in the press, but until this day there are no Lenin prizes. This, too, should be corrected.

In the notes to the critical edition of Khrushchev's Speech the editors say nothing about any connection between the cancellation of the Lenin prizes and the establishment of the Stalin prizes.

> The Lenin prizes were awarded for exceptional achievements in the fields of science, technology, literature, art, and architecture. They were established in 1925, and were not awarded between 1935 and 1957. In November [1955] to March 1956 the question of renewing of the Lenin prize awards was discussed in the Presidium and Secretariat of the Central Committee of the CPSU. From 1958 till 1990 they were awarded annually on Lenin's birthday.

- *Doklad Khrushcheva,* p. 161, n. 89

The idea of establishing prizes in the field of literature seems to have been first suggested by Gorky. Having read Stalin's speech to the unified Plenum of the CC and the Central Control Commission of the ACP(b) (January 7-12 1933), the writer responded with an enthusiastic letter.

January 16, 1933

> Dear Iosif Vissarionovich!
>
> The accumulation of materials for the first four volumes of the *History of the Civil War* has been completed by its secretariat.
>
> It is now essential that the main editorial group confirm the materials of the authors who have been mentioned for reworking, and I urge you in this regard. The authors must submit their manuscripts by March 31. I implore you to move this matter forward! I have the impression that the main editorial group is sabotaging this effort.
>
> I read your powerful, wise speech to the Plenum with a feeling of the deepest satisfaction and enthusiasm. I am completely certain that such a powerful echo will resound everywhere in the world of the working class. Beneath its serene, powerfully forged form lies such a resounding thunder that it seems that you have squeezed into your words all the noise of the construction of the years gone by. I know that you do not need any words of praise, but I think I have the right to tell you the truth.

You are a great man, a real leader, and the proletariat of
the Soviet Union is fortunate that at its head there stands
a second Il'ich by the force of your logic and by your
inexhaustible energy. I shake your hand firmly, dear and
respected comrade.

A. Peshkov.

On the reverse side of the writing paper in Gorky's hand are two notes,
in the second of which, among other things, is written the following:

Aleksei Tolstoy has in mind an All-union contest in
comedy – I hereby attach the draft revolution about this
contest.

Among our writers there is felt a strong sense of
renewed energy and the desire to work seriously,
therefore the contest might yield good results. But for an
All-union contest seven prizes are too few, we should
increase the number to at least 15, and the amount of the
first prize to 25 thousand – the devil with them! – **and
give to the prizes the name of Stalin** (emphasis added,
GF), for indeed this plan comes from you.

In addition: why only comedy? Drama should also be
included...

Forgive me for boring you.

A.P.

On February 3 1933 Stalin replied to Gorky:

Dear Aleksei Maksimovich!

I have received your letter of January 16, 1933. Thank
you for your warm words and for your "praise." No
matter how people may boast, no one can be indifferent
to "praise." Understandably I, as a person, am no
exception...

3. We will finish plans for a comedy contest soon. Will
will not refuse Tolstoy. We guarantee everything
according to your demands. **Concerning "giving the
prizes the name of Stalin", I protest most strongly
(most strongly!).** (Emphasis added, GF)

Greetings! I shake your hand!

J. Stalin

P.S. Take care of your health.

- Soima, Vasilii. *Zapreshchennyi Stalin.* Moscow: OLMA-Press, 2005, pp. 20-21. This volume is online at http://zapravdu.ru/index.php?option=com_content&task=view&id=79&Itemid=51

This passage is on the second "page" of the online book, at http://zapravdu.ru/index.php?option=com_content&task=view&id=79&Itemid=51?&Itemid=51&limit=1&limitstart=1

On December 21 1939 *Pravda* published a decree of the Council of People's Commissars of the USSR concerning the establishment of prizes and awards in the name of Stalin. The decree, issued under the signature of Chairman of the CPC Molotov and the business manager Khlomov, reads as follows (emphasis added, GF):

> In commemoration of the sixtieth birthday of comrade Iosif Vissarionovich Stalin the Council of People's Commissars of the Union of SSR decrees:
>
> I. To establish 16 prizes **in the name of Stalin** (of 100,000 rubles each), to be awarded each year to activists in science and arts for exceptional work in the following fields:
>
> 1. physico-mathematical sciences;
>
> 2. technical sciences;
>
> 3. chemical sciences;
>
> 5. agricultural science;
>
> 6. medical science;
>
> 7. philosophical science;
>
> 8. economic science;
>
> 9. historical-philological science;
>
> 10. juridical science;
>
> 11. music;
>
> 12. painting;
>
> 13. sculpture;
>
> 14. architecture;
>
> 15. theatrical arts;

16. cinematography.

II. To establish the **Stalin prize**, to be awareded yearly for the best discovery:

Ten **first** prizes of 100 thousand rubles each,

Twenty **second** prizes of 50 thousand rubles each,

Thirty **third** prizes of 25 thousand rubles each.

III. To establish the Stalin prized, to be awarded yearly for exceptional achievements in the field of military knowledge:

Three **first** prizes of 100 thousand rubles each,

Five **second** prizes of 50 thousand rubles each,

Ten **third** prizes of 25 thousand rubles each.

Chairman of the Council of People's Commissars

Of the Union of SSR *V. Molotov*

Business manager of the Council of People's Commissars

Of the Union of SSR *M. Khlomov*

December 20, 1939

Moscow, the Kremlin.

- "Premii bez prenii", *Kommersant"-Den'gi*, February 7, 2005. At http://www.kommersant.ru/doc.aspx?DocsID=544976

Thereupon still another decree was issued in which the question of the Stalin prizes received a further elaboration:

In addition to the decree of the CPC of the Union of SSR of December 20 1939 ... the CPC of the Union of SSR decrees:

One – for poetry,

One – for prose,

One – for dramaturgy,

One – for literary criticism.

Chairman of the Council of People's Commissars USSR

V. Molotov

Business manager of the Council of People's Commissars USSR

M. Khlomov

February 1, 1940

Moscow, the Kremlin.

From 1930 till 1991 the highest state award of the USSR was the Order of Lenin, not of Stalin. The Order of Stalin was indeed proposed but, as we have seen in Section 1 above, it was resolutely and successfully opposed by Stalin himself and never instituted.

> Concerning the Establishment of Two New Orders of the Union of SSR: "The Order of Lenin" and "The Red Star"

> The decree of the Presidium of the Central Executive Committee of the USSR [the highest State organ under the 1924 constitution – GF] of April 6, 1930:

> 1. To establish two new orders of the Union of SSR: "The Order of Lenin" and "The Red Star."

> The Statute of the Order "Order of Lenin".

> The decree of the Presidium of the Central Executive Committee of the USSR of May 5 1930.

> The Presidium of the Central Executive Committee of the Union of SSR … decrees:

> To confirm the statue below of the order "The Order of Lenin…"

- Text at http://glory.rin.ru/cgi-bin/article.pl?id=99

54. Stalin Suggested Huge Tax Increase on Kolkhozes

Khrushchev:

> What is more, while reviewing this project Stalin proposed that the taxes paid by the kolkhozes and by the kolkhoz workers should be raised by 40 billion rubles; according to him the peasants are well off and the kolkhoz worker would need to sell only one more chicken to pay his tax in full.

> Imagine what this meant. Certainly, 40 billion rubles is a sum which the kolkhoz workers did not realize for all the

products which they sold to the Government. In 1952, for instance, the kolkhozes and the kolkhoz workers received 26,280 million rubles for all their products delivered and sold to the Government.

Did Stalin's position, then, rest on data of any sort whatever? Of course not. In such cases facts and figures did not interest him.

Khrushchev, at the July 1953 CC Plenum:

Khrushchev: Unfortunately when there was a third variant [of a proposed tax increase] he proposed by the way to raise the taxes on kolkhozes and kolkhozniks to 40 billion, but the whole income is only 42 billion.

Mikoian: To raise the current tax from 15 billion to 40 billion.

Khrushchev: No, raise it 40 billion more in taxes. That is already, I don't know what.

Mikoian: That would be impossible.

-*Lavrentii Beria,* p. 171. This same story is repeated in the second draft of the same meeting on p. 313, but Mikoian's words are elaborated to take a dig at Beria.

Malenkov later mentions the same figure, but makes it clear that he had not heard it before the Plenum.

In the course of the work of the current Plenum you, comrades, learned the following fact. In connection with the problems of improving animal husbandry in February of this year comrade Stalin insistently proposed increasing the taxes in the countryside by 40 billion rubles. We of course all understood the glaring injustice and danger of such a measure...

Ibid.- p. 351. Note that Khrushchev had said Stalin mention this "by the way" or "as an aside" (*poputno*). Malenkov has turned that into "insistently" proposed.

Mikoian does not repeat this story of "40 billion rubles" in the account of this event in his memoirs. He says that it was Khrushchev that heard Stalin propose an additional tax on the peasantry.

Mikoian also fails to cite the "40 billion rubles" figure. "An extra chicken" per peasant family would not produce a large sum, much less this colossal figure – though Mikoian admits he did not ever hear Stalin say this! Evidently it was not Khrushchev, but "other CC members" who heard the remark about "an extra chicken."

It is interesting that Mikoian is very careful to state what he himself heard from Stalin, and to make it clear that he did not hear any of this himself. This could be interpreted as meaning he did not necessarily believe it, especially Khrushchev's figure.

> As always in the evening, when the other members of the Presidium were also at Stalin's, Malenkov laid out the essence of the matter in order to test Stalin's reaction. I was not present. Khrushchev later said that Stalin got angry and said that we were were renewing the program of Rykov and Frumkin, that the peasantry was getting fat while the working class was living more poorly. Other CC members told me that Stalin spoke out on this subject during the October [1952] Plenum and sharply criticized me for the very idea of raising the purchase prices on meat and dairy products. They said that he looked very mean, walked back and forth as he usually did, grumbled, and said about me: 'A new Frumkin has turned up!' But truthfully, I did not hear that. Then I heard he said we needed yet another new tax on the peasants. He said 'What's that to a peasant. He'll give up an extra chicken – and that's all.'
>
> And at that same discussion **Khrushchev heard about Stalin's proposal to levy an additional tax on the peasantry** and got upset, saying that if we were to raise taxes on the peasants then we needed to include people like Malenkov, Beria, and Zverev (the head of the Ministry of Finance) on the commission. Stalin agreed to that. After a time we actually met in our new composition. The commission discovered that both Beria and Malenkov considered it impossible to carry out Stalin's directive. This was explained, of course, in private conversations. They gave it to Zverev to do the accounting and explaining. In general, they drew this matter out as long as they could. Everyone considered

Stalin's suggestions about new taxes on the peasantry
without any increases in the purchase prices to be
impracticable. (emphasis added, GF)

- *Tak Bylo* (Mikoian's memoirs), Chapter 46, p. 578.

55. Stalin Insulted Postyshev

Khrushchev:

In one of his speeches Stalin expressed his dissatisfaction
with Postyshev and asked him, "What are you actually?"

Postyshev answered clearly, "I am a Bolshevik, Comrade
Stalin, a Bolshevik."

This assertion was at first considered to show a lack of
respect for Stalin; later it was considered a harmful act
and consequently resulted in Postyshev's annihilation
and branding without any reason as a 'people's enemy.'

Khrushchev is the sole source for this supposed statement by Stalin. This
quotation has never been located anywhere. No one else has ever claimed
that Stalin said it. Had it in fact been in a speech it would almost certainly
have been found long before now. We discuss this matter in the text.

56. "Disorganization" of Politburo Work

Khrushchev:

The importance of the Central Committee's Political
Bureau was reduced and its work was disorganized by
the creation within the Political Bureau of various
commissions – the so-called "quintets," "sextets,"
"septets" and "novenaries." Here is, for instance, a
resolution of the Political Bureau of October 3, 1946:

Stalin's Proposal:

1. The Political Bureau Commission for Foreign
Affairs ('Sextet') is to concern itself in the future, in
addition to foreign affairs, also with matters of
internal construction and domestic policy.

2. The Sextet is to add to its roster the Chairman of
the State Commission of Economic Planning of the

> USSR, Comrade Voznesensky, and is to be known
> as a Septet.
>
> Signed: Secretary of the Central Committee, J. Stalin.

What a terminology of a card player! (Laughter in the hall.) It is clear that the creation within the Political Bureau of this type of commissions – "quintets," "sextets," "septets" and "novenaries" – was against the principle of collective leadership. The result of this was that some members of the Political Bureau were in this way kept away from participation in reaching the most important state matters.

Edvard Radzinsky, biographer of, and extremely hostile to, Stalin:

> After Stalin's death Nikita Khrushchev in his famous
> report on the cult of personality waxed indignant that
> Stalin "diminished the role of the Politburo by the
> creation within the CC of certain "sextets", "quintets",
> to which were given special powers. ... "What a
> terminology of a card player!" – fumed Khrushchev. But
> he, addressing himself to the post-Lenin generation of
> the Party, did not know (or pretended not to know) that
> he was threatening one of the oldest Party traditions.
> "Troikas", "quintets", and other "narrow structures"
> created by the Vozhd within his leading group and
> known only to the participants and the Vozhd himself,
> had appeared in Lenin's day.

- Radzinsky, *Stalin*. Chapter 4. The Russian edition, *Stalin*. Moscow: Vagrius, 1997, is on line at http://militera.lib.ru/bio/radzinsky_es1/02.html

57. Stalin Suspected Voroshilov as an "English Agent"

Khrushchev:

> Because of his extreme suspicion, Stalin toyed also with
> the absurd and ridiculous suspicion that Voroshilov was
> an English agent. (Laughter in the hall.) It's true – an
> English agent. – p.48

Khrushchev's memoirs:

> Stalin even said to a few of us [lit. "a narrow circle of
> us," *v uzkom krugu*, GF] that he suspected Voroshilov
> was an English agent. Of course, improbable stupidities.

- Khrushchev, N.S. *Vremia. Liudi. Vlast'*. Kn.2. Chast' 3. Moscow: Moskovskie novosti, 1999, pp. 128-129. Online at
http://hrono.ru/libris/lib_h/hrush45.html

There is no other source for this story. None of Khrushchev's colleagues
in that "narrow circle" ever confirmed it.

58. Andreev; 59. Molotov; 60. Mikoian

Andreev

Khrushchev:

> By unilateral decision, Stalin had also separated one
> other man from the work of the Political Bureau –
> Andrei Andreyevich Andreyev. This was one of the most
> unbridled acts of willfulness.

Efremov:

> In the new list of those elected are all members of the
> old Politburo - except that of comrade A.A. Andreev
> who, as everyone knows now is unfortunately completely
> deaf and thus can not function.

- "'V Ch'I Ruki Vruchim Estafetu Nashego Velikogo Dela?' Neopublikovannaia rech' I.V. Stalina na Plenume Tsentral'nogo Komiteta KPSS.
16 Oktobria 1952 goda (po zapisi L.N. Efremova)" *Sovetskaia Rossiia*. 13
ianvariia 2000 g. p. 6. Facsimile online at
http://chss.montclair.edu/english/furr/research/stalinoct1652.pdf Also
at http://www.prometej.info/solnce/st03.htm

Konstantin Simonov:

> I remember only Stalin's reply about Andreev, who was
> not included among the members and candidates of the
> Presidium of the CC – that he had withdrawn from
> activity, and for all practical purposes could not work
> actively any more.

Simonov, *Glazami cheloveka moego pokoleniia* ["Through the Eyes of a Man
of My Generation"], 1988, p. 246.

Molotov; Mikoian

Khrushchev:

> Let us consider the first Central Committee plenum after
> the 19th Party Congress when Stalin, in his talk at the
> plenum, characterized Vyacheslav Mikhailovich Molotov
> and Anastas Ivanovich Mikoian and suggested that these
> old workers of our party were guilty of some baseless
> charges. It is not excluded that had Stalin remained at the
> helm for another several months, Comrades Molotov
> and Mikoian would probably have not delivered any
> speeches at this Congress.

Efremov:

> It's necessary to touch upon incorrect behavior on the
> part of a few prominent political figures, if we are
> speaking of unity in our affaiars. I have in mind
> comrades Molotov and Mikoian.

> Comrade Molotov - the most dedicated to our cause. If
> called upon, I do nt doubt that, without hesitation, he
> would give his life for the party. But we cannot overlook
> his unworthy acts. Comrade Molotov as our Minister of
> Foreign Affairs, having taken a little too much liqueur at
> a diplomatic deception, gave his agreement to the British
> ambassador to publish bourgeois newspapers and
> magazines in our country. Why? On what basis did he
> have to agree to such a thing? Is it not clear that the
> bourgeoisie is our class enemy and to disseminate the
> bourgeois press amongst to the Soviet people can bring
> us nothing but harm. This faulty step, if we were to
> permit it, would be a harmful, negative influence on the
> minds and world-view of Soviet people, would lead to
> the weakening of our communist ideology and the
> strengthening of bourgeois ideology. This is the first
> political mistake of comrade V.M. Molotov.

> And what about the offer by Molotov to give the Crimea
> to Soviet Jews? This is a crude error by comrade
> Molotov. Why did he have to do it? How could this be

permitted? On what grounds did comrade Molotov make this offer? We have the Jewish Autonomous Republic. Isn't that enough? Let this Republic be developed. And comrade Molotov out not to be an advocate of illegal Jewish claims on our Soviet Crimea. This is the second political error of comrade V.I. Molotov! Comrade Molotov does not conduct himself as befits a member of the Politburo. And we reject categorically his fanciful offers.

Comrade Molotov has such deep respect for his wife that no sooner has the Politburo taken a decision on this or that important political question, that it is quickly made known to comrade Zhemchuzhina. It seems as though some kind of invisible thread united the Politburo with Molotov's wife Zhemchuzhina and her friends. And she is surrounded by friends who cannot be trusted. Clearly, such behavior by a member of the Politburo is impermissible.

Now regarding comrade Mikoian. He, do you see, is categorically against raising agricultural taxes on the peasants. Who is he, our Anastas Mikoian? What is it that is not clear to him? The peasant is our debtor. We have a first unity with the peasants. We have guaranteed the land forever to the kolkhozes. They must render the due debt to the state. Therefore we do not agree with comrade Mikoian's position.

(see former references under "Andreev").

Khrushchev's memoirs:

And at the Plenum Stalin, in his speech, hit Molotov and Mikoian "upside the head," put their honesty in doubt. In his speech he insinuated political distrust of them, suspicion in some kind of political dishonesty. Well, well!

- Khrushchev, N.S. *Vremia, Liudi, Vlast'*. Vol. 2 Part 3. Chapter "19th Congress of the Communist Party of our country". Online at http://hrono.ru/libris/lib_h/hrush41.html

D.T. Shepilov, one of the few eyewitnesses to the Plenum who left a written account of what took place, said:

Stalin at the CC Plenum and without any basis expressed political distrust of Molotov, accused him of "capitulationism towards American imperialism" and proposed not to appoint Molotov to the staff of the Buro of the Presidium of the CC. That was done. V. Molotov accepted this without a single word of protest.

Standing at the podium Stalin with a suspicious expression spoke about how Molotov was intimidated by American imperialism, that, when he was in the USA, he sent panic-stricken telegrams, that such a leader does not deserve our trust, that he cannot be in the leading nucleus of the party. In the same tones Stalin expressed political distrust of A. Mikoian and K. Voroshilov.

… Molotov sat unmoving behind the table of the Presidium. He remained silent, and not a single muscle moved on his face. Through the glass of his pince-nez he looked straight out into the hall and only rarely moved the three fingers of his right had on the tablecloth, as though kneading a bit of bread. A. Mikoian was very nervous. He delivered a trifling and disordered speech. He too, defending himself from these fantastic accusations, did not fail to kick out at Molotov that, as he claimed, he had been friends with Voznesensky, who was himelf a terrible criminal.

- Shepilov, Dmitrii T. *Neprimknuvshii.* Moscow: Vagrius, 2001, p. 19; p. 229. Online at http://www.pseudology.org/ShepilovDT/11.htm

61. Expansion of the Presidium

Khrushchev:

Stalin evidently had plans to finish off the old members of the Political Bureau. He often stated that Political Bureau members should be replaced by new ones. His proposal, after the 19th Congress, concerning the election of 25 persons to the Central Committee Presidium, was aimed at the removal of the old Political Bureau members and the bringing in of less experienced persons so that these would extol him in all sorts of ways. We can assume that this was also a design for the future annihilation of the old Political Bureau members and, in this way, a cover for all shameful acts of Stalin, acts which we are now considering.

Efremov's notes:

Yes, we did hold the Congress of our party. It went very well, and many of you might think that, amongst us there exists full harmony and unity. But we have not this harmony and unity of thought. Some people disagree with our decisions.

They say, why did we significantly enlarge the membership of the Central Committee? But isn't it self-evident that we need to get new forces into the CC? We old people will die out, but we must think to whom, into whose hands we shall pass the baton of our great undertaking. Who will carry it forward? For this we need younger, dedicated people and political leaders. And what does it mean to bring up a dedicated, devoted political leader of the State? It takes ten, no, fifteen years to educate a state leader.

But just wishing for this is not enough. To educate ideologically firm state activists can only be done through practice, in the daily work of carrying out the general line of the party, of overcoming all sorts of opposition from hostile opportunist elements who are striving to slow down and interrupt the task of the building of socialism. And we must have political activists of Leninist experience, educated by our Party, in the struggle to defeat these hostile attempts and to achieve complete success in the realization of our great goals.

Is it not clear that we must lift up the role of our party and its party committees? Can we forget about improving the Party's work among the masses, as Lenin taught us? All this needs a flow of young, fresh forces into the CC, the general staff of our Party. This is what we have done, following Lenin's instructions. This is why we have expanded the membership of the CC. And the Party itself has grown a little.

The question is asked as to why we relieved some prominent Party and state figures from their important posts as ministers. What can be said on this account? We replaced comrades Molotov, Kaganovich. Voroshilov and others and replaced them with new workers. Why? On what basis? The work of a minister – this is hard, peasant labor. It demands great strength, concrete knowledge and good health. This is why we have relieved some deserving comrades from the posts they occupied and appointed in their places new, more qualified, workers who take initiative. They are young people, full of strength and energy. We must support them in their important work.

(see previous references).

Bibliography and Sources

Many primary and secondary sources were consulted in preparing this book. Most are in Russian only; as of the date of publication very few are available in English. This is one reason for the many quotations from primary and secondary sources in the text. All translations are by the author unless otherwise noted in the text.

To include the full text of the many hard-to-find primary sources, the text of Khrushchev's Secret Speech, and a full bibliography would add 15%-20% to the cost of this book. Therefore:

* The full text of Khrushchev's speech in the translation used by the author is available online at http://chss.montclair.edu/english/furr/research/kl/speech.html

* For the convenience of interested readers who can read Russian the author has made available many hard-to-find primary sources online. The URLs for these primary sources, as well as a full bibliography of primary and secondary sources, are available at http://chss.montclair.edu/english/furr/research/kl/bibliography.html

Editor

Index

53, 54, 55, 56, 57, 58, 59, 60, 61,
62, 63, 64, 65, 66, 67, 68, 69, 70,
71, 72, 73, 74, 75, 76, 77, 78, 79,
80, 81, 82, 83, 84, 85, 86, 87, 88,
89, 90, 91, 92, 93, 94, 95, 96, 97,
98, 101, 102, 103, 104, 105, 107,
109, 110, 111, 113, 114, 116,
117, 119, 120, 121, 122, 123,
124, 125, 126, 127, 128, 129,
130, 131, 132, 133, 134, 135,
137, 138, 139, 140, 141, 142,
143, 144, 146, 147, 149, 150,
151, 152, 153, 154, 155, 156,
157, 158, 159, 160, 162, 163,
164, 165, 170, 171, 172, 176,
177, 178, 179, 180, 181, 182,
183, 192, 193, 194, 195, 196,
197, 198, 199, 200, 201, 202,
203, 204, 207, 208, 209, 210,
211, 212, 213, 214, 215, 216,
217, 224, 226, 227, 228, 229,
231, 239, 242, 243, 249, 250,
251, 252, 253, 254, 255, 256,
258, 259, 260, 262, 263, 265,
266, 267, 268, 269, 270, 271,
272, 273, 281, 283, 287, 291,
303, 305, 309, 311, 315, 316,
318, 321, 322, 323, 324, 326,
327, 329, 331, 332, 333, 335,
336, 337, 339, 340, 341, 345,
346, 347, 348, 351, 352, 353,
354, 355, 356, 357, 358, 359,
360, 361, 364, 366, 367, 368,
369, 370, 371, 374, 375, 376,
377, 381, 382, 386, 387, 390,
393, 394, 395, 396, 397, 398,
402, 403, 404, 405, 406, 407,
408, 409, 410, 413
Kirov, Sergei M., 39, 40, 110, 120,
144, 152, 157, 223, 268, 269,
378, 380
Kobulov, Bogdan Z., 23, 113, 171,
178, 179, 187, 383

Kol'tsov, Mikhail E., 67
Komarov, P.T., 25, 59, 309
Konev, Ivan S., 90, 346
Koriman, Zinaida A., 319
Kork, Avgust I., 306
Kosarev, Aleksandr V., 44, 64, 65,
66, 67, 68, 69, 81, 152, 155, 159,
170, 171, 172, 182, 315, 319,
320, 321, 332
Kosior, Stanislav V., 54, 64, 65, 66,
81, 82, 152, 155, 166, 169, 181,
188, 190, 191, 255, 291, 315,
316, 317, 318, 319, 332, 382
Kosolapov, Richard I., 121, 253,
273, 392
Kossior. *See* Kosior
Köstring, Ernst, 297, 298, 299
Kotolynov, Ivan I., 40
Kozhinov, Vadim V., 84, 85, 93,
94, 195, 251, 334, 335, 337
Krestinskii, Nikolai N., 59, 174, 307
Krinitskii, Aleksandr I., 382
Kruglov, Sergei N., 71, 376
Krupskaia, Nadezhda K., 12, 13,
14, 15, 17, 18, 19, 232, 233, 235,
236, 237, 238
Kuibyshev, Valerian V., 45, 71, 120,
166, 206, 244, 326, 383, 392
Kumanev, Georgii A., 92
Kuznetsov, Aleksei A., 102, 367,
368
Kuznetsov, Nikolai G., 86, 91, 340,
353, 360, 366, 368

L

Larina, Anna M. (Bukharina), 44
Lazebniy, V.M., 299, 300
Lenin, Vladimir I., 7, 9, 11, 12, 13,
14, 15, 16, 17, 18, 19, 22, 27, 28,
31, 32, 35, 42, 43, 51, 90, 118,
119, 120, 121, 123, 126, 127,
134, 152, 153, 157, 213, 216,